5 Readers Reading

Books by Norman N. Holland

The First Modern Comedies
The Shakespearean Imagination
Psychoanalysis and Shakespeare
The Dynamics of Literary Response
Poems in Persons
5 Readers Reading

5 Readers Reading

Norman N. Holland

NEW HAVEN AND LONDON, YALE UNIVERSITY PRESS, 1975

Published with assistance from the foundation established
in memory of Oliver Baty Cunningham of the Class of
1917, Yale College.

Designed by Sally Sullivan
and set in Times Roman type.
Printed in the United States of America by
Alpine Press Inc., South Braintree, Mass.

Published in Great Britain, Europe, and Africa by
Yale University Press, Ltd., London.
Distributed in Latin America by Kaiman & Polon,
Inc., New York City; in Australasia and Southeast
Asia by John Wiley & Sons Australasia Pty. Ltd.,
Sydney; in India by UBS Publishers' Distributors Pvt.,
Ltd., Delhi; in Japan by John Weatherhill, Inc., Tokyo.

To Jane

Who koude telle, but he hadde wedded be,
The joye, the ese, and the prosperitee
That is bitwixe an housbonde and his wyf?

Contents

Contents

Preface

Blake has stated the problem this book addresses as succinctly as anyone.

> Both read the Bible day & night,
> But thou read'st black where I read white.

The question I would like to answer is: Why is this so? To be sure, Blake had in mind religious controversy as much as people's different readings of a text—

> The Vision of Christ that thou dost see
> Is my Vision's Greatest Enemy.
> Thine has a great hook nose like thine;
> Mine has a snub nose like to mine.

As it turns out, however, people read the same text differently for the same reason they have different preferences in religions or in noses: themselves. Answering the specifically literary question involves answers—or attempts at answers—to some basic issues in human psychology. How *do* people react to noses or, more generally, things, beliefs, other people (like Christ), or literary texts (like the Bible)? How does personality or society, filtered through personality, affect our interpretation of events?

I did not wish so large a problem. I began this book innocently enough, only to investigate literary response and specifically to confirm or change the "transformation" model of literary response I published in 1968.[1] I sat down with my colleague Joseph Masling, who had generously offered to help as a psychological consultant; we began to design experiments —and quickly ran into trouble. There seemed to me to be very little that would be "reliably reproducible" in the reading transaction. True, the literary text remained the same, but there seemed to be no meaningful way of relating one literary text to another as comparable stimuli. (The same genre? The same length? Two poems about seashells? Two "oedipal" dramas?) And I knew from my experience as a critic and teacher that the most skilled readers can diverge markedly in their interpretations even of widely accepted classics. (Think, for example, of the controversies and sharply differing reinterpretations of Marvell's "Horatian Ode," the Fourth Book of *Gulliver's Travels*, or *The Turn of the Screw*.) Of the usual methods of psychological testing—questionnaires, confirmatory judgments, the grids of personal construct theory, Delphi methods—none seemed really applicable to a situation in which each responder was as importantly unique as each stimulus *and* as each response.

I decided simply to fish for a method by seeing what issues emerged when I conducted more or less undirected interviews with a few readers who had taken standard personality tests. I still could not arrive at clearly testable hypotheses, mostly because I could not find fixed categories either for the reader or the work read or for what the reader said about his reading. Finally, then, this lack of method became itself the method, and I proceeded from the first exploratory group of graduate student readers to testing and interviewing a larger group of undergraduates from whom the "5 Readers" of my title come.

The major problem proved to be, not the interviewing, but analyzing the results. A simple procedure led to an extremely complicated problem of interpretation. Finally, however, this complexity subsided into a basic principle of personal interaction whose very simplicity adds elegance to its other claims on your belief.

Although this book concludes with a general psychological principle, its evidence comes from people's responses to literature—an early concern of mine that goes back past my adult and professional interests to childhood and no doubt stems from my own efforts then and now to cope with the interactions of people around me by finding generalizations from a safe distance. Professionally, I became interested in comedy and questions about why, when, and how people laugh. I was led, naturally enough, to Freud's theory of jokes, which impressed me for two reasons: first, it dealt with these miniworks of literature both in detail and totally, as aesthetically formed and unified texts; second, it showed how the purely literary (or quasi-literary) experience worked in terms of larger explanatory principles that applied to other areas of human behavior as well (dreams, slips of the tongue, or symptoms).

If psychoanalysis worked so well for jokes, it should be possible to apply it to literature in general. When I turned to psychoanalytic criticism, however, I found it very mixed in quality. On the one hand, there were some truly exciting insights and startling correspondences between psychoanalytic experience and literary works. On the other, only a small part of psychoanalytic theory was being applied, and that within a very limited literary framework. Often, for example, literary characters were studied like photographic copies of case histories, a naïve view of realism few literary critics would accept. Within psychoanalysis, little beyond symbolic decoding was being applied: the literary work was treated as a congress of phalluses, vaginas, and anuses, with token reverence to aesthetic mysteries, but no real attempt to analyze them or intellectual themes. Of the developmental stages, only the oedipal was applied to literature. As a result, the psychoanalytic critic could only talk about narratives or dramatic works that had father- or mother-figures, not poetry or prose as such. These procedures gave psychoanalytic criticism a very bad reputation in literary circles, which, I fear, it has not overcome even today.

Nevertheless, there were enough good insights from this school so that I wanted to explore it further, and I was very lucky at this juncture to be able to train at the Boston Psychoanalytic Institute. There I learned of other aspects of psychoanalytic theory and experience that were, by and large, not being applied to literature, notably those strategies for warding off anxiety and coping with inner and outer reality that I term, for brevity, defenses (instead of "defense mechanisms" or "defensive and adaptive strategies"). They emerge in literature as what literary critics usually call form, both in the larger sense of the selection and structuring of parts, and more specifically as rhymes, alliteration, stanza patterns, and the like. I thus found that one could use psychoanalytic psychology to talk about lyric poems and even nonfiction prose, not just dramatic or narrative versions of the oedipus complex. I also learned more about the pre-oedipal stages, those desires and fantasies that have to do, not with oedipal triangles, but one-to-one relationships or just one's own body. These, it turned out, played the key role in lyric poetry and other literature that did not tell a potentially oedipal story. Even in narrative and dramatic works rich with father- and mother-figures, these preoedipal fantasies served as deeper, more pervasive versions of oedipal material, as they do with real people.

Thus, I learned that people's responses to literature involved a transformation by means of forms acting like defenses, of drives, impulses, and fantasies back and forth from the most primitive strata of psychic life to the highest. Given such a model, one could understand the social, intellectual, or moral themes people found in literature as the highest level of this dynamic and continuing process of transformation. One could explain the way readers respond to literary characters as though they were real people, when they are patently not real and often not even realistic. One could interpret the feeling people have of being "absorbed" or "taken out of themselves" when engrossed in literature: their processes of transformation meld with the exterior work so that they no longer perceive a difference between "in here" and "out there." In short, drawing on other psychoanalytic concepts besides symbolism and the oedipus complex, notably defenses and the preoedipal stages, led to a complex model of literature-as-transformation, which in turn made it possible to explain a number of literary phenomena such as meaning, realism, the relation of the author's personality to his work, the role of embedded myths, the criteria behind evaluation, and so on. This model and some of its applications I set out as *The Dynamics of Literary Response* in 1968.[2]

At that point, I was again lucky: a substantial grant from the Research Foundation of the State University of New York made it possible to test this model, which I had derived fundamentally from a combination of psychoanalytic experience with introspection, and this book is the result of those tests. Essentially, *Dynamics* has stood up rather well, requir-

ing only the modification—or reminder, really—that psychological processes like fantasies or defenses do not happen in books
but in people. Within that framework, one can see five readers
who are the subjects of this book re-create the original literary
creation in terms of their own personalities, themselves understood as continuing processes of transformation. Specifically,
this book develops four principles governing the interaction of
the reader with what he reads, but these four separate principles are themselves simply four different ways of accenting one
more general and basic principle. This, it turns out, applies not
only to reading, but to a person's interaction with any external
reality, human or nonhuman. For example, in *Poems in
Persons*, a shorter and more literary book I was able to write
during the long gestation of this psychological and theoretical
one,[3] I showed how this one basic principle informed teaching,
criticism, theater-going, and the very act of literary creation
itself. Conversely, the same large principle seems to apply not
only to interactions of people but to interactions by anything
that can be said to have a style the way a person does: an
institution, for example, or a culture or a nation.

Thus, the study of this one phenomenon, reading, may pay
back to psychoanalysis the insight literary criticism has borrowed, giving as interest that long-sought passage that would
open up the intrapsychic model of classical psychoanalysis to
an interpsychic psychology. The psychohistorian, the object-
relations theorist, the social psychologist, anyone concerned
with the interactions of groups and individuals, may find in the
act of reading the basic principles that govern the human
activities he studies; for reading ever so curiously mingles
person and thing and person and person.

A project as long as this makes one conscious of a great
many debts and gratitudes of both a personal and an institutional kind. The Research Foundation of the State University
of New York has supported this research most generously.
Their three grants have not only made it possible for me to
complete this work, but they created the fertile ground from
which a major center for the psychoanalytic study of literature
could grow. Throughout, my department has created, by its

tradition of openness to new approaches and methods, an atmosphere in which discovery could and did flourish, making us all something more than an "Eng. Lit." department.

Among the many people who have helped, I am most immediately obliged to the "*S*s," as they would be called in the regular psychological literature. I wish I could thank them by name, for they gave of themselves in the most generous sense. I can only hope this book will give them something in return as constructive as what they gave me. Dr. Allen Zechowy, then of the Meyer Memorial Hospital, now of the Department of Mental Health, Prince George County, Cheverly, Maryland, worked with the preliminary group of graduate students. Dr. Andrew Corvus of Children's Hospital (Buffalo) worked with a larger group of undergraduates from whom these five readers were selected. I am grateful to them both for their adroit adaptation of established testing techniques to this new problem and for the skill with which they were able to convey their results and conclusions to me.

During the four-year germination of this book, many people have contributed to it. I am especially obliged to Mrs. Virginia White, Mrs. Helen Walter, Mme. M.-J. Truelle, and Mrs. Joan Cipperman, who stepped in at particularly critical moments to prepare large chunks of the manuscript. In this book (as in *Dynamics*) I am indebted to Sterling Lord who negotiated its publication. Whitney Blake and Jane Isay gave fine editorial guidance and encouragement. I am much obliged to Michael Brill for the astonishing diagram in Appendix A. Ms. Mary Z. Bartlett and Mr. Stephen Gormey helped create an immense bibliography of psychological studies of aesthetic responses. I am grateful to them and to Ms. Betty Jane Saik, who both by research and administration expertly steered the project over the greatest part of its course and set in motion the symposia and the research center that have developed from it. To her, not only I, but everyone working in the field, owes a debt.

Those who know this field will recognize how deep my intellectual obligations are to Robert Waelder, Erik Erikson, and Heinz Lichtenstein. In a more personal but no less incisive way, I learn something new about psychoanalysis each day I work with my colleague Murray Schwartz. I am grateful to my colleagues in the Group for Applied Psychoanalysis (Boston), who heard an early version of these ideas, and the similar G.A.P. in Buffalo and its parent organization, the Center for the Psychological Study of the Arts, who have heard them many times. I am thinking of Barry Chabot, Paul Diesing, Murray Levine, Richard Papenhausen, Lucian Pye, Robert Rogers, Stuart Schneiderman, Mark Shechner, Arthur Valenstein, Howard R. Wolf, and especially Leonard Manheim, Bruce Mazlish and Abraham Zaleznik, with whom I have shared the excitement of psychoanalytic discovery for lo these many years. Their many helpful comments have guided me through a highly complex process of re-examination and revision both of my thoughts and this book.

David Bleich has done outstanding work in this field on which I have drawn, but I am particularly indebted to him for his long and careful commentary on an earlier version of this book. He enabled me to make a transition I found extremely difficult: from a concept of reading as the reader's partaking partially of a process completely but potentially embodied in a text to reading as the reader's active re-creation of the text based on the materials he finds in it (as described below in Chapter 5).

It was after having written Chapter 8 that I came upon my colleague, Paul Diesing's radical sorting-out, *Patterns of Discovery in the Social Sciences* (1971),[4] which includes a searching and sympathetic understanding of the scientific status and the deep assumptions and aspirations within holistic, nonexperimental, case-study methods like those of psychoanalysis, literary criticism, and this book. I have added some references to his work, but footnotes alone do justice neither to the philosophical rigor and wisdom of his analysis nor to the encouragement he gave me for my own.

From the very first day of this project, Joseph Masling has magnanimously served as my psychological adviser. As it turned out, the book departs from his rigorous criteria for control and correlation, but it is a tribute to his educative mixture of firmness and tolerance that I understand the losses I am incurring by giving up experimental canons as fully as I feel the need to do so.

" 'That's all very hard to believe,' she said at length, 'but I do believe you, Buck Rogers.' " The words are Wilma Deering's, but they express admirably Jane Holland's amused patience, skepticism, and final confidence toward the "mad scientist" who sometimes emerged from my study. Dedication cannot express my appreciation deeply or complexly enough. Suffice it to say, I take joy in finding that this study of relations between people could not have gone on at all without our own.

NORMAN N. HOLLAND

Buffalo, N.Y.
September 1974

1 The Question: Who Reads What How?

The story was William Faulkner's "A Rose for Emily," and its one description of Miss Emily as a young girl was as clear as a description could be. The narrator, apparently one of the townspeople, says: "We had long thought of them as a tableau, Miss Emily a slender figure in white in the background, her father a spraddled silhouette in the foreground, his back to her and clutching a horsewhip, the two of them framed by the back-flung front door." Faulkner has pictured the Griersons as exactly as a photographer would, but that precision quite disappears when the description passes over into the mind of a reader. It disappears even if the reader is as well trained and fairly experienced as the five students of English literature who are the subjects of this book. Sam, Saul, Shep, Sebastian, and Sandra (as I shall call them) all spoke about this "tableau."

Good-natured, easygoing, dapper Sam singled it out as virtually the first thing he wanted to talk about in the story: "The father was very domineering. One of the most striking [sic] images in the book is that of the townsfolk looking through the door as her father stands there with a horsewhip in his hands, feet spread apart and between or through him you see a picture of Emily standing in the background, and that pretty much sums up exactly the kind of relationship they had." Sam was stressing the father's dominance and, in doing so, was positioning the townspeople so that they could see Emily between her father's legs.

This was part of what he found highly romantic in the story. "The frailty and femininity that that evokes!" he sighed. "Just that one frail, 'slender figure in white,' just those words there really show us the Emily that was and the Emily that might have been." Yet, almost at the same moment he was responding to this lacy, feminine Emily, he could say, "The word 'tableau' is important. While they [the townspeople] may be

1

envious and while they may be angry at the way that these people act, they yet need it, it seems, they in a way like to have it, much as one is terrified at the power of a god and yet needing him so much and, you know, sidling up to him and paying homage to him and in the same way I think Emily comes to function as this god symbol." A curious turnabout from frailty and femininity.

By contrast, Saul, a scholarly type, was circumspect. Sam, in his expansive way, trusted his memory, but Saul, when I asked him about that image, took out his copy of the story and read it over carefully to himself. "Ummm. I had remembered the word 'tableau,' and I had forgotten the rest of it. 'Horse-whip' there— rings— 'spraddled silhouette.' That seems right to me. That summarizes the relationship, I think. She's in the back in white, of course. I think of these white gowns in the plantation balls. The father a 'spraddled silhouette.' He's no longer stern and erect. He's spraddled across the door." Saul was seeing Emily's father exactly the opposite way from Sam, as a weakened, sprawled figure, at least until he read over to himself the sentence with the horsewhip in it again. "A horse-whip suggesting all sorts of nasty, sexual, sadistic overtones," but then he blurred that image. "Do they mean the horsewhip rather than his own stern demeanor? Or just the normal embod-iment of his traditions suggests the decline like 'spraddled' does? And then 'framed by the back-flung front door' just completes the tableau. It's a nice device. Faulkner makes that one work, too. That's a nice emblem." Well, maybe so, but Saul had so divided it up and dissolved it into questions and alternatives as to leave me quite puzzled about what he thought the thrust of the image finally was.

Shep presented himself as a rebel and radical, but his reading of the tableau seemed to me no more original or idiosyncratic than Saul's or Sam's. I read the passage to him, and he commented simply, "O.K. Protective image. That he's defend-ing Southern womanhood, perhaps, and defending it in that same sort of mindless way that says, 'Well, now, we've got to defend it.' " He went on to decide that Southern womanhood might well have defended itself and then to make a suggestion quite opposite to "protective image." "You could, I suppose, as an alternative interpretation say that the horsewhip is something which he's also adept with indoors as well as outdoors, but I don't think so. Maybe there's overtones that Daddy is sadistic enough—horsewhips being pretty sadistic things to carry around when you're greeting people, you know—that Daddy is sadistic enough where he wouldn't mind taking a belt at Emily once in a while, but I don't think they're much more than overtones.'' In talking about the tableau as such, he talked only about Emily's father, and in this curiously alternative or opposed way. Earlier he had recalled Emily as a young woman (and the tableau is the only place she is so described): "I can see her as a very good-looking, dark-haired girl who had a penchant for wearing dark clothes.'' Again, I sense in his substituting dark for white a will opposing the text, although at the same time, Shep said he liked this story very much.

Sophisticated, sardonic, somewhat cynical, a lapsed Catholic with aspirations toward aristocracy, Sebastian did not discuss the tableau as such, although he clearly remembered it in typing Emily as "the aristocrat of the Southern town, whose father is the original superego with a horsewhip, beating off suitors.'' "He's denying her access to suitable sexual partners.'' Often, Sebastian tended to distance and type the characters this way and to flirt with the actual, physical details. Here he saw Miss Emily as "the aristocrat,'' her father as "the original superego,'' but converted the "suitors'' to "sexual partners.''

Sandra, the fifth reader, was a tall, very attractive woman, gentle and subdued in her manner. She liked the story intensely, had read it several times, and had even, in her freshman year, written a term paper on it. Yet she recalled the tableau oddly: "They said they always had this picture of him standing, you know, sitting in the door with a whip in his hand.'' As for Emily, "I see her as very young and dressed in white and standing up, I guess she's supposed to be standing up behind her father, who would probably be looking *very* cross, say, if someone had come to call on her. No doubt, she would have a certain amount— Possibly fearful, but probably more regretful because she's being, they even say, robbed of something at that point. . . . There would be a great amount of strain on her face because of her inability to do anything except just watch.'' Sandra saw the emotional overtones in the tableau in a more subtle, empathic way than the four male readers did, so that she, too, had her own version of the image.

Indeed, one can say that each of the readers had a different version of Emily and her father. He was standing, sitting; erect, sprawled; domineering, weakened; sadistic, protective, and so on—sometimes even to the same reader. Emily was dressed in white, as for a plantation ball, or black; frail, but godlike; fearful, but ''the aristocrat.'' Some of these differences involve outright misreadings, but most do not. Conceivably, one could ''teach'' or coerce these five readers into consensus, but even so, whatever in each person's character originally colored his perception of the tableau would go on coloring his perception of every other element in the story. What is that something, that ineffable effect of personality on perception? That is the issue this book explores.

As the late Stanley Edgar Hyman once said, ''Each reader poems his own poem.'' Yet we know very little—practically nothing—about such ''poeming,'' about the way a reader re-creates the literary experience in himself. Today's literary critics are expert in pointing out an essence for any literary work. Today's psychologists—particularly the psychoanalytic psychologists—are equally adept at conceptualizing the essential dynamics of individuals. Yet we do not know how literature and readers interact.

We can find out, if you and I apply to what Sam and the other readers said, a combination of the close reading literary critics have so skillfully developed in the last decades and psychological methods of reading from language to personality. We shall move slowly—sometimes we shall seem to go word by word—but once we have put psychoanalytic interpretation together with the literary critic's, we shall have established four principles that account for the way readers read to fit their personalities.

As of now, however, in the words of a recent book on the problem of literary response, ''We know almost nothing about the process of reading and the interaction of man and book.''[1] In a manner all too common in the world of belles-lettres, however, the "almost nothing" we know tends to become complexity piled upon complexity, language explained by more language, authorities resting on other authorities—a splendid disguise of abstractions much like the emperor's new clothes. "Scholars and critics," Walter Slatoff writes, "who would distinguish carefully between various sorts of Neo-Platonism, or examine in minute detail the structure of a chapter or the transmutations of a prevailing metaphor, or trace the full nuances of a topical allusion, will settle happily for mere labels like distance, involvement, identification,"[2] labels that not only suffer from vagueness but deceive, creating the illusion that they refer to some real reaction people in fact shared and the critic in fact observed.

This tradition—assuming a uniform response on the part of readers and audiences that the critic somehow knows and understands—goes back to Aristotle's concept of catharsis, and his notions about people's apparently fixed responses to details of wording. Or this tradition might even have originated in Plato's assertion that poetry debilitates. Although the Greeks observed the phenomena that they ascribed to audiences better than later theorists, the tradition flourished after them, reaching a peak with the "rules" of the lesser neoclassical critics. Early psychoanalytic writers on literature followed, rather uncritically, this collectivist view from the litterateurs. Thus we find Otto Rank defending his oedipal interpretations of myths because, "The people imagine the hero in this manner, investing him with their own infantile fantasies."[3] Freud himself assumed a collective response to *Oedipus Rex* in the letter of October 15, 1897, in which he reported to his confidant Fliess, "I have found love of the mother and jealousy of the father in my own case too, and now believe it to be a general phenomenon of early childhood." "If that is the case, the gripping power of *Oedipus Rex,* in spite of all the rational objections to the inexorable fate that the story presupposes, becomes intelligible." "Every member of the audience was once a budding Oedipus in phantasy, and this dream-fulfillment played out in reality causes everyone to recoil in horror, with the full measure of repression which separates his infantile from his present state."[4]

Everyone recoils? Freud himself avoided this fallacy when he studied jokes as a kind of miniliterature; they have a "frame" and a text with especially sensitive formal balances and a response. What would one think of a theory of jokes that always concluded, "and so you laugh" or "and so you don't laugh," regardless of whether you did or didn't in fact laugh? After all, someone might have heard the joke before; someone else might be depressed; a third person might have no sense of humor, and so on. Indeed, responses to jokes are so various that, for a time, researchers (at Yale) were exploring a "mirth response test," trying to sort personality types by observing which cartoons they found funny.[5] Should we then postulate that responses to tragedy, something so infinitely more subtle than a cartoon, are fixed? No, and for some decades now we have, in fact, known the contrary.

It was in the 1920s that I. A. Richards asked his Cambridge undergraduates for the protocols that led to his ground-breaking *Practical Criticism.*[6] He asked his students "to comment freely in writing on" a series of poems, their authorship undisclosed. Richards found that these supposedly well-educated young Englishmen were evaluating very strangely indeed, misreading the plain sense of the poems, imposing cranky sets of preconceptions, responding in terms of stock sentimentalities, cynicisms, and other doctrines, as well as (perhaps) irrelevant memories. Richards, let us notice, was exploring his reader's conscious, verbalized responses to literature. Interested in education, he tended to concentrate on those parts of literary response that could be taught, and, indeed, his analysis of misreadings helped to reform, root and branch, the teaching of literature over the next four decades. Today, even among schoolchildren, one finds more sophisticated reading than Richards found among his jazz-age Cantabrigians.[7]

One would expect the giant entertainment corporations, with millions riding on each reel of celluloid, to have studied response far more carefully than impoverished English teachers could. But the published research in this field remains rather elementary.[8] There are many studies of effect, but they move casually back and forth between the transfer of information, the fulfillment of individuals' needs (for example, to escape), the impact on morality (typically delinquency), and immediate re-actions of "like" and "dislike." Indeed, the industry has de-veloped machines—the Lazarsfeld-Stanton program analyzer, the Cirlin Reactograph—with which an audience can indicate its fluctuating likes, dislikes, and indifferences. Of course, such a device cannot sort out variables—one cannot tell, for example, whether a member of the audience is disliking the whole movie or just the "bad guy" in it. In general, this one-dimensional quality carries over to the analysis of the content of films. The most sophisticated scheme I have seen only gets to issues like "Main story type," that is, "Is it a Western or a gangster movie?", "Marital status and changes of leads A, B, and C," "Sports (type and prominence)," or "Importance of part and characterization of unskilled labor." I understand that much research in this field is kept secret because of its commercial value. If what has been published is an accurate sample, there would seem to be little reason to do so.

Such simple categories show that a study of audience re-sponse demands at least one thing: some sensibly subtle way of analyzing the texts, both the text the artist creates and the text of what the audience says. I. A. Richards had that, with his marvelous sense of language, but his experience showed a second tool one must have to understand audiences. Without a psychology adequate to explain individual responses, one does not know what to do with them except pass judgment on them. "We rarely concern ourselves, for example," says Walter Slatoff, surveying the post-Richards critical scene, "with the problem of individual differences among readers. . . . On the few occasions we do entertain such questions we speak as though they were settled by reducing response to two categories—appropriate and inappropriate."[9] Thus, although Richards avowed a concern to maintain differences of opinion, he shifted the problem of evaluating poems to a much harsher dogmatism: passing judgment on "the relative values of differ-ent states of mind, about varying forms, and degrees, of order in the personality."[10]

Had Richards had a usable psychology of individuals, he would have been able, presumably, to see how his protocols were reflecting personality at all levels, not just the teachable surface of consciousness. Indeed, David Bleich has recently done just that: shown how some of Richards's protocols reveal the unconscious themes his Cantabrigians were projecting into the texts as part of their response.[11] "It has become a matter of course that any item of human behavior shows a continuum of dynamic meaning, reaching from the surface through many layers of crust to the 'core' "—thus, Erik Erikson,[12] articulating with his customary eloquence one of the most basic and widely confirmed of psychoanalytic discoveries. Freud's earliest case histories showed it and so did this morning's experience in hundreds of clinics and consulting-rooms. I know, for example, how the style and subject and method of this book stem from very early experiences of my own and my whole present character, including various half-conscious wishes and fears. Although these unconscious and infantile sources are by no means the only ones, if so conscious an act as writing an experimental and theoretical book has strong buried components, I find it hard to believe that responding to a play, a movie, or a poem does not. And, of course, it does.

As the remainder of this book will show, readers respond to literature in terms of their own "lifestyle" (or "character" or "personality" or "identity"). By such terms, psychoanalytic writers mean an individual's characteristic way of dealing with the demands of outer and inner reality. Such a style will have grown through time from earliest infancy. It will also be what the individual brings with him to any new experience, including the experience of literature. Each new experience develops the style, while the pre-existing style shapes each new experience. And this style can be described quite accurately (but not, of course, impersonally).

In short, psychoanalysis offers a powerful theory of individual responses to literature, and it has done so ever since Freud's 1905 study of jokes. (Interestingly, in that very early study, he also showed how social and economic factors would affect the pattern of inhibitions an individual brought to a joke and so affect his responses, but *indirectly,* as they filtered through his personality.) Other writers have extended this first psychoanalytic aesthetics, Freud's theory of jokes, to other genres and to literature generally.[13]

For the most part, however, psychoanalytic students of literature, like conventional literary critics, have looked not at the actual individual reading but at the text, the words-on-the-page. Then they have posited a response on the basis of the text. Thus, paradoxically, the psychology that more than any other deals closely and intensely with individuals—psychoanalytic psychology—has in this instance retreated from the living human being, the spirit, if you will, to the letter.

By contrast, conventional psychological literature offers hundreds of studies that deal with actual readers but that suffer from a lack of theory.[14] For example, physiological studies tell how heart rate, the electrical resistance of the palm of the hand, or its sweat pattern, vary as subjects watch a movie. Indeed, an Italian experiment even investigated the differing ways identical and fraternal twins fidgeted![15] But I find it hard to believe a single variable such as pulse rate or fidget frequency could represent a complex, multivariant transaction like a response to a film.

Other studies resort to personality tests, but I think it is not much of an improvement over the physiological approach to be able to say that reading gruesome passages from Edgar Allan Poe increases the anxious and aggressive responses to inkblots. Much closer to the method of this book is the study in which judges were able to match viewers' open-ended comments on a movie to their Rorschach responses. Again, however, the experiment merely shows the correlation; it does not suggest an underlying mechanism, only that "individual differences in the perception of a motion picture are a function of global aspects of personality as elicited by the Rorschach."[16] Different personality tests lead to similarly vague conclusions: "Movie attendance is related in some instances to the central aspects of personality." A child's choices among stories "cohere with other observable characteristics of his personality."[17] Other studies claim to have shown that men watch the men in movies more than women do; that boys prefer adventure stories, while girls prefer stories about love, private life, and glamor; that children who are already pretty aggressive identify with different characters in a Western according to the degree of their pre-existing aggression, their sex, and the ending of the film.[18]

No doubt, these studies (and hundreds more like them) follow out admirably the canons of experimental rigor. As a continuing line of research, however, they end most inconclusively, to judge, if nothing else, by the number of experimenters who turn to the same old issues over and over again. Instead of coherent research, one finds random observations. What these studies may have gained in rigor they certainly lack in theory.

One returns then to literary and psychoanalytic studies, weak in experiment but strong on theory. Not always, of course. I do not feel that my understanding of the differences in readers' responses is advanced by a literary critic's introducing an *"informed* reader" with (also italicized) *"literary* competence" or even a more generalized "reading self," who (or that) is roughly the critic's age, shares his ethnic background, "has experienced war, marriage, and the responsibility of children," and so on.[19] Some statements about response by literary and psychoanalytic folk do add more rigor and theory than these; some do suggest pervasive links between, on the one hand, the reader's personality (in depth) and his conscious reading skill and, on the other, his response. I am thinking of Morse Peckham's explanation of the effect of one's past aesthetic experiences on response, a theory supported by very detailed analyses from a variety of arts and corresponding to psychoanalytic notions of the role of the ego in art.[20] Similarly, child therapists like Lilli Peller and Kate Friedlaender have shown how children's stories reflect at a conscious level the child's unconscious fantasies, and therefore how the age appropriate to the fantasy determines the age at which a child will like the story. They, too, are showing a theoretical basis for combining the detailed analysis of a story with the depth analysis of the response.[21]

Such studies, in effect, deal with classes of readers. Psychoanalysis, however, is par excellence the science of human individuality (if there can be a "science" of uniqueness), and we would expect it to be most interesting about literary response when it speaks about individuals. However, it must then necessarily give up repeatable experiments. For example, a group of experimenters, in projecting films for hospitalized psychiatric patients, found that the viewers interposed their individual defensive patterns between themselves and the film to keep the affect something they could tolerate. Hence, one could not assume that any given film would necessarily arouse certain feelings. Similarly, in an example of "poetry therapy," David V. Forrest showed how disturbed patients responded to the well-known lyric, "Western wind, when wilt thou blow," in terms of their several personality types, paranoid, schizoid, hysteric, and so on.[22] These papers suggest structures relating personality to response (through defense mechanisms or diagnostic categories that combine defense and level of fixation). They do not, however, take the further step: going beyond types and categories to examine the work of art, the response, and the responder in detail.

One often finds analyses of the individual (but not the work) in case histories. Avery Weisman, for example, describes a rigid, obsessional man who could not face a sea captain's loss of authority in a movie and left the theater before the film's end. The whole setting—other patrons, streets, bodily sensations—seemed unreal to him: he had dealt with his guilt and anxiety by separating his intellectual processes of reality-testing from his conventional, pleasurable attachment to the dream world of the film. Edith Buxbaum, in a famous case, tells of a boy compulsively driven to read detective stories almost to the exclusion of any other activity. He was satisfying his aggressive wishes toward his mother by allying himself with the murderer. At the same time, he assuaged his guilt by feeling like the victim and also the detective. Thus his symptom served both defense and the gratification of instincts, and he became locked into it. Still more tragic was the patient of Gilbert J. Rose who committed suicide after witnessing a performance of Duerrenmatt's *The Visit:* he, like the hero of the play, felt himself the victim of a fantastically powerful bitch-goddess.[23]

Caroline Shrodes, however, has studied individual students' responses to particular literary works on the assumption that literary experience matches the therapeutic process: from identification and interaction with the work, to emotional catharsis, to insight into one's particular conflicts and relationships.[24] Less clinically, David Bleich in a growing series of moving and perceptive essays has analyzed the responses of ordinary readers, students usually, in order to elicit the unconscious themes of the text. In other words, he reverses the usual assumption of critics, that by analyzing the text one can understand the response; rather, he argues, by analyzing what readers find in it, one comes to understand the text.[25] And he is right to do so. To analyze the text in formal isolation as so many "words-on-a-page" (in the old formula of the New Criticism) is a highly artificial procedure. A literary text, after all, in an objective sense consists only of a certain configuration of specks of carbon black on dried wood pulp. When these marks become words, when those words become images or metaphors or characters or events, they do so because the reader plays the part of a prince to the sleeping beauty. He gives them life out of his own desires. When he does so, he brings his lifestyle to bear on the work. He mingles his unconscious loves and fears and adaptations with the words and images he synthesizes at a conscious level.

It is, therefore, quite impossible to say from a text alone how people will respond to it. Only after we have understood how some specific individual responds, how the different parts of his individual personality re-create the different details of the text, can we begin to formulate general hypotheses about the way many or all readers respond. Only then—if then.

At the same time, however, the reader is surely responding to *something*. The literary text may be only so many marks on a page—at most a matrix of psychological possibilities for its readers. Nevertheless only some possibilities, we would say, truly fit the matrix. One would not say, for example, that a reader of that sentence from "A Rose for Emily" who thought the "tableau" described an Eskimo was really responding to the story at all—only pursuing some mysterious inner exploration. In the basic question of this book, "Who reads what how?", there must be a "what," and our next task is to find out what it is.

2 What? "A Rose for Emily," For Example

The Model of a Literary Work

In "Who reads what how?", the "what" has so far seemed little more than a shimmering of possibilities, a pre-text for the reader's creativity. The work begins in the psychological dynamics of its author, and the act of creating it fulfills those processes—for him. The work finds its fulfillment, so to speak, when a reader gives it life by re-creating the work in his own mind. The text as such almost vanishes in the astonishing variability of different readers' re-creation of it.

Typically, the dynamics in any given reader's mind will not coincide with the author's processes, nor will one reader's experience match another's, and even the same reader, we shall see, will respond differently at different times in his life. To be sure, professional critics often write as though they were establishing a "correct" reading, but the fact is that critics themselves disagree more than they agree. Evidently, therefore, one cannot posit even for highly trained readers a "correct" response in any given reader's mind to something definitively "in" the text. We can only understand what a particular reader has experienced *after* he has experienced it and put forth his re-creation and synthesis beyond his own private mind.

We can, however, set out what readers do in general and we can specify that with some certitude. More than two millennia ago, Aristotle pointed out that one thing audiences do is try to find a unity in what they see, a central theme or meaning or idea around which the various details of the play or story come to a focus. It is a time-proven idea of literary unity or explication that says, if such a formulation is correct, one can interrelate through it each episode, each trait, even each detail of phrasing in a literary work. As a standard handbook of critical methods puts it, once one has "identified the [central]

13

theme," "the structural principle" of the literary work, one can "see the whole design of the work as a unity," as "a simultaneous pattern radiating out from a center."[1]

Stories, of course, do not present unities—only so many marks on a page. It is readers who provide the unity, and apparently for two reasons. There seems to be built into the mind a press toward unity. Freud, for example, remarks that "many experiences" lead him "to assert that the dream-work is under some kind of necessity to combine all the sources which have acted as stimuli for the dream into a single unity in the dream itself."[2]

Further, readers seem to need such a centering, although they vary, of course, in the degree to which they feel such a need. I happen to be the kind of person who wants a sense of unity very intensely, while others are content with much more easy-going explications. But all readers need to "make sense" of a text to some extent. Otherwise they complain of obscurity and express varying degrees of discomfort and anxiety. Evidently, then, the organic unity in literary works, which is really a unity people create for the work in their own minds, serves some kind of defensive purpose for the reader. "Meaning," that is, the act of making sense of a text, works as a defense against some source of anxiety.[3]

Each reader, therefore, will search out a unifying idea that matches his particular needs for sense and logic. Thus, one reader might see *Hamlet* as centering on the idea of human imperfection or failure, another as "about" the dichotomy between symbolic and real actions, still another as unified around an act of sacramental violence, and so on. Readers will press into service a great variety of ideas—moral, social, religious, or philosophical—to yield the classes and concepts into which they feel comfortable grouping the separate details of the work. And, of course, some readers have used psychological and psychoanalytic ideas—it is no accident that I mentioned *Hamlet*, the *ur*-example of psychoanalytic literary studies.

Freud found love of the mother and jealousy of the father first in his patients, then in himself, and then he was struck to find them in *Hamlet* and *Oedipus Rex*. Seventy-five years later, we are no longer surprised. We have by this time inferred psychoanalytic ideas from hundreds upon hundreds of works. Only the most naive of psychoanalytic readers of literature, however, would claim that oedipal fantasies have the same status as "meaning" that more conventional interpretations have. It is one thing to say *Hamlet* illustrates Goethe's dark maxim that to act is to sin or the great Aeschylean theme of learning through suffering. It is quite another to say *Hamlet* is "about" the parting and coming together of father, son, and mother. Our feelings toward mothers and fathers come deeper than and prior to the ideas of Goethe or Aeschylus. They are prior because they come earlier in life. In adults one sees mostly derivatives of such early imaginings, rarely the fantasies themselves. They are deeper in the sense that, in most adults, such fantasies tend to be unconscious, closer to the roots of personality in the body than to more consciously intellectual ideas.

Stories usually do not present infantile fantasies as such. Rather we infer fantasies from stories on the basis of what we know from clinical experience. For example, we can infer from almost any Hemingway story its author's painful imaginings about threats to the visible, physical sign of a man's virility, fantasies all too familiar in American psychoanalytic experience. We can deduce from almost any Fitzgerald story his equally common and vexing fears about unappeasable hungers that can only be satisfied by unreachable women or unattainable sources of riches. Hemingway did not write about penises as such (at least not often), but he did write about risking one's manliness, and his fiction abounds in such visibly virile activities as hunting, fishing, bullfighting, and soldiering. Similarly, Fitzgerald rarely talked explicitly about mothers who frustrate, but he wrote story after story about immensely powerful sources of riches, success, love, or admiration that eventually let you down. What we know about human psychology tells us that these fantasies about one's body and one's parents are likely to be unconscious and primitive, while ideas about wealth or manliness are likely to be the adult, conscious transforms of those early fantasies.

Thus—and this is surely a commonplace after seventy-five

years of psychoanalytic studies in the field—writers create by transforming unconscious wishes from childhood. Most people who are not creative writers know this transformational process best through dreams. Freud notes:

> Dreams frequently seem to have more than one meaning. Not only, as our examples have shown, may they include several wish-fulfillments one alongside the other; but a succession of meanings or wish-fulfillments may be superimposed on one another, the bottom one being the fulfillment of a wish dating from earliest childhood. And here again the question arises whether it might not be more correct to assert that this occurs "invariably" rather than "frequently."[4]

Just as all people (not just writers or readers) have a press or tendency to form unities, they also have a tendency to transform primitive, infantile fantasies toward adult themes. And both writers and readers use stories to do this.

The reader uses the literary work to create in himself a dynamic psychological process that transforms raw fantasy materials to conscious significance. In this process, he makes use of two basic agents of transformation. One is the press toward theme and meaning, a transformation analogous to sublimation or symbolization in everyday life. Thus getting rich may come to symbolize for him getting the power to win the unattainable Fitzgerald heroine. He may represent in his mind achievements with the visible, physical emblem of manliness by fishing, hunting, bullfighting, soldiering, and the other virile activities that permeate Hemingway's fiction.

The other agent of transformation (besides the process of meaning) is that catchall of aesthetic notions, form. Critics define form in its broadest sense as "all devices that structure content," but, of course, texts do not structure content—people do. Formal devices become part of the reading experience only as they become part of the reader's devices. If the process of meaning resembles a reader's sublimating, in using forms he looks as though he were using strategies from a more general set of defense mechanisms: putting dangers from inside outside or from outside inside, refusing to acknowledge them, trying to undo them magically, and so on.

In *Hamlet*, for example, I discover an elaborate set of dou-blings and splittings that divide my various feelings toward a father among several father-figures: Hamlet's dead father, Hamlet's remembered father, Hamlet's father as ghost, Ham-let's stepfather, Polonius, Old Fortinbras, or the Player King. My feelings toward women divide between earthy Gertrude and virginal Ophelia. I find Hamlet's attitudes toward fathers mirrored by the subplot around Laertes. In short, when I ex-perience *Hamlet*, I feel the unified cluster of my ideas about parents and rivals transformed by being split up: I have purer, stronger feelings because they are isolated toward different characters and events.

In its most general terms, then, this model of literature as transformation suggests that the inanimate literary work is not that, not a work in itself, but the occasion for some person's work (in the sense we give the word when we speak of the "dream-work" or creative "work"). That is, a reader, as he synthesizes and re-creates a piece of literature, works; he transforms his own fantasies (of a kind that would ordinarily be unconscious) into the conscious social, moral, and intellectual meanings he finds by "interpreting" the work. When I experi-ence *Hamlet*, for example, splitting familiar fantasies of love and hate toward fathers and mothers, I also find in the play generalized intellectual themes about the way thought and action split and work against each other. In almost any Hemingway story, I find my fantasies about the dangers of being helpless and unmanned transformed into a manly ethic of playing the game bravely and fairly in the face of inevitable loss—a loss I also feel in Hemingway's depressing plots and the way his reticent language withholds from me. In Fitzgerald's works, I sense another kind of loss, breathless, over-romantic exaggerations of language (as well as his depleting finales) from which I get a feeling of utopias undone, riches made unbelieva-ble, feelings derived, in my mind anyway, from longings toward a parental source of well-being.

Once we have recognized that literary works provide the opportunity for psychological processes in the reader analogous both to the writer's original act of creation and to sublimations and other defenses familiar from couch or clinic or, for that matter, everyday life in and around us, we are in a position to investigate response. We can begin to see how each reader creates from the literary work a psychological process in himself. We say we get absorbed in the act of reading or watching a film or play, but to speak of being "absorbed" by a book puts the metaphor the wrong way round. It is not the book that absorbs us; it is we who absorb the book. It is we who "devour" novels, who have a "taste" for science fiction, who are "insatiable" or "voracious" readers, who "take in" movies, who are "addicted" to murder mysteries or "sated" with academic novels, who find some writers a "treat" but end up being "fed pap" by "the tube."

As these figures of speech suggest, we enjoy literary works in a mode derived from our most primitive experience of gratified desire, that stage in earliest infancy when we feel at one with the nurturing mother who satisfies our hunger. We also speak of "losing oneself" in a book or becoming "at one with the work of art" or being taken "out of oneself." These familiar metaphors suggest a loss of self-consciousness or of a sense of one's own identity that also derives, ultimately, from that same at-oneness and merger with the earliest source of gratification.

"The work lives its own life within me," says Georges Poulet; "in a certain sense, it thinks itself, and it even gives itself a meaning within me." "Everything happens . . . as though from the moment I become a prey [*sic*] to what I read, I begin to share the use of my consciousness with this being . . . who is the conscious subject ensconced at the heart of the work. He and I, we start having a common consciousness." "When a man is 'absorbed' or 'immersed' in a story," writes Robert Gorham Davis, "the work . . . is thinking *him*. His ego has become object, not subject." "Let us observe ourselves," says Ortega y Gasset, "at the moment we finish reading a great novel." "An instant ago we found ourselves in [its place] with [its people], we were living with them, immersed in their air, their space, their time. Now suddenly without any intermission we find ourselves in our chamber, in our city, in our date."[5]

Probably the most exact adult analogy to this state of mind

derives from hypnosis. The hypnotist's subject sets up a sub-system within his ego answering to the hypnotist much the way a reader uses a literary work to set up a process of transformation from it in his own mind. One can think of a kind of "core" in the reader's ego that is regressed to primitive, magical thinking (primary process, in technical terms) based on the fusions of infant feeding. Surrounding this "core" is a "rind" of unregressed ego. The "core" contains the process of transformation that is the literary "work" as performed by the reader. Meanwhile, the "rind" sustains that work by such "higher" ego-activities as putting letters together to form words, remembering what has gone before and anticipating what will come next, synthesizing characters and events, and, most importantly, analogizing from the reader's own experience to the people and episodes of the literary work.

This model—the reader experiencing the work as a transformation within himself of unconscious fantasy materials through form and meaning—comes from *The Dynamics of Literary Response*. It appears here much as it did in my earlier book, but with an important change in emphasis, something I have slowly learned from listening to what real readers say about their reading. I often spoke in *Dynamics* as though these fantasies and their transformations were embodied in the literary work, as though the work itself acted like a mind. This, of course, is no more than a useful fiction and maybe less. A fiction certainly. Useful? I now think not.

Processes like the transformation of fantasy materials through defenses and adaptations take place in people, not in texts. They require a mind, either the writer's or the reader's. As Proust wisely said,

> In reality, each reader reads only what is already within himself. The book is only a sort of optical instrument which the writer offers to the reader to enable the latter to discover in himself what he would not have found but for the aid of the book.[6]

Proust's *mot*, like this whole model, tries to be universal and succeeds in being abstract. To make the model more tangible, to discover the "what" in "Who reads what how?," we can turn to a specific story, one that these five readers read. You have already seen one tiny part of their response, their comments on the "tableau" of Miss Emily and her father. Later, in Chapter 6, we shall see much more. At this point, however, I would like simply to show what a story looks like when understood by means of this transformational model. To do that, let us take Proust's counsel and look at what the story becomes in the mind of a sixth reader—me.

The Story: Themes

Evidently, a good many readers like what I like in "A Rose for Emily"—Faulkner's 1931 gothic vignette may be the single most popular short story in America. Anthologies by the dozens include it, as do textbooks and literature courses, while among the hundreds of teachers who must have taught this very short short story, at least twenty have published formal explications, developing social, moral, and intellectual themes from its details. Yet such conscious themes make up just the tip of the iceberg. Critics and teachers can use the story to achieve adult themes only because they also can use it to match defenses and adaptations and fantasies in themselves that reach back to the most primitive layers of their minds.

For me, the story's appeal comes from watching the artful way Faulkner "leaks" the final dreadful secret bit by intriguing bit. He begins with Miss Emily's death and the innocent narrator's recalling how the whole town went to the funeral of the old recluse who had shut herself away for many years in a decaying house on a deteriorating street. The teller of the tale goes on to a series of reminiscences: old Colonel Sartoris had remitted her taxes in 1894, and when the next generation tried to collect them, she faced them down. There had been a mysterious smell about her house that the town fathers had been too courteous to mention to her. Her father had chased suitors away with a horsewhip (in the "tableau" our five readers responded to so varyingly). Then, when he died, she had refused for three days to admit he was dead or to let the body be removed. She took up with Homer Barron, a Northerner and a day laborer, while the town speculated and gossiped about their affair or engagement. Miss Emily stared the druggist down when he tried to get her to comply with the law requiring her to say why she wanted arsenic. She bought a toilet set for a bridal present, but then Homer Barron disappeared and Miss Emily became a gray-haired recluse, living by teaching china-painting to the children of the town aristocracy, never leaving her house, tended only by an old Negro cook and gardener. Finally, she died and, once she was buried, the men of the town found a sealed upstairs room all decked out in rose, as if for a wedding-night, then, on the bed, the rotted corpse of the poisoned lover, finally in an indentation on the pillow beside him, "a long strand of iron-gray hair." And even knowing it is coming, I gasp at the appalling rightness of that final discovery.

Except for a few quibbles about the final clue as to when or how long Emily slept with the corpse of her lover,[7] a question that I think cannot be finally settled, one can safely say there is considerable consensus about the basic contrast in the story.[8] To be sure, different critics accent different forms of that contrast—I see three alternative ways of stating it: social, philosophical, and (less clearly) mythic.

Most critics speak of the tension in the story as social, between the South and the North, the old and the new, the traditional and the traditionless, and the gentility as against the middle or lower classes.[9] As Irving Howe says, however, to take the story as dealing just with the decadent South (represented by Miss Emily) and the uncultured North (Homer Barron) is to make it trivial. He finds instead a larger parable about the decay of human sensibility from false gentility to genteel perversion.[10]

If so, I would generalize the story still further as a breakdown of controls. Repressive rules give rise to violence,[11] and society itself becomes so weak it cannot enforce its laws and principles. Emily can withhold taxes, refuse to give the druggist her reasons for buying poison, or keep a public nuisance (the smell). Finally, she can commit and get away with murder—her final attack on society's laws and taboos, which society accepts. Yet, as Austin Wright points out, Emily does not simply reject society: the bridal decorations and the murder itself reveal a deep and lonely longing for marriage, which is a social institution.[12] Such a view matches Faulkner's own statement that it is a story "of a poor tragic human being struggling with its own heart, with others, with its environment, for the simple things which all human beings want."[13]

Other critics press these social readings of the story toward more philosophical issues. Ray B. West[14] sees the subject of the story as a man's relation to time, the past as represented by Miss Emily and her father and the present depicted through the unnamed narrator and "the next generation with its more modern ideas." Emily attempts, he says, "almost by force of will alone, to halt the natural process of decay and death." Thus, West finds (as I do) the center of the story in its statement: "With nothing left, she would have to cling to that which had robbed her, as people will."

West supplies an essentially psychological concept to unify Miss Emily's actions: *denial*, the defense mechanism that con- sists of the ego's refusing to perceive what it cannot tolerate. By clinging to the old (the very thing that had robbed her), Miss Emily denies the existence of what is new and painful: the deaths of her father and Colonel Sartoris, the authority of the new town officers—ultimately, "she denies Time, even to the point of ignoring . . . Death." "Emily pretends that it, like the sheriff's tax bill, does not exist." Similarly, she refuses to comply "with the requirements of the law, because for her they did not exist."

Cleanth Brooks and Robert Penn Warren in their justly famous textbook take the idea of denial even further: "Miss Emily . . . is one of those persons for whom the distinction between reality and illusion has blurred out." The dead lover seems still alive to her because she has lost "the distinction between illusion and reality, between life and death."[15] A denial of normal emotions, notes William Van O'Connor, in- vites a retreat into fantasy. Thus, one can see change or, more exactly, the denial of change as the story's central issue. As C. W. M. Johnson states the theme: "If one resists change, he must love and live with death."[16]

With that remark, I can put together the social ways critics have accented the story with the philosophical (or psycholog-

ical) interpretations to make a transition to a third kind
of reading. Miss Emily, by acting out social, moral, and
metaphysical denials, comes to symbolize the entire social
context of conservatism in the South; she becomes, in short,
the mythic emblem for the whole community and perhaps all
mankind. From this point of view, the descriptions of Emily as
an "idol," a church angel, and a "monument" take on special
force, and Emily, in O'Connor's phrase, becomes "the mystery
itself." Brooks and Warren call her "a combination of idol and
scapegoat for the community," and they suggest that the
story's comparison of her strained face to that of a lighthouse-
keeper shows that the light she sheds on the darkness of human
experience serves the same kind of public function mythic or
religious figures do.

This view of her, at any rate, would accord with Faulkner's
own: in rejecting a purely North-and-South reading, he said the
story dealt with "the conflict of conscience with glands, with
the Old Adam. It was a conflict not between the North and the
South so much as between, well you might say God and Satan.
. . . The conflict was in Miss Emily. . . ." Miss Emily, he is
saying, comes to symbolize "man . . . trying to do the best he
can with his desires and impulses against his own moral conscience, and the conscience of, the social conscience of his
time and his place—the little town he must live in, the family
he's part of."[17]

I also think Miss Emily is a symbol that, like the narrator,
sheds a dark light into the polarities of the community around
her. For example, the separation of the sexes. From its opening
sentence, the story sharply differentiates the roles of men and
women in the town: "When Miss Emily Grierson died, our
whole town went to her funeral: the men through a sort of
respectful affection for a fallen monument, the women mostly
out of curiosity. . . ." Miss Emily separates the sexes, as does
the narrator, yet one cannot tell whether the narrator is male or
female, old or young. The narrator uses the first person forty-
eight times, but always as "we," never as "I."[18]

Thus I feel the narrator, in some ways the most peripheral
person in the story, comes to parallel Miss Emily at its center,
for she, too, seems to me to be curiously androgynous. At first,

she is "a slender figure in white," looking, even at thirty, "like a girl, with a vague resemblance to those angels in colored church windows." When we last see her, it is with gray hair: "Up to the day of her death at seventy-four it was still that vigorous iron-gray, like the hair of an active man." Brooks and Warren speak of her "tremendous firmness of will."

She may even be one of those striking Persephonic figures that occur among Faulkner's women, holding in themselves mysterious forces of creation and destruction.[19] If so, then someone might see the final strand of hair as analogous to the Greek ritual of cutting off and leaving a lock of hair at the grave of a beloved person, especially since this beloved dead person is named Homer.[20] I would note, too, that the colors associated with Emily are those of the dread triple goddess (the colors Apuleius explains as being derived from the moon): black, yellow or gold, and red (here, "rose"). As a goddess of growth and decay, or the inconstant moon, Emily comes to "stand for" and ritualize for me larger entities: the American South or, ironically, all of us, as we reveal but fail to ward off the painful realities of time and change, all too horribly embodied in the final image.

The Story: Fantasies

When I stop interpreting so intellectually, however, and try to get at my "gut" experience of the story, I find I have a special feeling toward Miss Emily. She seems to me a sealed, opaque being, flat as a marble wall, but hiding within her something bizarre, wild, grotesque—and I want that something out in the open. No sooner do I say that, however, than I find myself associating phrases I picked out from various critics as well as background information from clinical psychoanalysis. Here, I have in mind a familiar and well-known symbolism—even so, the story spells it out. In "what had once been our most select street, . . . only Miss Emily's house was left, lifting its stubborn and coquettish decay above the cotton wagons and the gasoline pumps." The adjectives make the house into what Miss Emily has herself become: "stubborn" and "coquettish." Both Emily and the house are "monuments of the past" that have persisted into the present.[21] Twice the story calls Miss Emily "impervious," an adjective that could apply equally to a house that no white person has entered for years, that has not even a mailbox or a number. Judge Stevens also makes the equation quite explicit: When the younger generation complains about the smell around the house, " 'Dammit, sir,' Judge Stevens said, 'will you accuse a lady to her face of smelling bad?' "

Another symbolism seems relevant to me here: the "rose" of the title.[22] William T. Going wittily suggests that, given Faulkner's "subtle and gruesome treatment of odors in the story and the importance of the Grierson name, the title may well refer to Shakespeare's familiar lines from another tragedy of lovers:

> What's in a name? That which we call a rose
> By any other name would smell as sweet.[23]

The symbolism both of the house and of the rose makes me feel as though the story were talking distantly and obliquely about the externals of a body that, later we learn, has a nasty secret inside it, dust and darkness and, most strongly, smells: "a close, dank smell," "a thin, acrid pall," a "dust dry and acrid in the nostrils." Again, "It smelled of dust and disuse." The smell "was another link between the gross, teeming world and the high and mighty Griersons," and I'll even suggest that the adjective "high" conceals a particularly sardonic pun.

As I recite this litany of dirt, dust, and smell, I feel I am responding to the story, half-unconsciously, with a mixture of attraction and revulsion toward "dirty" body products. In any case, at an intellectual level, I recall that Freud identified a famous triad of traits: orderliness, parsimony, and obstinacy. All, he said, derive from holding on or letting go inner body "dirt" in response to outer demands, and I find all three traits in this story; although the orderliness is reversed with Miss Emily, not cleanliness but uncleanliness: smells, dirt, and dust. Emily is nothing if not retentive.[24] Faulkner himself said simply, "She had had something and she wanted to keep it." This theme of retention made sense for me out of one of the story's more startling images, a description of the aged Miss Emily: "She looked bloated, like a body long submerged in motionless water." "Motionless," West points out, links her to the absence of change, but more specifically to the kind of stasis that swells a body up. This is a story—at one level and for one reader—about the difficulty one has in giving up prized things from a certain house (or body).[25]

Given the familiar psychological association of the precious and the "dirty," I felt it fitting that some of what goes in and out is money: "the old thrill and the old despair of a penny more or less." Miss Emily does not pay money out in taxes. Instead, she defies the authorities who demand that she do so. "She gave lessons in china-painting"—one could hardly find a more obsessional pastime. Further, to learn this art, "the daughters and granddaughters of Colonel Sartoris' contemporaries were sent to her with the same regularity and in the same spirit that they were sent to church cn Sundays with a twenty-five-cent piece for the collection plate." As early as 1907, Freud had pointed out the similarity between religious practices and bodily "duties." This was even before he had brought out the special connection between parental control of inner physical products and obsessional controls of inner mental products and, indeed, of painting as a possible gratification of impulses to play with body products in an only partially controlled way.[26] Thus, the religious images we considered earlier play a part in establishing in my interpretation one level of unconscious fantasy on which the story builds: Miss Emily as "a tradition, a duty, and a care," resembling "those angels in colored church windows," "an idol," "an idol in a niche," and after her death "a fallen monument."

I do not, however, wish to give the impression that the only fantasy I find is at the level of controlling what is inside one's body—certainly not with a father like Miss Emily's. He is shown as penniless, violent, angry, having fallen out with the Griersons' only relatives. "We had long thought of them as a tableau, Miss Emily a slender figure in white in the background, her father a spraddled silhouette in the foreground, his back to her and clutching a horsewhip." Obviously, such a father evokes a child's feelings of fear and desire for him in Miss Emily—and in me. He dominates Emily, driving her suitors away with his horsewhip, and he continues his power, somehow, after his death. Even after her death, there was "the crayon face of her father musing profoundly above the bier."

From this point of view, the father controlling and dominating what goes into and out of his daughter, the very center of the story again becomes for me the narrator's remark: "We knew that with nothing left, she would have to cling to that which had robbed her, as people will." But Emily does more than cling to her father's body. After Homer Barron has apparently deserted her, she isolates herself, "as if," the narrator comments, "that quality of her father which had thwarted her woman's life so many times had been too virulent and too furious to die." He goes on to describe her hair as a "vigorous iron-gray, like the hair of an active man." She is described as a "lighthouse-keeper," as having "vanquished them [the town government], horse and foot, just as she had vanquished their fathers thirty years before." Maybe Irving Malin is correct when he says, "Her passionate, almost sexual relationship with her dead father forces her to distrust the living body of Homer and to kill him so that he will resemble the dead father she can never forget."[27] But, for me, it suffices to say Miss Emily identifies with her father, taking on his iron will, his strength, and his brutality, regressing from the little girl's wish to *have* her father to the more primitive wish to *be* her father.

In this context, despite the scandalized townsfolk (" 'A Grierson would not think seriously of a Northerner, a day laborer' "), her faintly "dirty" and sordid choice of Homer Barron seems surprising but right to me. Because he is tabooed, he can be a substitute for her father, the original forbidden lover. The very disapproval of the townspeople becomes tempting because it re-enacts that first, disapproved love, even as it guarantees the lover is in fact not the equivalent of a Grierson. As Freud says, "The condition for forbiddenness in the erotic life of women is, I think, comparable to the need on the part of men to debase their sexual object," both being ways of seeking "only objects which do not recall the incestuous figures forbidden" in childhood; however, "these new objects will still be chosen on the model . . . of the infantile ones."[28]

Thus, Emily keeps Homer's body as she tried to keep her father's. At the same time, her vengeful murder of Homer seems just the kind of thing her father would do; I feel she has incorporated much of her father's brutality in herself. There is, in effect, a man in Emily's house—or body—or mind. Even Faulkner tended to masculinize Emily in his description of the story to the students at Virginia: "the conflict of conscience with glands, with the Old Adam." "The conflict was in Miss Emily," including, apparently, Old Adam's glands.

By contrast, I feel, the town outside Emily's house sharply distinguishes men from women. The long opening sentence establishes just that: sexes are markedly different in this town, but Emily's house involves a peculiar combination of man and woman. "When Miss Emily Grierson died, our whole town went to her funeral: the men through a sort of respectful affection for a fallen monument, the women mostly out of curiosity to see the inside of her house, which no one save an old man-servant—a combined gardener and cook—had seen in at least ten years." Similarly, in the remission of Miss Emily's taxes, "Only a man of Colonel Sartoris' generation and thought could have invented [the story], and only a woman could have believed it." Colonel Sartoris was the one who "fathered the edict that no Negro woman should appear on the streets without an apron," but in Miss Emily's house the servant is a male cook. The narrator repeatedly insists on calling her supervising relatives, "the two female cousins," and, in general, it falls to the ladies to keep up standards in the town. " 'Just as if a man—any man—could keep a kitchen properly,' the ladies said; so they were not surprised when the smell developed." It is the ladies who get the Baptist minister to remonstrate with Emily about her relationship with Homer. The day after the father's death, "all the ladies prepared to call at the house and offer condolence and aid, as is our custom."

To my mind, the town, by sharply differentiating the sexes, recapitulates the kind of outside control Miss Emily had when her father was alive and before she had incorporated his masculinity into herself. Although Faulkner himself, as well as many readers, retained a vivid image of the delicately feminine Miss Emily, she actually appears in only one phrase, "a slender figure in white." Most of the time, we see Emily as she appears to the druggist, "cold, haughty black eyes in a face the flesh of which was strained across the temples and about the eyesockets as you imagine a lighthouse-keeper's face ought to look." "She carried her head high enough," driving with Homer Barron, and the word is applied at least two more times to the Griersons as a family. "Miss Emily with her head high"—her body, again, matches the house itself, "lifting its stubborn and coquettish decay above" its sordid surroundings.

This kind of character, fixed on body products, Karl Abraham notes,

> sometimes seems to stamp itself on the physiognomy of its possessor. It seems particularly to show itself in a morose expression. [Such persons] tend to surliness as a rule. A constant tension of the line of the nostril together with a slight lifting of the upper lip seem to me significant facial characteristics of such people. In some cases this gives the impression that they are constantly sniffing at something. Probably this feature is traceable to their coprophilic pleasure in smell.[29]

One could also, I think, trace it simply to controlling, "keeping a grip on," oneself.

Certainly control seems to me a basic issue of the story, not only for Miss Emily, but also in the town from whose point of view we see her. Repeatedly, we hear about the forces of law in the town, and such writers as Erik Erikson have shown the close link between law as that which "apportions to each his privileges and his limitations, his obligations and his rights" and the "sense of rightfully delimited autonomy in the parents" at that stage of development so involved with retention and elimination, with holding on and letting go, with shame and autonomy, control and will. All these things are important in "A Rose for Emily," particularly in view of what Ray B. West calls the "conflicting demands" of past and present.[30]

In the more modern period of the story, law takes the form of institutions or groups: "the post office," "them," "the sheriff's office," "the city authorities," "the town." It is a government of laws, not men. If there are men, they act on behalf of the law, as the mayor and the aldermen and the druggist do. In the older period of the story, it is a government of men, not laws, as government must appear to a child. It is Judge Stevens or Colonel Sartoris who controls, and this style of government is closely associated with Miss Emily's father. Thus, in describing the remission of her taxes, Faulkner uses the key word three times: "Colonel Sartoris, the mayor—he who fathered the edict that no Negro woman should appear on the streets without an apron—remitted her taxes, the dispensation dating from the death of her father . . . [and] invented an involved tale to the effect that Miss Emily's father had loaned money to the town."

In many ways, like that "edict," this kind of law seems to me more like a frightening unlawfulness, like her father's horsewhip or like justice in the Amerikan parts of America even today. Thus, the story shows a peculiar combination of violence with the weakness of the society in enforcing its principles against Emily. When Judge Stevens gets the Board of Aldermen to take the law into their own hands, "the next night, after midnight, four men . . . slunk about the house like burglars." Similarly, her father is described as "that which had robbed her." Then, if I think of the tenacity with which the South has clung to the "peculiar institution" that has cost her so much, I can find still another, regional dimension to the story's key clause: "With nothing left, she would have to cling to that which had robbed her, as people will."

Predictably, Miss Emily adopts this being "above the law" as her own lifestyle once her father has died. She puts the person in place of the law, as her father did, refusing to recognize the sheriff's authority—" 'Perhaps he considers himself the sheriff' "—or the Board of Aldermen's. Instead, " 'See Colonel Sartoris. I have no taxes in Jefferson.' " "Colonel Sartoris had been dead almost ten years"—like her father.

Such a government counts on the pride and dignity of its Sartorises, Griersons, and Stevenses. It punishes by the opposite of pride and dignity—like the aprons the Negro women must wear as a badge of servitude. Shame is a visual thing. Again, in discussing this phase of development, Erikson says, "Shame supposes that one is completely exposed and conscious of being looked at." "One is visible and not ready to be visible; which is why we dream of shame as a situation in which we are stared at in a condition of incomplete dress, in night attire, 'with one's pants down.' " In my reading, the control through shame occasions the many, many references to watching in the story, mostly references to the peeping, whispering, gossiping townspeople as they comment on Emily's actions.

This darkness and watching and shaming makes me nervous, but Emily seems unaffected. Indeed, she takes on a symbolic role as a result: "As they recrossed the lawn, a window that had been dark was lighted and Miss Emily sat in it, the light behind her, and her upright torso motionless as that of an idol. Now and then we would see her in one of the downstairs windows—she had evidently shut up the top floor of the house—like the carven torso of an idol in a niche, looking or not looking at us, we could never tell which." As the lighthouse-keeper, watching and watched, she becomes for me the visible symbol of an old "tradition" that based its hard training heavily on shame, like the educational systems of certain primitive peoples.

As Erikson notes, "Visual shame precedes auditory guilt," has more of the primitive about it, just as the Sartorises' and Stevenses' system of government does. Emily, ultimately, is not a well-governed person. "Too much shaming," says Erikson, "does not lead to genuine propriety but to a secret determination to try to get away with things, unseen—if, indeed, it does not result in defiant shamelessness."[31] Emily is both, shameless with Homer alive, secret with him dead. "Already we knew that there was one room in that region above stairs that no one had *seen* in forty years," and the participle I have underlined strikes me as psychologically exact.

Control, particularly control based on shaming, plays an important part in the stage of development in which the child learns to control his body products. It is important, too, to adults with characters fixated to that phase. And it is important to this story. Yet, as in Freud's original formulation, the most central issue of all is possessing or, in Erikson's phrase, "holding on and letting go." In this story, I feel that to love is to possess someone the way one would possess a thing. Emily holds on to Homer's body as, earlier, she had held on to her father's body. By contrast, I feel Homer's careless love is foreshadowed in the way he doesn't even own his horses but has to rent them from the livery stable. Emily takes possession of him by gifts: a nightshirt, a toilet set, and evidently at least the promise of herself. Conversely, it seems to me, to be loved is to be possessed like an object. Thus, the language of the story links love and death in "the tomb . . . decked and furnished as for a bridal," in "the long sleep that outlasts love . . . [that] had cuckolded him."

Always, however, in experiencing this story, I found I had in mind a parental figure (Emily's father, the narrator, or the town) who presides over what goes into and out of Miss Emily's house—or body. Erikson calls it the "battle for autonomy":

> If outer control by too rigid or too early training persists in robbing the child of his attempt gradually to control his bowels and other functions willingly and by his free choice . . . [among other outcomes, he may] pretend an autonomy and an ability to do without anybody's help which he has by no means really gained.
>
> This stage, therefore, becomes decisive for the ratio between loving good will and hateful self-insistence, between cooperation and willingness, and between self-expression and compulsive self-restraint or meek compliance.[32]

Miss Emily, like a child being trained, vacillates between shameless defiance of that authority (when it is the town) or totally introjecting its demands and complying with them (when it is her father). Against the parent trying to regulate a child's feces, Dr. Spock notes, the child is "apt to fight in rage and terror, as if he thought he was going to remove a very part of his body," or at least he will become "worried to see this object, which he considers part of himself, snatched away."[33] This is another sense in which I find central this statement: "With nothing left, she would have to cling to that which had robbed her, as people will." It is more than just a bad pun to say Miss Emily is a possessive woman. Miss Emily had "incorporated" or "introjected" the harsh controls based on pride and shame that her father embodied. Holding his body and Homer's, retaining them inside her house or body, is the outward sign of an inward adaptation. So also, I would guess, is her having become obese—a sign of incorporation at the beginning as well as retention at the end of her digestive mind and body.

To this highly specialized reading of the story, I associate an odd detail—Faulkner's handling of the voices. Fenichel sums up one psychoanalytic theory about speech: "The function of speech is frequently connected unconsciously with the genital function, particularly with the male genital function. To speak means to be potent; inability to speak means castration." Thus, virile Homer is associated with "a lot of laughing"; he was "a big, dark, ready man, with a big voice." "The little boys would follow in groups to hear him cuss the niggers."

By contrast, Emily's "voice was dry and cold," and, as for the Negro manservant, "He talked to no one, probably not even to her, for his voice had grown harsh and rusty, as if from disuse." Fenichel suggests that some of the feelings associated with putting excrement forth may become attached to the putting forth of words. Thus Miss Emily's taciturnity may be still another of her retentions; the Negro's, part of his utter subservience. The story shows still another significance Fenichel gives for speech: "In dreams, to speak is the symbol of life, and to be mute the symbol of death."[34] Thus, in a marvelously chosen adjective, we see Homer's "two mute shoes" in the sealed bedroom.

These references to speech and the voice—though only a small series of images in the story—nevertheless trace out the central psychological pattern I create from it. I find myself imagining the story in terms of going in or coming out, in several senses. That is, Miss Emily's father restricts the suitors who can enter her house (and thus her body). When she is deprived of sexuality, Miss Emily, and the story as a whole, seem to me to regress to a stage prior to male-female comparisons. She will hold on to what she has: first her father; then her father's tradition and style; finally, Homer Barron, the man who would have robbed her. (There may even be a play on "robber baron.") In contrast, then, to big-voiced Homer, who puts out sound freely, Miss Emily's silent house signifies the attempt to hold things in. He represents to me the new freedom from the North; she, the attempt to keep things as they are in the South, to stop process and change—a kind of social constipation.

The Story: Transformations

Intimately related to the fantasies I find in the story about controlling what a body has inside it are the defenses that I see developing and transforming those fantasies. As I look at my interpretation of the story, I find I have ordered it by forms that resemble two well-known defenses: denial and incorporation, refusing to perceive painful things (here, pressures to change) or keeping something precious by holding it within one's body. In more literary terms, a major agent of transformation for me is the narrator. He helps me to deny in that he controls what I know about the plot, and he incorporates materials in that he holds back the ghastly secret in dear Miss Emily's house until the end. He controls not only what I perceive but when I perceive it. As for me, however, I feel these defenses at work still more strongly in the character of Miss Emily.

Many of the regular explicators of the story called her resistance to change the central theme, whether one regards change in the specific context of the American South or in a larger, more philosophical way. In psychoanalytic terms, I think they are discovering Miss Emily's adaptive strategy (or maladaptive, really) of denial. She denies time, the law, and even death. "The distinction between reality and illusion has blurred out."[35] Miss Emily simply acts as though the "next generation," "newer generation," "rising generation," did not exist. She lives where she does despite the change in the street. She writes on "paper of an archaic shape." She becomes fixed like "the carven torso of an idol," and "thus she passed from generation to generation." She becomes "a tradition, a duty, and a care."

As I read its acceptance of her, the town incorporates this idol in a miniature version of Miss Emily's more drastic incorporation—one way the story generalizes into "Southernness."[36] The town copies Miss Emily. She keeps in her house the crayon portrait of her father, while the townspeople "had long thought of [both Miss Emily and her father] as a tableau." Miss Emily has for me a mythic dimension: the goddess slaying the year king, Homer, or her father, whose body she retains for the canonical three days. These Persephonic images become the feebly feminine religion of the "ladies" in the town.

In the same way, I feel the town goes along—up to a point—with Miss Emily's denial of her father's death. "We did not say she was crazy then. We believed she had to do that." Similarly, the townsfolk accept her becoming a recluse "as if that quality of her father which had thwarted her woman's life so many times had been too virulent and too furious to die"—a miniature version of Miss Emily's denial of his death. The townsfolk believe, " ' they are married,' " then become curiously silent on the subject when Homer disappears—again, they use a less mad version of her own denial. Ruth Sullivan has found a great many ways in which the narrator in particular parallels Miss Emily, as the watcher parallels the watched: for example, his opening sentence about entering the house corresponds to the final breaking into the sealed bedroom.[37] In general, he shares much of her pathology—as indeed one would expect (because the same fantasies and defenses permeate all parts of the story in any given reader's reading).

In all this doubling of Miss Emily's adaptations I am seeing what Ludwig Jekels long ago called "the duplicated expression of psychic themes." In my reading, both the town-narrator and Emily act out a combination of two defense mechanisms: denial and incorporation. The problem they must deal with is change. In external reality, the old is passing and being replaced by the new. Emily (and, in a more muted way, the town) deal with it in one of two ways.

The first is denial: she will say there is no new thing in external reality, as with the taxes, the mailbox, or the druggist. The second is incorporation: I still have the old thing inside me (in my mind or in my house or in my body). This defense takes its most drastic form in Miss Emily's keeping her father or Homer in her house, less drastically in her treating marriage as a possession or keeping the crayon portrait of her father. The townsfolk share this defense by their interest in what they take to be something precious or secret in the house, to be watched or approached "like burglars."

These two defensive strategies correspond quite neatly to the developmental sequence of the fantasies I found. Consider incorporation. At the level of sexual longings toward a tabooed or parental figure, Miss Emily holds onto her father and her tabooed lover. At the level concerned with differentiating male from female, Miss Emily acquires manly force. She succeeds, at the next level, in holding something precious inside herself against outside and inside pressures to let it go. Finally, at the deepest level of taking the things you want into yourself, Miss Emily takes Homer, the South takes Miss Emily, and so on. Clearly, all these are forms of incorporation, and all involve loving something.

I have, however, also found equivalent levels of aggressive fantasy. She defeats the taboo on a forbidden lover, having and destroying him. At the level of sexual difference and the battle of the sexes, this woman not only avoids being overcome by a strong male, she overcomes him. She defies (by withholding from them) outer authorities and controls that demand she give up the precious thing within her. At the most primitive level, she consumes and eviscerates a loved person. These are all forms of aggressive attack on outside forces felt as coercive or controlling. In effect, Emily gets rid of the parts of external reality she doesn't like—as denial does. By denying the requirements of the law, she destroys the law.

My reading, then, comes to two defensive strategies, several levels of unconscious fantasy, both loving and aggressive, and four ways of stating the conscious theme of the story. Such variety calls for as clear an exposition as I can give, and with appropriate reservations I think a chart would help:

A Transformational Core
for "A Rose for Emily"

Putting within yourself
and so controlling . . .

something that is outside where
it cannot be controlled but
seeks to control you.

Conscious themes:

Intellectual-aesthetic
"She would have to cling . . .
as people will."

"to that which had robbed her"

Denial of change

Inevitability of change

Social
The South and fixed traditions

The North and change

Mythic
The Persephonic idol

Forces of change

Defensive modes:

Incorporation
I will take and keep the
old thing inside me.

Denial
There is no new thing in
external reality.

Fantasy modes:

Oedipal
Identification with the
father

Destroying the tabooed lover

Phallic
A woman being a strong
male

A woman overcoming a
strong male

Anal
Keeping the precious-dirty
thing inside

Defiance of outer authority
and control; refusing the
inner inexorability of
excretion

Visual
The reader-townsfolk imagine
the violent sexual scene

Stillness, quiet

Being looked at

Staring someone down

Oral
Being in the matrix of
tradition

Being outside the matrix
of tradition, aristocracy

Obesity (inviscerating)

The skeleton (eviscerated)

In effect, the chart sets out the spine of "centers" that I am using to organize my experience of the story as a whole at every level. For me, as for many other critics, "A Rose for Emily" pivots on the issue of change and resistance to change, or (if we take into account the rich variety of unconscious themes) perceiving change as robbery and resisting that robbery by taking into oneself the outer being that seeks to force you to change. One conscious component of such a theme is the historical issue of South and North. Another is Miss Emily as the Persephonic goddess, traditionally both creator and destroyer, but in this story a lifeless and motionless monument pitted against social and industrial forces of progress.

Just as central, I think, is the story's own statement that "with nothing left," that is, with realities denied, people will "cling to"—incorporate—"that which had robbed" them, that is, the outer forces seeking to control and force them. *I will cling in fantasy to that which has robbed me of reality*—almost a direct statement of the way the defenses I find of incorporation and denial match the various levels of fantasy. To me, Emily becomes like her father. Then she destroys the tabooed lover's external reality and incorporates him in the house of her body. She becomes strong and masculine enough to conquer the father-lover who seeks to overcome her. She retains, inside her, the dirty but precious contents of her life despite external pressures to let them go. In terms of feeding, her body grows fat as she incorporates, while Homer's body is thinned into a skeleton. The sealed bedroom is depleted. It holds a secret stillness and quiet, while I feel I am left to create in myself the sights and sounds of the sex and the death-agony on the fatal night. Finally, the story withholds its secret from me, and I have to project my imaginings into the last scene.

In this last way, then, the story seems to me again to ask for an interpretation in terms of going in and coming out, but again (I hasten to add) this is *my* re-creation of the story. We come back to the question from which this chapter began.

What: Subjectivity and Objectivity

The pages above are *my* reading of "A Rose for Emily." The fantasies and themes, defenses and transformations I have described come from the ways *my* character structure absorbed the story. I re-created "A Rose for Emily" by means of a personality that combines a passionate desire to know about the insides of things with an equally strong feeling that one is, finally, safer on the outside. I have read Faulkner's story with the same mind that delights in photography and movies because they are surfaces that come out of the dark to reveal a reality behind them—yet never cease being surfaces. I read "A Rose for Emily" with a mind still heavily committed to the not-so-new New Criticism (because it explores depths by confining itself to the surface verbal texture), with the same mind that analyzed Restoration comedies (in my first book) as demanding that surface appearances fulfill and complete inner nature rather than mask it, or with the mind that (in this book) probes the depths of literary response but from a position neither "in" psychoanalysis nor "in" literary criticism. In short, interpreting "A Rose for Emily" by a theme of going in and coming out expresses my character just as any of my other activities does.

Naturally, I have supplied evidence for my reading, but as we shall see when we consider the other five readers reading this story, evidence or no evidence, the way one puts a story together derives from the patterns and structures in the mind one brings to the story. Someone else reading it, even from a psychoanalytic point of view very like my own, can arrive at conclusions rather different even though they draw on just as much evidence from the text. Indeed someone, Ruth Sullivan, has done just that.[38] The problem is not to decide which of us is right or wrong. Obviously, I am right for me and Ms. Sullivan for her, and either of us—or neither of us—might be right for someone else. The point is to recognize that stories (or evidences from stories) do not "mean," in and of themselves. They do not fantasy or defend or adapt or transform. People do these things, using stories as the occasion (with more and less justification) for a certain theme, fantasy, or transformation. The problem then becomes understanding, not the story in formal isolation, but the story in relation to somebody's mind. Not a mind hypothesized, hypostatized, assumed, posited, or simply guessed at—as we shall see, we can only work with real minds in real people.

All readings originate in the reader's personality—all are "subjective" in that sense. Some readings take close account of the words-on-the-page and some do not, but no matter how much textual, "objective" evidence a reader brings into his reading, he structures and adapts it according to his own inner needs. (Otherwise, if interpretation flowed structurally or necessarily from the text, why would critics sign their work?)[39] It is, as we shall see, impossible to subtract the subjective elements in a reading from the objective, for each helps create the other. Or, more precisely, *a reader responds to a literary work by using it to re-create his own characteristic psychological processes.*

Knowing this, however, I feel lost in a paradox that, characteristically, I find discomforting. New Criticism turns out to have been Old Subjectivity. A reader reads something, certainly, but if one cannot separate his "subjective" response from its "objective" basis, there seems no way to find out what that "something" is in any impersonal sense. It is visible only in the psychological process the reader creates in himself by means of the literary work.

We are not without a general principle, however. No matter who the reader is or how he reads, what he reads will take the general form revealed by this model: a fantasy transformed by defenses and adaptations to give pleasure and unity and meaning. But what fantasies and which defenses and adaptations he can use to achieve pleasure, unity, and meaning depend on his pre-existing personality, the fatality of defense and adaptation he brought to the literary experience. "What" the reader reads is finally, "what the reader reads." One can only find out in detail what the "what" is in "Who reads what how?," by analyzing the other parts of that question: "how?" and "who?" And so we shall.

3 How? The "Experiment"

There are two senses, one general, one special, to the "how" in our basic question, "Who reads what how?" In a general sense, "how" refers to the principles that inform all people's reading, and that "how" is the big question this book addresses. "How" in its more special sense refers to the conditions under which five particular readers did in fact read some short stories, and it is much easier to answer.

The "Experiment"

I simply brought a certain number of readers together with some literary materials, mostly short stories, to see what they would say about them. I began in an exploratory way with a small group of graduate students in English from my own university and finished with a somewhat larger group of undergraduate English majors from a neighboring college. (The "five readers" reported here came from this younger group.)

All my readers had volunteered. I circulated a questionnaire asking those interested in participating (for a modest wage) to fill in their name, address, and age, and also the names of some writers they liked. I chose those volunteers who mentioned writers whose works went beyond the ordinary reading lists of a literature curriculum but did not seem to be faddish or outré. I was hoping for sincerity and frankness. For this reason I preferred literature majors because they were used to voicing their reactions freely to literary works—whether those reactions were favorable or unfavorable, conventional or unconventional. Nonstudents or students from other disciplines often feel challenged to prove their cultural mettle and try to come up with the "right" answer. At least in the preliminary stages, since I was not working statistically, I decided there was no need to average across a spectrum of ages, genders, occupations, and so on. If I could discover the dynamics of response for this group, the same principles should hold, *mutatis mutandis*, for anyone. I have since found no reason to change this decision.

Although we occasionally talked about poems, plays, or films, I felt short stories would be most likely to elicit frank, uncomplicated comments. I tried, too, to pick stories that were not too difficult to interpret—you can see all too clearly in the readings of the Hemingway story in Appendix B what obscurity of theme does to readers. Trying also to avoid "stock responses," I chose stories that were neither respectably old nor fashionably new. Thus, although these readers would sometimes talk about classics like Dickens or Defoe or moderns like Cohen or Kesey, I focused the interviews on ten rather familiar stories of a few decades ago: Joyce's "The Dead," for example, or Mann's "Mario and the Magician," from a well-known anthology.[1] Here, I will report readings just of William Faulkner's "A Rose for Emily," F. Scott Fitzgerald's "Winter Dreams," and Ernest Hemingway's "The Battler." I first chose these to write about because I thought they represented three distinct categories of fantasy (in a psychoanalytic sense), and the responses to them should have differed accordingly.

I began, in other words, hoping to do an "experiment" in stimulus and response, complete with rigorous hypotheses, predictions to be confirmed or not, measurement, repeatable data, isolation of the experimenter from his material, and so on. I thought I could work with objective tests like questionnaires that could be analyzed statistically. Abruptly, and rather painfully, I realized that none of this fit the problem.

It has been hard for me to get beyond the simple stimulus-response model that some psychological systems offer. As a rather positivistic person, I find it an attractive simplification, and it is the model that I, like most literary critics, almost automatically assume. Literature "does something" to its reader. From this point of view, a story is a stimulus that elicits a certain response. Within the story, any given element, a character, an episode, a theme, a sequence of images, even particular words or rhythms, cause certain reactions in the reader.

Again, from this point of view, if a story is a "stimulus," one's first impulse is to say the "response" is what the reader feels at the time he reads the story. We have already glanced at a number of studies that try to measure feelings by hormone concentrations, heart rate, fidget frequency, and the like. As a practical matter, however, I did not regard galvanic skin reactions or palmar sweat patterns as useful indicators of response, and therefore I concentrated on the words my readers spoke. "Feelings" should be expanded to include "thoughts" as well, and one could also wonder whether one must limit responses to those "at the time." After all, sometimes a reader changes his mind in retrospect. Certainly the teaching of literature aims at sophisticating responses beyond that first impulse. It seemed I had to be interested generally in the interaction of a person with a story, and anything that was part of their relationship had to be counted as part of "response."

The very notion of a "response" presupposes a fixed stimulus, the "words-on-the-page" that formalist critics have examined so rewardingly these last few decades. The more I worked with real readers, however, the more I was reminded that a literary work is not a fixed stimulus. Rather, each reader must give the words meaning, and he can only give them the meanings they have for him. It is he who fills in the outlines to give characters appearances, ages, manners, or personalities. In our "tableau," for example, despite the particularity of Faulkner's description, it is left to each reader to assign Miss Emily and her father relative positions in the picture—her an expression, for example, or him a posture. In all stories, it is the reader who fills in motivations, themes, and plot continuities in order to bring the parts he has already experienced to bear on each new experience. To be sure, critics often make "objective" statements about works: "In 'A Rose for Emily,' we only see the young Emily once." "Emily does not want to obey the law and tell the druggist why she wants poison." "The narrator always talks as 'we.' " But a critic or reader says these things because he thinks they are important to his personal synthesis of the story. Another critic would single out other features.

We come back again, then, not to a "response" one can easily experiment with, but to what the reader said about his reading as a clue to a complete transaction. Accordingly, I gave up attempts at questionnaires and group experiments with statistical possibilities. I settled down to work in an informal way with a few subjects. I have given them names here that are recognizably human, although not their own: Sam, Saul, Shep, Sebastian, and Sandra. The alliteration testifies to an ex-engineer's lingering nostalgia for the rigor of statistical work with objective *S*s that so sternly commands attention in the psychological journals. But, in fact, I tried not so much to experiment as to empathize with and understand these readers' personal re-creations of the literary work.

I met weekly with each reader for a tape recorded interview of an hour or so on a story that we had agreed the previous week he would read. Each subject, of course, knew the interview was being recorded, watched me turn the machine on and off, and each also knew I was having the tapes transcribed. I tried to get each reader to say as much as he could or would about the story, either in statements he volunteered or in answers to my questions. Over and over again, I would ask, "How do you feel about" characters, events, situations, or phrasings, but I also had certain fixed questions for each of the stories. For example, in "A Rose for Emily," I would ask, "What do you think happened on the fatal night?" or, "Do you feel that Miss Emily took on some of her father's characteristics as she grew older?" I tried to predict my readers' answers to these fixed questions before our meetings. I would ask impromptu questions to draw out more material on a given point. Usually, I asked each reader to retell the story in his own words, although I had to give up that procedure for the more talkative subjects like Sam. Sometimes I would ask them about a specific passage that I read from the anthology. Sometimes they would ask me to read something to them or they would reach over and take the book from me in order to refresh their recollection. And some readers (like Saul) habitually brought the book with them to make sure what they were saying corresponded exactly to the "words-on-the-page."

By so informal a procedure I was hoping to get out free associations to the stories. I tried very hard never to express shock or surprise or annoyance or any sense that there was a "right" reading. I did try—always—to get the readers to say as much as they would about a given feeling or point or story until it seemed exhausted. And I did assume that, by and large, what my readers said about their feelings at the time they read the story was true, but this was not essential. Free associations are like the retelling of a dream—an invented dream will express its teller's mind just as a real dream will. So long as a reader was talking fully and easily, it did not matter whether he was recalling his emotions correctly or even if he was disguising them or making them up to suit my professorial mien—free associations reveal the act of synthesis and creation behind them. The reader's words held what I was looking for.

Thus, it was not necessary to compensate for what was, to me, a most startling process of filtration, the shift of face-to-face interview into written transcription. On hearing a tape for the first time, I never failed to be shocked at what had been lost by way of facial expression, gesture, stance, manner, and the like. Further, as the tape was transcribed, still more disappeared: the expression and tone of the voice, clues to sarcasm and irony, the length of pauses, and so on. I did, however, take care to note on the transcriptions any changes of meaning that the actual sound introduced (sarcasm, for example). Finally, what was left was what counted: the texture of significant words.

The words, all by themselves (with only my marginal notes on intonation), provided ample evidence of the way the reader had composed the story for himself. As psychoanalysis has been showing for three-quarters of a century now, the particular phrasings of dreams, jokes, free associations, metaphors, clichés, "Freudian slips," misreadings, and forgettings reveal the dynamics of the ego behind them. A transcription of informal, spoken comments will do the same, even if the gestures of body and voice have been filtered out, indeed, even if some of the verbal "filler" of spoken English be removed.

Although those of us working on the project transcribed the tapes absolutely literally, recording even *um*'s and *uh*'s and pauses, I soon found that quotations from such transcriptions made wretched reading. This, for example, is an exact transcription of the sentence from which Sam's first comment on the "tableau" in "A Rose for Emily" was taken:

Emily is, uh, the daughter of a very prominent resident of a small—is it Mississippi? Probably—town—small Southern town, and, uh, the father was very domineering. Uh. One of the most striking images in the book is that of, is that of, is that of the townsfolk looking through the door as her father stands there with a horsewhip in his hands, kind of, feet spread apart and between or through him you see a picture of Emily standing in the background, and, uh, and that pretty much sums up exactly the kind of relationship they had, uh.

In quoting such materials for you, I have quite freely begun and ended sentences within the flow of speech; I have silently deleted *uh, um, kind of, I mean, sort of, you know, like* (as in *like, man*), and other filler phrases without indicating their departure. I have, by and large, deleted false starts and repetitions. (But this is in reporting to you what the readers said—in my own thinking through each commentary I used the original transcript.) I can say with confidence I have not altered the meaning of any statement, nor have I deleted any substantive word within a quotation without indicating the deletion by ellipsis. To see the changes that did take place, you can compare this exact transcription with Sam's comment on the "tableau" as reported on page 1.

Interpreting What the Readers Said

The crucial data from the "experiment" were the words the readers used about what they had read. These phrasings evidenced each reader's synthesis and achievement of the story, his creation of it for and in himself. The nub of the problem then became interpreting what he said.

For me, the first and most obvious assumption to make is the ever-tempting one of the text as stimulus. One looks in what the reader says for wordings evoked by the text. For example, I find in "A Rose for Emily" a fantasy about holding on against inner and outer coercions to let go something precious and loved but also repellent and disgusting: dirty, for example, or smelly. That something is within or behind oneself, like a revered but cruel past or a lifestyle set by a harsh father or a scandalous love affair with someone admired but also "beneath one." Evidently, other critics, too, find a similar fantasy. "Perversion and decadence are a subtle effluvium from the story," says one. "Social pressure had been too great," says another about Emily's efforts to keep her father's corpse, "but she learned from that incident the necessity for concealment. The story is a success story—of success in maintaining an untenable position." I hear in other critics' phrasings the same unconscious meaning of Miss Emily's obstinacy, her "attempting, almost by force of will alone, to halt the natural process of decay," or her "obstinate refusal to submit to, or even to concede, the inevitability of change." All these phrasings reveal the body significance of "holding on" against external "social pressure" or internal "natural process" that demands one "let go." Brooks and Warren's summary statement continues the covert body imagery: "She is obviously a woman of tremendous firmness of will."[2]

Other critics, equally skilled, arrive at words that suggest they are responding to quite a different fantasy. Apparently, they see Homer less as something precious held inside, more as the lover implied and denied by the scene with which the story ends. Sometimes the critic's analysis holds that fantasy back from consummation, as when Irving Howe calls the story "one of those chill fables in which" authors "do not let quite enough 'life' break through the surface of their prose." Other analyses carry the fantasy out: "At the center of the story is the indomitableness of the decadent Southern aristocrat, and the enclosing parts reveal the invasion of the aristocracy by the changing order." Another reader speaks of "reverential connotations [that] cluster about romantic love, the bridal night, and Southern womanhood," but in the final image of that night, "these hallowed clusters are brutally violated." Themes of the sacred and profane, masculine and feminine mother flesh out another critic's fantasy of sexual intercourse: "We have, on the one hand, a rose offered in admiration to a woman of indomitable spirit who clung, in the very process of dissolution, to the vision of an ideal; and at the same time, we have the revolting spectacle of an aging and impotent culture couching with a corrupt materialism which its nobler components had rejected."[3]

Evidently, critics, no less than other folk, have their personality structures and unconscious fantasies; and even their highly sublimated insights express them. Not only do equally skilled readers show the usual variations in interpreting conscious themes and meaning; they also reveal in their wordings that they are creating the story and its meanings for themselves out of different unconscious materials: "break[ing] through" a "cluster" of "enclosing parts" as against obstinately stopping a "natural process." There would seem little point, then, in treating a story as a fixed stimulus embodying some specific unconscious fantasy of phallic mother, castrating father, interlocking genitals, or any of the bestiary developed by those psychoanalytic critics who simply decode literary works according to a "Freudian" dreambook.

One could arrive, however, at a more subtle version of the literary work as stimulus. It would be more in the spirit of ego psychology to treat the story as offering its reader certain formal, defensive, or adaptive maneuvers corresponding to ego strategies in people. One might then be able to correlate different readers' responses to a collection of comparable short stories with the different readers' characteristic patterns of adaptation, discovered by interview or projective test.[4] Very soon, however, one meets the kind of unexpected response I got from a reader in the preliminary group—call him Sheldon. Before one of the exploratory interviews, I had predicted (to myself) Sheldon would dislike Mann's "Mario and the Magician" because he did not like excessive control from others. This is what he actually said: "Great story! What atmosphere! The real reason I enjoyed it was because there was so much Italian in it. . . . I spent a little while at Acapulco once . . . " and he was off on a comparison of Latin types—Italian, Spanish, and Mexican—concentrating wholly on the beach scenes of the first half of the story and quite neglecting the overpowering hypnotist in the second.

Inevitably, one has to regard what the reader brings to the story (his personality, life experience, and so on) as prior to the stimulus of the story itself. Evidently, readers who differ about "A Rose for Emily" do so because they are themselves different. Therefore, one cannot predict what they will say about a story from the story—another kind of prediction is required, one based on the reader's personality or background. "A richly experienced reader will prefer Hemingway's 'The Battler' to Faulkner's 'A Rose for Emily.' " "If a particular reader of 'A Rose for Emily' has an unresolved oedipal problem (as determined independently of the story), he should emphasize themes of passivity and fatherhood." "If a particular reader is an 'anal' character, he should single out images of dirt, smell, and money." I did make predictions of this kind before every interview, and sometimes I was startlingly successful at anticipating what my readers would say about the story and my specific questions. More often, however, I got responses as unpredictable as Sheldon's excursion to Acapulco. More troubling than these errors was the fact I could not tell why I succeeded in some predictions and erred in others, even for the same reader on the same story.

I had to learn for myself what Freud had recognized and accepted a half-century before, that one cannot, in a truly psychoanalytic framework, predict:

> So long as we trace the development from its final outcome backwards, the chain of events appears continuous, and we feel we have gained an insight which is completely satisfactory or even exhaustive. But if we proceed the reverse way, if we start from the premises inferred from the analysis and try to follow these up to the final result, then we no longer get the impression of an inevitable sequence of events which could not have been otherwise determined. We notice at once that there might have been another result, and that we might have been just as well able to understand and explain the latter. The synthesis is thus not so satisfactory as the analysis; in other words, from a knowledge of the premises we could not have foretold the nature of the results. . . . we never know beforehand which of the determining factors will prove the weaker or the stronger. We only say at the end that those which succeeded must have been the stronger. Hence the chain of causation can always be recognized with certainty if we follow the line of analysis, whereas to predict it along the line of synthesis is impossible.[5]

Nevertheless, even after I realized there was no use in them, I continued to commit myself to written predictions before each interview, simply for my own self-discipline.

These predictions then drove home another point: to be applied ahead of time, the categories (both those to type readers and those to class comments) must be crude and limited compared to the actual words a reader would say. Categories like "anal" or "oedipal" or "experienced" or "emphasize" or "prefer" or "single out" (as in the predictions above) simply threw away most of what the reader said, often the very parts of his discourse that seemed most individual. It is when the critics of "A Rose for Emily" speak of "a subtle effluvium from the story" or "social pressure" or "the revolting spectacle of an aging and impotent culture couching with a corrupt materialism," that we glimpse the inner dynamics of their personal synthesis and achievement of the story. Categories like "anal" or "phallic" help a little to grasp those dynamics—but only a little.

The same need to listen to a reader's actual words applies to general literary processes as well as to the inner experience of particular stories. Consider, for example, the familiar feeling of "losing oneself" in a book or being "absorbed" in a work of art. These, we saw above, derive ultimately from feelings of being completely mixed into one's earliest, gratifying environment, sensations closely associated with nursing, and with mothering. Therefore, one might try to correlate the degree someone gets "taken out of oneself" by works of art with that person's degree of "oral fixation." Finally, however, prediction is impossible. Someone with a lot of "orality" could go either way: he might easily become absorbed in all kinds of experiences (not just literature), he might refuse to become absorbed, or he might work out a complex mixture of absorption and escape (as we shall see one of our readers, Shep, doing).

Further, the general category obscures the individuality of the response. Just the three critics we have already heard on this theme of being "absorbed" show considerable variation.*

* See above, p. 18.

Georges Poulet spoke of the way the work of art "lives its own life within me," and his becoming the "prey" of "this being [the author] ensconced at the heart of the work." I sense that Poulet feels as though the work of art were a being inside himself or as though it had a being inside itself—some form of mother and fetus perhaps. Either way, Poulet himself feels taken over, engulfed, or devoured like "prey." By contrast, Ortega y Gasset talked about "living with [the characters], immersed in their air, their space, their time," and he used three images of a timeless time, "moment," "instant," "without any intermission." I feel he is experiencing merger as Poulet did, but more in terms of fusion and union than being a "prey." Robert Gorham Davis also spoke of being "absorbed" and "immersed," but he accented the element of passivity in the experience: "The work . . . is thinking *him*. His ego has become object, not subject." Again, it is the exact words these writers use that tell us their experience, not the category "orality," although it is correct as far as it goes.

Evidently, the words that even a professional reader uses about what he reads reflect his personality, that "one myth for every man," in Yeats's phrase, "which, if we but knew it, would make us understand all he did and thought."[6] Congreve said it at greater length in terms of the metaphysical issues and the humours psychology of his era:

Our *Humour* has relation to us and to what proceeds from us, as the Accidents have to a Substance; it is a Colour, Taste, and Smell, Diffused through all; thô our Actions are never so many and different in Form, they are all Splinters of the same Wood, and have Naturally one Complexion, which thô it may be disguised by Art, yet cannot be wholly changed: We may Paint it with other Colours, but we cannot change the Grain. So the Natural sound of an instrument will be distinguish'd, thô the Notes expressed by it are never so various, and the Divisions never so many.[7]

Fond as I am of Congreve, I did not use humours psychology to interpret my readers' personalities and their comments. Rather, I count myself most fortunate to have had the help of two experienced psychological testers, Dr. Allan Zechowy, who worked with the first preliminary group of readers, and Dr. Andrew Corvus, who tested the larger, younger group from whom these five readers are taken. To each reader, they administered at least a ten-card Rorschach and a five-card Thematic Apperception Test (TAT). Later, on my own initiative, I myself gave the COPE questionnaire (designed to elicit defense mechanisms).[8] I had hoped to predict Rorschach and TAT outcomes from the readers' comments on stories; thus, some readers were tested after the interviews (here, Sam, Shep, and Sebastian). Later, I tried predicting readers' comments on stories from the tests; hence other readers were tested before the interviews (here, Saul and Sandra).

I could not make either set of predictions precise enough to be meaningful, and I slowly realized that with ten or so interviews with each subject, each interview running from twenty to forty pages, I had more than two hundred pages of free associations for each reader. I had, in other words, much more data from which to infer their personalities than even these skilled and efficient testers did because they had only worked with the readers a few hours. I decided the real service the tests rendered was to check my analyses of the readers' personalities, supplement my blind spots, point out themes I had missed, or make me re-examine conclusions I had come to too hastily. For the readers here reported, then, I have taken the interviews as the primary source of data on personality, the tests as only supplementary and to be overruled on the rare occasions where the interviews and the testers pointed to different conclusions.

To perceive the core of personality in someone, as I have tried to do with these five students, one listens with the proverbial "third ear." That is, one listens to what the other person says about himself or love or politics or friends or ideas or, to be experimental, to what he says about inkblots or cards with pictures on them—but above all to what he says. The "third ear" does not come to such words empty, however. One listens with an open, free-floating attention to the kinds of things people are likely to say or think about parents, their own bodies, authorities, desires, or fears. One listens, in short, with some knowledge of the issues clinical experience has found important. You have had brief samples of this kind of listening for resonances in phrases we considered from the critics about "A Rose for Emily" or the remarks of Poulet, Davis, and Ortega on literary absorption.

I wanted more, however. I wanted to bring together the overtones and resonances I heard from my readers, whose personalities I knew in a way I would probably never know my fellow professionals'. To interrelate their comments, I found I needed still another structure, one now overworked but still powerful and true.

The Concept of Identity

I brought to the interviews themselves my belief that, for all the infinite variations in his behavior, any individual also shows a deep and essential unity in his personality. I had, in other words, a concept of human character rather like Yeats' "myth" or Congreve's "humour." Later, I learned that the French critic, Charles Mauron, had applied the same assumption to the personalities of various authors, seeking a *mythe personnel* which would comprehend "both . . . the troubles of the living man and the obsessive metaphors of the author."[9]

In my own search for the unity in personality, I began with the first psychoanalytic characterology, which typed people according to their dominant drives as these developed from body zones. Despite its crudity, this rather simple system enabled psychologists to group a great many character traits in meaningful ways. It was partly because of this firmly established typology that I chose these five readers out of the whole group, because they give a range of such types. Sam's and Sandra's drives concern themes of strength and power, particularly as they relate to maleness and femaleness. Saul and Sebastian took pleasure in controlling their own inner creations, mental and physical, as against external authorities, while Shep showed strong aggressive drives associated with situations of food, talk, or dependency. You will see over and over again in their interviews traces of these phallic, anal, and oral modalities, but you will also see that these body-derived drives are far from fine enough to account for more than a small part of what they said about the stories they read.

Classing people only according to drives neglects the adaptations and defenses that give rise to the more complex traits we associate with character or personality. The classic psychoanalytic definition of character is Fenichel's: "the habitual mode of bringing into harmony the tasks presented by internal demands and by the external world." The word "habitual" stresses the way we sense ourselves and others as creatures with a sameness: "Character means that a certain constancy prevails in the ways the ego chooses for solving its tasks."

The remainder of the psychoanalytic concept of character rests on an idea put forward in 1930 by Robert Waelder, which has become one of the cornerstones of ego psychology. Fenichel describes it this way:

> Under the name of "the principle of multiple function" Waelder has described a phenomenon of cardinal importance in ego psychology. This principle expresses the tendency of the organism toward inertia, that is, the tendency to achieve a maximum of effect with a minimum of effort. Among various possible actions that one is chosen which best lends itself to the simultaneous satisfaction of demands from several sources. An action fulfilling a demand of the external world may at the same time result in instinctual gratification and in satisfying the superego. The mode of reconciling various tasks to one another is characteristic for a given personality. Thus the ego's habitual modes of adjustment to the external world, the id, and the superego, and the characteristic types of combining these modes with one another, constitute character.[10]

From this point of view, character *equals* specific methods of solution to inner and outer demands. Each person arrives at his own individual methods of solution, and they remain constant over long periods in his life.

Since they persist, these solutions must also give some pleasure—otherwise, he would seek out an adaptation that yielded more pleasure. It follows, therefore, that people choose methods of solution that also gratify their dominant body drives (oral, anal, phallic, and the like—in the older scheme). Thus people whose desires take the form of absorbing things into themselves might deal with the world primarily on the basis of identification. Others, whose pleasures come from the creation and control of inner products, might seek adaptations based on getting right down to the "nitty-gritty," dealing with what's "behind" the facade, "getting it right out in the open," and so on. Thus, the new characterology includes the old, because certain modes of adaptation tend to gratify certain drives, and thus these adaptations become permanent.

New or old, complex or simple, all characterologies must account for the continuity we see in ourselves and others, the sameness that Freud saw and mentioned as a clinician in 1908, years before he had theory enough to account for what he described:

> The sexual behaviour of a human being often *lays down the pattern* for all his other modes of reacting to life. If a man is energetic in winning the object of his love, we are confident that he will pursue his other aims with an equally unswerving energy; but if, for all sorts of reasons, he refrains from satisfying his strong sexual instincts, his behaviour will be conciliatory and resigned rather than vigorous in other spheres of life as well.[11]

Today, psychoanalysis explains this sameness by Freud's concept of the ego's defenses (developed and expanded after 1926) and the concept of adaptation (largely developed after Freud's death). Defenses and adaptations become habitual to the extent that they consolidate satisfactions and reduce suffering.

From this point of view, we consciously and unconsciously adopt strategies for minimizing the anxieties caused by conflicts like those between desires and reality, desires and guilt, or morality and reality. We also choose our strategies to achieve as much pleasure with as little effort as possible. In the familiar image of the donkey, we try to maximize the carrot and minimize the stick, all the while doing as little work as we can.

The individual may arrive at a balance that suits him through pathology: he may acquire a symptom, an inhibition, or a neurosis. Or he may adapt positively and creatively, finding a successful balance of pleasure and unpleasure, defense and relaxation, through love or work (to mention the two great regions for healthy living). Whatever the solution for a particular sphere of his life, once someone has achieved it, he tends to adhere to it. And beneath any one solution lies the deeper, more tenacious, general structure of drives and adaptations that changes little, if at all, even under the greatest stresses.

To express this constancy that informs everything a human being says or does, Yeats spoke of a "myth," Congreve of "humour," and Charles Mauron, of a *"mythe personnel."* In recent years, "identity" has become the most popular word to describe the modern psychoanalytic concept of character, although Erik Erikson's "ego identity" is more accurate and Heinz Lichtenstein's "identity theme" still more so. Because of the connections I want to make between literary man and literary work, I tend to adapt an old Adlerian term and speak of "style" or "lifestyle." Whatever the term, however, it must convey a constancy that colors every phase of an individual's life. It is what he brings from all his past to all new experience, and it is extremely difficult—perhaps impossible—to change. Yet, in practice, it can often be expressed quite succinctly.

The classic case that developed the idea of a concise verbal statement of identity is Heinz Lichtenstein's Anna S., a woman suffering through a pathetic and destructive round of alcoholic bouts, lesbian affairs, and businesslike prostitution. Lichtenstein concluded in working with her that her identity theme could be "transcribed" as "being another's essence."[12] That is, Lichtenstein asserts, for every individual there is a central identity "theme" on which he lives out variations, much as a musician can infinitely vary a single musical motif to create a theme and variations. By being a prostitute, Anna made herself her client's essence, the passive appendage that proved his masculinity. In her relations with her mother—the kind of woman of whom one would say, "She is nothing without a man"—Anna became that man: a lover and husband who sold brushes door to door or worked in a factory to support her. She sustained her lesbian partners' claims to masculinity by becoming very feminine and dependent and jealous in those relationships.

The point is that one can state an identity theme for somebody like Anna very briefly, yet that theme can ramify infinitely into all the events of her or anyone's life. Critic Charles Mauron, for example, takes all the texts (even of writers as prolific as Racine or Molière) and "superimposes" them. Mere comparison would keep a distinct view of the juxtaposed texts, but superimposition jumbles them in order to bring out the "*coïncidences énigmatiques*" or "*des réseaux d'associations ou des groupements d'images, obsédantes et probablement involontaires.*" From these groups and networks of images and associations he infers the "*mythe personnel*" that can then be interpreted as an expression of "*la personnalité inconsciente*" and its development, limited as need be by the comparison with the life of the writer. "The *perception* of the 'whole person,' " says Lichtenstein, summing up his own conception of this kind of interpretation of a personality, "means the process of abstracting an invariant from the multitude of [bodily and behavioral transformations during the whole life of the individual]. This invariant, when perceived in our encounter with another individual, we describe as the individual's 'personality' "[13]—or "myth" or "humour" or "character" or "ego identity" or "lifestyle" or "*mythe personnel*" or "identity theme."

When I say, then, that a certain reader wants to become a "thing" in a "system" or that another reader wants to draw closer and closer to sources of strength and nurture and never to see their loss, I am trying to state for them, as exactly as I can, identity themes that permeate their lives even as they create infinite variation on those themes. I am trying to state for them the "myth" Yeats wanted that would enable us to understand all someone did and thought, but I am arriving at such a "myth" by means of psychoanalytic ego-psychology.

Ego-psychology has, in Hartmann's words, "sharpened our eyes to the frequent identity of patterns in often widely divergent fields of an individual's behavior."[14] By 1966, Anna Freud noted, most analysts had begun to conceive of "a general cognitive and perceptive style of the ego," an extension of notions of defense to include besides the ego's dealings with danger, anxiety, affects, etc., also its everyday functioning such as perceiving, thinking, abstracting, conceptualizing. An ego style, in this sense, is linked with the concept of defence but by no means identical with it. It represents an attempt to embrace the area of conflict as well as the conflict-free area of secondary process functioning.[15]

Such a "style," as Hartmann had said earlier, would show how "a person's moral behavior is as much an essential part and a distinctive sign of his personality as is his character or his instinctual life."[16] In a more literary vein, such an "identity theme" links a man's prose style with his total personality.[17] Equally, ideologies, values, and all systems projected on the world, notes Abram Kardiner, will reflect the adaptation of outer, social forces by inner character, often in surprising ways. "The son of a millionaire may be a communist because it seems rational and desirable. Back of his endorsement may be an identification with the underdog. But he will present his endorsement in the form of a logical argument which has no reference to his unconscious identification with the 'underprivileged.'"[18]

Identities in this sense begin very early, presumably with one's biological endowment and prenatal influences—the vague kind of thing mothers recognize when they speak of an "easy" baby or a "good eater." Freud himself went so far as to suggest that a person's repertoire of defenses might be inherited (even though defense itself is an ego function), because id and ego begin life as one. To some extent recent observations of newborn children bear him out. We seem to come into the world with a certain ego style or "initial organizing configuration" that then becomes fleshed out with particulars as we pass through Freud's phases of development, Erikson's modalities, or the sequence of object relations some English theorists have recently stressed.[19] As the author of *Peter Pan* charmingly put the matter: "I think one remains the same person throughout [all the decades of life], merely passing, as it were, in these lapses of time from one room to another, but all in the same house. If we unlock the rooms of the far past we can peer in and see ourselves, busily occupied in beginning to become you and me."[20]

Lichtenstein, however, goes beyond the other theorists and nontheorists to suggest one specific phase at which the identity theme takes form: during the growth of self-object differentiation, as the child begins to recognize that his mother is separate and therefore that he is a separate being. Although born with a great range of possible adaptations, "the specific unconscious need of the mother . . . actualizes out of these infinite potentialities one way of being in the child, namely being the child for this particular mother, responding to her unique and individual needs." This way of being represents a "primary identity," "a zero point which must precede all other mental developments." Then, the child develops in a kind of rhythmic oscillation. He brings the identity he has achieved to each new experience, which in turn enlarges the identity he brings to it.[21]

Thus, in Erikson's closely related epigenetic theory, "Each successive step . . . is a potential crisis." Erikson uses that word, however, "to connote not a threat of catastrophe, but a turning point, a crucial period of increased vulnerability and heightened potential, and therefore, the ontogenetic source of generational strength and maladjustment," a point, in other words, where the individual's new growth subjects him to new weaknesses in order to open him to new powers as well. "Each stage becomes a crisis because incipient growth and awareness in a new part function go together with a shift in instinctual energy and yet also cause a specific vulnerability in that part." The crisis ends when the new capacities match the new opportunities "to become full-grown components of the ever-new configuration that is the growing personality."[22]

The central style or identity theme does not change but the individual does as he absorbs changed external realities or growth from within (biological changes, for example). These changes imply danger, and the ego must defend, often by affirming older patterns of adaptation. "Psychic development implies at all stages both progressive and regressive manifestations," notes Elizabeth R. Zetzel, summing the matter up. "Regression is thus an inevitable concomitant of forward progressive movement."[23] Roy Schafer puts the matter in structural terms: development of character involves "a series of hierarchically ordered id-ego positions, each of which acts as a defence against the position below it in the hierarchy."[24]

Once a person's identity theme is established it never changes, however. (Lichtenstein goes so far as to argue the "identity principle" is prior even to man's drive for pleasure. To give up identity one would have to become a thing—die.) At the same time, the individual can grow and change infinitely within that style. Similarly, the individual's theme is (probably) not in and of itself healthy or unhealthy—only what he does with it.

Anna's theme was "being another's essence." Before therapy, she expressed it in a series of self-destroying relationships, painful enough to lead her to seek help. After therapy, she found other variations. Yet one can see the essential continuity of her personality by comparing something she wrote before with something she wrote after. Anna had had fantasies of an imaginary lover, who was a "madman," and she would set them down in a kind of poetic form:

> Is that you beloved, is that you returning to Drown in my madness, to baptize me with the Sweetness of our foolishness? Oh, bring back the strange but happy love.—Bless you, and drink with me my blood to quench our starved thirstiness. . . . Embrace me oh madness, let my nakedness and nudity quench thy thirst for madness with love of a longing heart.
>
> When you leave I find my Self in a reality upon this God's hell on earth, to breathe only the contemptuousness of man's Sanity. Come back, come back, my Sweet love, don't turn me out, let me bathe my Soul in your torment, bleed my body of its blood for a Smooth Vintage of men's liqueur. Let me drink to your holy madness, to our love of Solitude. Oh madness, I love you, come back to keep me from Sanity.

In such prose poems, her images of being drunk by her lover, bathing or drowning in him or he in her, state her wish to fuse with him and become his essence—which is madness. Isolated, however, she is a "longing heart," turned out into a reality, which being sanity—separateness—is hell on earth. There is, to be sure, a Byronic grandeur in Anna's seeking the unattainable, but at the same time she was suffering—starving and thirsting —deeply enough to seek help in therapy. After that therapy, she wrote of her first real love affair:

> I feel so much part of him that when he tells me something that was unpleasant to him no matter what . . . I hate the thing or person for it. I feel it displeased him and that makes it terrible. If he is very tired, fatigue takes hold of me, and I seem to share his feeling, and usually end up relieving him of it. Does real loving make one feel a part of another? When he makes love to me I really feel that I'm way down deep inside of him, that his arms are my arms, etc. When he laughs . . . I am filled with sheer glee. When he is sad I long to whitewash all that has caused him his miseries and I feel compassion so deep that I usually have indigestion.

She is still "being another's essence," but now in a more loving and self-fulfilling or, at least (I assume), a less painful way.

In short, interpreting behavior through an "identity theme" explains how we remain the same, yet change. The essence of this view of identity is that we can see one theme or style permeating all aspects of an individual's life. In that sense, we have an unchanging self, but nevertheless reality and one's own inner drives demand that that self reach out to new experiences. It then grows by adding these experiences as new variations to its unchanging central theme. An "identity theme" is determined by past events, yet paradoxically it is the only basis for future growth and, therefore, freedom. It is the foundation for every personal and human synthesis of new experience, be it falling in love or simply reading a book. In understanding the principles within the one we learn something about the other as well, for the separate parts of life cease to be so separate.

It is tempting to say, as many critics do, that a given reader likes some story because it affirms his political or religious beliefs, and, in a partial way, that kind of statement is true. But one relates all fields of a person's behavior if one seeks out the underlying identity theme or lifestyle that *both* the story *and* the beliefs (*and* a great many other activities) fulfill. As we have seen, Sheldon liked "Mario and the Magician" because it reminded him of his own trip to Acapulco. Yet I know it to be more true that he was interested in Latins for their sexuality and in ethnic types in general because he felt controlled by his own matrix of tradition. To understand fully Sheldon's statement, "The real reason I enjoyed [the story] was because there was so much Italian in it," would take us very deeply indeed into his life.

Again, we come up against the difficulty or impossibility of sorting out the experience of literature into a discrete stimulus and a definable response. Each reader will bring all kinds of personal associations and experiences into the relationship between himself and the story—not least the very conditions of this "experiment." Obviously, I was myself one of the factors entering into what these readers said about their reading, and I need to face up to the biases and trends I may have introduced.

The Influence of the Sixth Reader

As you (the seventh reader) read the evidence, you will very likely ask yourself from time to time how and to what extent I influenced the things these readers said. After all, they were undergraduates in their early twenties and I a full professor in what one might call the prime of life. Some may have found the whole interview procedure (complete with tape recorder) arcane and threatening. Others may have taken my efforts at experimental neutrality for hostility or indifference. Still others may have felt frustrated that they were not told more of what the tests revealed, for I found that curiosity about oneself was the chief reason readers volunteered. All these readers knew of my interest in applying psychoanalysis to literature, and some of them tried at times to give me what they thought I wanted (interpreted through the usual undergraduate misunderstandings of psychoanalysis).

To ask how these factors affected what they said, however, is to proceed from the same cause-and-effect, stimulus-response model that we have already found inadequate. That is, the story did not "cause" their response—they did. Similarly, the interviewer and the interview situation did not "cause" their response. Nor did the current crises in their lives. But any or all of these might have—no, must have— entered into what they said about these stories. The point is: what "caused" what they said was their own inner style of creation and synthesis of everything they were experiencing at that moment.

It would be impossible to sort out all the factors that each of these readers worked over in his own mind to make up his personal synthesis of a short story. Could one "hold constant" Saul's anger at being jilted by a girl whom he thought like the heroine of the Fitzgerald story and still "vary" his fear of being overpowered by me in the contest that he took the interview to be? It is useless to think of the problem of Saul's experience of the story—or of me—this way.

Each reader "storied his story." He created his experience of the literary work from his own lifestyle. Thus, one of the five readers, Sebastian, thought the Fitzgerald hero simply silly, while Sam thought him sturdy and self-reliant and altogether admirable. Sam said he felt toward one of the characters in "The Battler" as toward a sinister and frightening Oriental torturer, a Fu Manchu. On the other hand, Sandra found the same character so gentle and reassuring, she positively glowed that he was in the story. These are the things to be understood, and they are not explained simply by saying Sebastian, Sam, and Sandra were reacting to me.

Had I been working with questionnaires or fixed-question interviews, looking for classes or categories of behavior that could be considered the same no matter who was doing the behaving, such contamination would have been fatal. Had a reader said in answering a questionnaire that he liked a story when he didn't, because he wanted either to please or to frustrate me, the experiment would have gone quite awry. This project, however, sought out the uniqueness of each response. I tried to get the reader to say more and more rather than to force his response into fixed classes and categories.

I was, therefore, more in the position of the analyst whose patient brings him a made-up dream. It doesn't really matter. Both a real dream and an invented one voice the dreamer's mind. So here, when Sam apparently misremembered and said that what Miss Emily taught the maidens of the town was knitting (instead of china-painting), I learned something about what was going on in Sam's mind. I learned that he transformed an activity with certain specific symbolic overtones into an activity with quite different overtones, and it would not make very much difference whether he did so unconsciously or deliberately.

In fact, I think his was an honest misremembering, quite impossible for me to "cause." And evidently the "words-on-the-page" (which are "china-painting") did not cause it, either. His misremembering is his unique act of re-creation, and even if a dozen readers misremembered the china-painting as knitting, the same reasoning would apply. I did not cause it. Neither did the text. Therefore, I would have to look for the explanation in the individual identity of each reader and his unique way of giving life to the story for himself.

In short, we come back to the basic data of this study—what the reader said. Once he has himself decided and said what he was going to say, the data, the two hundred or more pages of his talk, are fixed. What then comes to matter is the interpretation of this mass of material. In effect, the "experiment" becomes the putting together of those materials with the reader's lifestyle.

Two Kinds of Interpretation

The first interpretation involves looking through all the materials for the identity theme of an individual reader. Drawing on the tests as well as the transcripts, I looked through everything for general traits. I sought remarks on general topics, such as politics, marriage, friendship, sex, or family, and also general patterns that pervaded all those pages of talk: splitting dangers into two, looking for sources of security, seeing the world in terms of systems and inanimate objects—that sort of thing. You will find the results of this analysis in the next chapter, which describes the five readers in detail.

The second mode of interpretation was much trickier. It depended on the first which, after all, is a fairly traditional psychoanalytic approach to free or more or less free associations. Having already arrived at an identity theme for a given reader from all his interviews and tests, I looked through the transcript of only one of his interviews to find the principles at work in his highly personal synthesis of some one story.

As a practical matter, theory aside, my talk about a story with a reader for an hour or so would result in a transcript of from twenty to forty pages. To analyze this diffuse, discursive text, I would transcribe (in a shorthand form, so I could see it in a single overview) everything that reader said which could conceivably illuminate his response: opinions usual and unusual, misreadings, slips, special wordings, body symbolisms, and so on. In practice, I would leave out only those very rare remarks that said nothing about either the story or the reader. I would sort these separate items into from ten to twenty themes. Some of them would represent aspects of the story (a given character or episode or theme, an opinion on its merits, its style, and so on). Others would refer more directly to the reader's concerns (for example, a political association to the story, an association to some other work or an experience, or a special emotion).

Frankly, it took me a long time to infer from the reader's identity theme and the kind of reading he did the principles at work. I found, finally, that I sorted out the ten or twenty themes in his commentary on a given story into three interrelated and overlapping groups. First and simplest were those statements about his likes and dislikes of the story as a whole or of particular parts. Of course, sometimes I inferred a liking even when a reader did not say so explicitly but showed a lot of interest or enthusiasm at a certain feature. Second, I tried to see how, within his likes and dislikes, his wordings revealed fantasy materials: imagery of the body, for example, or significant persons or familiar fears and desires—the kind of thing we have seen reflected in the critics' wordings about "A Rose for Emily" or the phrases Poulet, Davis, and Ortega used about being "absorbed" in a literary experience. Third—and this was the subtlest part—I tried to see how the reader had adapted or managed various elements of the story. Had he stressed some and omitted others? I was interested in his rewordings and his interpretations, his perception of the story in the broadest sense. In particular, how did he see the characters? How did he interpret the various episodes? Had he forgotten parts (a name, for example)? Changed the sequence of events? Misremembered plot or wording? All these I took to be evidence of the way he had adapted the story to his own identity theme, construing it through his defensive structures.

These analyses of the separate interviews make up the most important outcome of an "experiment" which turned out to be not an experiment at all but the interrelation of two kinds of interpretation. Reworking and refining the interpretation of the individual readings in the light of the readers' identity themes led me to the general conclusions about the literary experience this book sets out. I offer them to you in two forms.

Chapter 5 sets out in general terms the four principles that I think govern the reading experience. They emerged slowly but definitely, with greater and greater clarity, from successive reinterpretations. Alternatively, I offer you the analyzed interviews themselves: five readers' readings of "A Rose for Emily" in Chapter 6 and the same five readers' readings of Fitzgerald's "Winter Dreams" and Hemingway's "The Battler" in Appendix B. In presenting these readings, I quote from 70 to 80 percent of what a given reader said about a given work, but I quote it in a more meaningful sequence and with considerable commentary from me to bring out the principles within the reading.

That, of course, is the real problem of the sixth reader here: that these conclusions rest on my interpretations, first of the readers' personalities, second of their comments. Consequently, my interpretations must necessarily express my own identity theme. The best I can do for the time being (that is, until the last three chapters) is be open with you and show you step by step how I proceeded. In analyzing the interviews, I was on my own, but for the readers themselves, Dr. Corvus's tests provide some confirmation and guidance. The briefest and gentlest of next steps, then, is to look at my style of interpretation as it applied to the search for the identity themes of these five readers. The next step is to see the "Who?" in "Who reads what how?"

4 Who? The Five Readers

They were undergraduates, advanced English majors, skilled and interested enough in reading so that all five were considering graduate school—in short, the kind of student a teacher of literature gets to know best. To know them only as students, however, is not to know why they experience a story or a poem or a drama the way they do. That calls for something more, a richer kind of knowledge, a sense of the essential core of the individual, his or her personal myth, lifestyle, or identity theme.

The data we have consist of Dr. Corvus's Rorschach and TAT results, the COPE test I sometimes administered,[1] and, most important, the two hundred or more pages of transcribed interview with each reader. To interpret the primary data, the transcribed interviews, I looked for each reader's remarks on his habitual likes and dislikes in people, politics, poetry—generalizations about anything. As I read, I kept in mind themes Dr. Corvus had singled out, such as feelings about gender and sexuality, attitudes toward aggression, preferred defenses, sensory modes, recurring configurations, and imagery of all kinds. I looked for them in the interviews and also for general clinical entities, personality types and themes, patterns of drive and defense, that occur commonly in our culture. And I also tried to keep an open mind.

In my own notes, I jotted down in shorthand form every statement a reader made that generalized beyond a particular text. I tried to recognize in the set of generalizations a central, recurring pattern of drive and defense, in short, an identity theme within the infinite variations of one individual's concerns. I was carrying out what Heinz Lichtenstein calls "the process of abstracting an invariant from the multitude of transformations," which is the principle of another person's "personality."[2] First and always, however, I had in my mind's eye the individual human being in front of me and my own feelings toward him.

Sam

Good-looking, tall, talkative, cheerful, and gregarious, Sam
was a favorite among the departmental secretaries, with whom
he gaily chatted and joked and flirted when he came for
interviews. He dressed dapperly, taking obvious pleasure in
himself and his world and the flattering attentions his world
bestowed on him. I must admit he quite charmed me, too: I
thought him one of the most likable readers I worked with. He
laughed with ease, and he lounged through his interviews with
me comfortably and engagingly. I sensed a certain lack of drive
or aggression in him, but a striking ability to project himself
imaginatively into people and situations, lending his own good
nature freely to his guesses about the motivations of others.

As he told me more about himself, I realized how much Sam
wanted to be supplied esteem and admiration, particularly as a
tall, handsome, stylish, affectionate young man. He found
conflict menacing and either fled fights literally or refused to
recognize them. At his most successful, he wooed and placated
whatever threatened him until he and it could serve each other
in the mutual admiration Sam liked.

This pattern of drive and defense, this hunger for outside
supplies of self-esteem, which was to be satisfied through
mutuality, colored Sam's personality as he revealed himself in
offhand comments on various events and aspects of his life.
For example, he told me that he tended to be rather "square"
in matters literary. "I suppose my taste is just terribly traditional," he said, contrasting his likes with more "experimental" fare, and by the word "traditional" admitting he sought
reassurances from the past (or perhaps confirmation from me).
Similarly, although he held liberal enough political views, he
liked established institutions, even Lyndon Johnson (at a time
when almost all his fellow-students were gnashing their teeth at
him). "I've a great deal of sympathy for [him]. He's got a
rotten job." In a period of long hair and body odor, Sam held
out for "social amenities and graces and stuff like that."

> They at least seem to me to be much more abiding. Those are
> the things that carry down through the generations. . . . Sure,

they're ephemeral and they're superficial. Fine. But those are the things that seem to be more worthwhile to master than any particular credo that may be out of style in five years. And besides, you don't effect any changes anyway. I'm very pessimistic about that.

Sam's pessimism about political actions showed the passivity implicit in his desire to deal with reality by cozying up to it as a child would. Thus, he could laugh at his own response to a movie, "I enjoyed the color—as I and a child of five would —and I enjoyed all the motion." At movies, "I just literally lose myself in it. I think of nothing else. I think of no one that I'm with. I think of no problems that I have. I just literally sit back and watch the movie." Similarly, he described a theatrical performance: "This was a case of my really being carried away by what was said, by the lines." People, by contrast, did not merge with him so easily as he with works of art. "If you ever feel in any mood, don't ask someone that you're feeling it about what they're thinking, because the answer is inevitably something that will destroy you totally. . . . because they're not thinking anything attuned to my mood."

In phrasings like "being carried away," Sam often put his feelings of regression and identification in terms of body movement. "I think that the movie, with its greater scope and with its more intense powers of pushing you wherever the camera goes, has greater capabilities as far as audience participation (of sorts) goes than the play does." Sometimes, Sam's phrasings turned toward a sexual passivity, as when he spoke of John Updike's poetry: "I think what he set out to accomplish, or what it seems to me he set out to accomplish, he accomplished in me." Often, he phrased his likes and dislikes as body movements. Hawthorne's "Young Goodman Brown" was "too extreme, too much of a pull on the imagination," while Katherine Mansfield's "The Garden Party", he said, "never got you into the nitty-gritty of any great universal problem." A story "has to at some point lead you to more basic things."

The feminine identification he implied by being so passive showed in Sam's style of study, particularly in the house-wifely ways he avoided anxiety:

Let's say I have a paper to do . . . I will do anything. I will
find— You know, I'll mop the floors so as not to have to start
to do that paper. I will wash dishes. I will page through a
magazine that I haven't looked at and should be looked at
because the new one's coming in and if I don't look at it, I'll
never look at it and so on. As long as it's a reasonably valid
excuse. I'll dust. I'll empty ashtrays. I'll straighten my desk.
I'll take care of any little trivia until, like if I've got a week to
do a paper, there is nothing left to do . . . except to sit down
and do the paper.

This passive trend affected his reading habits: "I want to have
a couple of hours to sit down and read [a book I'm really into].
That's why I do most of my reading at nighttime, when all the
dishes are done, the bathroom is clean, and all that stuff, and I
can just sit down." I got the picture of someone being clean,
orderly, or erect on demand. Thus, Sam said he read *The New
Yorker* for a store of amusing ephemera, because "I find myself
a lot of times in social situations where conversation has to be
kept going and whether I am actually responsible for it or not,
I find myself feeling that something's got to be done, and that
I'm the elect— So things have to come up out of nowhere."

Thus, Sam would stop being passive or housewifely and
"come up" with something, because he felt he was being chosen or demanded of and someone might judge him adversely if
he did not play a more active role. Also, a fear of the unknown
—such as difficult poetry—would bring him up: "If I'm sitting
down to read [Wallace] Stevens, I'm on the edge of my chair."
"You've got to be ready to catch the things he throws out."
"I've got to be on my toes. I've got to be constantly thinking
of what I'm doing." "I am sitting on the edge of the chair, so to
speak, pencil in hand, ready to underline words, and to watch
out for syllables and stuff like that." By contrast, with Updike's poetry, which Sam took to be "an exercise in language
play," "I find myself able to sit back in the chair. I can put my
pencil down and just read him and it's nice."

Sam was again brought up into an erect position in his
response to D. H. Lawrence's "The Blind Man," a mysterious
story that plays a theme and variations on fears of injury. Sam

defended against the blindness by watching. "Wow! It's *some*thing!" "It was strange." "I wasn't terribly comfortable. I was always kind of hanging on . . . trying to grasp just what was going on. It was kind of unfamiliar." "I wasn't exactly sure what I should have my eyes open for . . . and it seemed to me that he [Lawrence] kept trying to *say* something, kept trying to tell everybody something, and that I had to keep aware for what it was." Similarly, with "experimental" litera-ture, "Perhaps it is just that I don't understand it. Maybe I'm just a bit afraid of it, but I just think that there is a lot of other stuff that one could be bothering about."

These two last responses outline Sam's two basic adaptations to threat: in the second, flight to get close to some other, nonthreatening thing; in the first, trying actively to "grasp" or see or understand what was going on—preferably so as to achieve a loving, passive identification, the "it's nice" he felt when Updike accomplished something in him. "I'm romantic enough to like the idea of touching and of that meaning some-thing." "I'd be perfectly willing to adapt myself to an Italian sense of touch."

> A lot of my guards are dropped immediately, when I'm put in with Italians, because that's where two men can walk down the street arm in arm and not be—not have water poured on them from high windows and stuff like that, and girls can hold hands as they walk down the street, and these are things which I find personally charming.

In general Sam tended to retreat from heterosexuality to a simple friendliness, faintly sexual, between men. For example, at a critic's making a good point, he quipped, "I simply pat him on the flyleaf for being clever," or

> I have great sympathy for the . . . sacredness of touch, especially among friends, more so among friends than among lovers, where, you know, . . . you have so many other things to worry about . . . [but with friends] even the slightest touch becomes meaningful . . .

. . . and, one should add, a means to identification.

Dr. Corvus described Sam in clinical terms as a well-put-together, almost classical, hysteric, that is, to oversimplify, someone who deals with reality in terms of male and female bodies. Thus, Sam showed the ability to range, in his Rorschach responses, from parts and fantasies of people to real, whole human forms. For example, he could move from raw, unrepressed "cock" and "phallus" to symbolizations like "bowling pin" or "snake head," or from an area of the inkblot to an actual, well-known person. What problems Sam showed in the Rorschach seemed to stem from aggression. When he perceived aggressive material in the inkblots, he would flee, as it were, to the edges. To inkblots that ordinarily evoke aggressive responses, Sam's associations suggested that, for him, aggression chiefly had to do with biting or the mouth: he would see "something crabbish or clawish," "tigers," "wolves," "a fox," "a manta ray," or, most explicitly, "an angry mouth." He also seemed to retreat easily from masculine aggression to an infant's hunger, as when he moved (in a series of responses) from "scrotum" to "breast" or from "a [David] Levine caricature of a nose" to "breast and tummy." Never, in his responses, was he the aggressor. Rather he cast himself as a wooer, trying to placate others and get them to like him, perhaps, Dr. Corvus suggested, as a reaction against his own aggressive feelings.

One would guess Sam feared and denied his own anger because he feared the anger of others who might retaliate physically. Such a dynamic showed, for example, in the TAT story Sam wrote for Card 13B which pictures a boy sitting in an empty doorway.

> The boy sat stooped and huddled and small against the black depths of the darkened house beyond the doorway. The sun slanted against the side of his face, catching the glisten of his eyes and the gold of his hair. He thought: "Father is away and gone for the day. I wish he would never come back and mother and I would be alone together and mother would be different and we would love each other as it was once before father ever came back." The father walked into the yard, glinting fire-eyed, red-haired, to the boy—towering above him, daemonic, fiery. The boy shuddered as the father

stooped to pick him up. The father gave the boy a kiss on the forehead and set his bare feet back on the dust of the ground. The boy thought the blood [*sic*] that ran from the calf's throat when his father killed him last week, and how it ran into the dry dust of the ground.

I cannot help feeling that Sam was trying to please Dr. Corvus or me by giving a pair of "Freudians" the kind of transparently "oedipal" story he thought we wanted. Also, I think the diction of the story shows he was trying to be "literary." One does not disguise oneself, however, by being literary and psychological.

Sam identified easily with the boy, readily projecting his thoughts into direct quotation. The first feelings of smallness or loneliness or depression ("the black depths") Sam canceled out by picturing the light of the sun enhancing the boy's appearance and by having the boy imagine an earlier union with his mother. This wish to go back prior to the father's importance remained only a wish, however, although the fears and anger associated with it were clear enough in the defenses against them. Sam mollified the fiery, daemonic father: all he does is kiss his son. In the description of the towering, red-headed father and also in the rough equation of the boy's body on the ground to the cut calf ("his father killed him [whom?] last week"), Sam almost treated the father-son relation as a contest of two phallic demons. "The boy thought the blood" (a "Freudian slip"?) suggests Sam's fear and anger toward the father, but, presumably, Sam partly identified with that fiery, devouring father, too. The anger, Sam denied by seeing the man as a loving father and the son as misunderstanding. The fear, Sam denied by, first, wishing the father away, then, by seeing him as only loving. Loving and being loved, then, seemed Sam's most pervasive answers to his own aggression and the aggression of others. He would deny inner and outer realities, if need be, to find love and admiration among father, mother, and, indeed, "sun."

These same patterns of defense showed more schematically in Sam's COPE test. In five out of six queries, Sam picked as his preferred response (eighth decile): "He realizes that the fault for [X] lies completely with himself and with no one else." The designers of the test call this "turning-against-the-self," "a way of dealing with anxiety—blaming the self rather than others who also may be available." By defining his fault himself, Sam avoided having it either in or defined by "others."

Conversely, Sam's *least* favorite defensive maneuver (last choice out of five, four times out of six, hence first decile) was: "He feels that he may [do or be X], but with help from someone more experienced, he could change." As the test designers say, this item "implies recognition of the anxiety and a statement of the need for help, employing the use of a parent-figure," and this was not something Sam liked to do at all—have a parent recognize deficiencies in himself. By contrast, Sam loved to relate himself to others in a context where both would see things to admire.

To use all this testing to understand Sam's reactions to literary works, we need to translate it into precise terms of drive and adaptation, and then into an identity theme. We can think of Sam as driven by two kinds of hunger. First, he hungered for admiration of his boyish virility and charm, most specifically, of his erectness in all senses of the word. Second, he longed for affection and thought he would achieve it through "touch" leading to merger with some reassuring person. He resisted his own aggressive drives—instead, he wanted to be given affection and admiration in a passive way.

Sam's adaptations had a duality that matched his drives. Primarily, Sam tried to deal with dangers by creating situations of mutual admiration and reassurance leading to identification, particularly with the very person whose aggression he feared. Through this kind of identification, Sam could gratify at least three drives: to receive admiration and love by wooing them from that other; to penetrate, fuse, or merge with the other; to act out aggressions vicariously and guiltlessly through the other. Secondarily, Sam dealt with dangers by external flight or internal avoidance: denial (refusing to perceive dangers); repression (refusing to acknowledge that he had perceived a danger); regression (a retreat to an earlier state of mind), and so on. In still more clinical terms, Dr. Corvus remarked *la belle indifférence*, the Pollyanna and counterphobic denials often seen in the classical hysteric.

Flight, however, especially a flight from passivity, could itself let Sam assert power and gratify drives to express his manliness, as when he could "come up" with a joke or an interpretation. Flight could also make a bid for outside supplies of admiration or affection: "See how I stand up and fly, free of wrongdoing. Admire and love me." Inner flight, particularly a regression toward childishness, could open still another way of receiving a flow from outside of love and admiration from an environment partly seen as mothering him. And all these adaptations could either aid identification or avoid aggression and so help Sam achieve the popularity on which he thrived.

In briefest terms, Sam's fantasies and defenses came together around wishes to take in or get out, taking in passively or getting out actively. Thus, Sam wanted to take in love and admiration of his own self-contained masculinity. He defended against threats to this solitary maleness by getting out of dangers into an isolated boyishness or by coming close to and taking into himself reassurances about his maleness from outside. Ideally, he achieved the most satisfaction by combining both these defenses and his hunger to be loved as an intact, boyish male by fleeing to a source of admiration. He did not want a sexual woman (who might pose dangers to his isolated virility) so much as he wanted desexualized brothers, fathers, or mothers—provided they seemed strong enough to him to be sources of security against his own deeply buried and quite unconscious hostilities. We could state this as an identity very laconically indeed: to get out of dangers to his maleness and to take into his body love and admiration.

To be sure, this must seem to you much more of an X ray than a portrait. Only a short step, however, takes us from Sam's identity theme—with its polarities of loss and gain, taking in and getting out, male and female—to the very real, very ingratiating and dressy young man seated before me, confessing his concern for manners and external appearances, touch between friends (but not lovers), *The New Yorker*, housekeeping, and Lyndon Johnson. In all such preferences and interests Sam re-created those polarities—and, of course, in his experience of literature as well.

Saul

The first thing I sensed in Saul was self-possession. He had an inwardness, intensity, and concentration that one associates with the traditional image of the scholar. Yet this self-contained quality masked a number of paradoxes. Although he was the most scholarly of this group of readers, Saul was also the most quirky and unexpected. He sought a precision and clarity far beyond anything the others tried for, yet more often than not the result was shadowy, vague, and elusive. He seemed eager to participate in the project, but when it came to the interviews themselves he so managed and controlled them as to be distinctly uncooperative. He talked, but he seemed to talk mostly to himself. He would muffle his words in his beard, embodying his tendency to slur in a modern hairiness. Matters got more difficult the more he talked, for, to get things very exactly, he would read quickly, softly, in a mumble, as if to himself, long sections from the stories, making his tapes painful and difficult to transcribe. Nevertheless, whatever his unconscious feelings, he brought to our enterprise a conscious commitment and enthusiasm that I appreciated.

Dr. Corvus thought Saul showed a good deal of originality in his Rorschach responses. He would come up with things like "a Gemini capsule" (Card II), "gibbons" instead of ordinary monkeys (III), or an image like "gophers holding hands with elephants" (VIII). He was much involved with trying to make the whole card make sense, and often he would use his ingenuity to synthesize and master the entire blot.

He had trouble, however, with colors. He would say things like, "The colors don't support this well." "The red and white conflict with a sense of fact" (Card II). "The red is spatially different" (Card III). In Rorschach testing, Dr. Corvus said, discrepancies perceived between the colors and the shapes often signal discrepancies felt between emotions and intellect. Saul tended to use harsh or degraded animal imagery for sexual material, and this might have been the basis for such a feeling of conflict.

Saul seemed preoccupied with another set of images: smallness and largeness (for example, the gophers and elephants).

Often (as in Card VI) he saw the relationship as "a small creature towing a large one." Other responses—Draculas, fat cats, a fat professor, various images of food—introduced situations in which the "large one" was eating the "small creature." Saul repeatedly used the word "odd" for the blots, and he concerned himself with the "strangeness" of the various images and how well they "fit" the totality. Thus, he would often turn from big or "important" sections of the blot to concentrate on innocuous details. Dr. Corvus's first metaphor for him was, "He's a photographer, searching for reality, peeking at small facets, rather than the total view." This, I take it, was what he accomplished by his scholarly, Talmudic style in his interviews with me, when he would take pains to read out exactly the right wording of some relatively unimportant passage while the larger question I had asked him went unanswered. "Circumspect," in its original Latin sense of "looking around," would describe Saul exactly.

In his COPE test, he avoided the defense of "denial" (in the sense of "a lack of recognition of feeling toward a significant object . . . . a lack of recognition that the discrepancy between actual and ideal behavior occurs . . . . . The 'don't worry' aspect"). He chose denial *last* six times out of six, placing it firmly in the zero decile. Saul did not like at all the idea of not seeing something. By contrast, Saul did like to have what he saw confirmed by others. He favored the defense of projection (defined in this test as "reversing the subject and object of the feeling"; "the anxiety problem is accepted but the motivating source of the behavior is perceived as being in the object rather than the subject"). Thus, in his Rorschach responses, he would sometimes preface an image by saying, "You can see . . ." meaning, "I see," or, perhaps, "I hope you see what I see."

Another way he would strengthen his sight was to argue his perceptions into validity. Thus, in Card IV (the "father" card), he saw a tall man leaning against a tree. "That [the tree] is to account for the odd appendage." In effect, he would comment on his comment, his fantasy becoming more real than the inkblot that gave rise to it. Once, at least, Dr. Corvus said, he physically turned away from the card so as not to be distracted by it as he developed a particularly interesting fantasy. Sometimes, he would give his images tactile values: for Card VIII, "cotton candy, but it's the wrong consistency." At other times, he would produce three-dimensional pictures with angles and perspectives.

As with the other subjects, a TAT response gives a good sample of Saul's style. This is to the boy in the doorway:

Appalachia—boy's family not desperately poor (he has shirt, overalls in decent repair) but still they live in hand-hewn house. Poor enough that the boy is succumbing to the emotional blight that poverty confers on the inhabitants of the other America. Boy's unhappiness partly this, partly his *father's absence*—he has been gone, looking for work, for a month (when the mines pulled out 3 years ago, dad lost job)—father not broken yet by the poverty (only extreme last 3 yrs.) but affected. The boy is affected by father's progressive demoralization.

Saul's response is the shortest of all the subjects', and this is as long as his TAT stories ever got. His writing was tiny and crabbed, and in this story there are eleven places where he crossed out his first word to replace it by a more considered one, not, I would say, with any great difference in subtlety or grace.

Yet in the content of what he wrote, he showed the same careful scholarly attention to details such as how the house was made or how good the boy's shirt and overalls were. But only these few details caught his attention, since the story overall remained quite elusive. Unlike Sam, who put a mother and a red-haired father in the picture, Saul saw it entirely in terms of loss, absence, and deprivation.

Specifically, he saw a large, vague, superior force; "poverty," he called it, using only that word but using it twice. "Poverty" was attacking an equally large, vague victim— "Appalachia," "the other America"—and dealing out nebulous harms—"emotional blight," "progressive demoralization." The specific people are, vaguely, "succumbing" or "affected." Against these shapeless ills, Saul tried to balance details and set exact limits. He carefully distinguished two different causes for the boy's unhappiness. The family was "not desperately poor," the father "not broken yet." The poverty has been "extreme" only the last "3" years (expressed with a digit) since the mines left.

In general, Saul sought a precision to avoid vagueness (but unconsciously he often sought vagueness itself). He was preoccupied with "fit." He was alert for the "odd" or "strange," and he would hedge, qualify, and redefine in his interviews until he reached what he thought was just the right match. Incidentally, this revising also controlled the interview according to Saul's terms, not mine. "A logician," Dr. Corvus called him, "a systems analyzer," and this defensive pattern accounted for some of his literary preferences. "The prose works with authority and precision," he said of an author he liked (Flannery O'Connor), "specifies something." "I like the precision in defining this emotion with a good deal of— Well, after 'precision,' I don't know for sure what to say. That strikes me as absolutely right. That's another way of saying 'precision.' " " 'Crystalline' is another word." "I get back to these vague critical terms like 'conciseness' and 'efficiency' and so forth, which I groove on." In particular, he liked "that kind of precision, utterly no nonsense, precision in delineating the inadequacies and grotesqueries." I decided Saul took especial pleasure from women's controlling these grotesqueries, for he praised a very frilly, feminine story as "perfectly realized," "perfectly described," "perfectly clear." "What the mother does . . . fits perfectly," Later, he described that mother as "frightening terrible." Similarly, when he was discussing a Poe story, he said to me, "I felt as though the prose was like iron bars between me and great shadowy shapes on the other side of them." In effect, as an English major and an aspiring writer, he felt free to avoid the great shapes and concentrate on the exactness of the controls.

Another way Saul's guardedness came through in his interviews with me was his habit of quoting authorities. In a given interview, he might quote critics and writers half a dozen times, often rather oddly. Thus, "I *learned* from Fitzgerald. I learned more about how America works." He quoted another novelist as an authority on what men's sexual fantasies were like. He even cited me, as a critic, to myself and fed me psychoanalytic terms he thought might please me, confessing meanwhile, "I'm still pretty innocent in this terminology." He also quoted a great deal of text and felt uncomfortable when I posed questions that asked him to imagine events not explicitly described. "Uh, now we're talking less about the text with that question. It's not really clear. . . . That one was one of the questions I was asking myself, obviously. Um, textually, um [pause] textually, I think it suggests . . ." and he began to quote again, thus evading my question and keeping his imaginings about the text quite to himself.

I took Saul's inwardness and scholarly intensity to represent at the visible level a deeper inner need to hold knowledge and situations in himself. Saul was a remarkably guarded and secretive young man, much concerned with issues like: Who controls whom? Who is big and powerful and therefore likely to control? Who will be exact and hard and therefore force the other to let go of something, particularly something sloppy or vague, hard to hold onto, whether it is inside or outside one's self? At his deepest level, Saul seemed most to fear being a small, passive object with some big, vague power threatening to take something out of him. He was afraid that a "mine" would be "pulled out." He seemed to expect the threat from a large, sadistic person, most likely a woman (for Saul tended to see women as threatening, aggressive, or austere).

Saul's scholarly and logical search for precision was the creative way he avoided this danger. He became an intellectual who got things to fit or match in an exact balance that he could control. He bargained terms with that superior force, fearing a disproportion that would lead to an unequal bargain and a situation where he would be overpowered and forced to give up something precious. He constantly searched his environment for anything big or vague that might pose a danger. He needed to see all threats before they could become dangerous; to leave nothing hidden or uncertain; to control situations; and, in particular, to hew to measured balances between closeness and distance, emotion and intellect, acceptance and rejection, or man and woman. If he could not get such a match or bargain, he would avoid the whole situation, physically or psychically, and look for a world of safe precision elsewhere.

Shep

Of all the readers, Shep most intrigued and most saddened me. I found him mixing in the most striking way, stereotype and original, morality and pathology, maturity and immaturity. He held forthright and progressive ideas but in a bitter, wronged way. Shep presented himself as almost a prototype of young alienation—radical, hip, and hostile. His clothes had achieved a kind of monochromatic brown patina. Indeed, he proudly told me one day that everything he had on his back was used clothing he had scrounged for free. His hair was very long and very much in a state of nature. In the interviews, he sprawled and slouched, and his flat Southwestern *a*'s often trailed into snarls. He tended to be taciturn or at least to measure his words carefully.

He could also be evasive. Consistently, he diverted literary talk into his own sweeping generalizations about revolution, drugs, sex, and a sort of at-oneness with the cosmos. When he did confine himself to literature, he began almost automatically to analyze it, skillfully phrasing clever comments and modern dogmatisms, but talking almost to himself. He was quick and good at literary analysis, but he preferred to seem impulsive, and often, I thought, he deliberately and self-consciously created the mere appearance of spontaneity.

I got the impression from seeing Shep among other students that he had no close friends. Certainly, he never mentioned a close relationship with another person (as Sam talked about walking with friends and lovers or Saul about his girl troubles). Shep did complain of his parents, both in his childhood and in his life at the time of the interviews, and he did mention various writers and celebrities. In a manner almost mythically American, he would speak of fleeting figures he had met on his travels—Shep as the archetypal hitchhiker, the stranger on the train, the frontiersman. But he never spoke simply of being with someone. Instead, he seemed to relate to people in terms of systems, abstractions, and ideologies. To be sure, most of us in Shep's milieu in 1969 applauded Shep's values but, even so, he gave them an oddly bitter, relentless flavor.

Dr. Corvus told me that Shep would typically project something into the test materials but then deny his own projection, insisting someone else had put it there. In the first cards of the Rorschach, for example, he spoke of the images he gave as "the arrangement of ink." "It was designated that way," he said, mixing his saying with the blot's design.

Similarly, in one of the interviews, he remarked, "You're leading me down the primrose path just to see how much I can fabricate." True, I was much interested in his "fabrications," but why did he think fabrication a "primrose path"? Why would he say of my request that he retell the story in his own words, "That sounds like a trap question"? Before taking the TAT for this study, he recalled, "I think I had one of those once, and it didn't make any sense, because the pictures all aimed toward a certain story that wasn't what I wanted to see in it." I thought he was saying he preferred his own fantasy free from what he took to be a controlling intelligence in the pictures. In the same way, Shep tended to see the Rorschach cards as literal, not in an "as if" way. Many of his responses to them were hostile: images of projectiles or ripping and tearing apart. In Card IV, he saw a bat, but it was "not particularly out to get me," he said, as though he had to remind himself he was not under attack. Dr. Corvus said he got the impression Shep felt watched by a harsh superego.

As I reminisce about Shep, I find myself thinking that his mind adapted to the world as a small or frightened animal would. That is, he related to reality by perceiving it in terms of threats. Indeed, a vulnerable organism has to react this way in order to keep constantly on the alert. In this mobilized state, Shep coped adroitly with the world's actual dangers (and those he projected into the world) in one of two ways: either he hid or he fled to a point from which he could fight.

For Shep, hiding meant becoming a mere object among other objects in a "system." Flight meant exile and resistance. "That's a damned everyday occurrence in my life, the fascism of this country. I carry a piece of paper in my hip pocket," he said one day, referring to his draft card, "that tells me about it any time I care to look, and that will probably drive me into exile." Like so many in 1969, Shep felt that he had only the choice of submitting like a mere piece of paper to an all-powerful state or fleeing elsewhere to fight another day, and the political setting exactly matched these two modes of adaptation.

The United States of 1969 also matched his need to perceive the world as threatening and to threaten in return. In all our conversations, Shep had a tendency to push out from the material at hand into general themes and issues, usually political and social, where he could, in effect, pick fights. Some of these generalizations and comparisons seemed sensible enough, some seemed silly, but all gave me the same feeling in the interview situation. I felt challenged and, in hearing or reading our interviews again, I often detected a testy note in my questions—as now I feel a distinct tendency to be defensive in writing about those discussions. Shep was forcing on me (and on others he described in his interviews) occasions to take offense or to retaliate.

These assertions functioned multiply in Shep's character. He was talking the "language of escalation," generalizing more and more widely and so maximizing the possible areas of disagreement. He thus created the aggressive atmosphere that mobilized his adaptive strengths. In one mode, he cloaked himself in generalities. In another, these general themes and issues worked as a kind of flight for Shep, away from my literary questions into something he himself had chosen; and there, he could fight.

One day, for example, he announced he had come across a review that said an author had "raised fiction to the level of a sport." Is this what one says to a singularly nonathletic teacher of literature? He talked about Shopper's World, a local mall: "It's really a scary place, not so much the people, but as a whole plastic environment covering acres and acres." He, by contrast, was "into" Zen and yoga and so did not need a hi-fi, did not even like light shows or the Fillmore. I found myself feeling I was damned if I did (but cowardly if I didn't) argue with him about the aesthetics of shopping plazas or the technology of acid rock. Yet if I had, I suppose we would have settled into a distant sniping, each secure in the fortress of his own value system.

Shep's adaptation of "hiding" himself in a system showed
with particular clarity in his response to TAT Card 13B, the
picture of the solitary boy in the doorway. Ordinarily, this card
elicits depressive material, thoughts about the loss of nurturing
persons, for example, or loneliness or hunger. Shep quickly
developed the ambivalent themes one might feel toward a withholding mother, but he applied them to the government. (His
writing was all small capitals, as if there were no difference
between big and little letters.)

POVERTY IN AMERICA. THANK YOU, DEPARTMENT OF
HEALTH, EDUCATION + WELFARE. WHAT ABOUT THE DE-
PARTMENT OF HELL, INTIMIDATION + WARFARE IN THE
OTHER PART OF THE BUILDING?

A BOY CAUGHT IN THE ONE NATION IN THE WORLD THAT
SHD. BE ABLE TO DO SOMETHING FOR HIM—BUT IS MORE
INTERESTED IN WASTING LIVES + PROTECTING CORPORATE
INCOME.

WHICH ALL SOUNDS PRETTY MARXIST, I GUESS. I REALIZE
THAT IN HUMAN TERMS HIS SITUATION IS NOT UNLIVABLE,
MAY IN FACT BE MORE LIVABLE THAN THE CONCRETE-LINED,
AIR-CONDITIONED SUBURBANITE'S CHILD'S IS. YET HE LOOKS
HUNGRY. WHICH IS A DRAG. WE ARE PART OF THE SAME
BODY (AND I DON'T MEAN BODY POLITIC) + I OBJECT TO THIS
BOY GOING HUNGRY WHEN THE RESOURCES ARE ADEQUATE
TO FEED HIM. IF HE WANTS TO GO HUNGRY AFTER THAT, IT'S
PERMISSIBLE, OR SHD. BE. I AM NOT TALKING ABOUT
"ACCULTURATING" HIM.

NOR AM I INTERESTED PERSONALLY IN DOING ANYTHING.
IF THE BUREAUCRATS DID THEIR WORK RIGHT, THERE
WOULD BE LITTLE OR NO NEED FOR VISTA, LET ALONE A LOT
OF THE PRIVATE AID GROUPS. THE HOUSE IS NICE. IT SHOULD
BE A GOOD PLACE TO LIVE IF YOU'RE NOT HUNGRY. OR MAL-
TREATED BY YR. "PROTECTORS" (THE POLICE—I TAKE THE
TERM TO INCLUDE ALL *ORDERING* INSTITUTIONS OF A
SOCIETY, ALL THOSE WHOSE DECISIONS CAN BE IMPOSED ON
YOU, INCLUDING COURTS, EMPLOYERS, ETC—ARE NOT SUF-
FICIENTLY TOLERANT WITH RESPECT TO THE POOR,
WHOEVER THEY ARE.)

A PUBLICITY PICTURE, DESIGNED TO STIR CERTAIN EMOTIONS. IF I WERE MORE IMPLICATED IN THIS SOCIETY, PERHAPS MY REACTIONS MIGHT HAVE FIT MORE CLOSELY. ANGER, BUT NO VIOLENCE.

Obviously, in a political setting, Shep's tirade could make perfect sense, but he was taking a psychological test, and he was asked to tell a story to an obviously fictional picture. As in his interviews with me, Shep has fled from a situation that might be revealing in order to snipe at it from the safe distance of an otherwise highly acceptable system of moral and political priorities.

Nevertheless, Shep's response strongly suggests that he did not achieve in early childhood some of the full, stable trust that makes later growth easier. Chief among these earliest gains is a sure sense of one's own boundaries, the dividing line between inner and outer reality, parent and child, and so on. Shep, however, as in this TAT response, felt himself "part of the same body" with the boy in the picture and identified himself with "the poor whoever they are." Hence, too, he mistook the level of reality appropriate to the picture, seeing it as a "publicity picture" (perhaps for some government agency's sinister plans).

In merging with the world around him, Shep partly converted his own massive feelings of anger into a feeling that he was being dominated by some sadistic being outside himself. Thus, he did not distinguish society's indifference to the boy from a system of "ordering institutions," a "department of . . . intimidation." And behind these sadistic "protectors" I sensed Shep's massive, early resentment of some mothering person. Dr. Corvus also concluded Shep must have felt greatly deprived in childhood. From this deprivation came his feeling that he must either coerce or be coerced and his feeling, too, that to be dependent was (ultimately) to be eaten—just as his upper case letters absorbed the lower case. As Shep said to TAT Card 18GF, "Proximity could breed murder."

Shep's narrowed sense of self showed up in the way he thought of the body as a destructive machine, particularly when taking something in or putting something out. "In Spain," he recalled, "you can pick up a thing called *turista* which causes vomiting and diarrhea, and I found that most encounters with the people called *turistas* tend to induce the same reaction on my part." "When a junky shoots up, there's a narcissistic closed circle from the right hand through the needle into the arm—complete isolation—and I think Hemingway sitting there with the rifle in his mouth, or pistol against his head, or whatever it was, there's that same sort of closed circle from the hand through the weapon to the body. They seem to be caught in the same sort of evil bag," he concluded, suddenly giggling.

In the same way, Shep found security (of the "hiding" kind) in surrendering the separateness and edges of his self. For example, he commented on the blind man in D. H. Lawrence's story of that name: "If he's going to know objects this way ['in a way more intimate and more primal than . . . others know,' Shep had said], he's going to . . . have to exist as an object, in the flow of things, surrender to the world, be totally dependent upon it, but not really, because he's an integral part of it—there's not the separation that makes for dependence. If you get into the stream of things enough, you don't have this subject-object dichotomy anymore." Similarly, he recalled the anti-Negro prejudice of the town he grew up in: "About the most you can do is grant that they are separate human beings, and you don't get around to think of them as being part of your flesh and blood until sometime later." In effect, he was saying, to be close, to empathize with someone, is to become the same body as that person or to be engulfed by him; and this is something that happens to the black, the blind, the deprived boy in the doorway—and Shep.

As against these weakened victims was "the sort of bureaucratic putdown you run into all over the place," a mysteriously powerful controlling force: "Ultimately fascism is black magic. It's an attempt to control the environment absolutely, by forces hostile with [*sic*] the current of things." He saw this aim of controlling the bodily currents of others as "the old con of government anywhere, that we're doing for you what you can't do for yourself and proceed and take over all sorts of things that you *can* do for yourself, such as regulate your sexual habits or your intake of chemicals." Here, I felt that behind the specter of the state stood his parents, particularly as they controlled his body's taking in and putting out. Thus he dismissed clothes as "externals . . . defining who you are rather than the internals . . . It's a heap of trash." Of Richardson's *Clarissa,* he said, "These people [her family] treated her like shit . . . and by accepting this treatment, she accepts their judgment of what she is in order that they can treat her that way. She becomes an object."

In short, in Shep's psychic economy, to be close meant being threatened or controlled, which then implied being made an object, perhaps even being consumed or gobbled up. Alternatively, being close could mean being the same as, part of the same body, loved and loving. In effect, one could be safe if one gave up identity and became an object in a system. One could even, in a way, be loved: "There's not the separation that makes for dependence."

Alternatively, instead of being close, Shep simply fled, both physically and psychically, into that "exile" he so often referred to. "We grow out of it, grow out of . . . being a child. We lose it." "She's a bitch," he said of a character in a story, "but she's a lot like my mother. She can be a bitch, but she'll be very nice out in public. And she probably regards her own family as public." "I've always liked snow . . . and if I were to walk outside right now [and see a] pile of snow on the ground, I'd think it was great. Keep snowing all spring," he said, as though he were addressing the weather gods. "I'm feeling like I've got to get to the roads again, probably take off over Easter and hitch to Denver."

Besides, or beyond, flight, the further step toward not being controlled that Shep would take was aggression: "Violent resistance." "Maybe that's the only thing that would do it," "protect you from fascism." "If you don't dig killing people, if you would rather have [someone else kill the tyrant], then eventually you may come to realize that the only thing left is exile."

These extremes—merger as an object in a system or total separation through flight and fight—carried over into Shep's attitudes toward reading and literature. He contrasted times when "I get captured by what I'm reading" with analytical puzzle-solving. "Take an aerial photograph of it. Then I'm very

much the separate observer," reading "like a damn critic,"
thus, like the "damn" man he was talking to. Flight served,
like merger, to evade human contact, but literary flight gave
Shep a way to re-create his own autonomy: "[What] I'm concerned with in reading is trying to make sense out of my own
life." "That's why I'm in the whole English bag," he said,
because it offered more "insidious reading" than other subjects. Whether he intended "insidious" to mean "tending to
entrap" or not, he found in literature a way of actively re-
establishing that earliest passive closeness he had fled. "The
important thing is making life assume a wholeness both for
yourself and for the people you happen to contact through the
classroom."

The dehumanizing common to Shep's merger and his aerial
detachment showed again when he recalled "the quote attributed to Mussolini's son bombing Ethiopia, that the bombs
down there looked like little red flowers. I find that a very
distasteful thing intellectually, and yet I'm still taken by it because in a way, they must have looked like little red flowers,
and I'm almost morbidly fascinated with the detachment of a
man who could look down there and see only the flowers."
Yet, as he went on, he seemed to say that the cruelly indiffer-
ent response was the direct, intuitive one "preceding the intel-
lection of it." "The Mussolini image is a striking image before I
even start thinking about it in terms of an abstraction, and it
was just the experiential thing of, here, you drop something
over the edge which explodes and blossoms like a red flower
before even thinking about what exploding things do." I could
not tell whether Shep knew that Vittorio Mussolini had really
been referring to the *bodies* of Ethiopian cavalrymen making
roses when bombed.[3] If so, Shep's association doubly suggested the rendering of people into things.

The essence of Shep's identity, this search for thingness,
seemed to come from his reacting against an original, mothering utopia that ceased to be a nurturing bliss and became a
depriving, disgusting emptiness. "Once Eden goes through the
Fall, it becomes the most desolate place on earth. I think that
sort of mythic inversion is almost necessitated. You have to
maintain the intensity even though you don't maintain the po-

larity. So that this [place in a story] has gone from being the navel of the world to perhaps being the asshole of the world."

Shep seemed to me the kind of adult whose infancy had turned into extremes of rage and who had developed thereafter, not so much in fulfillment of his first experience of the world as in reaction against it. He moved, as we all do, from his first relationship, based on what went into his body, to what might even have been quite average processes of control of what came out of his body, body products and body actions. But Shep seemed someone who had perceived that control in terms of his own massive rage. Control came to represent for him a total taking over of his being. Similarly, in the romance of the boy for his mother or his identification with his father, it seemed to me, judging from the adult Shep, that his aggressive feelings as a child had so colored these later phases of development that he treated the crucial others in his life as things, institutions, or abstract forces that threatened to engulf him.

As an adult, Shep singled out this sort of relationship to reject it: "If two people can't exist as individuals with complete freedom of agency in the world, if one has to possess the other as an object, you don't have a love relationship—you got a property relationship. If I ever decide to make children in the world, I want to marry, not incorporate." In fact, however, in his constant response to others as things or systems, he was aggressive enough toward them that he seemed to feel secure only if he were himself also a thing among them: the boy in the picture or "the concrete-lined, air-conditioned suburbanite's child."

In a more positive vein, he admired people or institutions for "exercising possibilities in the world" (which I took to be a conscious moral value derived from his unconscious need to adapt through activity and flight). Choice was a good thing in Shep's economy—he needed lots of emergency exits. Alternatively, he could appreciate situations of "no choice" as "natural" and gratifying if they produced "thingness," that is, if they assigned one a secure role in some matrix, like a position in a myth (he delighted in mythic interpretations of literature) or in one of the Indian tribes he so admired (part

of his conscious primitivism) or in a social or literary theory
he approved.

As an adult, Shep showed in our interviews a warm desire to
be a sensitive reader and teacher of literature coupled with an
incomplete sense of self that sometimes helped him to be that
sensitive reader and at other times gave rise to fierce aggressive
impulses. These aggressions would lead him to respond to people in and out of books as abstractions ("red flowers," "being
part of your flesh and blood"), not as people with lives of their
own. Within this limitation, however, he responded at all
psychological levels (oral, anal, phallic, oedipal—in technical
terms), unlike, say, Saul, who responded primarily at one. At
all these levels, however, he polarized stories and themes into
two extremes of merger into "thingness" or flight-and-fight.
Often, Shep seemed unusually mature because of these modes.
Certainly his loosened boundaries corresponded to the new directions in American culture. Yet those same loosened boundaries made the world a far more angry place for him than it
needed to be.

Sebastian

A complicated, engaging young man, Sebastian had a sardonic
sense of humor that made for lots of jokes and for amusing
interviews. He was a surprisingly worldly and sophisticated
person, the most self-consciously "literary" of these five readers. Clever with words, he was also much attuned to economic
class and social status—possibly because at the time we had
our interviews, he was working his way loose from family,
religious, and ethnic values he had formerly held quite strongly,
and he talked a good deal about himself as a lapsed, or lapsing,
Catholic. Tall, well dressed in a hypermodern way, hair flowing
freely, his eyes wandering a bit, he impressed me as a slightly
incoherent, impulsive person, almost too eager to accept new
fads and fashions, hurrying to get somewhere without quite
knowing where. Although highly articulate, he had a curious
way of slurring his words, as though to make them still more
casual than they already were, but I felt underneath his seeming ease, his manner was studied. This mixture gave him an

intriguing style that mixed nervous energy with "cool."

These are only my impressions, however. With considerably more precision, Dr. Corvus found two patterns or directions in Sebastian's responses to the Rorschach, which he stated in technical and clinical language. Sebastian would deal with threatening materials in the inkblots, said Dr. Corvus, by flight or avoidance or denial, typically substituting his own intellectual products for the materials given him or "dressing them up." Alternatively, he would sexualize things that caused him anxiety, particularly aggressive material, often going to the extent of identifying with them in a pregenital tenderness that was, in Sebastian's own phrase, "definitely benign." Although the tests are "as if" situations, Sebastian would tend to get absorbed by them (as he did, for me, with literary texts). At the opposite extreme, he would, in Dr. Corvus's words, "arbitrarily brush aside, omit, compartmentalize," thus returning to his first mode of adaptation. He would use "inconsequential things to blot out disturbing images." Dr. Corvus sensed, in this side of the pattern, little "self-involvement," "lots of responses, but shallow, moving away, not pulling together." In both patterns, that of substitution or that of passively fusing with threatening materials, Sebastian, Dr. Corvus said, showed a pervasive lack of affect, a stiffness, an inanimacy.

Sebastian's COPE questionnaire (considerably less reliable, to be sure, than Dr. Corvus's more supple tests) shed a different light. Far from lacking affect, Sebastian had plenty of anxiety; he did not divorce anxiety from "the discrepancy between [his] actual and ideal behavior" (in the words of the test manual). Isolation was his *least* used defense (first decile). His most used (ninth decile) was perceiving "the motivating source of [his] behavior . . . in the object rather than the subject." That is, Sebastian often felt controlled by others, not himself (as, in the Rorschach, he would blur himself into threatening material).

If I were to try to state Sebastian's identity theme as exactly (and therefore as connotatively) as possible, it would be: *to give an intellectual creation of his own and to be given a fleshy control that he could fuse into or withdraw from*. With that theme in mind, read Sebastian's story in response to the "depressive" TAT card of the solitary boy in the doorway:

He lived almost without props. Had none of the paraphernalia of American boyhood. Had only the unchanging faces of buildings. So what developed—almost ex nihilo—was a system of memory. Ex nihilo because the content of his consciousness was almost non-existent. He trained himself in speech—a self taught rhetoric—memorising and elaborating the laconic exchanges of his dour parents, lank creatures both so exhausted from scratching a bare living out of their West Virginia soil that they could spare nothing for conversation. He imagined rooms of a great house and corresponding to each room and to the contents of the rooms he would fit segments of his neat speeches. Interior monologues that lasted whole sunny days as he sat on the log doorsill. They called him dull.

No event in physical reality could begin to compete with the rich ornate rooms full of weighted objects heavy surreal furniture of a crystal mind.

He sat while a bright yellow truck came to deliver a farm implement anxiously contracted for months previously appeared at the crest of a hill a quarter mile distant. He watched, silent, his parents walk to the rough gate to greet its long awaited coming. He saw the panic-eyes of the driver a stranger as he did not, could not stop as the truck careened madly sliding, its rear end thrashing through space to softly thump his silent parents almost silently out of existence and watched without moving as its lumbering yellow shape smashed his fragile blond skull into the rough floor of the seed cabin.

He wrote with conscious artistry, and with a dualism running through his story (as well as that lofty disregard of commas and other niceties so characteristic of the English major).

There are really two stories: one, an investigation of mental products inside the leading character's head; the second, a violent scene "outside." The first half shows Sebastian's exchange of mental creations for a physical reality—particularly a reality that gave nothing, "nihilo." "They could spare nothing for conversation." Whatever its origins in Sebastian's early relation with his parents, this pattern provides the basis for his ability to use intellectual and verbal products creatively to maximize his possibilities for happiness in the world of the adult.

The second plot in Sebastian's TAT story about the boy in the doorway introduces the theme of control—or, more exactly, the violence that results from the lack of it. The truck of "a stranger," silent as the son himself, crushes with its "rear end" and "yellow shape" both parents and child. It represents a kind of violent physical match to the first mental plot in the story. In the first, mental possessions substituted for physical. In the second, the "rear end" silently thumps the silent parents. The "yellow shape" smashes the "fragile blond skull."

The question of stopping a "rear end" brings in themes associated with early experiences of controlling (or having others control) our body creations. The story speaks of "soil," "weighted objects," "contents," and "interior mono*log*ues . . . as he sat on the *log* doorsill" (italics mine). This TAT also shows a scene by a gate—"his parents walk[ed] to the rough gate to greet its long awaited coming." Admittedly, Sebastian has much transformed the body meaning of these words. Nevertheless, I think I discern fantasies about the control of soil and a fear (or wish) that failure to control what physically (as against mentally) comes through the gate could lead to the violent destruction of self or others.

In general, then, I find that Sebastian showed two patterns. First, he would seek a control he could join himself to (like the boy in the TAT "memorising and elaborating" his parents' "exchanges"). Often, Sebastian would see control as an exchange and often (although not in this TAT) the controller as a sexually desirable woman. Second, he would substitute his own mental product for these external controls. Thus, these two patterns could combine to make a third, Sebastian's ideal: a mutual giving in which he came close to a sexually desirable controller who gave him something physical, fleshy, or "dirty," to which he responded by giving his own mental products.

These patterns provided the unconscious basis for Sebastian's distinctive intellectual style: a sophisticated search for models he could emulate, often expressed in imagery like the "soil" or the "rear end" of the TAT stories. For example, he said that in parochial school, "I felt that I was standing hip deep in my own tradition, and I really liked it. . . . I've sort of backed out of it." "I have a tendency now to put my eggs in the hippie basket, like I really identify with that kind of business."

Of his own ethnic tradition, he said, "It's never as great as it's painted. They really have feet of clay. The only people that are as grand as they say they are are the English. They're flawless, their parades, and their things, and they've got the money to do it right." He admired "that peculiar British business, which goes from the top to the bottom, practically. . . . They just seem to have insulated themselves from their violence in a way we haven't done." Violence in an English (as against an American) novel "would be somehow comical. It would be seen through two or three panes of glass somehow. It would be distorted and far off and not merely somebody actually being thrown out [of a window] and the sense of guts on the street, the loving care for the physical details." Thus, as in the TAT, Sebastian revealed a faith that sophistication and wit would provide alternatives and controls for the rawly and perhaps violently physical.

It is also worth noting, I think, how many of Sebastian's phrases in his ordinary speech are classic psychoanalytic symbols for the body products on which the child's earliest controls are focused: standing hip deep, putting eggs in a basket, paint, clay, the rituals of Englishness, money, bottom, or guts. He was constantly acting out the substitution of mental products for physical ones. Similarly, it is striking that the controlling forces that appealed to him were precisely those that classical psychoanalysis links to sphincter morality: a ritualistic church and an authoritarian government. "I liked T. S. Eliot [in school]. I liked the idea that there was a kind of acerbic certainty. I was sort of a fascist in that prep school way." He liked novelists who worked out the Catholic and conservative tradition he was being educated in at that time. "I was totally in it [English aristocratic fiction] . . . for me, at that point, something in the nature of ritual. . . . some kind of celebration of something . . . a liturgical quality. And then just total delight with [their] sharp, aristocratic vision."

All kinds of reading, however, even criticism, could give Sebastian the mixture of control with giving that he liked. After learning from good criticism, he said, one would read a story "with a sense of treading over familiar ground and coming on familiar and loved landmarks." Sebastian always sought the "familiar" in his reading. In effect, he liked being given himself. "I was always looking for evocations of the kinds of things that I went through." "I like John Updike, for instance, very much. Anybody that's working the childhood memory vein always appeals to me. Salinger, for instance." He felt most entertained when "you realize that you're just being entertained. There's no real demands being made on your consciousness at all."

Indeed, for Sebastian to identify fully with others, they had to give to him, not he to them. For example, he said of political figures, "It's part of the charisma of any leader that in some way he's giving up something, he's making a sacrifice. . . . Even though he embodies the group ideal, somehow it's a drain on his energies to be the group ideal. . . ." Similarly, he said, the Church had taught him "that we've got all the truth here, and we'll give you some."

By contrast, Sebastian did not like authors or authorities who kept things within themselves. He was "offended" by Thomas Mann, "by his burgherish quality. It's heavy. It's like a Victorian parlor. It's liberal and broad-minded and tries to take everything into its scope, but it's ponderous in the way that it includes everything. . . . There's no mercurial quality to it, which would make it so much more pleasant"—indeed, witty like Sebastian himself. But with Mann, "Everything is ponderous, that elephantine quality." Ultimately such inclusiveness and self-sufficiency seemed a withholding: "Because he is aware of everything, he's also a suitable censor." Sebastian disliked people and institutions who withheld from him, whom he could not get close to.

Naturally, someone who so disliked being withheld from, liked being given to, even being given by the authorities of church and school the choirboy ethics he now rejected. "It thrilled me. I loved it. I liked all the stuff that I had been fed since I was [a child], of the Christian intellectual tradition and

how deep it was, and how groovy it was, and how everybody
finally comes down to it, like you can't get away from the
Church." His word "fed" tells us this giving was important to
him at all levels of his being, even or especially the earliest but
also later stages. "I accepted the categorical imperatives absolutely, and I bought that completely." "I liked almost everything that I was given [to read]." At a less intellectual level, he
enjoyed thinking about women in passive situations: "It was
titillating, that a sort of placid Southern beauty like that
would— All that passiveness would be just exemplified and
there she is, you know. 'Take me.' It was sort of exciting."

Conversely, if an author or an authority gave to Sebastian,
Sebastian would not only sexualize and merge into the situation, he would give in return. Thus, at the movies, "if it's done
right at the beginning, if I sense any kind of imagination at all,
or any kind of depth at all, "I'll just accept all the *données*
without much trouble and I'll buy the whole thing, all the prem-
ises, and scream and yell and just be as much a part of it as
anyone could want." Similarly, with the theater: "I always
thought of myself as terrific [as an actor] potentially, and so I
respond to plays on the level of . . . thinking about the actors
and how they're doing it, and could I do that?" Like so many
English majors, he wanted to be a writer, and he often tried out
his own creativity alongside the author's, as it were, when he
read fiction or poetry, asking whether he would have written it
that way. Being given a story, he gave one in return.

Yet there was something odd about Sebastian's giving in
return—it seemed (as Dr. Corvus had concluded) to limit his
merger. To be sure, he could say, "When I'm in a movie . . .
I'm really *in* it." "I guess my state of mind is total identification with what's going on." "I sort of forget the fact that I'm
in a public place and have a tendency to laugh a lot or to make
verbal comments on what's going on, as if the movie weren't
particularly on the screen but were on my eyeballs instead."
Yet, how many of us, when we are totally engrossed in a
movie, are making comments on it? It seemed to me Sebastian's own giving provided him an escape from his fusion with
the silver screen—verbal creation. Giving out words in return
for getting images meant he could set the terms of his fusion

into cinematic or literary experience. As he said of literary skills, "It's a technique. It's a way of going about it that you can respect, but you know that it's limited. You know that it's not partaking of darkness."

In short, Sebastian's intellectual statements about life and letters said to me that he had created a sophisticated and worldly-wise view of things from a combination of two deep patterns. First, Sebastian longed for closeness to an authority that was not heavy or demanding or withholding or self-contained by its own ideals. Rather, the authority was to give freely. (It was the "take me" attitude that led me to decide such an authority must have derived from a giving mother.) Second, Sebastian would give the authority something in return: eggs in the basket, a portion of truth, a drain on his energies, business, ore from the vein of memory—he'd "scream and yell and just be as much a part of it as anyone could want." Most of all, Sebastian would give by means of literary or other intellectual techniques for distancing and isolating: verbal comment, wit, a violence made "somehow comical," "seen through two or three panes of glass," "distorted and far off." "I mean it's very easy to ridicule your own deepest feelings or to catch yourself being swept up in magazine rhetoric." Ultimately, he could flee altogether into his own intellectual creations, rejecting completely the bargain with the controlling authority, as he was apparently doing with the religion of his youth.

Always, however, he wanted to avoid situations of either total withholding or total merger (either of which, he seemed to feel, could give rise to massive, overpowering violence). He wanted an intimacy limited by means of giving and getting in return. As I suggested above, he acted so as to combine three possibilities: closeness to an authority, being given something warm and fleshly by that authority, giving in return a mental or verbal creation of his own. And it was in this atmosphere of mutuality that our very pleasant interviews took place.

Sebastian, however, introduces another issue—creativity. Although this book has to do, not with writers' creations but readers' re-creations, Sebastian nevertheless illustrates a point that should be made, because he wanted to be a writer. I do not know if he will go on to become a successful writer in fact or, indeed, a writer at all, but we can see how, if he does, his writing will serve him as an adaptation to certain early wishes and fears, in his case, about the control of physical and mental products. Thus, should he prove "creative" (that word sometimes being narrowly limited to productive artists), his creativity would not be a special faculty but part of the whole pattern of adaptations that makes up his lifestyle. Whatever Sebastian creates, and the very fact of his creating it, will exist on the same basis as his early fondness for the Church or Englishness or passive girls who say, "Take me."

Consider another TAT story Sebastian wrote, this one in response to Card 2, a scene in the manner of Thomas Hart Benton. In the foreground left is a girl carrying books. In the foreground right a woman leans against a tree—occasionally she is seen as pregnant. In the background a man, naked to the waist, is doing farm work. Sebastian wrote of it:

> The farm—isolated, fertile smelling of loam, manure sweat ammoniac and pungent. The hours—earliness—scrabbling poultry faint dawn light harsh noonlight piercing afternoon. Escape.
>
> I can escape. How? One way. The mind. To shut out smells, sounds, excepting. The brain a fragile flower perched closed but timidly opening on—manure fertility.
>
> I am here and gone at once. I am double. A woman. My hips broad. . . . [*sic*] my breasts round small. Him. His huge reeking presence in twilight mud clotted wrists. Pole thick coarsely hairy wrists.
>
> I am as fertile as this hateful farm and as and as [*sic*] the white pages of my life giving book.
>
> The girl, Mona, 16 has lived on a farm in Ohio for all of her 16 years. She has lately become more and more engrossed with a literature unknown as the city world is unknown to her muscular brothers to her faded eternally pregnant mother.
>
> She longs to escape the confines of the farm smells. She enrolls in a correspondence course offered on a matchbook

cover. Is accepted. Applies to a boarding school near Cincinatti. Something of her brooding unrest communicates itself to her examiners. She is admitted.

The time comes for departure. But she senses that in leaving the soil the sinewy muscular sunlit world of labor and childbirth she becomes a prisoner of that departure. Wandering. Error. The girl errant. In the harsh light of late may in the waning heat she waits at the farm gate. Awaits the station wagon to remove her from her thick environment. The sound of her brothers cries is harsh. Her mother, father dead, is silent. Proudly tearful.[4]

Obviously, we are in the presence of considerable literary talent.

Despite the somewhat self-conscious artistry, however (or because of it), I think Sebastian says a good deal about himself. That is, the first and most obvious thing about Sebastian's TAT protocol is that he did try to make it a short story, a literary production. Indeed, he shows no small talent in such fine imaginings of detail as the ad on the matchbook cover or Cincinnati or his arty stringing together of words in the first two paragraphs (which look almost like a first draft). Given a picture, Sebastian gave back a story—a correspondence course, in a way, a "match book."

Second, Sebastian got right into the scene, smelling it, emoting to it, recording a series of impressions in a manner quick as life. He was so "into" the scene that for the first few paragraphs I was not sure who the "I" of his story was. Third, Sebastian readily identified with the girl in the picture whom he associated with books and school—he identified with females in three out of four TATs.

Fourth, as with his other TAT story, much of the incidental imagery consisted of familiar associations to body creations: "loam," "manure," "pungent," "reeking," "smells," and so on. He partly saw as entrapping and "hateful" the "farm smells," the "manure fertility," and the coarsely hairy wrists, thick as a pole (a pun?), to which he limited the muscular (and I think, sexualized) brother.

He saw, however, an alternative mode to that physical,

smelly, muscular fertility, namely, "the brain" or "literature." He called it an "escape" that would shut out "smells," but also an "opening on—manure fertility." The girl escapes, but she is also "a prisoner of that departure."

Really, then, Sebastian based his story not so much on an escape as on two modes of adaptation, each of which could be an escape and each a trap. "I am here and gone at once. I am double." In one mode, he felt immersed in physical, sexual, smelly earthiness, as earlier he said he was "hip deep" in his ethnic tradition. In the other mode, he rose above that "thick environment" to be a fragile flower of brain, mind, and literature, and it was in this second, adaptive mode that his intellectual and verbal talents flowered. Thus Sebastian could say, in a key sentence, "I am as fertile as this hateful farm and as"—blocking on this figure of speech—"the white pages of my life giving book." He was fertile, then, in both modes, in his fusion with a fertile but controlling or authorizing environment and in his own intellectual or literary creativity. Whether he becomes a writer or not, I suspect, depends on which of these modes dominates the other. When last I saw Sebastian, he was on his way to a commune, and I had the impression that, for the time being anyway, an authorizing environment was going to be more important to him than giving out his own creations.

So be it. Nevertheless Sebastian is paradigmatic. One can see the vital possibility of creativity in his character and see also its role in meeting his outer and inner needs, some of which go back to very early infancy. For any human being, the literal, historical sources of creativity lie deeply buried in the haphazard experiences of infancy, which are difficult to learn about, differ for each child, and are quite unpredictable in their results. For the adult, however, one can see the dynamic. Artistic creativity, whether Faulkner's, Sebastian's, or Hilda Doolittle's,[5] is simply that particular human being's way of meeting the demands he faces from an outer and an inner reality. That reality can reach as far back, for example, as Sebastian's apparent decision in the very first year or two of his life to give his mother mental products in response to her physical control, nearness, and warmth.

Sandra

Sandra was graceful and stylish, although subdued in manner. "Maidenly" was the adjective Dr. Corvus applied. She tended to be rather blocked and rigid in the interview situation, turning our sessions into a question-and-answer quiz. Indeed, it was not until several had passed that she was able to ramble on freely or even look at me directly. Always, she hedged and qualified her conclusions: "Every touch was pretty perfect." An insight was "a definite addition, I guess." Nevertheless, she was an extremely intelligent and perceptive reader, thoroughly cooperative in the "experiment."

Obviously, one salient fact about Sandra is that she was a woman. I know I responded to her differently, and presumably she talked to me with a set of constraints different from the male readers'. One could say therefore that she brought to both the stories and interviews a set of expectations and experiences not comparable to the male subjects', but this would be to treat her femaleness as though it were "maleness-with-a-difference," a very old-fashioned and clumsy way of thinking psychoanalytically about women.

In this, the eighth decade of the development of psychoanalysis, one could try instead to understand any human being, male or female, in terms of his or her identity theme. The experience of being female helps develop that identity theme in one-half of a given culture's people, just as the experience of being male does in the other half. And being male or female in a given culture is one of the realities to which each individual must respond by means of his developing identity. There may be some identity themes that are inherently male or female (such as Erikson's concept of "inner space"), but no one, so far as I know, can say for sure as of 1975. To me, Sandra's identity theme seemed the same kind of statement as the male readers'.

If I put all her tests and all her interviews together, I am led to the following theme for Sandra. To begin with, she perceived the world as a kind of mystery; and sometimes, by words like "trap" or "trick," she conveyed the feeling that the mystery posed dangers. To find out if it did, one had to look at it, and vision dominated Sandra's sensory patterns to a quite extraordinary degree. If the mystery looked as though it might overpower her, she responded by what psychoanalysts call the "flight" defenses. She might physically avoid the danger, or she might refuse to look at it ("deny" it in the strict sense of avoiding the perception of it). She might perceive it but then erase it from consciousness ("repress" it), or she might perceive it, but refuse to feel any emotion toward it or make any intellectual connections with it (that is, "isolate" it by not letting it "touch" other things in the mind). In short, having seen the situation and found it threatening, she would arrange to see it no longer. Vision was crucial.

If she found it promising, however, she would try to see more of it, see it from closer up. In literature, this seemed to mean technique. More than any of the other four readers, she responded to the techniques and devices of literary works, and she would often, in her comments, play literature off against life, using each to keep the other in balance. Again, if the situation continued to look promising, she would draw still closer and begin to use images or imaginings of touch leading to a more intimate exchange.

"Promising" in this context, or "exchange," had special values. For Sandra (as for Sam), many of the themes and issues that concerned her involved abilities and achievements of all kinds, especially power as a thing in itself and also the power of eye, voice, mind, arm, body, and the like. Clinically, these concerns derive from the child's longings (after, say, the age of two) to have the same abilities to dominate the world (and himself) as his bigger, more powerful parents do. In that same stage, the physical differences between male and female take on heightened significance, and the child becomes much concerned with his own appearance, activity, and abilities. Many fantasies equate the whole body or mind or person, their rise or thrust or penetration (in various idioms), with the physical fact of maleness or femaleness. Both pleasure and anxiety focus on the theme of "bigger is better," as it applies to the differences between parent and child, between one child and a competing child (often a sibling), between bodies and parts of bodies, and also between boy and girl.

For Sandra, touching and drawing close seemed to offer an equalizing of such differences, a flow of power from stronger to weaker. "Promising" also meant for her the simpler, earlier pleasures of nurture and food (associated, perhaps, with the stronger mother giving of herself to a weaker child). These, too, would be given her if, after seeing and finding it safe, she drew near the promising source.

Very generally then, we could state Sandra's identity theme this way: *to see and approach more and more closely a source of power and nurture, but not to see its loss*. This is indeed abstract. My first concrete evidence of Sandra's character came from Dr. Corvus's tests. "A good hysteric," he called her—about as high a rank on the scale of normality as a clinician is likely to give—that is, someone whose fixations (on the body, typically) occurred sufficiently far along in development to leave only superficial, easily healed limitations. Nevertheless, he said that she showed "significant repression and denial," using, for example, the word "gray" in her Rorschach responses more than most people do. What colors she did talk about, she tended to mute. In Card X, for example, she began with "blue-gray-green caterpillars" and moved on to "yellow—some sort of horses." Others she mentioned were a "pinkish-red cat" and an "olive-drab beetle." Nevertheless, she seemed generally satisfied with herself and her life, he said. She was "comfortable with her femininity," but seemed rather in awe of male vigor, power, and protectiveness. She wanted to see more of these things and, curiously, it was precisely seeing that she regarded as a way of participating in or drawing on masculine strength, possibly because she was herself (in the appropriate idiom) very easy on the eyes. Thus, she recognized male-female differences but in order to minimize them. She both saw a great deal and refused to see a great deal.

The artful story she told to the blank TAT card showed how some of these patterns worked in her thinking:

Emily opened her eyes. "Nothing," she said. "There's nothing there." She'd been blind since birth, and her parents had tried everything. Finally, they had brought her to Vienna. Dr. Herzinger would take her into his hands. The famed eye surgeon had worked miracles. Her case was a challenge. Emily remembered hearing him sigh all during the initial examination. "I'll be honest with you," he told the girl. "Chances are 80-20 against you." But, well able to afford the operation, her parents had consented. The girl herself built up no false hopes. "Nothing," she said. "Of course." She stared straight ahead at the white expanse. Then came her father's voice: "Emily—" he said. "The doctor wants you to try moving your eyes. You've been staring at his stomach for five minutes."

The happy, even witty, ending shows the wishes and adaptations that are important to Sandra: deficiencies in the girl will be minimized through seeing, through being close to benevolent males (father-figures in Vienna—where else?), and through receiving from others strength (through stomach or eye—I?). The less happy opening shows one line of Sandra's defenses, not seeing: " 'There's nothing there.' " At the same time, the surgeon's realism and Emily's refusal to build up false hopes suggest the positive, adaptive role of seeing in Sandra's psychic economy: exactly and realistically defining sources of strength and sustenance.

This story of the seeing but not-seeing girl foreshadowed the same adaptations her COPE test revealed in a more schematic way. Sandra preferred as defenses denial, isolation (in the test's special sense of denial of affect), and projection (in the test's definition, recognizing a feeling, but finding its source outside, in another, rather than inside, in oneself). All three of these defenses ranked in the ninth decile, the last two quite highly so. One recognizes in this schema the "flight" defenses we have already mentioned that make up various ways of not seeing. Nevertheless, Sandra did want somebody to be dependent on, for she totally rejected "blaming the self rather than others who may be available" "as a way of dealing with anxiety"; she chose, for a defense, turning against the self last in all six test situations, putting it in the zero decile. This is Sandra's longing for an outside source of strength and comfort.

Sandra's TAT story was quite self-consciously literary, and, in general, in our interviews, Sandra spoke far more than any of the other readers about literary techniques. "I can't help —Almost as soon as I respond— I suppose I can't respond to any story, you know, straight, emotionally. I think, as soon as I read it . . . 'Isn't that good!' " "I have a feeling that, powerful as the characters were, I would still always think of the way something was being told and the things that were being used, and certainly it adds to my total enjoyment (or not) of the story itself." "I seemed to be quite taken up in what was really happening with the people, but at the same time (not first) I was noticing the story, the sort of short sentences and very strange language sometimes." Her concern with literary techniques led her to quite astute observations that in turn augured well for her own success as the English teacher she wanted to be.

At the same time, this concern for literary techniques made Sandra a certain kind of English teacher's ideal reader—slightly pedantic. (Indeed, she even said of D. H. Lawrence, "A high school English teacher might fail him . . . because sometimes he would put the strangest combinations of sentences together.") Because she employed attention to technique both as an early warning system and as a source of pleasure, Sandra —alone among all the readers I have ever studied—found it easier to become "absorbed" in complex, poetic language than even the most overpowering movies.

> Most of the time I'm reading and I'm at a certain distance where I'm saying, "Isn't this good?," "This is really perfect here," or—you know, and I'm saying this to myself as I go along. I'm still, quote, caught up in it, but at a distance of time. Then every once in a while, I suppose it's when you get to a passage that—What would you call it? Maybe "lyrical," although that's a pretty overworked word—then I stop saying, "Isn't this good?," and I don't know, I have a feeling that I'm moving with whatever's being said, rather than standing away and watching what's going on.

Often Sandra described her sense of absorption this way, as a kind of mutual movement.

For example, talking about a poem (and again, showing her

unique ability to lose herself in quite formal writing), "Even
without saying it out loud, I respond to the sounds, the movement of it. It's got a fairly soft and I suppose you'd say 'un-
dulating' movement. Even the shape of the lines falls into that
wave-like pattern." Similarly, she could become "absorbed" in
something as complex as Henry James's language precisely by
being aware of it, "the way he narrates in there, fairly long
prose passages, and the kind of dialogue that he uses in charac-
terizing the people of this little world that he makes. So that I
think it's kind of possible to enter into the world that he's
creating." She would recall in a story, "the first thing that got
me" or generalize, "Even if I read something fast, if there's
really something that I'm going to like in it, it gets me the first
time." She could speak of the way "a book really gets me" or
say of a story, "It's really powerful. It's kind of a dreamy
thing. It just takes you right up in it."

By contrast, in movies (where most people find it all too easy
to go into a trance), Sandra concentrated on technique, even
in a film that apparently hit her pretty hard (Roman Polan-
ski's terrifying study of a schizophrenic girl, *Repulsion*):
"God, wasn't that amazing? I just couldn't believe it. It had
an amazingly horrifying impact, but I was really awed by his
photographic techniques." Sandra's wordings ("amazing,"
"couldn't believe it") show her using her more drastic defense,
not seeing, before settling for a balanced concern with technique. "It was amazing that he could bring that kind of horror
to the screen and still not overdo it. Every touch was pretty
perfect." Further, technique could rescue even the unsatisfac-
tory, such as a Hollywood film she didn't at first like. "The
story itself leaves a lot to be desired. But as far as acting and
directing and that, I was pretty well impressed with that and
that really made it."

Technique, then, verbal or cinematic, served Sandra as
something to see and judge before she would give in to the real
pleasure of literary works for her: entering their world and
getting close to the people in them. "In so many stories," she
confessed, "it's so hard for me to separate or to forget that the
story is told in a specific way and to react to the people in the
story, that I don't know if I ever could really do [it]."

But she did. Sometimes the person she sought would be the author. Thus, "I think it [biographical information about Joyce] made me like it ["The Dead"] more. I don't know why, particularly. Maybe . . . because it makes you, ever after that . . . always conscious of a person behind it, too, which is a definite addition, I guess." Sometimes, a narrator would attract her, perhaps because his apparent power over the story played into her interest in strong men. "I have to admire the writing, because if it weren't so well done, and if it weren't for that specific narrator, I think I probably wouldn't have liked the story at all." And, about the fatherly narrator of Mann's "Mario and the Magician": "I *liked*, I really liked the narrator. I really enjoy his voice telling this kind of story very much." "The narrator is your person to hang onto." (Sebastian, you remember, disliked this narrator for being "ponderous" and "broad-minded.")

At the same time, her responses to the hypnotist's dictatorship in that story showed that there had to be a limit on power. She felt it necessary to remind herself that hypnosis could not make you do everything: "I had always thought that *really* the unwillingness of a subject would prevent it." Yet, it was precisely her need to limit the hypnotist's power that enabled her to make an interpretation of the story broader than the usual allegories of Hitler and Mussolini: "It's about freedom in very basic and important ways." To credit the story, "You would almost have to believe that there is such a thing as power that one person could have over another person, no matter where he gets it from . . . although I think you could reject this kind of story on a factual basis and see it in a larger perspective of power of any one person over another person." Sandra's fear of that kind of power made her reject entirely a dominant Fitzgerald *belle dame sans merci*.

Alternatively, she could, as we have already seen, defend by concentrating on formal elements. "Powerful as the characters were, I would still always think of the way something was being told." Thus, she liked Henry James's *Europe* for its formal isolation. "It was another world. It's like long gone and far away." "It's like a story was opened up in front of him and then closed, but . . . he still has it that he can show it to other people.''

Her visual images here recall her major sensory mode. She seemed to enjoy stories that gave her the sight of a mystery: ''They're mysterious people, and I suppose that's part of— I keep thinking, 'fascination' or 'intriguing story' and it applies to both stories.'' Apparently, for her, these sights related to unconscious themes of thrust: ''These two stand out as having something very strange about them, just on the face of the stories themselves, beside whatever interpretations a person would put to them.'' Or lack-of-thrust themes. Of a woman in a story, she said, ''I think of her as a person that's not integrated into a whole purpose, and even if she does have— I'm not even sure if— Or what there is really right at the bottom of her that is her real self or what would be being herself. I'm not sure what it would be.'' And then she changed the subject, ''That gets into the whole theme in the story about seeing.'' (I think ''whole'' here had an unconscious meaning for her as the word often did for Sam.)

For Sandra, seeing gave power. ''Looking at a person,'' she said, ''with them not being able to look back makes it kind of helpless for the person that's being looked at.'' She recalled ''Sartre's idea of the stare where a person . . . has another person in control when they stare at them and the stare is kind of even a stare of hatred, I think he calls it, where you objectify a person for yourself. And the only time that you can get back and get your self-possession back is when you stare back at the other person.''

Seeing also meant she could control or limit others, for example, Gabriel Conroy in ''The Dead,'' whom she thought weak and impotent. ''The most interesting physical characteristic, to me, is the way Joyce describes his . . . glasses glinting in his face, and you can see these wireless glasses, and it's almost as if they take the place of eyes.''

Seeing had another kind of power, clearing up mysteries, which otherwise made Sandra anxious. For her (as for Sam with his symbolisms masculinely ''holding up''), interpretation took on an almost physically penetrating quality. ''When you're worried about a problem like 'What does that mean?',

you want to find the key, because it is so important. . . .
If not maybe the key to the story, but a key to making it
all hang together, because it is something that's been working all the way through." Of an interpretation she agreed
with, she said, "I think he's really got it here." "It's pretty
impressive."

For Sandra, as for Sam, the act of reading took on overtones
of mastery, but, of course, Sandra had her own special themes,
as one can see from comparing her TAT story to the others for
the picture of the solitary boy in the doorway. Like her other
TAT story, it shows her characteristic concern with power and
strength.

> If you walk by this hut any afternoon of the week, you'll see
> the boy on the stoop. His father's out in the woods working
> at the funny machine the boy peeked at once. All the older
> boys are there, too, for they're big enough to help run the
> machine and drive the pick-up truck to and from the hollow.
> Ma is working the small, dusty plot that provides a few
> wizened vegetables every week. She'll be back soon to start
> supper for the boys. He can help a little then. That's about
> all he can do. There aren't any other kids his age for miles.
> He'll just sit here and wait to grow big.

As with her other story, the "plot" deals with the deficiency in
the central character, here, the boy's helplessness and loneliness, but the cure does not require surgery—he'll just "wait
to grow big." By contrast, the father has a "funny machine"
the boy "peeked" at once. (A still? promising oral pleasure?).
The older, bigger boys help run that funny machine and the
"pick-up truck," both, I think, symbols of virile erectness
and penetration to be contrasted with "the hollow." That
may belong to the mother—the story is ambiguous—but
mother certainly works the "small, dusty plot," barely productive, while the men make things. Even so, despite her concern with deficiency and paucity, Sandra created the kind of
environment she liked: a world of cooperative effort and mutual reinforcing of old and young, male and female, parents
and siblings—all having shared, if unequal, strengths. The
story acts out her identity theme almost literally: to see and

approach more and more closely a source of power and nurture, but not to see its loss.

Abstract but Individual

Obviously, a description like that resembles an anatomy diagram more than a portrait, yet it is by some such schema, which is both abstract (that is, general, universal) but also individual, that one can grasp the dynamics of a reader's recreation of a literary work. General as these identity themes are, they suggest that other categories would be just as abstract and far less individual. I cannot, for example, imagine how one could account for any given reader's imagery about a story by means of "objective" categories like social group, years of education, or economic class.

Similarly the characterology of early psychoanalysis would be abstract and offer only a slight individualization. It would type Sam and Sandra as a pair of "phallic" characters or, as Dr. Corvus said, "hysteric." Saul and Sebastian would form another pair ("anal" or "obsessional" characters), and Shep, whom Dr. Corvus diagnosed as a "paranoid character," would be, in body terms, an "oral" personality. Yet, as we shall see, readers of the same general type "storied" the same story quite differently, even at the simple level of liking and disliking. Saul, for example, liked the authority of "A Rose for Emily," while Sebastian found it too defined and "discrete." Evidently, to deal with people's experience of literature we need something more individual than the traditional categories, even though they do reveal some convergences in personal dynamics.

It is for that reason I have turned to identity themes even though these are drastically open to the biases of the interpreter's own style. Just as they are five readers reading stories, so I am a sixth reader reading their readings. It can't be helped. One must simply acknowledge the personal concerns of the interpreter.

It is in that spirit that I point out that each of these five identity themes involves a dualism. Each consists of a going away from and a drawing close to. Shep, as I see him, dealt with the world either by exile to a point where he could resume his fight or by hiding and becoming a thing in a system. Saul could draw close by means of a defined bargain with a defined adversary, or he would escape to a safe precision elsewhere. Sebastian sought out an exchange of his wit for fleshly dirt from some authority figure—or else he escaped by concentrating entirely on his own verbal or intellectual creations. Sam either fled into an isolated, boyish masculinity or sought out mutual admiration leading to a passive identification with a stronger male or asexual figure. Sandra could proceed through a sequence of seeing, touching, moving with, and drawing from a source of strength and nurture or she could flee to a different source.

These dualisms could come from the ambivalence that pervades every human interaction. They could also come from the sixth reader's characteristic concern with inside and outside. But it is also worth noting, I think, that the flight sides of these identity themes quite resemble the closeness sides. That is, Shep fights to the death on either side. Saul seeks precision and Sandra sources of strength on either side. Sebastian creates with his mind and Sam becomes boyish on either side. In a broader sense, we might hypothesize that an identity theme is not dual but single, although it may look different depending on the balance between pleasure and pain in the particular setting where we see it. We will see it more as flight if the environment arouses anxiety. We will see it more as a drawing close if the context promises more gratification. In literary terms, as we shall see, not only does a reader like a story in his own characteristic way, he dislikes it in his own way, too.

Identity themes give us a way of understanding a whole character, relating moves toward pleasure to defenses against unpleasure. One abstracts an identity theme from the myriads of ego choices a person reveals much the way one abstracts a central theme to express the unity of all the many words in a literary work (each an ego choice of the writer).[6] Just as several literary works might be described by a single theme (appearance versus reality, for a familiar example, although even more precise statements would do multiple duty), so a single identity theme might satisfactorily describe more than one person. Individuals and the details of their lives are, like literary works, unique. Themes, being abstracts from unique sets of particulars, are not so individual. Yet, as we shall see, they offer powerful help in accounting for unique events such as the one this book is devoted to: the creation of a unique experience of a work of art by a unique perceiver of that work or, in Donne's lovely word, their interinanimation.

5 The Answer: Four Principles Of Literary Experience

A scan of all of Sam's, Saul's, Shep's, Sebastian's, and Sandra's interviews leads to a style for each of them that pervades everything he or she says or does. They and all of us live by creating variations on an identity theme that is our essential self. "Creating" is a key word, for such a view of human nature implies not only sameness but differences that we create. Each of us creates at least his own way of walking, talking, smiling, sitting, sleeping, loving, fighting, eating, and all the rest. Presumably we also create our own ways of seeing films and plays or reading poems and stories.

Identity implies, too, that all these creations have a unity, particularly that we meet and create external reality by the same strategies we use to manage internal reality. As Joyce wrote: "We walk through ourselves meeting robbers, ghosts, giants, old men, young men, wives, widows, brothers-in-love. But always meeting ourselves."[1]

Just how we meet ourselves in the books we read is the question I am raising, and the answer this book sets out is four principles that describe the inner dynamics of the reading experience. I would have liked to let the interviews themselves tell you these principles, with a minimum of comment from me, but that would require you to do the work I did—more, I think, than any author has a right to ask of his reader. I therefore present them here, before the evidence in which I found them.

The Four Principles

In a way, all four can be summed up in one overarching idea; we can think of it as the first of the four:

Style Seeks Itself

In general, if a reader has responded positively to a literary work, he has been able to put elements of the work together so they act out his own lifestyle. Alternatively, if he has no reaction to a literary work, or a negative one, that tells us he has not been able to use the work to reenact his own style.

We need to talk about something more precise, however, than just "the work," because readers often respond in a half-and-half way, positively to some parts and negatively to the rest. For example, Sandra was pleased by Hemingway's descriptive style, but repelled by his dialogue. How does one explain such partial responses? Partly by specifying details within the work, partly by focusing on the relevant aspect of lifestyle.

If a reader responds positively to parts of a work, he has composed them to act out for him one specific part of his lifestyle, namely, his expectancies toward other, separate entities. That is, each of us approaches a new experience with a certain characteristic cluster of hopes, desires, fears, and needs. We want this economy of expectancies acted out by that separate entity in such a way as to net us pleasure. We expect the same from literary works. Moment by moment, line by line, word by word, we try to make the characters perform, the plot evolve, the language resonate, and all the parts of the work coact to yield a balance of gratification.

Our first principle, then, is the following: if we have responded positively toward certain features or combinations within the work, we perceived them as acting out within the work our hopes at any given moment toward the whole work as a separate entity. But if we responded negatively or not at all to some elements, we did not perceive them as acting out within the work the kind of balance leading to gratification we would like from other beings.

Notice that there has been a kind of right-angle turn. The reader who is responding positively perceives the work and elements within it as acting out in its own linear sequence the hopes that run from reader to work. To put it another way, the reader responding favorably feels no difference between what he perceives as going on "in the work" and what goes on between himself and the work. If the work pleases him, events "out there" become events between "out there" and "in here." The reader merges with the book, and the events of the book become as real as anything in his mind (so Poulet, Davis, and Ortega have described "absorption"). In the more technical terms of Roy Schafer's analysis, this feature of literary response comes from a particular split in the ego, a "suspension of the reflective self representation that pertains to the act in question," here, reading.

> The term reflective self representation refers to the implicit or explicit notation accompanying realistic thought that it is thought (e.g., memory, perception, anticipation, etc.) and not concrete reality. When the subject suspends his reflective self representations, he disappears as thinker and experiences his thoughts as though they were concrete realities,[2]

as when we are "absorbed" in a literary work and willingly suspend our disbelief.

Each reader will achieve this absorption in his own way—if he achieves it at all. He will therefore deal with the work by means of the adaptations and defenses he ordinarily brings into play with external realities. Hence the pivotal relation in his experience of a literary work—and the second of our four principles:

Defenses Must Be Matched

If the reader has a favorable response toward a work, he must have synthesized from it all or part of his characteristic structure of defense or adaptation. He must have found something in the work that does what he does to cope with needs or dangers.

By "adaptation," one ordinarily means the progressive, constructive, and maturational mastery of inner drives and outer reality. "Defense" means a mechanism put into action automatically and unconsciously at a signal of danger from within or without. Thus, the two terms can overlap in any given situation. When the ego projects, it deals with a danger by seeing it as outside, but projection may also be a way of empathizing with another person, seeing his point of view. Introjection puts a threat inside, but it may also provide a basis for stable inner governors to keep a psychic balance. Denial avoids threats by refusing to perceive them at all and repression by not acknowledging the perception, but either may be adaptive in protecting the ego from intolerable fear.

An older tradition in psychoanalytic writing often treated defense mechanisms as though they were blocks to normal pleasure, in and of themselves pathological, undesirable, and to be removed in therapy when possible. A more modern approach, based in ego psychology and the concern with man in society that one finds in Freud's last writings, sees defenses as necessary adaptations to inner and outer reality, not obstacles to pleasure but preconditions without which pleasure would not be possible. Here I shall use both words with the understanding that they often refer to the same activity but looked at differently: "defense" in a context of merely avoiding pain; "adaptation" in a more positive context of constructively coping with inner and outer reality.

Each individual evolves his own style of defense and adaptation, which becomes, simply, one part of his total lifestyle. Particular defenses and adaptations in particular contexts just represent variations he plays upon the one identity theme. And evidently, to judge from five readers' readings, each of us passes all his experiences through the filter of his personality, particularly in a defensive way to avoid pain.

As we shall see with our five readers, this re-creating of one's own defenses from the materials of the story becomes very delicate and unpredictable. Sebastian (whom you may remember as the lapsed Catholic and would-be aristocrat) dealt with dangers from controlling forces by offering his own creations of a verbal or intellectual kind. When he read the Fitzgerald and Hemingway stories, he held the heroes in contempt, although these men offered creations of their own, because their creations involved business success and athletic manliness. They were not verbal or intellectual enough for him. He objected to the two heroes as "simple-minded."

For a reader to match his defenses by means of elements in the story, he must be able to satisfy his ego with them at all levels, including his "higher" intellectual functions. Thus, it is the matching of defenses that draws on a reader's concern with language, his experience of prior works, his critical acumen, his taste and all the things people bring to bear when they deliberately evaluate literary works. As we shall see when these five readers explain their value judgments, their perceptions of the text, even the most subtle and intellectual ones, rest on their need to match defenses. Thus, Sebastian's comment on the two heroes looks like an objective reading of the text, but he would not read them that way except for his need to meet the world by offering an exchange of inner creations. Sam, the boyish and dapper seeker of self-esteem, found those two heroes quite satisfactory, because their independence matched his defenses, so very different from Sebastian's, his need to reassure himself with admiration. I, with my concern for inside and outside in "A Rose for Emily," paid little attention to the narrator, while Sandra found him one of those reassuring sources of strength she needed. She responded warmly and positively to him, taking him to be one of Faulkner's considerable achievements in the story.

In short, these matchings of defense involve subtle balances. I find them quite unpredictable, but once made or not made, I can see very clearly what took place. Much less tricky, much less delicate is the other mode of using the work to re-create one's own style: matching, not defenses, but fantasies or drives. This is the third principle governing literary experience:

Fantasy Projects Fantasies

That is, each reader uses the materials he has taken in from the literary work to create a wish-fulfilling fantasy characteristic of himself. The fantasy does not lie latent in the work—only the materials for the fantasy that each reader will then create for himself in the terms that give him pleasure (and the fantasy the reader creates may or may not coincide with the fantasy the writer had while writing).

This principle—that the fantasy is not "in" the work but in the reader or, still more accurately, in the creative relation between reader and work—marks a departure from an older psychoanalytic concept of literature. I and other psychoanalytic critics have often written as though each literary work had a fixed fantasy content. As a matter of common sense, however, works do not have fantasies—people do. Fantasies are clusters of wishes deriving from the stages in which children develop. These stages focus on particular issues such as being fed, giving up one's bodily creations, accepting limits and controls on physical and sexual strivings, accepting the difference between the sexes and the generations, and so on. Further, these stages seem linked to parts of the body in a biological timetable that does not vary from culture to culture, although, of course, different cultures do vastly different things with these various themes and issues.

What in the child were early and later stages become in the adult "higher" and "lower" levels. All coexist, however, and it becomes possible to think of personality at least partly in terms of fixation to one or more levels. In adults one recognizes derivatives of these childhood issues by wordings that reveal connections between adult activities and particular body parts, parent-child situations, or other psychological issues associated with one or more of these stages. Thus, to use familiar literary examples, one can identify a class of writers (Jonson, Dickens, Gogol, and Balzac come to mind) whose writings deal extensively with the underworld or the lower classes, whose vision is dominated by images of dirt, dust, garbage, gold, money, mud, fog, or smells, and whose plots balance off pettifoggery, pedantry, miserliness, or obstinacy with sadistic violence or unnatural purity. We recognize in such writings adult creations transformed from childhood concerns with the control by outer authorities of inner creations, mental or physical, dirty or precious. If we were to work with specific books, we could be still more precise, moving from a broad sense of phase or level to the specific fantasies that give rise to Dickens's themes of parental betrayal or Balzac's sense of overpowering impoverishment.

None of this, however, says the fantasy is "in" the work. Rather the fantasy is "in" the writer, and we read the work as evidence of his creative transformation of the unconscious themes that concern him. We read "through" the story to the mind behind it as we would read a TAT story. And above all, one tries, by honest self-analysis, to recognize and take into account tendencies to use the interpretation to express one's own identity theme.

As one listens to these five readers talk about particular stories, the last illusion of a fixed fantasy content should fade away. Each reader used the materials of the story to create a fantasy at the level of development that mattered *to him*. No matter how convincing a case I can make for "A Rose for Emily" as a story built on wishes and fears about the control of body products, Sam perceived the story in terms of the masculinity that concerned him, and Saul fantasied about overpowering authorities. Each reader placed the unconscious fantasy content of the story in the level or levels of fantasy where his own mind habitually functioned. For example, Miss Emily, according to the story, taught the young ladies of the town china-painting. One would assume that such an activity symbolizes a control over smearing and daubing, turning paint, messy, perhaps, or soiling, into something pretty, delicate, and precise. Sam, much concerned with boyish virility, remembered china-painting as knitting, replacing any "symbolism" of smearing with an act of penetrating with a long, pointed object. He used—or misused—the story to create a fantasy at the level that mattered to him.

Moreover, the reader will use the materials of the story to build, not some fantasy ostensibly "in" the story, but his own characteristic fantasy. I do not mean to imply that each reader has only one fantasy, but it is good to recall that he has but one recurring structure of defenses and that defense and drive are really only different points of view on a single phenomenon: his lifestyle or personality. Hence, as we shall see, Sandra, who needed both defensively and libidinally to draw close to sources of strength and nurture, tried to fantasy them in the stories she read. Saul, who wanted to meet the world in a precise bargain, used the materials of the stories to create bargaining situations. Each of the five readers drew on the characters, episodes, and language of what he read, but he structured them into the specific form of fantasy that gave him pleasure, just as he had matched his defenses.

Thus, fantasy and defense are intimately interlocked in literary response because of their deep relation in the mind. At the earliest stage of our development, we live through an ambivalence: our mothering source of sustenance is by that very fact a source of frustration as well. Good development means tolerating that early mingling of love and hate so that the first relation with another can form a structure for all later relations, which will include that first ambivalence. As a psychoanalytic maxim has it: what we deeply fear, we also wish; or, you could state it the other way round: what we wish we also fear. Either way, it suggests a final limitation on human happiness as well as the means by which we gain pleasure in this mortal coil.

For any given individual, his preferred fantasies and his structure of defenses will deal with the same kind of thing (just as his first human relation had to be attached to a single person), things like Saul's bargains and controls or Sandra's sources of strength. In order to bring a reader's defenses and adaptations into play, he needs to perceive the thing he fears. For Sandra, for example, to bring a story into her world, her kind of experience, she must bring her adaptations into play. To do so, she must perceive the very overpowering she so much fears—then, and only then, can she construct defenses to manage it. From another point of view, however, that overpowering also makes up the power source that Sandra enjoys being close to. To gain pleasure, then, she must perceive the work in terms of power. To make it important or even real for her, she must project into it the kind of thing she both fears and wishes; that will enable her to use the work in her defenses and thus to accept it and enjoy the pleasure of being close to a source of power.

In effect, we are understanding the psychology behind the literary maxim: form and content are one. That is, as we saw in developing identity themes for these five readers, a single theme permeates all the mind's multiple functioning. Much the same language will describe an individual's adaptations as his drives, because, although those two functions operate between different agencies confronting the ego, any given mental transaction will combine elements of drive with defense and adaptation. In the act of reading, drive corresponds to content, which corresponds to fantasy, while defense corresponds to form, which corresponds to management of fantasy, both triads taking place, not in the text, but in the reader's mind. Thus, in a psychological sense, much the same language will describe form as content. "Form and content are one," but they exist, not "in" a text, but in the unity of the reader's personality. Saul's bargains, Sandra's sources, or Shep's systems serve both to ward off dangers and to secure gratification, and, as we shall see, they transform the stories they read into the bargains, sources, and systems they desire.

Form and content differ, however, in an important way. As we shall see, the reader's relation to a story becomes tricky and subtle as he synthesizes his defensive structure from it. By contrast, he has no trouble at all using the story to get the fantasy content he wants. Put another way, once he has achieved the defensive forms and admitted at least part of the story into his psyche, he easily goes on to transform what he has admitted into his preferred level and type of fantasy. Form-defense differs from fantasy-content this way because they are associated with different actions of the reading mind. The reader defends against the story as a potentially dangerous external reality. He actively shapes it before allowing it into his own mental processes. Therefore, the act of defending operates against the story, to keep it out of the psyche. Only what precisely matches the reader's defenses gets through. Once in his psyche, however, the story becomes swept up in the general press every human being has toward gratification. The reader's psyche uses, adapts, and transforms whatever it has taken in from the story that will yield pleasure. The ego's defenses act like a doorkeeper carefully checking invitations against the list of acceptable guests. Once the guests are admitted, however, the party turns out to be not stuffy at all, but quite easygoing, even a bit rowdy and disreputable.

Once the reader has achieved both the delicate matching of all or part of his defensive structure and the much more open adaptation of what he has matched to suit his fantasies, the fourth principle comes into play:

Character Transforms Characteristically

He will "make sense" of the text. By means of such adaptive structures as he has been able to match in the story, he will transform the fantasy content, which he has created from the materials of the story his defenses admitted, into some literary

point or theme or interpretation. In doing so, he will use
"higher" ego functions, such as his interpretive skills, his
literary experience, his experience of human character, in
general, his subtlety and sensitivity. He will bring to bear the
social, moral, or political ideas that already embody congenial
transformations for him. He will, finally, render the fantasy he
has synthesized as an intellectual content that is characteristic—and pleasing—for him.

In effect, our four principles have closed the circle. In
characteristically fantasying, defending, and transforming, the
reader works out his own personal style through the story.
Since he has a positive relation to the story, his style must have
found itself in it. Had any of these three points of connection
failed—in particular, had he not been able to match his defensive structure—he would not have been able to synthesize and
recreate the story within his lifestyle, and therefore he would
not have a positive relation to it. It is interesting that Freud
hints at this idea as early as 1900 in the concluding, metapsychological chapter of *The Interpretation of Dreams*.[3] The
individual cannot work with an idea in a secondary-process
way—that is, in the intellectual and aesthetic transformation
that makes up our fourth principle—unless he is in a position to
inhibit any unpleasure that may proceed from it (except, of
course, for a signal to start the inhibiting process)—that is, in
our terms, unless he can match his defenses.

The circle closes another way. The first principle ("style
seeks itself") describes the reader's relation to the *sequence* of
events in the literary work. As each event does or does not act
out his characteristic expectancy, he does or does not establish
a positive relation toward it. Our fourth principle ("character
transforms characteristically") describes his relation to the
story as a *totality* of separate events, as the "organic unity"
critics since Aristotle have described. Now, however, we see
that that unity does not reside in the mere work. The reader, by
means of his ego's ability to organize and synthesize reality,
creates a unity from his positive relation to the story. Each act
of reading is constructive. It makes something new, something
human, something personal—or else no real act of reading
takes place.

Finally, then, these principles assert that it becomes both useless and impossible to separate the act of reading from the creative personality of the reader. Thus, I found that I could not separate the principles themselves from actual readers reading; I could grasp these four principles only by studying single interviews about particular stories in the light of the reader's personality as revealed by the whole series of interviews and tests. Having once arrived at these principles, however, I realized I could have reached them directly, by deduction: they follow abstractly from the concept of identity, particularly identity as a style of multiple functioning.

Reading and Identity

Identity we have defined as an essential sameness in the human personality, and we have understood it as an identity theme on which the living organism plays out variations as a composer might. Each variation he plays functions in multiple ways (in Waelder's term). That is, whatever a human being does —dream, tell a story, acquire a symptom, take up a vocation, make a friend—he does so as to achieve a maximum of pleasure and minimum of pain with a minimum of effort.

Waelder went on to relate this basic inertial principle to the structural view of the personality. It is the ego that must passively respond to and actively seek out solutions to the demands of inner and outer reality. Specifically, four "agencies" act on the ego in a highly symmetrical fashion. The reservoir of drives (the id), presses toward blind, immediate satisfaction, while the internalized pressures of parents and culture (the superego) trigger defenses in the ego that inhibit or change the raw drives. The ancient inertia of self tends to make the ego solve its problems as it did before (the repetition compulsion), while reality (the fourth agency) constantly confronts the ego with new tasks that demand new solutions. The ego acts between paired alternatives: to satisfy the drives or deprive them, in new ways or in old. And what we have been calling defenses or adaptations are the solutions the ego adopts, either by being acted upon or by itself actively testing the pressures of inner and outer reality.

The concept of identity puts in systematic form the observation that the ego habitually adopts the same general style of solution. Within this sameness, however, there is an important difference. An adaptation or defense acting on external reality will look somewhat different from the same strategy acting in internal reality. Within, one finds magic, animism, primitivity, in the formal term, primary process thinking. The ego looks outward more carefully and warily, using, in psychoanalytic terms, secondary process thinking or problem-solving intelligence. "The inner world has its origin in an animistic world view, a world view dominated by man's helplessness in the face of separation and death," writes Arnold Modell, while the ego's relation to reality has to do with the ability to give up imaginary satisfactions and really act upon one's environment. But the line is not hard and fast. Particularly in symbolic thinking, and thus in art and language generally, Modell suggests, "Private and public modes of thinking interpenetrate" just as, in action on the world, "the created environment and the autonomously perceived environment interpenetrate."[4]

In reading, the text serves as the external reality that the reader meets as he meets any object outside himself. His ego maneuvers it carefully to consciousness through his system of defenses and adaptations. Hence, our second principle, the touchy and delicate matching of defenses: if the reader has a positive relation to something he has read, he must have been able to find in it a total or partial match to his characteristic pattern of adaptations. True, the individual's pattern is constant, but facing outward, toward reality, he accents secondary-process thought and the warding off of dangers more than the taking in of pleasures. Conscious intelligence, logic, experience, and other "higher" ego functions play active roles as does style in its more primitive modes: physical avoidance, the unwillingness to perceive unpleasant realities, dehumanizing oneself or others, seducing a dangerous force, dividing up reality to deal with it in little bits—to mention defensive modes like those of our five readers.

Once a reader has been able to draw a work into himself through his system of defenses, however, the accent changes. Facing the inner world, the ego accents the search for pleasure more strongly. In reading, we eagerly draw on the various elements of the work to make up a satisfying fantasy, much as the first builders of churches reassembled the censored marbles of pagan temples for their own purposes. Working within, the ego acts freely, creatively, and imaginatively, with far less concern for danger since here, where reality does not threaten, it has no need to fear real anxiety or shame. This is the third principle, the third component in the reader's synthesis: fantasy projects fantasies.

Even in the world within, however, the ego does not simply fantasize. Rather it imagines, partly consciously, partly unconsciously, a satisfaction that balances the competing demands of the three inner agencies and the external reality of the text. That is, fantasies represent a compromise among the drives toward pleasure, the warding off of guilt and anxiety, the tendency to repeat old patterns, and the creative push to achieve a new satisfaction from this new experience. Thus, the fourth principle: Character transforms characteristically. From whatever part of the work he has filtered through the structures that he keeps between his inner world and his outer environment, the reader creates a fantasy within his individual style. Then he transforms that fantasy using his characteristic modes of defense and adaptation and the words that he has matched to them.

He will transform the fantasy he has created into a synthesis and unity that he finds consciously integrative and satisfying. The political man will confirm his interests in personality or leadership. The moralist will find a reinforcement of his ethical views. The scientifically minded man will see verifiable realities. And each of them will have transformed the literary work by means of the same ego balance of drive and defense that supports their conscious orientation toward politics, morality, or science. Or else they will not have established that positive relation to the literary work that means, really, sharing in the act of creating it. The reader's ego uses the text to build from his own unconscious drives through his own patterns of adaptations and defense toward a conscious significance and unity that matters to him. Either he has that positive re-creation or he wards off the story, keeping it separate, out of his lifestyle, and he works out his fantasying without reference to the words. He becomes able to think Miss Emily an Eskimo.

This fourth principle (characteristic transformation) defines the reader's relation to the whole work as a meaningful unity. He must also make the work fit the principle of multiple function in the momentary, sequential, word-by-word process of literary experience. Our first principle, style seeks itself, states that at each moment, as well as in the total experience, the reader tries to have the various elements of the literary work enact what he expects from it as a separate being. That is, he will try to make the language, events, or people he creates from the text function in multiple directions to work out the compromise among the demands of inner and outer reality that is his own style. But in this particular context, his momentary response, he will try to use words, plot, and characters to act out that part of his lifestyle which defines what he expects from an other. To the extent he succeeds, the boundary between self and gratifying text will blur and fade. He will become "absorbed."

The literary work I read today represents the latest in the long sequence of gratifying others to whom I have related, beginning with the nurturing mother of earliest infancy who actualized in me a certain lifestyle. In particular, however, each literary work caps the sequence of literary works that preceded it and before them the mixed human and literary experience of being read to. As Selma Fraiberg points out,

> There will come a time in childhood when pleasure in reading and in language achieves a certain degree of independence from the human partners who had served as teachers. The dialogue that had originated between the child and his family and the child and his teachers is no longer the indispensable component in learning and in pleasure. The book itself has taken over as a partner and is invested with some of the qualities of a human relationship.[5]

Thus, we come full circle: The "expectancy" we bring to reading makes up one small aspect of lifestyle, but that expectancy also inherits and stores early interpersonal experiences around reading—as lifestyle itself crystallizes from early relationships.

In our print-oriented society, children learn to read through personal relationships, and reading itself becomes an extension of these relationships. Other is other, be it book or mother, casual friend or total environment, and we relate to that other in terms of our particular identities. The English psychoanalyst, D. W. Winnicott, takes man's cultural experience back to a "potential space," originally between baby and mother, then child and family, later individual and society or the world. "This potential space is a highly variable factor (from individual to individual)," and "it is here that the individual experiences creative living,"[6] that is, through regressing to the experiences of earliest infancy. There is no reason, however, to limit this potential space to cultural experiences—all experiences of an other take place at that interface and take place in terms of an identity that continues the theme laid down in the new human's first human relationship.

In effect, our four principles define the way self and other interact in such a potential space. Self warily takes in some of other through its system of adaptations and then freely and creatively uses what it has taken in as part of its own system for transforming drives toward pleasure and meaning and wholeness. From this larger point of view, the four principles involved in reading quickly coalesce into one. Id and superego, drive and defense, look less like psychic entities in themselves, more like functions, and still more like ways of looking at one central relation, between the individual (taken as variations on an identity theme) and an other.

If we look at the identity theme as a strategy for warding off anxiety and pain, we are looking at it as a defense. Then, it acts like a lock that must be exactly fitted to admit the intruder. If we regard someone's identity theme as a strategy for maximizing gratification, however, then it looks like a greedy amoeba soaking up whatever its chemistry will tolerate. If we regard it as a strategy for dealing with the outer world, we are taking it as an adaptation, wary, calculating, reality-oriented, and secondary-process. If we observe it applying only to inner reality, however, it seems archaic, primitive, magical, and primary-process.

Yet inner and outer, primary-process or secondary, reality-oriented or compulsively repeated in response to inner cues, defense or pleasure-seeking—these are only modifiers for accenting one facet or another of a single principle of interaction that is the result, the "answer," this study yields. *A reader responds to a literary work by assimilating it to his own psychological processes, that is, to his search for successful solutions within his identity theme to the multiple demands, both inner and outer, on his ego.*

We began with a simple fact: the variability of literary response (Blake's "thou read'st black where I read white"). We have come now to the reason for that variability: two interacting forces that define human motivation, an identity principle of continuity and a pleasure principle of change. Louis Sullivan's Irish maid Julia summed them up as well as anyone. The great architect describes in his autobiography a childhood visit to his former home and a conversation with Julia about the many Irish immigrants fighting in the Union Army. She recalled a man from Kerry who joined up:

> And wan day as he was out a-walking fer his health, and faring to and fro, he came upon a blanket lying on the ground; and at once he picked it up and with great loud laughter he sed, sed he: Sure I've found me blanket with me name upon it: U fer Patrick and S for McCarty; sure edication's a foine thing, as me faather before me wud say.
>
> Oh, Julia [said Sullivan], I don't believe that's true. That's just another Irish yarn.
>
> Will, maybe it isn't true and maybe it's just a yarn; but I belave it's true and I want to till ye this; the man from Kerry had a rale education. Ye may think I'm a-jokin' now, but when ye get older and have more sinse ye'll be noticin' that that's the way everywan rades; and the higher educated they are, the more they rade just as Pat McCarty did, and add some fancy flourishes of their own.[7]

True enough. As Julia suggests, what we have found out for reading does seem to apply as aptly to blankets as to books.

One has only to state this basic principle to realize that it need not be limited to reading. The individual (considered as the continuing creator of variations on an identity theme) relates to the world as he does to a poem or a story: he uses its physical reality as grist with which to re-create himself, that is, to make yet another variation in his single, enduring identity. In short, what started as an explanation of literary experience begins to become a general account of the relation of personality to the perception and interpretation of experience. Or how we can all make "U.S." into our property. But before going on to such larger, empyrean speculations, we should look at what gave rise to this theory, what it was designed to explain, namely, five readers reading.

6 The Evidence: Sam, Saul, Shep, Sebastian, and Sandra Read Faulkner's "A Rose for Emily"

The Story

In my own reading of "A Rose for Emily," I found two basic structures. Incorporation: I will take and keep the old thing inside of me. Denial: there is no new thing in external reality. Within a core defined by these defensive patterns, I could transform the events and words back and forth from a variety of primitive, bodily fantasies about Emily and her house to social, intellectual, and mythic themes about the conflict between the denial of change and its inevitability.

As a professional critic, I would like to be able to say this reading is in some objective sense "true," but, in all honesty, I cannot. As we have seen, readers (including professional critics) respond to a story by re-creating their own lifestyles from it. Therefore, my analysis of "A Rose for Emily" in Chapter 2 remains just that—my analysis. Objective analysis of a text in seeming isolation reveals only the story as it was re-created in the mind of the analyzer with all his conscious and unconscious concerns.

As thorough and accurate as I may think my analysis of the story, few of these five readers' comments correspond to what I found "in" it or "there." Each reader created the story anew for himself, and he alone can say what he has created. Therefore, what these five readers say is the final evidence for this general theory and four particular principles of literary response. One must turn to them to decide whether the four principles are satisfactory answers to the question, Who reads what how?

I have chosen, however, not to present the interviews simply verbatim. It is extremely difficult to discern from simple transcripts the underlying dynamics without more reflection and work than any author should demand from his readers. I have instead quoted extensively from the interviews, developing various themes and issues in what the reader said, more than he could have on the spot.

This chapter consists, then, of commentary by our five readers on Faulkner's "A Rose for Emily." In addition, I have provided (in Appendix B) their comments on two more stories: F. Scott Fitzgerald's "Winter Dreams" and Ernest Hemingway's "The Battler." To see the diversity in different readers' readings of a single story, you might choose simply to read straight through this chapter. Alternatively, to experience the continuity within one reader's readings, you might choose to follow one reader through all three stories. In either case, you may want to glance back at the description of a given reader in Chapter 4 before reading any of his remarks. The essential thing is to experience the sameness one reader brings to different stories and the difference different readers bring to the same story. Only then will you be able to test the explanatory power of these four principles or to pass judgment on the general principle that literary response expresses not the text alone but the reader's re-creation of the text within his identity theme.

Sam

Sam showed in his other readings and in his tests a pattern of defenses that one might very briefly summarize as "in" and "out": to get out of dangers to his maleness and to take into his body love and admiration. In addition, Sam, who had once attended a class on this story, may also have brought to "A Rose for Emily," either through his own reading or his instructor's, comments by Faulkner and by Brooks and Warren (if I recognize some faint echoes correctly).

In general, Sam wanted to draw close to a source of strength, while Miss Emily wanted to draw a source of strength into herself—a very threatening prospect for Sam, one would think. In his "in" mode, however, he could deal with dangers by identifying with them, adopting a position of being mothered or

nurtured or admired by what he had found dangerous, ultimately taking it into himself. He could also deal with dangers
by getting them "out," fleeing them psychologically, by denying their existence, for example, or holding off the feelings they
aroused, forgetting them, or displacing them (as he would shift
from the center of an inkblot he found threatening to its edges).
Through these denials Sam was able to relate to levels of the
story that did not threaten his own intactness. "I think that I'm
romantic enough to— I would have loved to live as moneyed
and landed gentry in the Old South before the War." "I'm
romantic enough to have liked that kind of life." "I kind of
think that it's nice that things were once like that. It's good that
they're not like that now, because it is so grossly unjust. But
it's interesting to see that they were once like that."

The Old South charmed Sam by re-creating an order into
which he could, as it were, cuddle right up. "That kind of
smallness," he called it.

> Things were so ordered then. It seems that everyone did
> have their place, not only the Negroes to be kept in their
> place, but the whites to be kept in their place, and it certainly
> involved more liberties and the like, but everything was nice
> and set, and one knew what one had to do and what one was
> expected to do, and one did it happily if one was rich, be-
> cause there were nice things to do. There were parties . . .
> and everything else. I would certainly not want to be a Negro
> in those times, but they did exist, and if I were living at the
> time and had my choice of who I wanted to be, and had my
> choice of being a born baby to one of these people, I would
> certainly pick the richest Southern family in the whole South
> and live my life probably very happily. Because I think that
> I'm lazy enough and selfish enough and I'm shortsighted
> enough when it comes to my interests that I would be able to
> do this kind of thing with very little qualms.

In that disquisition (and Sam was nothing if not a talker), a
number of his themes emerged. Again, we hear him talk about
the sense of security he wants, nurturing showered on him, all
decisions made for him, in short, being a "born baby." To get
this nurturing matrix, he was willing to give up a good deal of

reality (be "shortsighted") and one senses in that plaintive phrase about the times or the slaves, "they did exist," a steady pressure to deny painful realities. Others would have to remind him: "If I were asked, you know, if you asked me . . . 'Well, what would you feel about this if you were a Negro's son who had to be in the thing?' and then, of course, different answers would come." Yet, evidently, he would still be a "son," a "born baby," and it is with those words in mind that one has to hear his notion of "the top." "I just like the order of it all, especially when, in this wishful kind of way we're talking now, I can place myself at . . . any level of that order, which, of course, would be the top."

In effect, Sam would be the loved baby by virtue of denying harsh truths, and he was honest enough with himself to recognize this. "Had I lived then, I don't think I would have had any moral qualms." "The whole slavery issue and that whole aristocratic life amidst so much poverty among whites and Negroes is not justifiable in any sense. Yet I don't think that I would have worried about that, as you seldom do when you're in that kind of position."

Sam was less conscious of the aggressive pleasures I think he felt at being on "the top." "I would have been a great plantation owner, and I would have whipped my share of slaves, and all these other terrible things that now would never enter your mind [*sic*], but these were established things then, and it seems that one didn't question whether they were right or wrong." Similarly, when I asked him about the 1894 edict created by Colonel Sartoris—"he who fathered the edict that no Negro woman should appear on the streets without an apron"—Sam was candid again:

> I hate, I hate to say. I like it. It's terrible. It's the worst thing. I mean, it's not terrible for me to like it. It's terrible that that kind of thing ever once existed. It's inhuman. It denies so many basic rights of everyone involved. It treats the Negro as animal. The Negro is *not* animal. But I can't help but be charmed by the naïveté, by the total lack of concern that such a position of power places one in.

At another point he acknowledged a more sadistic pleasure.

"I react with kind of a smile that says, 'Oh, those were the good old days' type of thing, when I read that with the apron on the street." I do not mean to be harsh on Sam—all five readers said very similar things—but it is clear that whipping, or the edict, or his wishes to be on "the top," "in that kind of position," "such a position of power," all let him get a taste of the pleasures of tyranny, of masculine dominance in its crueler forms.

In short, to put his response in terms of our four principles, Sam could match one of his basic defensive patterns to one he found in the story. Once he was sharing with the story a denial of threats to himself (but not to others), he could project a fantasy content into it. Notice, however, that Sam's fantasy content did not include the fantasy I found of holding on, despite pressures, to something precious inside one's house-body. Rather, Sam fantasied at levels that concerned him more: cuddling in or being "on top." Cuddling in as a born baby referred to holding on at a level of nurture—a level more primitive than one's control of body products. Being "on top" in Sam's sense referred specifically to the preciousness of maleness and dominance by one's body. Thus, both are ways of holding on, to be sure, but in modalities earlier and later than those I found in the story.

Sam's need to confirm physical masculinity came through most clearly in what he said about Miss Emily's father. "She lived under her father. Her father made the decisions. Her father kept things up. Her father was the leader, the member of the town council . . . a very strong male figure in her life, and she was totally dominated by it" (*sic*—and notice that, as if he weren't strong enough already, Sam elected Mr. Grierson to the town council). Almost the first thing Sam picked out from the story, as we have seen in Chapter 1, was the "tableau." "The father was very domineering—one of the most striking images in the book is . . . her father stand[ing] there with a horsewhip in his hands, feet spread apart and between or through him you see a picture of Emily standing in the background." Again, she is "under" him, although in a different way.

Through Emily's father we can see the double value of phallic strength for Sam. It could deprive or it could provide a nurturing matrix to support, in Miss Emily's case, her femininity. "I think she had as much of a chance to be [feminine] at the beginning, had she lived in a world where her father's rules worked, as at one time they did. I think everything would have been fine. She would have had a thousand niggers* around to do her work for her, and she would have been happy, and she would have met a man of the quality—in quotes—and everything that everyone expected."

Emily's position would have matched Sam's as a "born baby," but her father made the tradition destroy rather than support. "I think at one time she had the grand chance just to be the darling lady throughout the whole of her life. It seemed that her father, and all he stands for and all you can make him symbolize, ruined this." He "forced her life down roads that perhaps it wouldn't have taken," by "turning suitor after suitor away, with each time he's doing it, casting her in— ruining her life more and more."

Sam imaged this as the father and tradition physically obstructing suitors seeking to get to Emily. "Her father stood in the way of many suitors because of aristocratic and traditional reasons." "Her father . . . stands for the old way of life against the new incoming way of life." Given Sam's concern with virility, I believe phrases like "whole," "stand for," or "incoming" had not lost their bodily meanings for him.

Similarly, new and incoming Homer involves a sexual symbolism, as does Emily when she "begins seeing Homer Barron, which is probably the only gap that the story had." "Perhaps . . . she feels this kind of chance ought to be given." "Anyway, it's a strange kind of leap of faith that you have to take there." Again, Sam juxtaposed symbolic acts: "She receives him into the house. She goes out with him in the carriage, is seen around town with him unchaperoned."

In general, Sam regarded Homer as standing "for the new road of the future coming down, and again, for the North as

* Sam, like the other readers, was using this epithet deliberately to "try on" a slaveholding frame of mind, not to cast a racial slur.

opposed to the South, which her father was." "For 'Barron' to make any sense," said Sam, working on the name, "you'd have to apply it to Emily, the kind of thing he brings down from the North." "It is this that really renders her barren, or renders her as the last of her generation and the last of her kind, and so what he brings is sure death for the aristocracy and the race that Emily comes to have to symbolize." Loss was another Barronial theme: "She lost her honor to Homer Barron." "As far as Emily is concerned, what this kind of newness brings . . . is barren, is death." "She, too, must die until finally there is nothing but Homer Barrons running around." Homer, in other words, contrasts with the tradition as lover does with parent, but just as the hypermasculine parent was double-valued, so Homer's love and sexuality carry with them death and sterility.

Homer and Mr. Grierson brought out Sam's attitudes toward masculinity. Miss Emily presented a much more complicated character to relate to, involving several kinds of fantasy and defense. For Sam (as for all the other readers), the house came to symbolize Miss Emily herself. "Other things that stand out strongly in the story are the picture of the house as being a picture of her whole way of life. [It] comes out much more clearly, with much more force than I've ever given it."

Partly, the house stood for Miss Emily's body as a container of prized objects, living and dead at the same time. "When her father died, Emily put up some sort of a hassle about taking it—about taking him—out to be buried." Here, Sam's wording does remind me of the struggle children sometimes put up against the loss or taking away of their body products, also the familiar confusions in children's thoughts about their feces: Are they living or dead, part of "me" or just an "it," or, in this case, "him" and "it"?

She seemed to me to be terribly strong inwardly . . . she had a lot of inner fortitude, and the only way it behaves . . . shows itself is in what she dedicates her life to doing as far as the house— In other words, progress will march along, but it will stop and then pick up after it reaches Emily's house. It's just not going to be there, and this takes a fierce determination.

Stasis and obstinacy—these are the traits Miss Emily's body-house expresses, "her determination to maintain things as they were."

But Sam did not settle for Miss Emily's anality—he made her over into his own levels of fantasy, expressed in hassles, strength, and fierceness. "Other things stand out that are impressive . . . that of the house, that of her, as character, as strong-willed, tragic hero." For Sam, Miss Emily and her house had some of that power to "stand out" that her father had; in another genital sense, she made up for what she lacked of male power by holding on to some man's. "She lost her honor, and what else could she do but keep him [Homer] forever, make him hers in the only way she possibly could?" What, indeed? "He is seen going into the house by someone that night and is never seen to leave it." "Lord knows what they had been doing inside the house, anyway, whether . . . she had compromised herself in other ways." Sam showed his phallic transformations most graphically by misremembering Emily's obsessional china-painting: "The house is closed up. She doesn't receive the knitting students anymore, or whatever she was teaching them." Penetrating needles replace painstaking brushwork.

Someone as narcissistically masculine as Sam, however, wanted to emphasize the difference between the sexes. Here, Sam would often see Miss Emily as intensely feminine, as in his framing her in the "tableau" between her father's legs: "That pretty much sums up exactly the kind of relationship they had." "The frailty and femininity that that evokes!" sighed Sam, thinking of the "tableau," "just that one frail, 'slender figure in white,' just those words there really show us the Emily that was and the Emily that might have been." At one point he called her "the darling lady"—a woman with a chance to be "feminine." "She was probably still attractive" and "thin" when she met Homer, he decided.

Sam was no feminist: he turned Emily into someone wholly passive, with marriage the only sensible aim for her life. "What hit me throughout the story was the total lack of any freedom. It wasn't even a question of fate. It was just environmental and preconceived mental sets that had governed this poor lady's life from the onset." "She's caught between memories of her father and the kind of life that he stood for and desires inherent in her. And it seems that she's trapped by what Homer Barron does, probably inadvertently, by taking her out and riding her in the carriage [*sic*], therefore getting the whole town to think that they're going to marry." "She refuses to bow to this [namely, the fact that aristocracy no longer exists, and everyone pays taxes, and tells druggists why they're buying arsenic]. Were she to bow to this, she would have to say, 'Well, then, why in heaven's name am I not married with family when I could have been?' " Only the belief in her own aristocracy can "make her life at all worthwhile, at all dignified. Otherwise, it becomes farcical, that you have this sad lady living in, just let's say, living in a three-room apartment in some part of the town and yet not marrying and not doing this and not doing the other because she's aristocracy."

Again, typical for a male concerned with physical masculinity, Sam thought of Emily partly as threateningly strong, partly as frail and helpless. Although she was destined only for marriage, he also saw marriage with her as potentially dangerous. "She killed as the only way of marrying him." They were "not actually married and not married in Homer's mind. I think this was kind of a melodramatic wedding for Emily. It doesn't seem to me that she could have gotten Homer up there [*sic*] if she had mentioned anything about its being a wedding." The only way she could "make him hers . . . was to kill him and have him there." "They go to bed again, one last time, and everything is laid out [*sic*], and she puts the arsenic in the wine . . . the goblets, or whatever, and kills him." And after this deadly wedding night, "She's eminently faithful to him, even after she kills him. She is as good a wife as any wife could be." Again, Sam said,

> I don't think the idea would ever come into Emily's mind after the murder, to marry. She *was* married. It *was* for Emily a marriage and of a very sacred sort. Had a man come along and fallen in love with her, who was everything that both she and her father put together [*sic*] could ever have hoped for, of such lineage and such money, and the like, that

it can't be imagined, I don't think that she would have married him, because to her mind she was a married woman. She lost her honor to Homer Barron, and in order to regain her honor, married him, and would only lose it and go deeper in sin type of thing, if she ever considered marrying again.

Again, after the marriage, "If you're going to take that salt and pepper hair found on the thing as indicative that she did go back and lie with him . . . she was almost consummating the marriage every night and lived as a married woman would, I suppose, in her own way." "Sleeping with him," Sam described it, "as I'm reluctant to say . . . after he was dead, or just perhaps lying by him." This marital fidelity "puts us more in sympathy with the kind of pathos of her life," "the whole pathos of her situation."

Once Homer was dead, however, Sam tended to see Emily as made of sterner stuff, "something like Scarlett O'Hara, not quite as gaddy." "While she was younger this [total dominance by her father] was not something that was unwelcome. I think she began to resent it as she got older." "The solitude of her life . . . does not make for femininity and the hardships, the lack of money." "She's fiercely independent. The townsfolk hold her in great respect that isn't really due but almost because of fear." A similar tendency to make her strong showed when he said, "Perhaps she was by anybody's standards insane by the end and hard and unnatural in the sense that she slept with this corpse and a murderess, by all standards. I think, though, that her situation evokes a lot of sympathy." "As she grew up and as she took looks at herself and saw what her life was, it seems that she became hard, independent as hell, especially after her father died." Of her various refusals, Sam would say, "That stands out definitely." "Other things stand out that are impressive," and he continued with other, similar masculinizings.

Thus, Sam ran a gamut in his attitude toward Emily. At the gentlest level, he said something like what Faulkner had said: " 'Rose for Emily' seems like kind of tribute paid . . . now tell the story in a ballad-type way about Emily whose life was awfully difficult." Or Brooks and Warren, who saw "her as . . . strong-willed tragic hero." "I think," Sam could say in this masculinizing vein, "that she handled herself in a Hemingwayish way, in a kind of manly way, didn't cry and didn't complain and kept up all appearances as best she possibly could." With a sterner attitude, Sam noted that one of the men, after throwing lye around the house, "sees her in the window with the light behind her . . . a kind of Buddha idol—that's the image that it evokes. It's kind of an idol for the town, for a whole way of life, for a whole frame of mind, this kind of old, traditional Southern way of life, and she became its goddess." Sam spoke of "gothic grandeur midst absolute poverty." "She began to be as the townsfolk look at her, legendary, a kind of pagan deity to all that they'd have her stand for." And that "stand for" signals a change of sex. "While they [the town] may be envious and while they may be angry at the way that these people [the Griersons] act, they yet need it, it seems, they in a way like to have it, much as one is terrified at the power of a god and yet needing him so much and, you know, sidling up to him and paying homage to him and in the same way I think Emily comes to function as this god symbol."

Sam was able to accept the harshness of an Emily who was both feminine trap and masculine god because he could construct denials for himself out of Emily's. "In an effort to just live her life out, [she] would close off whole areas of reality and not even look at them." "When her father died, Emily . . . kind of in her own mind, refused to believe that he was dead." When a complaint is made about the smell around her house, "She refuses to listen to it, so the townspeople themselves have to go and spread lye." This is a "Freudian" misremembering—the complaint came to the Board of Aldermen, not to Emily. It is as though Sam needed to have *her* deny, not anonymous townsmen. Similarly, "She won't sprinkle the lye because that's ridiculous." But nobody asked her to.

In many ways, then, she provided Sam with denials of impotence: "She refuses to cope with the inroads of the present" (an echo of Homer's "incoming" road; perhaps), and, Sam suggested, "The total physical deterioration . . . could easily be seen as symbolic for mental deterioration, too." "So much of what she had grown up under," Sam said, having just mentioned her father as symbol for the tradition, "and come to see as life was not real and was dead and was changing and moving on." Yet, Sam felt, Emily could not accept this change; to do so would be to make her "bow," "collapse," and otherwise lose her erect strength. He imagined Emily saying to herself: " 'My entire life has been formed and pointed toward this kind of an existence. I'm not married. I'm not really happy because of it. And if it's held such sway in such important areas of my life, I am certainly not going to let it override me now.' " Sam seemed to mean by "it" the whole concept of the aristocratic Southern tradition, and for it to "override" Emily meant for it to overtake her and ride over her in its rush to change—but, admittedly, his usage is odd. " 'Besides, I'd collapse. I'd fall down. My mind would unhinge by all the contrasts suddenly there if I were to let it. So I must go on as if everything were the way my life of loneliness shows that it should be.' In other words, it would be the only thing that would make her life at all worthwhile, at all dignified." " 'If I accept this, that I have to pay taxes like everybody else,' " Sam imagined her saying, " 'and yet I can't do so many other things like everybody else . . . ' this would just be totally conflicting and it wouldn't work." Sam's Emily, like Sam, has to deny in order to be "formed and pointed," and not "collapse," "fall down," or "unhinge."

At the beginning of the interview, he had talked about her fierceness, her grand manner, her becoming an idol or a god, even with masculine phrasings about her "standing out" or "standing for." However, once he had imagined the "disgusting" part, her lying with Homer, he shifted to feeling sympathy for Emily, and then shifted again, this time to stressing her passivity, how she was never free, totally bound by her tradition, "under" various pressures. From passivity, he went on to the very feminine; frail Emily, then back to the mannish, strong tragic heroine. Evidently, triggering these shifts was what Sam knew about the dirty secret or what Emily knew.

I said to Sam that we really only see Emily as "bossy, domineering, tough," but that he was suggesting she was

"feminine in the early part of her life." "So then, what's the
thing that made her change?" I asked. "The realization that her
father was dead," he quickly answered. "And I think a kind of
awareness that things were moving on, that things were changing, and yet, a similar awareness that she was unable to change
along with them." Yet it is precisely this change that Sam
thought Emily denied by her style of life.

It might be most accurate then, to say that Sam felt that what
you know and what you can avoid knowing determine whether
you will be frail, feminine, and passive ("under") or masculine
and cruelly domineering ("on top"). And this idea applied as
much to Sam's relation to the total story as to that segment of it
called Miss Emily Grierson. Following our principle of the
matching of defenses, Sam found a defense in the story: denial,
or the whole question of what one can tolerate knowing. Having selectively denied, Sam made the story's words about holding in something precious into his own preferred fantasies
about holding on to a nurturing matrix so as to thrust forth in a
virile, aggressive way. Then, following our concept of "characteristic transformation," he transformed those fantasies into
intellectual themes in his own style.

Thus, Sam decided on "the reason of this story": "I think
the thing we talked about, about the future and the past and
what one should carry out of the past with one into the future,
is pretty much it." "The past should not be totally ignored,"
he had said, "and yet it should not be totally lived in, and some
sort of a compromise has to be made."

> What he [Faulkner] is asking you to do is bring the good of
> the past to bear upon the future . . . bring the valid of the
> past to bear upon the future . . . bring the valid of the past to
> bear upon your life in the future. In other words, that tradi-
> tion which is helpful, that tradition which is good, that tradi-
> tion which gives solid [*sic*] and reason to your life, is fine. To
> do, as perhaps is suggested Homer Barron does, and throw it
> immediately over one's shoulder and never look at it, for
> what counts is the future, that's not good either. To do
> what—we can't say her father, because he died—but to do
> what Emily did, and to base her whole life on an idea of the

past, can easily lead to the kind of tragedy that Emily's life does. Neither is good. A kind of middle road, a kind of compromise seems to be what is suggested.

Reasonable as this interpretation is, it also derives from Sam's own wishes for an early (or past) matrix from which he would draw supplies (of love? strength? self-esteem?) in order to push on into his later life in a virile way acceptable to his own need to be admired as a young man. Further, when we looked at what Sam meant by that past, we found that he built it up from a series of romantic denials of reality.

Even so, Sam felt a little nervous about what he did and did not know in this story. He did not find his expectancy of supply and support so simply gratified by the ante-bellum world of "A Rose for Emily" that he could just merge into the story. He contrasted "A Rose for Emily" to the only other ante-bellum story he could think of: "I enjoyed it very much . . . but I didn't really lose myself in the sense that, well, that you could lose yourself analogously in *Gone with the Wind.*"

> The story was complex enough to . . . keep me on my toes, in the sense that I felt that I had to be on top . . . I did enjoy it thoroughly, and was involved with it, but didn't lose my-self in the sense that I could just really sit back and let the story unfold, because the story didn't. It unfolded all right, but I always had to figure just how the hell it was unfolding. And 'What, now! That was twenty years ago!' like you had to have a pad of paper next to you to figure out the time thing.

Even so, Sam took pleasure in the puzzles of "A Rose for Emily." "I enjoyed the kinds of mechanical demands it made on you to figure out what happened where and everything else." "Another one of the things that . . . I felt I was being forced to do as a reader was to dig between and beneath just what was being said, to find out real things, especially with the ending." As we have seen, Sam wanted to penetrate things in a variety of senses.

One way he did so was to project himself into the situations and characters, understanding them by playing them out—for example, that mysterious wedding night. "Perhaps she said, 'This will be our own little common-law wedding, dear,' and Homer, 'Heh, heh, heh,' you know, and 'I'll skip town tomorrow,' would say 'All right,' 'Fine,' type of thing." Homer, he said, left "perhaps telling Emily where he's going, perhaps saying, 'No, I will not marry you. I never had it in mind to marry you.' "

Another way he went into the story was less projective and more critical: he tried to "solve" it like a problem or a puzzle, and this too may have had a thrusting, probing, virile significance for him. "It was, in a way, a mystery story." For example, he had said Emily's taking up with Homer "is probably the only gap that the story had." Later he said that he, as a reader, puzzled in order "to try and fill in a lot of gaps."

In this problem-solving, however, Sam handicapped himself by a variety of denials, although, to be sure, he frankly confessed them. Thus, he admitted he was "reluctant to say" whether Emily had been sleeping with the corpse or not. "You really can't— You don't know, and you're kind of loath to think about it, because it's kind of disgusting." Because he didn't want to look at the event itself, he looked instead (as in his Rorschach tests) at the periphery. He drifted helter-skelter through the possibilities of that wedding-night until finally he concluded, "It all boils down to the fact you have to interpret the last paragraph where the hair is found. . . . There is dust on top of the hair." "It sounds as if it's [the hair] on top of the dust or at least not that heavily covered over by the dust." Limited as my housekeeping skills are, I nevertheless suspect that trying to decide whether a strand of hair someone has picked up had been on or under dust would puzzle the most compulsive duster. The story, at any rate, gives no clue.

This concern with the position of the strand of hair matched another pattern in Sam's response. It showed, for example, in his recollection of the tableau: "the townsfolk looking through the door as her father stands there." Actually, the story describes "the two of them framed by the back-flung front door," so the townspeople must have been outside the house and the Griersons on the porch or other space in front of the front door. Later, Sam called the tableau, "the picture of her shown by her father." Both errors shift the position from which the event is seen. Similarly, he recalled Emily's wedding present, not as "a man's toilet set," the story's phrase, but "the silver backed combs and things like— Or was that his to her? Do you remember? Or was that hers to him?" In the same way, he spoke of Emily's "chatter" with the druggist. Hardly accurate. The only chatterer one could possibly associate with that scene is Sam himself. Again, Sam described the method of narration: "All the secrets, if any, that you're privy to, are just ones of general speculation and rumor." How can one speak of "rumor" as a "secret"?

All these slips and self-contradictions carry out denials: Sam avoided seeing something he did not want to see by concentrating on something peripheral. As such, his denials use the way the story omits and slides over its clues so as to build toward the final, awful discovery. This shared denial, this matching of defenses, established Sam's basic and pervasive contact with the story.

Indeed, it was precisely Sam's ability to regard the South as benevolent even when perpetrating slavery, violence, and humiliation on Negroes that provided his deepest point of identification with the story (as a "born baby"). Having established the South as a nurturing matrix, Sam could then pursue his other libidinal aims: being "on top," in "a position of power," "a great plantation owner," whipping "my share of slaves." Miss Emily's father illustrated this same double value: he provided a matrix in which she could have been "the darling lady," but as things turned out, his values destroyed her life. So, too, Homer Barron's phallic powers had this ability to give Emily a life or take it away.

Homer had something else as well that was important to Sam, the ability to elude the matrix of the South, to fly free. "He returns, it seems to me, because Emily sends for him. That would be the only reason I can see of his coming back." Sam rendered Homer's freedom in images of air. Homer Barron, "catching wind" of the threat of marriage, leaves. "She was too clever to put any claims on him forcibly, because I think he would just have blown the joint." And there was perhaps the faintest grisly echo of these images when Sam de-

scribed the entry into Emily's house after her death: "The
townsfolk pour into her house . . . to air their curiosity."

Homer did not fly, however, but Sam was able to accept his
demise by taking the murder as only a meal and a marriage. In
the development of the story, the South ceased to be a useful
matrix, and so did Miss Emily. Sam, however, could accept a
masculine version of Miss Emily as a "god" to whom one
would sidle up. He took on a masculine role himself, penetrating and probing the story's secrets (but using denials to avoid
anything too threatening), and enjoying his power over it. "I,
feeling that I was more or less successful with it ['the time
thing'], I enjoyed it. It was kind of an easy crossword puzzle
type of thing to be doing on the side." In effect, Sam had
wanted to get on top of the story and force his way into it by
actively interpreting it. By the end of the interview, he felt he
had been fairly successful in doing so, and this gave him libidinal and aggressive pleasures of a thrusting, penetrating kind.
From his vantage point on top, following the principle of expectancy enacted, Sam responded favorably to Emily. "She has so
many conflicts that she has to resolve," and he sympathized
with her for facing and solving her life problems as he had
solved his problems of interpretation.

In key with his shift from a kind of passive nurturing in the
motherly bosom of the Old South to a more active probing of
the story, Sam took the intellectual theme to be carrying forth
something from the matrix of the past to thrust into the future,
a theme akin both to Homer's tentative flight and Sam's shift
from a passive enjoyment of *Gone with the Wind* to an active
solving and filling in of the Faulknerian gaps.

As for Sam's characteristic transformation, he did not develop the fantasy I did, having to do with the control of inner
things. Instead, he introduced the virile themes of strength,
domination, and penetration that concerned him, and he transformed that fantasy of being on top (through denials he created
from the story) into an active, male theme of—the missing
defense—flight. At that (phallic) level, I thought the story
showed Emily's becoming a strong, masculine woman, but Sam
did not see it that way. For him, the story seemed to be
Emily's proving he was right in his fears about women. Emily's

killing Homer equaled marrying him, and Sam took the theme of the story to be, "what one should carry out of the past with one into the future." That is, Sam would like to be able to carry "what gives solid and reason to [his] life" away from such a woman (or matrix) and "bring [it] to bear . . . in the future." To the extent "A Rose for Emily" made that difficult for Sam to do, he parted company with the story. Not, however, before he had, in his completely individual way, demonstrated the four principles of literary response.

Saul

Scholarly Saul, as we have seen, guarded himself very heavily indeed against the danger that more would be forced out of him than he wished to give. His need—to find a balanced bargain in which he could be sure he would not be overpowered—governed not only his response to the story, but his attitude toward the interview. "I had to sit here and face that question when you asked me that." When I asked him what he thought actually happened on the night Homer was killed, "It's another question I have to face right now." In effect, he perceived the interview (not without reason) as my demand that he deliver answers. This, alas, was exactly the opposite of what Saul wanted to do. He wanted rather aggressively to control the pace and direction of what came out, and he had to "face" me because he feared being forced by someone he could not see, someone behind him, for example.

"I knocked it ["A Rose for Emily"] off in the last twenty minutes," he announced at the beginning of the interview, thereby imposing his own limits on the depth and seriousness of our conversation. Introducing an "analogy" he had to the story, he said, "I'm not sure how [it came to me]. I wouldn't want to defend that for very long. That's one of my quick associations to it. I did another thing wrong . . ." Evidently, to associate freely and quickly was "wrong." Saul needed to control the interviews, because (I think) he feared that if he freely associated, talked "away from the text," for example, he might let more out than he wanted to.

In general, a reader's experience of a literary work depends first and foremost on how closely he can create his adaptation from the work. Saul needed to see forces that might make him let too much out—alertness was one way he coped. Bargaining with forces he thought might take something away, however, was even more Saul's way of dealing with the world, as, for example, in the interviews.

To apply this mode to "A Rose for Emily," he had to find a person with whom he could establish his bargain, and he did: Faulkner himself. Then he took this approach *via* the author to be the proper "Eng. Lit." way of doing things. "I'm more prone to do this on Faulkner than I was on Katherine Mansfield's story, read it like a graduate student, fit it in to what I know about Faulkner, and so forth." Yet this bargain, too, required further defending, as when he read out a sequence of adjectives that had caught his fancy, but commented, "I said, 'Yeah!' two ways. One, a kind of gut reaction way. The other in a 'Gee, this kind of sums up Faulkner's attitude toward' [way]. You know, in the footnote."

Even his enthusiasm had to fit within bounds. He liked the tableau of Emily and her father: "It's a nice device. Faulkner makes that one work, too." "I like [the story], if only to start with this on the level of authoritative prose." To another sequence of adjectives, "I don't get much 'gut reaction.' I just see it fit in the pattern." " 'Authority' is the word I get most with Faulkner."

In the course of our ten interviews, he praised several other authors in almost the same words. This sense of the writer as an "authority" seemed to play an important part in Saul's feelings toward literature in general and Faulkner in particular. "He knows, he knows. He always gives the impression of knowing what he's doing." "He's just so goddamned good . . . with such masterful authority. He knows what he's doing every time he puts a word down. You know, he gets away with lots of things that not too many people can." "I think there's something about his rhythms."

Yet, true to his concern with holding on and releasing, Saul needed to feel that his authoritative writer dropping each word according to his rhythm and intention could, if he wanted to, simply let go: "There's a wild, wild paragraph," he said of

Light in August, "in which he just lets out all the stops." "I think he makes some of this work the way it seems Whitman makes things work. He just yells them. It's got kind of 1840's public oratory." "I think that's probably the way he's doing it. . . . He, like Whitman, mixes Latin and Greek derived words with slang. He does everything *wrong*, and it works."

As in that echo, doing things wrong, Saul readily identified with Faulkner. "I've got to assume, at least Faulkner is assuming, that arsenic takes a while to act." Saul's sense of being in an equally balanced bargain with Faulkner even led him into the *hubris* of competing with that brilliant writer: "I would never dream of trying anything like that, and he makes it work!" "The bastard can out-write me. He writes just magnificently!"

Yet, as one would expect, he also undermined the very authority he seemed to admire. "I sometimes suspect Faulkner of being just a little stagy in some of this," by which Saul meant working things out too neatly, and, therefore, manipulating him, getting responses out of him he did not wish to give, responses that he, Saul, might feel guilty or ashamed of. "I suspect Faulkner again there [in connection with the old Negro]. No matter how much I like Dilsey [in *The Sound and the Fury*], I suspect in her case, too." "Even after you think about it [his prose] a while, he's managed to fool you." "Sometimes you smell a little staginess," when "he gets away with things that . . . he shouldn't be getting away with." And, common though it may be, the idiom of 'getting away with things' exactly expressed Saul's fear.

In much the same way he traded with Faulkner, Saul singled out the nearly invisible narrator of the story. "The thing with 'we,' I like the way he handles that. It's really nicely done, I think." Curiously, he found this the realest thing in the story: "There aren't quite any real people . . . except maybe the 'I' that's speaking" (although the narrator always speaks of himself as "we"). By supplying a nonexistent "I," Saul revealed his relationship to the narrator as another person with whom he bargained for the story's information, shifting and displacing items, particularly the emotional weight to be given them. Saul identified with this controller as he had with Faulkner. For

example, who is the "I" in this sentence of Saul's? "I managed
to deal with what happened to him [Homer] by saying he went
away somewhere." Is "I" Saul or the narrator?

Similarly, when he responded positively to Miss Emily, he
did so because she resisted the controlling forces of others. She
had "a certain amount of power, not a power that females
would have had in the old traditions. But it's not the same kind
of power that her father or the mayor [had]." He said this in
answer to my question about whether he thought she took on
some of her father's force in her later, withholding years. "It's
a defensive and resistant power, not particularly masculine
power." That she "vanquished" the city council, he said,
meant, "She wouldn't listen to them, just as she wouldn't yield
to having the mailbox and the numbers put on her house for
free mail delivery."

"As the last holdout, she's doing very well at it," "She *is*,
you know, the last holdout of these old traditions." He was
describing a contest of wills, not unlike my efforts to get responses from him. In this vein, he made an interesting slip
while reading part of the story aloud to me. " 'She looked back
at him, erect, her face like a stained flag' " (instead of
"strained"). Again, "The house is the last holdout on that once
most select street." He liked the tableau of Miss Emily and her
father and the front door. "They're framed in this door of this
old aristocratic house which now stands alone among cotton
gins . . . and gas stations. It strikes me as right. I can't say
[why]."

We can, however. Such a "framing" or holding was just
what Saul wanted. He had been able to strike a balanced bargain with Faulkner's authority or the narrator's. Having
achieved his major defensive pattern of withholding within a
frame, he was able to enjoy the story. And he was able to
respond to persons and actions with the story (notably Miss
Emily) who acted out for him the balance of outer control and
inner withholding that was Saul's expectation toward most of
life. Thus, Saul liked Faulkner's language, singling out phrases
like "stubborn and coquettish decay," "decorated with
cupolas and spires . . . in the heavily lightsome style of the
seventies," "the cedar-bemused cemetery." Here Saul was

finding the limited controls he favored in Faulkner's balances of positive and negative values ("coquettish decay," "heavily lightsome"). Then, in their unconscious significance, these phrases could link human traits to decay. They could express the body's experience of the loss of its precious but disgusting, living but dead, products in a larger, more totally human experience of the death, decay, and loss of a tradition.

This matching of defense, drive, and therefore expectancy made up Saul's positive response to the story. He also had negative responses, particularly when he felt threatened or overcontrolled. He had two characteristic ways of dealing with these threats to his autonomy. First, he might push the opposing force away, make it disappear, as it were. Second, he might deal with it logically so as to "cut it down to size." He could then strike a new, more favorable bargain with it, dominating it or even, perhaps, getting rid of it entirely. Consider the way he commented on Emily's father: in effect, he blotted him out by dividing him up into inconsistent alternatives until one could see him no longer. "How do you feel towards him?" I asked. "I think of [George] Wallace supporters," he replied, but went right on to say, "I think he was partly, at least, like the mayor who had fathered the— You know, more in the image of the aristocratic white Southerner with benevolence towards niggers—to a point."*

"This constrictive benevolence," he called it, and the adjective reveals the sense of coercion and control that mobilized Saul's defenses. Thus, he dealt with the tableau of Emily and her father in the doorway by splitting it. " 'Horsewhip' there— rings—" "A horsewhip suggesting all sorts of nasty, sexual, sadistic overtones." Yet, even as he gave him this sadistic sexuality (again appropriate to Saul's fears of authority), he took it away. "The father a 'spraddled silhouette.' He's no longer stern and erect." True, "sprawled" is one possible meaning for "spraddled," but many people would take the word in this context to mean "spraddle-legged" or "straddled," that is, with legs spread wide apart. Saul took the word to mean a decline in Mr. Grierson's powers, and then he pro-

* As noted before, the epithet is Saul's experimenting with a racist attitude.

ceeded to qualify the image even further. "Do they mean the
horsewhip rather than his own stern demeanor? Or just the
normal embodiment of his traditions suggests the decline like
'spraddled' does?" Frankly, I cannot tell very clearly what
Saul meant, but what is clear is that he was controlling the
tableau by dividing it into separate words and then dividing
even those words again.

Similarly, when I asked him about the edict that no Negro
woman should appear on the streets without an apron, he
shifted to the participle that introduced that appalling law:
" 'Fathered' . . . is the word you're asking about, I suspect,"
and he promptly rewrote it to " 'sponsored.' It means practically the same as 'sponsored,' I think. I don't know. Although I
suppose you could talk about paternalism and stuff but—" It
was typical of Saul to try to make a tyrannical father into
"paternalism," which then vanishes.

It was equally typical of him to blur, qualify, and so weaken
the substance of the edict. "It's just a matter of, you know,
Negroes are not allowed to be people, only servants. That's a
social class thing." Even holding the book, he had changed
"Negro woman" to "Negroes," and still holding the book, he
phrased the edict: "No one should appear on the streets without an apron. That's just identifying the servants, that they're
not allowed to dress up in their Sunday best on the street." The
effect is to deny all the force and cruelty of the original, to take
the coercion out.

He applied the same equalizing technique to other
authority-figures in the story. "The druggist . . . asking her
what she's going to use it for, is like the people saying that
'We're the ["city authorities"]'— They're the same representa-
tives of the same order of things." And he had already seen
them defeated. He blurred distinctions further in recalling,
"The people— they all think about 'in their brushed Confeder-
ate uniforms'—they talk about having danced with her." But
these words in the story describe only "the very old men."

He felt Faulkner, with Miss Emily's servant Tobe and Dilsey
of *The Sound and the Fury,* was "romanticizing the good house
nigger," "making of her more a literary symbol and less a real
person, which is what apparently the entire social structure . . .

of the house militated to do: make people into figures in the white man's psychic drama of some sort, rather than allowing them to be people on their own." Yet, despite the touch of Fanon in this speech, it was Saul, not Faulkner who erased, in these words, blackness into "people," or said of this utterly baffling servant who shared Miss Emily's ghastly secret all those years: "There's not much to him, except she clearly— he's in her control or he willingly— Well. That sounds like two different things." "Devoted while he's her servant for forty or fifty years. There's something, and he's so much associated with her when he's— He has something and knows— He's complicit somehow in this murder."

I tried to open up Saul's enigmatic view by offering him the suggestion (which I had got from another reader) that Tobe had masterminded the whole thing. To this bizarre idea, Saul commented, slowly and sagely, "Well, he appears and disappears appropriately," then, after a long pause, "I don't recall anything in the story . . . anything that suggests she was in any way captive by anyone living." "But why would he go out to the market? 'Show these gentlemen in.' 'Show these gentlemen out,' " he quoted, as if to prove that no self-respecting mastermind would be coerced into a servant's role, not in complete control of appearances and disappearances.

As for the real murderer, Emily, he saw her as the controlled, rather than the controller (not, as I saw her, someone changing those roles in midstory). "She had pounded into her head . . . that she is better, that she's one of the chosen, one of the elect, one of *the* better people." "That's one of the more important mechanisms of how she's trapped in this heritage." "I don't find her as frightening terrible as I do, say even the mother in Mansfield's story." "There's something pathetic about Emily." "I perceive her as more a victim." "I'm sympathetic to the sorts of things that have happened to . . . the lost Miss Emily." "I perceive her as less terrible, partly because of a kind of sympathy, maybe because she's more shadowy."

In general, he tended to make Miss Emily unreal. Of the murder scene he said, "I can't imagine them having tea in their nightgowns." "This is more like it's being acted out in a dusty museum case." "I think I react sort of like a museum grotesque of some sort." If he could not make her passive or harmless, a "victim," he made her threat remote and therefore not dangerous. "She manages to conceal all this and be still thought of with a certain amount of reverence, until after her death." Thus, when I put forward my idea that Miss Emily took on some of her father's brutality and force, Saul would have none of it. "It hadn't occurred to me because I don't think of her as quite that real." "She's still too wispy and shadowy and, you know, wispy gothic, for me to think about it that way, masculine."

This was Saul's other way of establishing his own controls against forces that looked as though they might be able to control him. He would push the opposing force away, make it disappear, by, in effect, changing the subject (that is, the grounds of the bargain). This was Saul's "originality." Inevitably, he felt that, to talk about "A Rose for Emily," he had to tell me about *The Sound and the Fury, Light in August,* and movies of the 1930's set on glorified plantations. Less predictably, he talked about a Katherine Mansfield story and *Miss Lonelyhearts.* Still more originally, he decided Faulkner's prose style worked the way Whitman's poetry did, and rather than discuss any of the language of this story, he cautioned himself, "Let me stick to Whitman." Almost the first thing he said was, "The analogy of that strange Christ figure in Flannery O'Connor's *Wise Blood* came to me."

Despite his willingness to compete with Faulkner, Saul showed blind spots when he tried to talk about the prose rather than just quote it. "I had remembered the word 'tableau,' and I had forgotten the rest of it." In the amorous language of the last scene, "I haven't the slightest idea what 'cuckold' . . . what it's doing here." Again, unless he was controlling its terms, he refused the bargain.

In the same way, he associated an unreal Miss Emily with an unreal South, a sense of Miss Emily as monument and idol—"It just fits the death of the old traditions." Saul knew nothing about the murder but his own "filmy guessing." "There's something finally unreal about Southern gothics," like Miss Emily: "wispy and shadowy," "less terrible . . .

because she's more shadowy." Saul associated to this ideal a specific image of things appearing and disappearing: "this gothic world where figures appear and disappear much more readily than they do, say, in the streets of Buffalo, in the real world out there."

To some extent, Saul's whole response seemed to pivot on this sense of things appearing and disappearing, which sometimes was good, sometimes bad. Part of his "negative reaction" to the story came because it got "shadowy." Yet, losing something calls for restitution. "After they lost the war, they had to idealize something. . . . The aristocratic conditions, like the movies of the plantations in the '30s and '40s and '50s. All these great plantation balls and the white gowns floating around and all this lovely, lovely world." "They tried to enforce that," he said. "It's no longer possible to maintain it." "That can no longer be maintained with sanity after that world disintegrated." "When the tradition no longer had the hold on life to protect them, you have to get stern to hold on," and this word, he thought, described Miss Emily's manner better than "masculine."

Saul's concern with "holding on" led him to respond especially to things appearing or disappearing, and this concern in turn led to what resembled denials, deliberate ignorances, in his perception of the story. They were not denials, however, but distancings he himself imposed. Saul had to be on guard. He seemed almost aware of his tactics, for just as he had called old Miss Emily "cockeyed," he could speak of "the cockeyed way I perceived the story." "Five paragraphs from the end they talk about the one room that hadn't been opened in forty years, and, until I started reading that, it hadn't— I had faced the question [*sic*] of what happened to, um, the man's name— " and he had blotted out Homer Barron. "I didn't think of the smell or anything. I managed to deal with what happened to him by saying he went away somewhere. He left." And, at a later point, he said, "I managed to ignore the poison when I was dealing with what happened to Homer Barron."

These statements that he had "managed to deal with" or "faced the question" make his reading seem like a highly logical affair. So, in a way, it was; for logic and dividing into

particulars was Saul's alternative to his other strategy of blur-
ring distinctions and making parts of the story appear and disappear. "The moment I read this line [about the unopened
room] . . . . at that point it was all predictable." "*That* and the
smell and so forth hit me, obviously. The smell was him decaying. Had it not been for the smell, it wouldn't have been so
certain." Recall the way he divided up the sadistic tableau. At
another stage in the interview, he developed four logical possibilities for the way the murder could have taken place,
mumbling and maundering about the speed with which arsenic
works, putting on and off clothes, having the Negro carry
Homer up the stairs, wondering whether they would have had
tea in their nightgowns, and so on. The fact of the murder got
lost as he concluded, "The only thing that's clear is that she
has this 'iron gray' hair they find on the pillow next to his
pillow." "The whole end of this story is rather obscure, to tell
you the truth. I suspect we're supposed to project our own
gothic horrors into this kind of Rorschach blot on the last
page." Exactly right, I think, certainly righter than those critics
who have tried to ferret out exactly what happened on the fatal
night. The point is not, however, whether Saul is right or
whether he seems right to me. The real question is, How did
he—the most guarded and defensive of these five readers
—accept so open a reading of the final, threatening mystery?

Of our four principles, the most basic is that of "expectancy
enacted." A reader responds positively to certain elements,
when he feels those elements do within the work what he expects toward the work; he responds negatively to those elements in which he cannot match his own structures of defense
and adaptation. Saul responded positively to Faulkner's "masterful authority," the managerial narrator, the "resistant" Miss
Emily, and the language and images that "framed" their content. These things he saw as deliberately controlling what they
would let out or hold onto. They thus acted out exactly both
Saul's defenses and his drives. Indeed, the story came so close
to his own patterns that he saw the theme of the story quite
conventionally: holding on to tradition. He found, in effect, just
the opposite of what he found in "Winter Dreams," holding on,

rather than letting go " 'transient beauty' and all this decadent crap."

Saul responded negatively to people or episodes in the story who seemed to him not limited or contained and who seemed to show overwhelming power: Miss Emily's father, the more demanding parts of Faulkner's prose, the edict against Negro women, Emily's enigmatic servant, Miss Emily as a murderer, and the final fact of the murder itself. He interpreted these as situations in which the bargain did not take place between equally balanced opponents. Rather, one side demonstrated overwhelming power. To such a situation, Saul applied one of two defenses. He might deal with it logically, dividing up strengths as he divided Mr. Grierson until he was of manageable size or as he qualified various forces: the druggist, the city council, the cruel edict, the murderess. Or he might push the large force into the distance, making it remote and unreal, as he did Faulkner's more complex prose or the Old South—or the "inkblot" of the murder. *It* cannot control *his* response: "I suspect we're supposed to project our own gothic horrors" —with the implication nobody was going to frighten Saul that easily (so that his "open" response was really another kind of wariness).

In effect, Saul dealt with the world (and, within the world, this story) in terms of things appearing and disappearing. Would he be coerced into letting something out from inside himself where it lay hidden? Would he be forced to make something of his own, which was invisible, appear? Or would he be able to coerce the coercer and make that other appear or disappear according to his, Saul's, will? This more rigid defense led to his logically mastering that other, qualifying it until it became small or remote or unreal.

It was perhaps inevitable that Saul's last words about the story would be split between his two negative modes, pushing away and logically dividing. "My only negative reaction would be, um, well, two." On the one hand, "It does get a touch shadowy." "It's sometimes just a little mawky, stagy, and pat." ("Mawky," I decided, was a portmanteau word, from "mawkish" and "murky.") On the other hand, "It works itself out maybe a bit too neatly. It's a masterfully unfolded pattern, but maybe if you know the pattern already, and it unfolds so easily, it's less thrilling a story to read."

Shep

Radical Shep liked "A Rose for Emily." This story, he said, comparing it to others in the anthology we were using, was "up on a level with the Conrad ["The Secret Sharer"] and the Joyce story ["The Dead"]. It's kind of midway between the two, with Joyce somewhere up near the top." Shep's enthusiasm means he interpreted the story's form and structure to yield a match for his own strategies of defense and adaptation.

Shep, we have seen, had two related patterns, both aimed at preserving a sense of identity in the face of an other perceived as overwhelming and all-powerful. First, he might try to become a passive victim, a "thing" in a "system." Alternatively, he would flee the matrix to fight it from a distance—exile and resistance, as he said, speaking of his underground lifestyle. This flight-and-fight strategy, however, could cut him off from a story, at least if applied at the outset.

From time to time, Shep would use his interest in "systems" to throw out a digression in such a way as to mobilize opposition—although I think these maneuvers had more to do with his response to me than to the story. Often, he stated these digressions as conflicts. "The Southern tradition, I think, is preferable to the tradition of the McLuhanistas, that kind of pop tradition" (a curious phrasing). He felt, even in Faulkner's own writings, one could do better than the Griersons. "The thing that Sam Fathers was into [in "The Bear"], it was very much a better tradition to be in than the slave-owning aristocratic one. Even the Snopes tradition was a little bit better before they started making money." "Something like [William] Burroughs' cut-up method . . . is an attempt to regain—and I would, in fairness to Burroughs, say, regain in a better form than the old Southern aristocratic one—an attempt to regain that form which Faulkner at least writes as though he has." In effect, Shep brought in McLuhan to be put down by Faulkner; Sam Fathers, and even the Snopeses, to put down the Griersons; Burroughs to put down Faulkner, and so on—he was acting like a fight promoter, particularly when he changed from intellectual and literary preferences to more tender topics.

"I don't like it [the Southern tradition] for the same reason that I don't like Christianity. . . . I don't like Christianity from some of the things that it's done trying to stay alive." Or his comment on Miss Emily's father in the tableau: "He's defending Southern womanhood . . . in that same sort of mindless way that says, 'Well, now, we've got to defend it.' " "He [Homer] can build roads like a mother, you know. He's great at building roads, but the roads don't go anywhere. They're no real connection. They're that phony geography that ends up on Esso travel maps." I sensed in Shep a hostility just looking for something to pounce on. He seemed constantly to be tossing in baits to see if he could draw me into an argument of some kind —about the falsity of Esso maps or Christianity or McLuhan or Southern ideals or whatever it might be.

Shep's other defensive strategy, however, played much more of a role in his response, because he could so easily match it in "A Rose for Emily." That is, half of Shep wanted and needed to find he was incorporated into a matrix, even, if necessary, as its victim. For me, much of "A Rose for Emily" builds on the formal strategy, "I will take and keep the old thing inside me": Miss Emily's keeping of Homer, for example, the town's affectionate tolerance of Emily, or Faulkner's flashback form. If Shep also saw the story that way, he could match his style exactly.

Shep himself longed for a nurturing and sustaining system, "some sort of contact between self and environment," he called it, and he saw the whole Southern milieu of the story in these terms. "For Massa, it represented something valuable and some way really tying in with what was around him, with the world that he lived in, and also with the time that he lived in, and the times preceding and following that." "These people were integrally and viably connected with what was around them, with their environment in general, be it social or physical, and . . . consequently they didn't exist as individuals in the sense that most fiction deals with. They, in a way, are seen in a mythic dimension, or maybe a heroic dimension would be a better way to put it."

Either way, Shep did not react to the characters as individuals but as abstractions, as words. "Names," he concluded, "are magical. Names mean something." He felt sorry for Miss Emily, "regardless of the slave-holding bit and what the Confederacy stood for. The metapolitical oneness, the action which was identical to its object, the energy transmission of the scene was a very good one, so I did sympathize with her." "In a way," he said, "the two are inseparable, the person and the situation. . . . I found myself feeling as though she and virtually everyone else in there, as well as the things like houses and so forth, were extensions of a whole group of things, a whole piece in the historical geography of the place."

He saw time the same way. For example, in his retelling the story in his own words, he said, "I think that I tend to sort things out and arrange them in this historical sequence because I don't have the sort of thing that Faulkner had and that the people in the story had about some sort of an integral tradition, some sort of connection with the past, in terms of geography, in terms of the way events tend to accumulate and make places meaningful, and that's the real geography of the area." He referred again to "that geography of experience," "historical geography," and it was this sense of an eternal now that seemed to be the chief appeal of the story to him.

"I got quite hung up in it, particularly along the temporal-spatial continuity that exists for the people in it and that makes possible his [Faulkner's] violating chronological forms. . . . the fact that things in Jefferson coexist in past and present." Again, it was this particular feature that made him admire the mere technique of the story: "The movement is perfectly logical, but it fits in with the flow of the story, because those movements are all there in the present that he's writing in." Although he recognized that he himself could not sustain such a mode—"My own words would probably tend toward the chronological"—he was also able to recount in exact detail the complex narrative sequence of the opening paragraphs of the story.

He had, in fact, better recall than any of the other subjects of the way Faulkner made past and present coexist, and he admired it more. "What he manages . . . in that first section, of getting you to accept the eternal moment through which he sees things, is beautiful! It makes the whole story worth reading, just to catch what he's doing there and to watch him continue to do it the rest of the way through."

Shep, however, saw both the timelessness of Faulkner's time and the matrix of Southern tradition ambivalently. On the one hand, the tradition made freedom for some people. "Insofar as it does manage to make (for only the whites involved in it) a way of fulfilling their possibility as human beings in the world, of gaining some sort of contact between self and environment, insofar as it does just that, I like it, because it's something that I wish *I* had." On the other hand, it posed two dangers.

First, it could trap people: "The aristocratic tradition could exist only if you had an adequate number of serfs around. If there weren't enough people willing to be serfs, you had to just take some and make them be serfs and fight to defend your right to do this. Wow!" Nor was the danger confined to serfs. Miss Emily, he said, took over the burden of decay from her father and so became shorter, older, and "drastically ugly." "It wasn't a matter of going into something naturally, the way, say, Indians in the same tribe—their children move into the adult position naturally. I think she had to. It was expected of her . . . because there was a choice now and there didn't used to be a choice. Earlier, it could have been natural." "She was perpetuating the same ethos in which [*sic*] her father lived."

That was the second danger: a stultifying rigidity. The tradition, he said, "started out as a way of exercising their [the aristocrats'] possibilities in the world and exercising them to a fairly maximal amount, but . . . it eventually became a retreat behind which they could find shelter from some of the new things that were happening." Thus, the tradition became "aristocratic, heavily ritualized, and increasingly more formal." "They had a very rigid formal code and it was perhaps very much a dead code by the time she got her hands on it, but it represented something which the new people weren't able to offer an adequate substitute for."

Given this rigidity and no substitute for the tradition, it became a source of deadly force—at least, that is what Shep seemed to be answering when I asked him where Miss Emily got the strength to kill Homer Barron:

> The strength is there in the rigidity of the code that she lives in. That rigidity gives her the capability of functioning even this way, I suppose, particularly in that, as the code has fewer and fewer people attached to it in any sort of meaningful way, it becomes more and more rigid, as she becomes more and more rigid in her confrontations with the town. . . . It's a very rigid posture and that rigidity is her strength, even if it be inverted into destructiveness. Really, that's all her strength is, an inversion of the original positive rigidity of the code, the rigidity as ritual, as structure of life.

In effect, Shep was describing someone both in and out of the trap of tradition.

Time, too, he saw as something nurturing but also entrapping. His very first words about Colonel Sartoris's ugly edict that Negro women had to wear aprons were, "He was mayor in 1894, so, according to the time scheme I just ran him through, he'd be into the formal, the protective stance of this ethos." Even his more isolated comments linked the edict to time: "I think of that edict as being a stupid and rigorous way to try to protect himself from change." "By the time of 1894, when Colonel Sartoris is [*sic*] mayor, it [the tradition], it's dead formalities."

Similarly, Shep's misreadings of the story tended to cluster around issues of time. For example, he was nonplussed when I reminded him that the hair on the pillow was gray. "Wow! Wait a minute! Yes . . . Let's see, was her hair gray when she married him? I just assumed that it would be gray when he came back that time the neighbor saw the Negro let him in, that her hair would be iron gray. Otherwise, it would be a black hair, I guess." He went on to fumble with the various clues about time, and possibly it was his pleasure in mingling past and present that accounts for his strange idea that what Miss Emily did with Homer's body was look at it. The hair, to almost every critic I have read (whatever their other differences), proves that she lay down beside the body at some time. But

Shep decided it meant "probably that she would come in there and lock him away, to keep it, that she wanted to use the body for something, if only to look at it." Similarly, he had a unique notion of Miss Emily's motive for killing Homer, that by putting her lover through a process of decay ("and coming to relish the sight"), she could offset with a kind of sympathetic magic the social decay around her—again, one senses an attempt to bind up past and present in timelessness.

In effect, Shep derived from the story a special match to his need to find a sustaining tradition, an inner geography of experience, a timeless mingling of then and now, a positive version of the infant's early experience of nurture and mothering. Shep felt toward this matrix a sense of security and satisfaction leading to a loss of personality in a larger mythic or heroic realm. But he also felt this security as a dangerous rigidity that harbored a murderous power to kill and enslave. He opposed it and decided that he, Faulkner, and Emily were all, in varying degrees, able to take an active role toward this social matrix, manipulating it, watching it, and rearranging it.

In other words, we are seeing come into play Shep's first defensive strategy, flight-and-fight. His other defense enabled him to find in time and tradition a matrix or system into which he could subside, losing his individual identity. It could nurture and sustain him or it could entrap and engulf him with rigid, murderous force. He found both need and pleasure in fighting that matrix, thus bringing his first defense to bear and creating the ambivalent pattern that permeated the way he saw the story's themes and ideology. Now we are beginning to see how this second defense also governed Shep's perception of the story's people and episodes.

Consider, for example, a minor, although ideologically fraught, character like Miss Emily's Negro servant. As we have seen in the TAT story he told for the picture of the solitary boy, Shep tended to identify with the downtrodden. He did so here, making the Negro part of the whole Southern aristocratic tradition (as he himself, he said, wished to be), relating him to Miss Emily, therefore, as the presiding goddess of that tradition. "He also maybe is one of the last of his kind." But he is the opposite side—"He comes out of the same ethos as Miss

Emily, but he comes out of the dark side [*sic*] of it, where he's accepted his inferior position.''

In effect, the matrix—and my maternal pun is always intentional—oppresses the Negro, and thus oppresses Shep. ''He comes out of the side that undermines the ultimate effectiveness of her and her father's ethos, the side that's being denied, and it becomes a way of life simply because they [the Negroes] choose to accept their denial. It's kind of a political asceticism.'' But blacks (and I think Shep would identify with them) will no longer ''shuffle and say, 'Yassuh, boss,' . . . [and] work almost to the point of death.'' ''The new order will take over.'' (Shep might have known the Hitlerian overtones of that phrase.) ''Then, with the blacks at least, the new order has the possibility of creating that viable ethos again after a hundred years, because apparently they're being able to do something with their blackness and turn it into a positive way of life.'' First Shep saw the Negro as a thing within a system. Then he saw a reversal of that order, with the Negro escaping the system imposed on him and asserting his own against it.

In effect, we are seeing Shep work the characters in the story into his flight-and-fight strategy. First, he would ''flee'' a character, making him abstract, ignoring or mistaking his motivations and relations with other characters. Then he would describe him in a confronting or aggressive way, often by means of a displacement onto a distant or radically different system, which, indeed, he would identify as such: ''the new order.'' He opposed Emily's father this way—perhaps indicating what he would like to do with his own father.

First, he made Grierson trivial. ''There isn't that much said about her father, except that he dies and that apparently he made her lead a very restricted life.'' ''Her father is, I think, a very incidental figure. He's next to last, and next to last is a bad place to be.'' ''Effectively he was dead when he was alive . . . the dead hand of the past.''

In part of Shep's mind, anyway, Mr. Grierson seemed a mere appendage to Miss Emily's actions, notably her keeping of his body. ''Why she wanted her father's valuable— I mean, that's for the Electra complex people to decide.'' Shep sensed Miss Emily as powerful or maternal, and he suggested that she was the diabolic planner of all the events that had to do with Homer. "Perhaps [*she*] even might have been nourishing her father's false hope that if she could marry this man [note that Mr. Grierson had died before Homer appeared] . . . then she might have figured that if she could have had children by this man, she could have seen that they went straight." In effect, Miss Emily is so capable, she "nourishes" her father by totally controlling her children.

Once Shep had invented this strong Emily, however, the other part of his psychic pattern came into play, and Mr. Grierson became her powerful antagonist. When he discussed the tableau of Emily and her father, at first, the horsewhip was "a protective image" (!), but he added:

> You could, as an alternative interpretation, say that the horsewhip is something which he's also adept with indoors as well as outdoors, but I don't think so. Maybe there's overtones that Daddy is sadistic enough—horsewhips being pretty sadistic things to carry around when you're greeting people—that Daddy is sadistic enough where he wouldn't mind taking a belt at Emily once in a while, but I don't think they're much more than overtones.

Yet these overtones exactly fit Shep's pattern of avoiding the story's threat and then actively re-establishing the threat on his own terms.

He did just this with Homer, at first denigrating him as a lover, "a fairly crude guy, building roads." He felt Homer's name meant, "You're supposed to picture some of the worst of the people that came down, very simple, very lower class, very much beneath Miss Emily's former station . . . the ignorance of the poor boy from the country." He tended to reduce Homer's sexuality: "She has sort of a lover in this Northerner." Barron, he took to mean "Barren, you know, the thing about having no possibility of creating something that will work."

Gradually, however, toward the end of the interview, he began to admit a tenderer Homer, one central enough to be the rationale for the story's title. " 'A Rose for Emily' could represent either Homer Barron himself as a lover for Emily or his attentions to her in the sense that a rose can be symbolic of all

the gifts and attentions that he had paid her." A curious reading, I thought, for the story seemed to show Homer callously
using Emily. Shep went on to make Homer into a thing by
suggesting that the dead Homer was a monument to Emily.

At first, he would not say there was a marriage "certified by
any civil or religious people, in which she lived as a wife and
. . . he treated her as a husband [sic]." But, he said, "She
would have had to—in her own mind—decide that they were
. . . married, in order to even get into bed with him." And by
the end of the interview, he was saying, "She did marry him.
She changed her name to Barron."

What had happened midway was his sexualizing of Homer.
Perhaps somewhat annoyed at me for asking him to infer mo-
tives about which the text was silent, Shep invented a conversation between Emily and her lover to explain Homer's going
away and coming back just before the murder:

> Maybe he wanted to go off and said he was visiting his folks,
> but she knew his parents had been dead for twenty-five
> years. . . . She knew also that he had this, this woman in this
> other town. He says, "I want to go up to Memphis to visit
> my people." She'd say, "Your people live in Illinois." He'd
> say, "No, they're coming down to Memphis." She'd say,
> "Who are they staying with—that woman up there?" And
> he'd say, "No, it's my parents," and leaves and comes back
> and says, "Wow! Had a great time with my parents," and
> she decides to let him back in just long enough to do him up
> right. Maybe even says that she wants to live with him as
> man and wife, and he gets hip to what's going on. He
> wouldn't mind a little more of that. . . . But that's all
> hypothetical.

In effect, just as Shep himself had made Emily's father aggressive, he also made Homer sexual—after he had denied the
story's versions of those threatening traits. Shep tended, at
first, to weaken Emily, to deny her the mythic, heroic role
derived by some of the story's critics (Brooks and Warren, for
example). "In a way, Miss Emily is a descendant of the culture
hero, except that she's a descendant of the culture hero in his
waning phase." Earlier, he had used that word, "descendant":

"She was her father's descendant, the end of the [line]," "a woman of the old order of the South," who had to be protected by dead forms and formalities like the edict. "The generous gesture . . . of the remission of the taxes—it's a way of denying the fact that taxes could be a burden on Miss Emily."

Also weakening her (and also in line with his pleasure in merging past and present), Shep said he saw Emily in "several coexistent images. I can see her as a very good-looking dark-haired girl who had a penchant for wearing dark clothes." The only picture we get of the young Emily, though, shows her in white—I am reminded not only of Shep's countering the tableau but also of his complicated associations to themes of blackness, particularly sexual desires between black and white people. "And I can see her," he went on, disposing of her by means of time now, "as a middle-aged woman beginning to get sloppy around the edges, and her hair is gray, and beginning to become increasingly isolated from the people around her because hers is a different life pattern. Then I can see her as that last image that the townspeople see her as, the short, squatty, screwed-up, dark-haired woman." Again, Shep seems to have made a slip: when middle-aged, her hair was gray; now, old, her hair is dark.

Shep, however, ignored the slip and began to nag at the question "How did she get short from being relatively tall?" (another way of weakening her). And yet another: "I don't think of her as being womanly," he said. "I think of her as being ladylike." "Feminine, in that she is nice and ladylike . . . but not female in that she doesn't realize the body aspect of what it means to put down 'Sex: feminine' [e.g., on an application] as opposed to 'Sex: masculine.' "

Later in the interview, however, Shep began to toy with the idea of a stronger Emily. For example, he related the title to a phrase concerning the aldermen trying to collect taxes: "If you read it as in parentheses, 'They (arose for Emily),' it's a sign of social respect to her." Similarly, he emphasized Emily's strength with the druggist (or, more accurately, her obstinacy). "She won't violate the code about 'Never lie,' but on the other hand she won't violate it far enough to treat this man as anything more than he is—her servant. She walks in there. That is

her store, and he's there to get for her what she wants."
Psychoanalysis would trace this kind of obstinate adherence to
codes to a specific source: the child's concern with the rules
about surrendering his body products and the contests that
often spring up as to who will dominate in that situation. Thus,
Shep went on to recall "Mark Rudd's remark about the job of
the [university's] administration is to keep the johns clean. If
the johns are dirty, it's a bad administration."

In this context, Miss Emily's obstinacy resembles that of a
child determined to get and to keep, and so Shep saw her
motive for the murder. "She decided that they got her father,
and they weren't going to get him [Homer]." Shep could accept
revenge against Homer as a motive for the killing, but, he said,
"There is a great deal of flamboyancy added to the thing. She
did it with style. She was no simple murderer, and a simple
murderer would have been concerned only with the revenge
motive."

Shep went so far as to suppose that Emily contrived the
whole affair with Homer to kill him. "It's possible that she
could have done the whole thing from the beginning with the
eye towards seducing him and destroying him." She intention-
ally became a "fallen" woman: "She maybe never would have
stepped down at all if she hadn't intended to destroy him in the
end—but I don't think so." He preferred to think that Emily
decided to kill Homer only when "she felt he was going to
leave." She bought gifts to convince people they were married,
"plotting revenge already." Hence, he decided, Emily bought
the gifts and the nightshirt all as camouflage, a "cover," to
make it appear they were married.

Making Emily so deliberate makes her that much stronger,
particularly as a rebel against established society—the role of
hers that corresponded most closely to Shep's own lifestyle and
his flight-and-fight adaptation. In one respect, however, Shep
needed to limit Miss Emily: he insisted that she could not have
been sleeping by the corpse (even after we had discovered his
mistake about the grayness of the hair on the pillow). "I just
don't see how she could and leave the dust undisturbed, not
from the standpoint of sanitation, but from the standpoint of
physical realities of dust." Yet most critics of the story think

Emily lay by Homer long enough for her hair to turn gray and then stopped long enough for the dust to gather. "Do you think they were making it before that night?" I asked him. "I don't think so," he said, "not the way the room was decorated, 'this room decked and furnished, as for a bridal.' It sounds like it was done as a special occasion and fairly recently." Yet the narrator of the story, the town gossips, and even Shep himself in other contexts, have all decided that at this point "poor Emily" has "fallen" through some hanky-panky in the yellow-wheeled buggy. Shep, however, had assumed that any sexual intercourse must have taken place in the bedroom as part of a murderous act of rebellion against the "new order." In the same way, he had been unable to accept closeness from women in other stories. Not even his strong defenses would enable him to accept sex or nurture from a woman who had not been turned into a "system."

With that one important exception (more important in life than letters), Shep's twinned defenses permitted him to enjoy a variety of fantasy satisfactions from the story. According to our four principles of response, if the reader can create his defenses from the work (as Shep does so richly here), then the reader will go on to project into the work those fantasies that most concern him. Shep was most involved with a matrix that he could merge into or flee from. He both feared and wished nurture from such a matrix, for it threatened—and promised—a total control in which he would lose his own separateness and identity. Such hopes and fears stem from the infant's first taste of the world—quite literally through eating from it. Then his awareness of himself as a separate being comes as he learns he must wait for that world, that other, to come lovingly or threateningly to ease his hunger.

The one thing, then, that Shep could be sure of in Homer's murder was its oral component (although other readers felt less certain as to the eating and drinking involved). About "inward things," Shep found the story indefinite, but

You can conjure up with not too much problem some of the formal things that they must have gone through. She must have asked him to come in to eat dinner so she could get the poison into him somehow, or maybe it was in the drink before they bedded down. Anyway, she offered him this loaded refreshment, and he accepted it and thanked her and . . . that sort of thing fits in just fine because that's what anybody would do in that situation.

Food was a weapon.

So also was speech. Thus, Shep described Miss Emily's confrontation some years later with the men of the town about Colonel Sartoris's remission of her taxes: "And here she meets them verbally and just draws the line and says, 'Don't step over that,' and refuses to let them." As part of his weakening of Homer, Shep did not mention Homer's "big voice," although the story singled it out. The first thing he mentioned about this Negro servant was, however, that he had lost his voice. "Anybody who would forget how to talk because he hadn't had occasion for it is really a first-rate Uncle Tom—which is weird, because Uncle Tom stood up and said, 'Fuck off, you guys,' a lot more strongly than 'an Uncle Tom,' as an epithet, would."

In effect, mixing up a mild Tom and an angry one, both purely metaphoric identities, suggests the anger and destruction Shep could mobilize by being separate and having his own voice. Thus, at many points, he said of Miss Emily things like: "She had so little choice." "There was nothing left for her but the tragic event." And we have seen him feel the opposite: that the Southern tradition could, for all its oppression, provide "some sort of contact between self and environment . . . something that I wish *I* had."

Similarly, when he thought about Faulkner (for he always sought out the person who created the matrix), he found nothing "that enables you to tell whether this is simply a job of good writing or whether it's actually his [Faulkner's] way of perception, his day-to-day experience that it would be impossible for him to write in any other way." That is, was his writing the act of a being totally controlled? Or was it the act of a deliberate, separate other? Reluctantly, Shep settled for the latter. "It's possible that it's something that he's learned, because it's something that seems to go above what he had in

something like *Soldier's Pay* or *Mosquitoes*," which Shep
called "the really sloppy period at the beginning."

The word "sloppy" signals another level of Shep's fantasies,
those associated with the child's messes—his body products
—and the efforts of himself and others to control them. Shep
singled out the problem of Emily's smells. "She has one confrontation with the men of the town about smells coming out of
her house, in which she doesn't even really speak with them.
She sits in the window, watches them do that thing about keeping the town neat, and scorns them for it." In effect, Shep
thought the authority-figures *should* tidy up after Miss Emily's
smells, as university administrators should clean up the toilets.
In this way, he seemed to confuse identities: the dirt is Emily's
or the students', but the fault is the authority's.

Shep's response to the theme of dirt and disorder led him to
a highly idiosyncratic theme for the story. He decided Emily's
purpose in the murder was: "offsetting it ['the social decay that
she realized her time and her people were undergoing'] with the
physical decay of this representative of the new period." As he
described it, she was almost doing sympathetic magic. "Social
decay and physical decay are not that far apart. They're no
further apart than body and body politic."

> She can reverse the social decay process by putting her
> lover, representative of all of them ["the newcomers"]
> through a physical decay process and coming to relish the
> sight. This would also give some sort of, quote, explanation,
> unquote, for her necrophiliac hangups. The fact that she
> wanted her father's body around to . . . preserve it from
> decay—she was denying the end of the line thing symbolized
> by putting it underground and letting the earth have it.

Shep became even more repellent as he expanded his image:
"She's is doing the same thing in social terms that her father's
body is doing underground." "There's this process of putrefaction."

Repeatedly, he referred to Miss Emily in terms of the "end"
or "behind" or leaving something behind. "She knew she was
the end of the line." "The situation had, in a way, been inflated
by her, her lastness, her finality [so] that the only event equal

to it was what she did." "Homer Barron dead [was] kind of a monument behind for her and behind— you know, showing her triumph, monuments being, I suppose, designed to show the triumph against time." "At the beginning, she is a fallen monument." "The monumental aspect of roses [*sic*] is another one." Her own putrefaction, Homer's, and the opposite—the sweet, ephemeral perfume of roses—all make odorous monuments "behind" Miss Emily.

In response to my standard question about Emily's introjecting her father's values, he answered, "She doesn't so much become like her father as she takes over the burden of decay from him. She becomes uglier, shorter . . . shorter in my mind, older (pretty obviously, you gotta do that). You don't have to become quite so drastically ugly as she does, though." "She's . . . not so much a tragic figure as a little, short, squatty, fat, screwed-up woman in a tragic position," and he emphasized, "the short, squatty, screwed-up . . . woman." He, too, was puzzled as to how she got short: "I leave that to the physiologists. I understand that does happen though, that you start losing height as you get older . . . maybe she could get at least several inches shorter."

Although he mused about bones and cartilage bending, it seemed to me that he was really thinking of Miss Emily being shortened and weakened by losing something—ultimately, or in the "end," leaving something behind. At the same time, by seeing her as several inches shorter, squatty, screwed-up, in a tragic position, I thought Shep was introducing still another level of fantasy. A child becomes aware of the differences, particularly in their ability to thrust their wills on the world, between parents and children and men and women, and he fantasies about bigness and the sexual behavior and genitals of grown-ups as the sources of power. He wants to be bigger than they are. Thus, Shep used up-and-down imagery quite generally to describe conflicts in the story: Miss Emily, for example, was "a woman of the old order of the South . . . [who] goes through a series of generally downward-pointing happenstances." "The people with whom she was associated were undergoing this process of decay." She, therefore, was going to "triumph over the social decay," "outliving and triumphing over" the newcomers.

He saw his own interpretations as this kind of being above and penetrating the story: "You could write all sorts of things on top of it, but it doesn't really make it definite." "There are so many open points [in Faulkner's description of the fatal night] that it's hard to conjure up anything . . . definite." "The right explanation" of Emily's giving gifts "would be to make it fit in and function as well as possible." He could imagine the purely formal events of the murder: "That sort of thing fits in just fine." But, "Not having the emotional givens of the situation, I don't think you can fill in a conversation." A common-law marriage, "That sort of 'married,' you know, it might admit." Homer would be "most obvious to work on because he was new to the area and was from the North and obviously an outsider, and here she's offering him an excellent way to get inside in all sorts of ways."

Sensing the marital situation as a getting in, Shep spoke of the sexual act between Emily and Homer as a war or a trap. Her buying the nightshirt was "camouflage," "bought as some sort of cover." The initialed toilet set, for example, "he wouldn't have been too much grabbed by that." As for the murder, "I'm sure she wouldn't have done it to him if he hadn't hacked her off in some way"—and he explained the idiom for me—"caused some sort of an argument . . . dissension." After that quarrel, "She decides to let him back in just long enough to do him up right." To let him bed her, however, she would have had to decide they were "in some way permanently entangled with each other, married." At the end of the interview, on the supposition that Homer died while deflowering Miss Emily, Shep cried with outright glee, "Tremendously symbolic! The old vagina dentata myth rides again!" But, of course, it had been riding, more or less explicitly and consciously, throughout these phallic fantasies.

Shep did not show much, if any, fantasy from the level psychoanalytic criticism has traditionally considered the most important: the oedipal love affair of child, mother, and father, for example, Miss Emily's domination by her father and her own domination of her tabooed lover, the Northern day-laborer. To some extent, he treated Emily as a mother who nurtured the father-aggressor and punished the son-lover. But it was not a major part of his fantasying. That remained pre-oedipal.

Having composed his defenses from the story, and having created fantasies at three unconscious levels, Shep transformed those fantasies by means of the defenses toward a conscious theme. He arrived at his own characteristic transformation of fantasy to theme.

He began with his idea that Emily was performing a kind of sympathetic magic, but failing. "She feels personally that with Homer she managed to offset the decay process around her and, for that matter, within her, as she represents the tradition. . . . she doesn't really do it." "Becoming 'Barron,' she didn't prevail in the way that she thought she had. For her, maybe she went to the grave triumphant, but for everyone else she went to the grave dead. I think that's the judgment that has to be made, after all. Aw, hell—drive through Jefferson, Mississippi, Oxford, Mississippi, and you can see this judgment has to be made."

I felt I was getting a strange, at least idiosyncratic, reading of the story: the killing and keeping of Homer Barron was some sort of planned aggression against the environment—a very different reading from, say, Sam's notion that it was an act of marital fidelity or Saul's that it was a defiant "holdout." Different, yes, but, on second thought, Shep's reading does not differ all that radically from, say, Brooks and Warren's finding a scapegoat in Miss Emily, or the very generally held idea that she is some kind of prototype or exemplar.

In sum, Shep liked the story, and therefore it and he together were acting out his basic pattern of expectations. More critically, he derived formal and structural patterns from the story to match his defenses. Still more exactly, Shep expected to relate to the world as if it were an all-powerful other, source of both nurture and suffocation. One way he dealt with the world so perceived was to flee to a safe distance and attack from there (flight-and-fight), but in talking about "A Rose for Emily" he seemed to apply this strategy against me only, not the story.

Second, he could accept domination by the all-powerful and become a thing, a victim, in a system.

It was this pattern he applied to the story, finding mythic values both in the South and in Faulkner's skillful collapsing of time into a mingled past and present. These, he said, furnished a life-giving "contact" between himself and the environment. Finally, however, they also could entrap and stultify with deadly force.

He therefore brought into play his strategy of flight-and-fight, but not against the whole story. Rather, he defended within the context of his first acceptance of Faulkner's mythic and time-less world. He went through a pattern of first evading, then strengthening Emily's servant Tobe, her father, her lover, and Emily herself. He varied her, for example, from a short, squatty, screwed-up, ladylike victim to a flamboyant, deliberate killer, rebelling against society (although he could not let her lie down close to dead Homer).

Within his two defenses, he projected into the story fantasies rooted in all but the highest developmental issues of childhood. He found in time and in the South a nurturing matrix that fed but totally controlled or destroyed, from which an infant might have to rage himself free. He found fantasies of resisting the controls of others and leaving a smell or a monument behind for those others to clean up (whether they were the parents of his childhood, the town fathers of the story, or the university administrators of his current life). Fantasying from a still later level of development, he thrust his own masculine interpreta-tion down into the open points of the toothed trap—so he characterized Miss Emily and her story—and dominated.

At the most intellectual level of his response, he transformed these fantasies by means of the defenses he fashioned from the story to arrive at a theme or, as he called it, "a judgment that has to be made." He interpreted the story as developing a mythic paradigm: Emily, he thought, put Homer through a magic putrefaction to offset the social, political, and bodily decay around and within her. But she failed, and that was the tragedy.

Finally, then, our four principles close. The transformation of fantasy to theme that Shep created in the story and the deeds of the characters as he saw them worked out his characteristic expectations. Thus he created the external story into a vital inner experience. As Shep himself might have put it, he had found a way of exercising possibilities in the world.

Sebastian

Sebastian had read "A Rose for Emily" as a freshman and liked it very much. Now, however, his final response was negative, at least as compared with his former enthusiasm. " 'A Rose for Emily' comes off more—I don't know the word I want—programmatic, . . . outlined. It seemed more stark than it had seemed in my memory." "There's a discrete ending." "It should be mitigated somehow, the explicitness of it. And it's not a very explicit story, really . . . It tries to save it for the end and be suggestive, but it seemed too strong."

Nevertheless, there were some things Sebastian liked about the story. He could wax rhapsodic over something like a tradition, for example, Sartoris's edict about Negro women and aprons. "In a way, it's a caricature. The thing is that I suspect that there probably were such edicts. I'm sure there were, and worse ones too. That the edict itself was almost a part of Americana. You know, it's thrilling, really, to have such things in this country's past. Past, nothing!" And he went on to muse about chain gangs. "The South seems to be the repository of that authority. Absolute subjection. And it's interesting. I mean very, very interesting, and thrilling again." "Even the rulers have no choice, because they're so completely determined, by the system that they work under," that "so limits choice that anything that departs from the rigidly formal system . . . becomes so unacceptable that in some way violence has to be done."

Yet just this authority or control was what he singled out in the story to dislike, its being "discrete," "concrete," "strong," "programmatic." He preferred a Katherine Anne Porter story ("Flowering Judas") because it was "more suggestive, although 'A Rose for Emily' is fine, too, but the thing is that with a concrete necrophilia, you're working with a—you know," and he broke off. In other words, it was not that Sebastian disliked the story's controlling him, but he wanted that control to be a continuing tradition, a relationship, not a single exchange or a "discrete ending." By comparison with other stories, he said, "This one, being more of a shocker, is so much more lurid that it keeps you outside it."

Again, we can understand his complex reaction in terms of our four basic principles. Where Sebastian responded positively, he was acting out, by means of the story, his own characteristic expectancies toward the world. Specifically, he must have been able to feel the story acting out one of his two related modes of adaptation: it was either allowing him to exchange his own intellectual products for the story's or providing him with a control he could couple himself to in a sexual way, an "absolute subjection" that was "thrilling."

In his first mode, Sebastian needed to project his ideas into the story, and obviously they would not suit every story—or even many. (It is worth noting, I think, that of these five readers, Sebastian was the only one who said he disliked all three of the stories here reported.) Where a reader's projections do not fit easily into a story, he will tend to drive himself away from the story as most people conceive it, creating distortions or tangents. Thus Sebastian romanticized about "Those Southern names . . . Slade. Kincaid. Hunnicutt. All those that have gone into the West." (Or the Western movie anyway.) Sebastian distanced parts of the story he didn't like by turning them into works of art. For example, when Emily stares down the druggist, "it's sort of satisfactory because it's concise . . . Especially cinematically, it's a nice moment." He turned the story into a play by saying, "The story is almost told by a chorus. In fact, it *is* told by a chorus." At various points, he spoke of this "chorus" as dispensing justice, appreciating gallantry, speculating about Miss Emily, and so on. Once they have brought Emily's relatives, "chorus-like, their sympathies switch back to the underdog." "The chorus, meanwhile—more involved than Greek choruses seem to be—switches sides like rooters at a football game."

All his conversions of the story into a work of art combined with his feeling the story was sharply defined to keep him (in Sebastian's own word) "outside." Another way he kept himself outside the story was by his own tendency toward abstract language, his strange circumlocutions in trying to describe particulars as traditions. "There's a consciousness of the valuation of medieval remnants." "The notion of the patriarchal, feudal business was striking." As for the chorus, "They're the modern consciousness faced with the attractiveness and the decomposition of that kind of world, that *Weltanschauung* that Judge Stevens took to his grave." He talked about other characters, too, in this abstract way. Grierson was "the original superego." Homer, he typed as "a Yankee scalawag, labor foreman." "You can't quite fix the generation of the teller because it spanned so many generations." He generalized Emily into simply "the aristocrat." He interpreted the title as Faulkner did: "People have been presenting roses to her all her life as acts of homage . . . I mean, they're not for her exactly, but they're for an abstraction, too, that she living represents." He also abstracted from Miss Emily's black servant Tobe, accepting the story's term "nigger," as did the other readers, but with an especially studied indifference. "It's not an abrasive use of 'nigger' at all, because we know that the chorus only thinks in terms of 'niggers.' It's not really a term of disparagement . . . It's just a description. I mean, it's just a word. It's a noun of no—at least for them—no particular opprobrium. That is, you're just describing, uh, 'niggers,' part of the landscape," as he said the Negro women (whom he thought sexually victimized by Sartoris's edict that they wear aprons) were an "integral part" in "a landscape."

In short, by a variety of techniques, Sebastian took himself (or people in the story) out of and away from it by means of his own intellectualizing. He made them into artifacts of an ancestral tradition. In his other mode, Sebastian moved in just the opposite direction. He tried to draw himself close to and into a controlling force by making it tender and loving (and also his sexual imaginings could serve as his own productions to supplant the story's). Thus, he responded with a set of sexual theories extraordinary even for this rather kinky story. By contrast with, say, Sam, who was "reluctant" to admit any sexuality, Sebastian said casually, "I think they were having an affair." He seemed to see Miss Emily using her sexuality on the druggist: "Sexuality is involved in her resistance to modernism or, if not modernism, legalism." Unlike the other subjects, he visualized Miss Emily with Homer's body (using an unconscious pun). "As far as the necrophilia goes, I wonder how far it really extends. I mean, obviously, there's the physical limitations of that particular combination." I asked him to explain. "Well, it's possible for a male to perform an act of complete necrophilia on a dead female, but it's impossible the other way around. So there has to be an element more of fantasy for her involved, too. But there obviously is, you know, some physicality. I think she's probably been sleeping with the corpse a long time."

Sebastian responded to Colonel Sartoris's edict about aprons in the same sexualized way. "I react to the term 'fathered' the edict," he said. (Saul, the other obsessional personality, also singled out this word—see above, pp. 151–52.) "That was a strange phrase to use," Sebastian went on. "Fathering the edict seems to, you know, in some way be fathering the women, to be fathering that state of affairs. So it implied for me the sexual—well [and he laughed]—intercourse that took place between whites and Negroes."

Still more unusual was what he said about Emily's keeping her father's body for three days. "I began to wonder, what about the father? I mean, if Homer Barron was fair game later— Even though I doubt that there was necrophilia at that point . . . that reaction flitted through in my mind." "You mean she had a necrophilic relation with her father?" I asked. "Well," he said, "if not physically enacted, even so far as the one with Homer, at least the fact that she was maintaining a corpse . . . as if it were alive. It's there. I mean that, I think, in a way qualifies it as necrophilia." Perhaps the word had by this time lost its genital sense for him.

Even so, I was startled to hear him comment on the Negro: "He has to be in some way perpetrating her ends. He was an accomplice all the way, and he never deserts her, and he obviously knows what's going on in the house, since he's the only person other than herself who gets into the house the last part of her life." He turned to abstraction. "The role of the Negro as sexual accomplice in the South," he mused. "It's just a thought, but it was, you know, part of it. I mean, because he's originally presented as being somewhat attractive, young, and vital.'' In fact, the text actually says, ''The only sign of life about the place was the Negro man—a young man then—going in and out with a market basket.'' The one other time Sebastian used the word ''vital'' was in describing the outpouring of Miss Emily's memories: ''The one vital thing in her life . . . was the affair with Barron.''

In effect, Sebastian was setting up sexual relationships for Emily. I asked him, ''What would Emily be like if you met her?'' ''Could you describe her?'' ''Vulnerable,'' was the first thing he said, ''but only to a prolonged and sensitive siege. That is, to meet her, I take it in the terms of really meeting her, which is to get her to let down her defenses, to let you inside her house, the same house physically that she's been keeping people out of.'' ''She knows that she's weird and getting weirder. That's why I say she's vulnerable, but there would be that embattled aristocratic veneer, which is more than a veneer—it's an armor plate that would be very tough to crack.''

Without some such sexual relation to Emily, Sebastian found he could not like the story. ''How do you feel toward Emily?'' I asked him. ''Unsympathetic,'' he bluntly said, ''and the reason for it is because of the opening description . . . 'What would normally be simply plumpness was in her obesity.' The physical picture is so unattractive that it casts a pall over what is really a sad story.'' ''We see her in her most unattractive phase, and so I'm out of sympathy with even the phase of attractiveness, where her face was like a strained flag,'' and, one should add, where she was buying poison. Every woman's most becoming moment? ''In the situation with the druggist she still had her sexuality going for her. She was still attractive and . . . her vitality in that case, her slimness was to her advantage, and so I liked her, as she faced the druggist.'' ''I was compelled to admire the *young* woman. She could get away with it. The old woman gets away with it, too, but since . . . [I] can't transfuse sexuality into it . . . I'm just unwilling to go along with it.''

As Sebastian's word ''compelled'' suggests, much of his

sexualizing of the story is aimed at its traditional or parental authorities and controllers. For instance, he described her father "with a horsewhip, beating off" (in one phrasing) "suitable sexual partners." The sexuality in such fatherliness shows in what Sebastian called Grierson's fierce insistence on her "unspotted virginity of demeanor."

Sebastian's own sexualizing of authority pervaded the way he thought the townspeople felt toward the aristocrats' authority. "They respond first to the aristocracy, to the notion of Grierson family superiority. They tend to resent it. At the same time, they tend to accept it." Similarly, "There's a consciousness of the valuation of medieval remnants, Judge Stevens, Colonel Sartoris. The kind of gallantry that they'd indulge in is still appreciated and very much by the townspeople." Later phrasings—Miss Emily as "feudal daughter," her resistance to tax collection as "feudalism"—link medievalism to sternness and authority. "The notion of the patriarchal, feudal business was striking," he said, effectively bringing these ideas into a cluster: parenthood, patriarchy, and superego (with a horsewhip); total, sadistic control; medieval and feudal gallantry, romance, and sex. And, I suppose, among the "medieval remnants" must have been Sebastian's childhood Catholicism.

Thus, Sebastian partially matched one of his two adaptive strategies. Although the story did not provide a receptacle for his own intellectual products, he could find in it a picture of continuing sexual control. Given this match, we would then expect Sebastian to go on and put into the story a fantasy that matched the early drives and early relations to others that mattered to him.

As we have seen, Sebastian concerned himself with intellectual and verbal products that seemed to him to derive originally from body products. He was much occupied with questions of control and the mutual giving of these creations from within the self. From a merely clinical point of view, one would expect Sebastian to see in this story a fantasy of violations of authority by means of dirt, smells, stains, and the like, and of compliances with authority by obedience to rule or by paying out money or other precious goods. Again, from a purely clinical point of view, one would expect him to see that authority as

rather sadistic. Someone like Sebastian might also be concerned with the story's ending and with things in "back," according to Jones's and Abraham's classic descriptions of this
personality type (as including a "tendency to be occupied with
the reverse side of various things and situations" or "marked
curiosity about the opposite or back side of objects and
places").[1] Much of this we have seen already in the partial
meshing of Sebastian's adaptive patterns with the story's.
Now, however, we see his response more from the point of
view of his drives for pleasure.

Thus, more than the other readers, Sebastian spoke of the
smells in the story, intensifying them with gamy descriptions.
"She's probably been sleeping with the corpse a long time and
that," he said laughingly, "gives a certain pungency to Judge
Stevens's remark, 'You can't go up and tell a lady that she
stinks to her face.' " "It's pretty ripe." His concern with
smells worked creatively for him. That is, he achieved an insight no other of these five readers did. The title, he decided,
was "almost unforgivable irony in one sense: 'A rose by any
other name would not smell half as sweet.' There's not much
sweetness about *her* rose. So I think the title refers to the
decomposition of living matter, and so I take it ironically."
That is, reversed, as he had himself reversed the quotation
from *Romeo and Juliet*.

Not sweetness, however, but decay was Sebastian's theme.
"She's sleeping with it while it's decomposing," he said. He
extended the theme of rottenness from Emily to the townspeople, whom he made sadistic. "There's a satisfaction in her
decomposition, a maliciousness that suggests that they, too, are
part of the general decomposition of the town." Not only the
town, but the entire way of life Miss Emily represents "embodies that kind of decay. It *is* decay. It was decay from the
beginning. It was decayed in 1500."

In this vein, as we have seen, Sebastian responded strongly—and somewhat negatively—to the "dirty secret" quality
he felt in this story, its (in his phrase) "discrete ending." "It
tries to save it for the end and be suggestive, but it seemed
too strong after the . . . other story." These words—"end"
and "ending," "discrete" (or "discreet"?), "strong"—all

took on extra meaning for me from Sebastian's concern with inner products. "Because of the end, everything in the beginning has to be colored by suspicion." Sebastian turned other things backward, too, like the quotation from Shakespeare or his contradiction in terming Homer a "Yankee scalawag" (scalawags being Southerners who sympathized with the North) or saying the town "switches sides like rooters at a football game" when rooters are precisely those people who would rather fight than switch.

These are only trends, however. At least twice during this interview Sebastian developed more complete fantasies treating Emily in terms of the body's output. In general, he spoke of her in his own distinctive metaphors. "She's carrying around such a great weight of perversity . . . she's been strained." He found her a bit attractive "where her face was like a strained flag. It's poignant, but it just doesn't carry the day, so I don't like her." "If she sensed your sympathy, she might relax, but what the relaxation would involve, I don't even dare to think about [and we both laughed]. The outpouring, I think, would be dreary." He generalized from Emily (and generalization, we have seen, was a characteristic way Sebastian created "products" of his own): "Even though I don't like *her*, I can feel more sympathetic with other old ladies because the story does serve the purpose of distilling the odium that's connected with her, with all old ladies with memorabilia." (As so often with Sebastian, his choice of words seemed just odd enough to make me wonder if he did not take "odium" for some variant of "odor.")

Paying out money served as another image Sebastian associated with Emily. Thus, when she refuses to pay taxes, she shows "she can stymie that basic a function of collective civilization." Alternatively, "She's already paid her taxes to that town plenty of times. The taxes she paid weren't in money, of course, but they've gotten their taxes out of her, and they're still getting it [*sic*] just in terms of conversation. She's providing a wealth of material for that town."

This was one major mode in which Sebastian saw Emily, as someone closely watched by various authority-figures—like her father or the townspeople—to see if she had something inside, which had to be either found out, forced out, or concealed.

This led to Sebastian's wording of Miss Emily's refusal to let them take her dead father out of her house. "When it becomes obvious that *hauteur* is not going to work, that is, there are certain things that the moderns, that the tax collectors and the druggists will not stand for, and one of them is that stink or even the possibility of such a stink, she does break down." One recalls Dr. Spock's description of children's fears about parental rules during toilet training forcing away a precious part of the body. Emily's dirty thing had to be forced out and taken away.

Accordingly, shame played an important role in Sebastian's version of the story. "She takes up with Homer Barron very publicly, riding around in a yellow, spoke-wheeled buggy, disgracing herself in the eyes of the townspeople." Both Sam and (as we shall see) Sandra found Emily's motive for murder in her wish to keep Homer, in a sense to marry him; Sebastian, however, decided she was driven by shame. They weren't married and he wouldn't marry her, and that was "the only reason she would have killed him." "The reason the lover has to be killed appears tied up largely with the relation between . . . the community and herself. That is, she can't abide this disgrace." Yet Sebastian himself realized a weakness in this reasoning. "That's something that I really haven't thought through. . . . In effect, he does go away. As long as he's out of sight, and she's stuck in the town, then it seems that outwardly conditions are the same," as if she were disgraced. But Sebastian could not take the further step and say that Miss Emily, because she was a Grierson, simply didn't give a damn what the rest of the town thought. Sebastian's attitudes toward authority were too complicated for that, and he attributed to her a tendency to cringe and hide.

In a manner typical of shame ethics, she could deal with the authorities by concealing the dirty secret. Thus, he said, the relationship between Emily and her father was "bound, probably, very much by prescribed forms." "As long as she'll maintain this pose of respectability, he'll be able to do the same thing. The fantasy *has* to be maintained." But why did he see this as a "pose" or a "fantasy" or mere outward behavior? There is not the slightest hint of unmaidenly conduct on Miss Emily's part until after Homer's appearance. Sebastian was the one supplying the inner dirtiness.

Because of his own psyche, Sebastian could supply a sensitive account of the way such a quirky conscience, which will tolerate murder but not jilting, develops from a parent's insistence on the appearance of perfect behavior. "When that state of affairs is threatened, his violence will show itself, and it upsets the applecart." Loss of control leads to spills that are like violence. When a child adopts that style of self-control himself, the threat of violence persists. "It's . . . probably much more his [Grierson's] obsession to begin with than hers, but once he's gone, that superego control is magnified, and so it's her obsession now." In effect, Emily's father put something of himself in her, a sense of shame so exaggerated that it motivates even murder. And finally that inner shame and violence leaked out at the end of the story.

Sebastian developed another fantasy along the same lines, this having to do with the black servant Tobe and the idea that Miss Emily's house is like her body. Tobe disappeared after Emily's death. "When they walk into the house, he walks out the back door and disappears." He generalized, "Those Faulkner servants, lower caste Southerners, who just disappear when a state of affairs comes to an end by the onrush of modernity. They just walk out back and that's *it,* y'know. Into the wilderness or into— someplace." He seemed to be attributing this going "out back" simply to a habit of Faulkner's writing, which seemed odd to me. Mindful of the South, I suggested, "He might have thought he'd get in some trouble when they found the body upstairs, because he would have been an accomplice, as you point out." (Indeed, Sebastian thought Tobe specifically a sexual accomplice.) "Somehow," he replied, "I never thought of that when he left." He simply felt the chorus dispensed justice so casually and since Miss Emily was able to "stymie" the tax collectors, "then it seems that the Negro could be forgiven or ignored, because he is so much a part of the background, yet is so essential a part, that somehow I think they would let him go. I don't think any effort would ever be made to look for him. He would just disappear." Something black, lower caste, forced out the back into "someplace" to disappear in the wilderness when affairs come in an onrush to

an end—I think we have come to the unconscious fantasy
Sebastian found and created in this story. For Sebastian, "A
Rose for Emily" dealt with a fantasy about putting something
loved and dirty into a body and taking it out by violence or
shame or just the pressure of time.

Our four principles of response say that, to the extent Sebastian responded favorably to the story, he had made from
it his own strategies for coping with life, and he had projected
into the story a fantasy or cluster of wishes from his preferred
level of drive. Now, this fantasy, according to the principle
of "characteristic transformation," he transformed toward a
theme or "point" to the story. I did not want to turn our
interview, designed to elicit free associations, into an exercise
in literary interpretation, and so I did not question him closely
about themes. He did, however, volunteer a rejection of what I
took to be the central moral idea of the story ("With nothing
left, she would have to cling to that which had robbed her"):
"It's a sensitive enough thing," said Sebastian, "but my immediate reaction was to reject it. I said, 'That's too bad.
Shouldn't have put that in, Bill.' "

Of the four themes developed for this story in Chapter 2,
Sebastian ignored one, the mythic, misquoted another ("We
always wind up holding onto the thing that denied us") in order
to reject it, but he endorsed the third, the social theme that pits
Southern tradition against Northern change. "I knew that he
[Faulkner] was a Southern writer, and so I was ready for all
sociological references. I wanted to see an insider talking about
it [sic]. I wanted to see what unconscious things he would
reveal about the South." At least, this had been Sebastian's
"theme" as a freshman. Now, he seemed to find a "point" for
the story in the idea of "decay," "a woman victimized by a
tradition she had no control over," which itself "embodies that
kind of decay."

Notice that, having partially matched his adaptive strategies,
Sebastian did not feel the need of a theme at all severely. And
he contradicted himself easily and frequently without much caring. He would complain about the "absolute subjection" but
find it "thrilling" at the same time. He would call "naive" and
"common" something as bizarre as Miss Emily's keeping her

father's body. He would speak of similarities between Homer
and Mr. Grierson, then decide Homer was everything Grierson
was not. Sometimes he would sexualize characters (like Sartoris or Tobe); then he would see them as types and abstractions. He could sexualize much of the story, but he could not
"transfuse sexuality" into Miss Emily when she was old. On
the other hand, this lack did not pose an insuperable bar to his
enjoyment. He could still sexualize the edict, the "thrilling"
subjection by Southern authority, the Negroes, and so on.

It was only to this limited extent, however, that he could
match his adaptive strategies, and only, therefore, to that limited extent did he enjoy the story. He did not find a match for
his other defensive maneuver (substituting or exchanging his
own productions for those the story gave him). Indeed, he
felt the story overcontrolled. To the extent, however, that he
could find a controlling authority "thrilling," he developed a
fantasy of that authority coercing something loved and dirty
out of a body; he transformed this fantasy into a theme of
decay by controllers and controlled, each with his dirty secrets. As "expectancy enacted," Sebastian was substituting
some authority-figure's grandiose, historical, traditional, sociological "dirt" for the physical dirt and smells the story was
giving him through its "ending."

But "It didn't seem as rich as it had the first time I read it."
The change from Sebastian's freshman reading shows the role
of so-called "higher" ego functions in literary response—here,
his maturing in political and literary ways. The need for authority persisted, because that is deep in Sebastian's lifestyle, but
the particular authority that would satisfy his need—that was
open to change. As for Southern aristocracy, he said, "I'm just
too modern or wishy-washy or removed from it to really like it
anymore. I'm too far from the aristocratic thing myself to stand
for it. I just don't like it. It's too right-wing." Almost reluctantly, he sided with the newer generation, although he saw it
as part of the "general decomposition of the town," that they
abraded Miss Emily's medievalism. The druggist "was just
doing his job." Even the "town clerks" (notice that the story
speak of "the Board of Aldermen," "the city authorities"),
"they have their job to do. They're limited, but I don't buy the

implication that one simply looks down druggists." He still
needed to feel that people were governed by authorities and
had their "job" to do, but the adult no longer romanced about
aristocracy as the adolescent had.

Sandra

She liked the story "very much," she said. "I admire so much
the way it all hangs together." "I would read it again because
every time I read it, I find something else that's more interesting in it. . . . It's got that much in it for me as a piece of
literature, besides having a strong impact."

Evidently, then, to judge from her enthusiasm, Sandra's
adaptive processes had found their match in the story. She had
two defensive or adaptive modes. Which one came into action
depended heavily on what she saw. If what she saw was
threatening, she took steps not to see it any more: physical
avoidance, blocking or denial of perceptions, repression, emotional insulation, or other ways to "unsee." If, however, what
she saw was promising, she tried to see more of it, to come
closer, and to touch and participate in it as a source of strength
or nurture. She wanted an equalizing exchange, a flow of power
or sustenance from older to younger, parent to child, man to
woman, stronger to weaker, and so on.

One begins to study the dynamics of Sandra's response, then,
in terms of sight. In talking about the story, she often used
images of vision for knowledge or understanding: "I wouldn't
see any reason for . . ." "I wouldn't see any point in doing
that." She told the episode with the druggist almost entirely in
images of seeing:

> He's afraid to even see her again after questioning her. . . . I
> can picture the kind of person in a scene like that. I would
> place myself over opposite her and imagine . . . looking at
> her over a counter and seeing her face. I don't see . . . the
> druggist at all, which is not really the important part. I think
> you're supposed to see the way *she* would look.

It is worth remarking, I think, that she does not wish to look at
the actual overpowering.

Sandra managed not to see in other situations with overtones of robbery or deficiency. "As he says, the remains [of Homer] were in a posture of embrace . . . which I didn't even notice until this time." In talking about the rose-colored room at the end, "I kind of liked . . . the rose whole idea," she said, a curious inversion, perhaps connected to the fact that although she had read the story several times before and had even done a little paper on it, she had, she said, "never really thought about the title."

Throughout this interview, as in her others, Sandra repeatedly interjected a sense of uncertainty. She spoke much more than she needed to in terms of "I think," "probably," "maybe," "perhaps," and so on. She used sentences like "I'm not saying she was schizophrenic or anything, but . . ." She began her reply to one of my questions by saying, "That would be the absolute answer," but she finished with, "It's certainly not to be dismissed as a possibility." She ended her puzzlement about Homer's death with, "That's what I think happened. You know—you have to think something," as though she wouldn't if she didn't have to.

In a mannerism we have seen before, Sandra would turn from coercive events in the story to another reality. For example, in talking about what I think is the key line of the story ("With nothing left, she would have to cling to that which had robbed her, as people will"), Sandra said "I didn't pause and muse over that for a long time, but when I did stop and think, it didn't occur to me right away that I could think of any case where somebody did cling to 'that which had robbed her.' And what robs you except for a person, I suppose?" She went outside the story to interpret the edict requiring aprons on Negro women as "something like making Jews wear a star."

She would take the interview situation as another reality to play against the story as, for example, in the pleasantry with which she began this interview. I asked her how she felt toward Emily. "You mean, like if I really met her?" she asked. "Well, of course, she didn't meet people so I suppose that's not really right to think of it that way." After having had some trouble remembering something, she sighed in relief: "I'm glad that came to me, because you were probably starting to think I was

a little off." Again, when I asked about her feelings toward
Emily, she replied, "I always forget to think about these
things." Sandra's unseeings seemed to ward off sights relating
to loss or deficiency and they had the secondary effect of creating momentary deficiencies in Sandra herself, brief helpless-
nesses, appealing and charming, that might elicit support from
someone else.

They lead us to her other adaptive mode: the wish to balance
off deficiencies. Sandra mentioned that she had written a paper
on this story for an English class—the subject could hardly
have been more appropriate for so visual a person: "Color
imagery is used really effectively: and this is what I had written
about when I was a freshman." "It's really fascinating, and I
enjoyed even looking at it again," she said, as she went on to
develop her visual thesis. "Any color that's even mentioned is
. . . either a metallic color, like gold or silver, which is usually tarnished, or a very pale . . . off-white, a faded color,
or a yellow." "The only yellow talked about is on the carriage wheels and on his glove when he [Homer] holds the
reins." So far, so "objective," but then Sandra added her subjective view: "Even that yellow I picture as more of a jaundice color than the lemon yellow or something pretty." "You
wouldn't imagine that it was probably a real bright yellow."
This was precisely the way she had muted the colors in the
Rorschach cards.

In general, Sandra got into the story in this equalizing,
balancing way, by seeing, but sight was only a first step, touch
its natural second. Thus, in talking about Emily's staring down
the druggist: "I can see, I can feel," how it would be. "When
she said 'No,' there was no question about it. The next step
would be physical force and you just wouldn't . . . touch this
person." Similarly, "with the aldermen, their next thing . . .
would have to be an *arrest* or something, and that is just *known*
to be out of the question."

These contexts make Miss Emily forbidding and the touches
hostile, but they were not always so in Sandra's mind. After
her father's death, Miss Emily had "become hardened" because she lacked "a beneficial kind of social contact." Evidently, "contact" could soothe and ease, as in Sandra's own

reactions to the story. She could speak of various elements as "a great little touch," "a beautiful touch," or the whole story's "having a strong impact," "a fantastic impact."

When Sandra talked about the persons of the story, she balanced and equalized them, making people stronger and weaker, better and worse, kinder and crueler so as to avoid unequal contests. For example, she made a protective figure out of the narrator, although Professors Kempton and Sullivan, two professional critics who have studied that character in detail, say that he is very vague indeed: the reader does not know the narrator's age, sex, or role, and he, in turn, seems to know only the most superficial and widely shared anecdotes about Miss Emily.[2] Even so, as my choice of pronouns above suggests, I find it difficult not to speak of him in the masculine singular, although *he* always calls himself "we." Sandra managed, for part of the interview, to keep up his plurality. "They talk about her hair turning gray." "They said they always had this picture of him standing . . ." "Once where they say, 'We always thought of him as a picture.' "

That picture must have been a turning-point to Sandra, for her plural applies correctly to the narrator, but the singular is incorrect for the picture itself: "We had long thought of *them* as a tableau," says the story, describing Emily dominated by her whip-wielding father. After talking about the tableau, however, she made the narrator singular in all senses. "He's really quite the perfect kind of narrator for this story." "I think it's almost definite that he's a man. He speaks about what 'the ladies' say, and he knows more than the usual townsperson." He also speaks about what "the men" think and do, and it is not clear that he knows more than the others; but, for Sandra, he took on the qualities of an omniscient narrator. "I think he knows everything that would be said in the town, but he knows a few things I'm almost sure he couldn't have known about her."

Sandra added still another dimension to this vague, plural being: "He's extremely sensitive, and he's got an amazing perception of why people act the way they do, why the townspeople are happy if she's being married or happy if she's getting her come-uppance, and he makes this little psychological conclusion on Emily, too—why she kept her father's body." Yet, when I asked her about that line, "We knew that with nothing left, she would have to cling to that which had robbed her, as people will," she hedged: "I don't really think that everybody knew in just those many terms. He knew, and he probably knew that most of the people sensed— But I'm certain he's much more perceptive than his fellow townspeople, really." Sandra had, in effect, created a narrator of vision, who saw the way she did, a man who could be wise and supportive but not overpowering.

Miss Emily's father proved harder to equalize. Sandra dealt with him by blotting him out as a person. "I admire the way he works in the story," she said when I joked with her about how much she disliked him. "That's one thing. As a person, no, no, certainly not!" In an odd description of his harshest deed, she simply eliminated him, speaking of Miss Emily's "having had so many suitors forcefully rejected from her." Yet this way of dealing with a strength that threatened to overpower her had its adaptive side, too. Because she needed to contain and limit this tyrannical force, Sandra was able to see a feature not even the professional critics pointed out:

> It's amazing the way that it's presented. He's never flesh and blood. He's talked about as a silhouette one time. He's talked about twice as a face in a crayon portrait, which is, again, that pallid color, waxy, deathlike hue. Where they say, "We always thought of him as a picture," I think he's wearing black. Well, he's really an ominous presence. His face is there looking down at her from the crayon portrait when she's on her deathbed, I believe, and that's really chilling, very effective.

In the same vein, tending to match Emily a bit more evenly with her adversary, she imaged his "spraddled silhouette" as "standing, you know, sitting in the door with a whip in his hand."

Similarly, she reduced Sartoris's cruel edict about aprons on Negro women: "I smiled a little bit, sardonically, I'm sure, because it's a great little touch of ironic humor. I think Faulkner meant it that way, and I think [of] the voice in the story as meaning it that way. Proclaiming it. 'He who fathered the edict.' Using these heroic terms to describe such a petty and obvious extension of bigotry.'"* She took this phrasing to be the narrator's wise irony. "I smiled but not with—I'm trying to think of the levels of humor here—not with mirth. A little bit—I don't mean bitterly or even sardonically, but just — I smiled almost at the way *he* said it because it was such a perfect undercutting of the heroic Colonel Sartoris." (Imagining the narrator's "undercutting" of "He who fathered" was not, I think, accidental.) She remembered how Sartoris had remitted Emily's taxes—"His expansive good nature, but only to . . . gentle folk of his own class. And if this is—as he singles this out—his most important piece of legislature [*sic*], that's pretty good!" And Sandra not only smiled, she laughed out loud.

Sandra had to equalize Miss Emily's servant, old Tobe, by making him bigger. In the text, he seems scarcely more than a physical object with a "rusty" voice. At first, she had "no personal reaction." "He just fits more with the setting against which she is placed." Then she made him more ominous. "He's a dark presence. He fits in with the whole coloring of the household." Next, a classic symbolism appeared: "It's [a] very strong impression I get of this 'dark presence' sort of, coming in and out the old, dirty, white mansion with his market basket." Then Sandra shifted from the menace of power to the promise of nurture. "As he . . . gets older and shuffling . . . he's really like the chain of life which keeps her going, as remote as she is and as self-sufficient . . . food, I suppose, is really about all he goes out for." Tobe almost seems like an umbilical cord in the image of the chain, and his mistress as "remote" and "self-sufficient" as an unknown baby. Then, from these images of nurturing and feeding, Sandra shifted Tobe into the role of a very weak successor to Miss Emily's father. "It's really a beautiful touch that finally he's a very old man. He finally gets to be about the only communication anybody would have from the outside world if they had the temer-

* Notice that Sandra thought "fathered" a "heroic" word, while Sebastian found it sexual. One cannot take for granted the meanings of even the most basic concepts apart from readers' adaptations of them.

ity to come to the door." He replaced Mr. Grierson, "in the
door with a whip," who "would not let any young man across
the door."

Sandra strengthened Tobe, but Homer, like Mr. Grierson,
she had to weaken. In particular, she did not want him to be a
Lothario.* "You don't see him with any other women, I don't
think, except Emily. He's even described as 'a man's man,'
I think, drinking with the young men, and 'I'm not the marrying kind of man,' and that kind of thing." A movie star occurred
to her, "something out of a musical comedy I'm trying to think
of. . . . He's barrel chested. Um— Howard Keel." In effect,
she had made Homer's "big voice" visual by translating him
into a movie musical.

Even so, she had some trouble visualizing Homer to her
satisfaction, for she somewhat cryptically remarked, "Even
though he . . . probably has fewer lines to describe him; I think
you can see him a little bit. Well, not *see* him, no, because each
one has a pretty vivid enough description and personality. But I
would say that I would be more *drawn* to him." In effect,
Sandra was showing the sequence of her needs to see strength
and thereby to fuse with it. "Drawn to" replaces "see." "I
would be more drawn to him, his open nature, and he's described as always the center of a laughing group." The lover,
the narrator, the servant—she had made each a good man of his
kind so that she and Emily could be "drawn to" them.

Conversely, she felt that Miss Emily's isolation deprived her
of strength (or so I interpret the idiom "cut off"). "Obviously
she wanted to cut herself off." That phrase was hardly the only
symbolism that cropped up in Sandra's language. We have already noted her astonishing inversion, "the rose whole
idea"—an echo, by the way, of something she had said about
Rorschach Card X: "Too many colors. They don't go together.
I'm trying to see the whole." In the story, she linked the symbolic values of rose and room: "I think that the rose is kind of a
large term for . . . all her expectations about that room because
that was like her real . . . bridal chamber." "I suppose its the
one colorful or beautiful—in her own way—kind of thing she

* Contrast Shep's fantasy that he had a mistress in Memphis (above, p.
166).

has," she said. "I didn't think it specifically a flower at all, although it could be." She recognized that it was "faded rose," but recalled a brighter stage. "It works very well against all the other colors," which she had muted. "Yellow," which she made "jaundice" rather than "lemon" or "bright" yellow, "is the most vivid color, if you want to call it that, used at all in the story up until the point of entering the room and seeing the rose colors." "Room" involved symbolism; so did "end." Thus, "The only time the rose is mentioned is at the very end in the colors of the bridal room that they have set aside" [*sic*].

To be sure, merely speaking of the "end" of a story does not demand an interpretation in terms of genital symbolism. However, I recall Sandra's fears in the Fitzgerald story about a man and a woman crushing each other in the "end," and I suggest that one might keep such a possibility in mind. As another example, when she said, "It's got a fantastic impact for me at the end . . . the punch, the ghastly kind of surprise ending of a good thriller story or something," I asked her if she could describe it more (indeed, what I said was, "I know it's a hard thing to talk about"). "Yeah," she replied, "It's awful hard to say. It's just sort of a gasp at the end . . . You, you recoil a little bit, but it's just so perfect." In another context, describing the ending she preferred, "I would rather have her stay up there to the end." "She'd just want to *die* up there." "As soon as you know, you kind of gasp; you kind of say, 'That's perfect!' because it's perfectly horrible," she finished, laughingly.

One need not, but one can, interpret such phrasings as giving the unconscious significance of a genital enclosing or containing to the story, a sexual unity ending in orgasm. We have already heard Sandra say: "It's got that much in it for me as a piece of literature, besides having a strong impact." "There's a lot in it." "I admire so much the way it all hangs together," she said. "The remains were in a posture of embrace . . . which is all the more to add to it." "It's like all those things are tied in together."

Evidently, Sandra's positive response to the story pivoted on things being *in* and *together*, mutually giving. Miss Emily, however, did just the opposite: "She sealed off the top of the house." "She'd sealed off the upstairs." Earlier, Sandra had

said, "Obviously, she wanted to cut herself off." Perhaps
Sandra was describing something in her own life (whatever had
led to her watching so many things) when she visualized Miss
Emily in the tableau, "possibly fearful, but probably more regretful because she's being—they even say, being *robbed* of
something at that point. There would be a great amount . . . of
strain on her face because of her inability really to do anything
except just watch."

Being 'cut off,' Miss Emily became "just a carved-out, hard
figure." I read Sandra the passage comparing Miss Emily to an
idol, a flag, a monument, and she reinterpreted her into a hard,
ungiving, rigid parent, maybe a mother. "I think they convey
some of her *stony*—I see it as a stone kind of idol—a stony
exterior, very rigid, with the same expression all the time." As
a monument, "it doesn't matter so much what she looks
like—it's just what she stands for to the other people in the
town. It's somewhat of a forbidding image." "People may
come to her and look *at* her, and even though they're sent to
learn something from her, you don't get a sense that there's
any real possibility for a return of feeling from the idol to
the—not the worshippers; I don't want to use that word—but
the people who come to look at it."

Seeing is the modality, but as always it was mutual giving
through seeing or touching that Sandra wanted. "Over the
years she's become hardened through the repeated denial of
. . . a beneficial kind of social contact." "At the same time as
being hardened," Miss Emily became "very, very proud,
confident, sure . . . of her own social standing [Sandra had
trouble getting this out], which is an important factor when
she's dealing with . . . the new breed." In fact, she was thinking of "the new breed of city officials who are not the old-line
aristocracy class," yet Sandra was building up a complicated
picture of Emily as combining in herself a rejecting mother and
a refusing child.

By contrast, Emily saw the townspeople of the older generation as sustaining and caring for Miss Emily. "The women go
to call on her when her father dies. . . . And you imagine it's
the women, the mothers that are sending their daughters to the
china-painting, I think." Then, these women resent not being

able to mother Emily. "Their custom is to . . . bring food and
try to do for her after her father's death. . . . And they *resent*
being cut off from being able to do whatever they want, kind of
take care of her."

At the same time, the younger townspeople become like
children resenting a parent-figure who will not be close to them.
"I didn't stop to think about it, but now, I would imagine these
women are mostly like 'new generation' wives or something,
neighbors. I don't see them as too old." Symbolizing the taboo
between child and parent, she said, "There's a social difference
there." Because of the change in the neighborhood, "Now the
people that would be there would not be the kind of people that
lived there when the house was new." "They probably resent
being cut off, and I'm sure they're . . . doing most of the
thinking that Miss Emily probably didn't know, I think they
say, her proper place, because they probably, a lot of them, are
financially much better off. They might keep their property a
lot better too; and here she is, cutting herself off from them for
probably reasons which they can't help but take as snobbish."
Probably? The story says, "Only Miss Emily's house was left,
lifting its stubborn and coquettish decay above the cotton
wagons and the gasoline pumps."

For her, the new generation was being "cut off," and the
answer to that was to see. "Their custom is to . . . bring food,"
but even this, she thought, might mask a visual motive.
"Again, I can't help thinking that . . . they probably would like
to see the house." Sandra responded to the passages drawing a
distinction between men and women: "I think it puts the
women in a—I hate to say—unfavorable—but it's the first word
that comes to mind. I see the women as sort of busybodies.
They're *dying* to see the house and all this. The men . . . have
more *respect* for a fallen monument." For her, seeing was intimately bound up with mutuality between people, either in
feeding or, in the sexual, Elizabethan senses of those words, in
falling and dying.

Touching, for Sandra, came next. In her reading of the story,
touching appeared as Miss Emily's various introjections. That
is, just as she combined in herself rejecting mother and refusing child, a rose and a rigid, standing stone, so she took into

herself—or her house—both Homer and her father. Thus, sleeping with Homer was "just sort of a token gesture, something that she could have maybe on her own terms." Her motive for seducing and killing him was "so nobody else would have him. She would even have him in a way on her own terms—just to keep his body around." At the same time, "the affair with Homer is probably somewhat of an act of defiance. It's all those things, I guess, in together, which would probably argue (if you were looking at it from that kind of angle) for her bringing him right into their house, the house where her father lived and probably would not let any young man across the door." In effect, she was saying, getting close to Homer gave Emily the strength to defy her father.

At the same time, Sandra, among all the five readers, accepted most readily my reading of Emily's motive. "To what extent do you think killing Homer is like something her father might have done?" "Oh, absolutely, I think," she instantly replied. I hope she was not just agreeing with the professor, and she did seem to take to the idea eagerly. "There'd be no question about it, and I never even thought of that. If her father were alive and knew that Homer had gotten as far with her as he did, I think that would be the absolute answer." On her own, she applied this to Emily's mind. "I'm not saying she was schizophrenic or anything, but the father's side of her might just come out and say, 'Look what you've done to me, Homer,' or something and do it that way." In effect, getting close to her father gave her the strength to destroy Homer. She thought of "fathered," remember, as a "heroic" word.

For Sandra, Emily combined in herself old and young, bright and faded, the rose and the stone, the "cut off" and the erect or rigid, mother and child, father and lover, the enclosing and the forbidding woman. Thus, Emily and the entire story came together as introjection: absorbing parts by sight or touch into one's very body so that in the "end" or "whole" of the story all its opposites would be "in together," notably the male and female polarities, so that the strong figures would be weakened (like Grierson and Sartoris) and the weak made strong (Tobe or the narrator). In these terms, we can see why Sandra enjoyed Faulkner's Emily but not Fitzgerald's Judy. Judy was a strong woman who weakened a strong man, but Emily's feminine weakness was compensated by Homer's and her father's masculine strength.

In sum, Sandra responded positively to just about everything in the story. In terms of "expectancy enacted," she must have felt most of the story was acting out her own style of dealing with experience, specifically with her defenses of not seeing or seeing, then touching and becoming part of a center of power and sustenance. The narrator in particular managed "not to see" in Sandra's sense, and at the same time served as a source of strength and insight through whom she could see and feel. Other characters did not fit her defenses so easily, but she was able to weaken the threatening ones and strengthen the supportive ones without alienating herself from the story.

With defenses so matched, Sandra obtained a satisfying fantasy from the story. Not, to be sure, the fantasy that I arrived at, based on themes of possession and control of body products: in short, fantasies from that stage in childhood when the child struggles with his parents over the lawfulness of that within him and the inner and outer pressures to give it up. Rather, Sandra found what concerned her: getting power and sustenance into herself from a strong person she drew close to. Thus, Emily gained power this way, while Tobe, Mr. Grierson, Homer, and the narrator—they were all in her together in language that suggested this union had the same unconscious meaning for her as her idea of a sexual climax.

This is what we have called "characteristic transformation." For example, when Sandra talked about an image like dust, which one would interpret classically in terms of "dirty" body products, she rendered it in terms of amount and exaggerated size: "And when they come in, it's been so dusty that you have the sense that it's, it's so covered with dust that"—and she could scarcely finish—"you don't get the sense that the dust is brushed away at all!" She was transforming a symbol (if you will) for excrement into her own concerns with size and strength and whether the special thing in question is there or "brushed away."

In short, Sandra used the story to create a set of pleasurable unconscious fantasies personal to her. In trying to avoid our interviews becoming tutorial sessions in literary analysis, I did not ask her to formulate a central theme. Even so, her microessay on the story's color imagery showed how "purely" intellectual interpretations transform unconscious wishes. And to judge from her drawing close to the various characters so as to balance off their strengths and weaknesses, she might well have interpreted the story in terms of the incorporative half of the theme developed in Chapter 2. After all, "Putting within yourself and so controlling . . ." does not differ very much at all from Sandra's final verdict, "It's got that much in it for me as a piece of literature."

7 The Terms of Subjectivity

Tableau, Identification, Symbol

This book began with a tiny question that we can now—finally—answer. Confronted with Faulkner's tableau, "Miss Emily a slender figure in white in the background, her father a spraddled silhouette in the foreground, his back to her and clutching a horsewhip, the two of them framed by the back-flung door," five readers came up with five dramatically different readings. Our question was, What is the something in each of their characters that made their perceptions of the tableau differ?

Now, we have seen that is is not one thing, but the entire personality—that "invariant" abstracted from "the infinite sequence of bodily and behavioural transformations during the whole life of the individual"[1]—which I, following Lichtenstein, have been calling the "identity theme" on which the living, creating individual plays out innumerable variations. To look at reading in detail, I have isolated four principles involving defense, drive toward pleasure, characteristic sublimation, and characteristic expectation from other persons. But these four separate entities simply accent different aspects of one basic principle. Each reader takes in what he reads as the raw material from which to create one more variation on his continuing identity theme. *Style re-creates style*, and from this basic principle one can understand a reader's re-creation not only of a total literary work but of a small fragment such as Faulkner's little tableau.

Sam, as we have seen him, hovered between being feminine and masculine, passive and active, or weak and strong. He wanted to be helpless so as to take in supplies of love or admiration from outside; but then, by identifying with the source of those supplies, he would make himself strongly, safely, and separately male. When he re-created the tableau for himself

(see pp. 1-2), he composed a perspective in which, by identifying with the townspeople, he saw a frail, feminine Emily
positioned between her domineering father's legs. At the same
time, he thought both Grierson *and* Emily the possessors of
godlike powers that the townsfolk needed to sidle up to. In
short, Sam saw the tableau through his preferred defense, dealing with a source of threatening male power by identifying with
it. He gratified this passive, childish wish to have power given
to him by closeness to a male source in his picture of the frail
but godlike Emily between her father's legs and his image of
the townspeople sidling up to the lordly Griersons. At the
same time, however, he asserted his own safe separateness by
the long perspective he put between the viewers and Grierson's horsewhip.

Saul sought from the world balanced and defined exchanges,
in which he would not be the one overpowered. Although he
admitted he had at first "forgotten" all but the containing word
"tableau," he managed to like the picture for being "right,"
"nice," "of course." Miss Emily was a Hollywood figure in
white, and he cut Mr. Grierson down to nonthreatening size by
seeing him as "no longer stern and erect." At first the "nasty,
sexual, sadistic" horsewhip conflicted with the containment he
wanted, but then he decided it, like Grierson's posture, suggested his "decline." Containment was completed by the frame
the door, making a "nice device," a "nice emblem."

Shep characteristically evaded human relationships, which
were charged with aggression for him, by polarizing them into
extreme opposites. Typically, he would either exile himself or
he would relate to others by fusing himself to them as victimized things in an impersonal system. He followed out the
pattern by making Faulkner's highly aggressive tableau even
more so. First, he turned it into part of the system defending
"Southern womanhood." Then, he concentrated on a thing,
the horsewhip, suggesting that perhaps "Daddy . . . wouldn't
mind taking a belt at Emily once in a while." Having established one pair of extremes between "outdoors" and "indoors," a "protective image" and sadistic sexuality, he then
went on to express another opposition by giving Miss Emily

"dark clothes," although she is here described as a "slender figure in white."

Sebastian wanted to unite himself with forces of control, to which he would give something verbal or intellectual, hoping to sexualize them and get back something warm, dirty, or erotic. Talking about the tableau, he distanced and typed the characters: Miss Emily was "the aristocrat" and (more intellectually) her father was "the original superego." Having thus established his own terms and controls over the material, he could relate sexually to Mr. Grierson's act of withholding by converting his first word, "suitors," describing young men like himself, to "*suit*able sexual partners."

Sandra sought to avoid depriving situations and to find sources of nurture and strength with which she could exchange and fuse; in doing so, she used seeing or not seeing as her primary sensory mode. She wanted, therefore, to see only situations of balanced strength, not an easy thing to do with this tableau. At first, she put considerable distance between himself and the scene: "They said they always had this picture . . ." She tried to bring Mr. Grierson down to manageable force by changing him from "standing" to "sitting" and "looking *very* cross"—surely a dainty way of referring to a father "with a whip in his hand." Emily would be "standing up," hence somewhat strong, "regretful," rather than "fearful," because "she's being . . . robbed of something." Seeing was the key element in her distress: "There would be a great amount of strain on her face because of her inability to do anything except just watch." That would be the worst thing for someone with Sandra's character structure, to have to watch oneself being robbed of a source of strength or care.

Quod erat demonstrandum. Readers read differently because of their different personalities, and we can understand both the large and the small interactions of a reader with what he reads by relating them to an invariant "identity theme" abstracted from his ego choices. In other words, this holistic approach asks that we go far beyond the psychological terms customarily offered casually by literary critics as explanations of response: the two most common are symbolism and identification.

Identification is a complex concept in psychoanalytic psychology; it has a range of meanings no one of which seems to coincide with what literary people mean by the term. That is, when critics speak of identification they imply an individual or an audience putting itself in the place of a character on the basis either of sympathy for his predicament or a superficial similarity between the character and themselves—salesmen identify with Willy Loman, boys with Huck Finn, and so on. The psychologist, however, sees in identification a permanent change in someone's ego: we all develop by identifying in various ways with others, chiefly parents, and these identifications remain, permanently structuring our egos.

"Identification with X" literally means "making someone the same as X." There was not much of this kind of identification in the responses to "A Rose for Emily." We did hear Sam trying out the role of a "born baby" in an ante-bellum aristocracy. "I just like the order of it all, especially when, in this wishful kind of way we're talking now, I can place myself at . . . any level of that order, which, of course, would be the top." "It's terrible. It's the worst thing. . . . It's inhuman. . . . But I can't help but be charmed by the naïveté, by the total lack of concern that such a position of power places one in." Similarly, we can hear Sandra aligning herself with the druggist in Emily's showdown with him: "I would place myself over opposite her and imagine . . . looking at her over a counter and seeing her face. I don't see . . . the druggist at all, which is not really the important part. I think you're supposed to see the way *she* would look." But when I examine these identifications with the experience of the tableau in mind, I realize that I am not seeing an identification of a fragment of Sam's or Sandra's personality with a fragment of the story. Rather, they are each re–creating a part of the story within their whole style of response: Sam is putting himself into a source of power and admiration; Sandra is watching, warily, a source of strength that may overpower or rob her.

A still more striking illustration of the holistic nature of literary identification occurs in the responses to Hemingway's "The Battler" (see Appendix B). The story deals with the venturing of young Nick Adams. At a hobo camp, he comes upon a punch-drunk fighter, Ad, who threatens him, and Ad's Negro companion, Bugs, who wards off the violence. If literary identifications proceeded from superficial resemblances, one would expect young male readers to identify with the young male adventurer, Nick. Yet not one of the young male readers of this story—not one!—identified with Nick. "I just don't like making it, I guess," said Sebastian of Nick's initiation into manliness. Even Shep, who had traveled around the country just as Nick was doing, dismissed the whole story for not providing an initiation ritual, while Sam felt, "We don't get much into Nick's mind" and seemed (at least jokingly) to identify more with Bugs, his feminized (?) companion. Only Sandra identified with Nick. "I almost can't think of how I feel toward [Ad] without thinking how Nick feels, because it's true of what I'm feeling." Even these brief phrasings, however, tell us that identification was taking place not on the basis of superficial similarity but in terms of the reader's identity theme: Sebastian's need to succeed with his mind; Shep's craving for a system; Sam's wish to be given strength; Sandra's need to get close to sources of strength.

Identification simply does not take place on the basis of surface similarities between reader and literary character. Nothing in this study will support that idea or suggest that superficial resemblances of gender, age, culture, or class (in a Marxist sense, for example) have any important role in and of themselves in response. What counts are the deeper structures of adaptation and lifestyle. To be sure, surface similarities between a reader and a character may indicate a deeper psychological similarity and so may seem to provide a point for identification. Identification as such, however, takes place not because of external likenesses but because of an internal matching of adaptation and defense within a total dynamic of response. We identify when a certain character (or even milieu, as with Sam or Shep) enables us to achieve a close matching of our own defenses within a total re-creation of our psychological processes by means of a literary work. Then we, like Sandra, feel what the character feels. We "identify"—in the literary sense.[2]

Symbolism is another psychoanalytic concept loosely and

lightly (and sometimes heavily) applied to literature. Here again, however, we drastically reduce the explanatory power of psychoanalysis if we treat the symbol as an isolated thing, entire unto itself. Certainly, the horsewhip that Mr. Grierson brandishes as he blocks the door to Emily's suitors looks like an obvious phallic symbol. Miss Emily's house makes an equally obvious and familiar symbol for her body. (Indeed, I relied on this symbolism in my own interpretation of the story in Chapter 2.) Yet not one of our five—six—readers read the story without adapting these symbolic values to his or her own personality. Then what purpose does the familiar kind of symbolic decoding serve that so often substitutes for true psychoanalytic understanding?

I do not mean to say that our readers did not themselves use symbols. On the contrary, I am quite sure that when Sebastian spoke of Miss Emily's black servant as just going "out back" and "into the wilderness or into—someplace" "when a state of affairs comes to an end by the onrush of modernity," he had, probably unconsciously, interpreted Tobe's elimination by a body model of elimination—a defecation. But merely decoding his remark adds little to my understanding of his response to the story.

Often these readers showed symbolisms in their own descriptions, not so much of the story, as of their mode of response. I am thinking of Sam's concerns about his interpretations "standing up" or "keeping up," or Sandra's phrasings about the end of "A Rose for Emily": "just sort of a gasp . . . you recoil a little bit, but it's just so perfect," and so on. Her phrasings would equally well fit an orgasm, his a phallus, but again, simplistic decodings accomplish little. At best, they can serve as first steps toward a richer, more general understanding of Sam's or Sandra's total response. Settling for mere translation from ordinary speech into genital terms simply shuts down further discourse.

Moreover, translation faces a basic confusion. "Orgasm" means something special to each of us, and so do all the other terms a symbolic decoding might introduce. Sandra spoke of "the rose whole idea" in this story, and I interpret this odd inversion (and other things) as meaning that she was unconsciously thinking of a woman's genitals in relation to the story. Later, for example, she spoke about the way things would come together in the story as a "whole." Sebastian, I think, was using the same symbolism quite consciously when he said there's "not much sweetness about *her* rose," but then he went on to talk about smells. Merely to say that the rose or the story "stands for" feminine genitals would blur the deep differences between the two readings.

Consider the statement that Colonel Sartoris "fathered" the edict requiring Negro women to wear aprons on the street. One would think that so basic a word has a fixed meaning, but for Saul, "fathered" became merely "sponsored"—because he needed to tone authorities down. To Sebastian "fathered" meant "fathering the women" in the sexual intercourse between Southern whites and their black victims, for Sebastian wanted to sexualize authority figures. Sandra said "fathered" was a "heroic" word—she wanted to make parents into sources of strength and support, preferably not sexual.

The point is that symbolic readings can never be more than a useful shortcut (and Freud made himself very clear on this when he added the sections on symbolism to *The Interpretation of Dreams*).[3] One ought not to stop at simply decoding symbols, translating them abstractly, like fixed mathematical equations. Rather, psychoanalytic insights into symbolism should lead to a human context and convergence, a total sense of the full meaning of the symbol to some actual person. Only then can they serve in the only way (so Freud tells us) they were meant to serve: as supplements to free association in interpretations from manifest to latent content or surface to deep structure; as meanings of words, objects, or relationships within a context and to some particular person.

Experience with readers, particularly the example of the word "fathered," also makes it possible to refine some of the distinctions that have been absorbed under French influence into recent literary criticism from the pre-1910 linguistic theory of Saussure. I am thinking of the distinction Saussure draws between *langue*, the social collectivity of language, and *parole*, the individual, executive act of speaking or performing language, which is psychological and variable. By contrast, says

Saussure, *langue* is homogeneous, the social side of speech that the individual can never create or modify by himself. It governs the process of audition in which sound images are translated into fixed visual images. Thus, for Saussure, language consists of signs, each one composed of a signifier (*signifiant*) bound to a signified (*signifié*), and these bonds are socially fixed—unalterable.[4]

Our experience with these three hearings of the word "fathered," however, and indeed this whole "experiment" of listening to what people read and hear in stories in terms of their personalities, asks that these Saussurean fixities be opened and flexed. There seems to be no unchanging union of meanings to sound-images (a signified socially bound to a signifier). Rather, each individual, as he hears or reads language, re-creates that relationship through his personal system of defenses by discernible laws that can be set down and whose operation can be observed. For our five readers, audition was not passive and collective, but active and individual, proceeding as the individual accented certain transformations over others when he interpreted surface structure into deep structure in the manner described by Chomsky, Katz, and Fodor.[5] That is, the grammar of a language offers each of its speakers a myriad of transformations with which to form sentences. Each speaker makes up his *parole* or "performance" (in Chomsky's term) by choosing among them. Some, obviously, he will choose simply in order to communicate with other speakers of the language. Others, with which he has more freedom of choice, he will choose so as to express his personality, for example, Faulkner's fondness for relative clause embeddings, Fitzgerald's use of negative prefixes, Arnold's nominalizing of actions, and the like. But we have seen that when people *listen* to language or read it, they accent certain transformations and meanings according to their identity themes. In other words, the principles we have discovered can extend the concept of performance to listening as well as speaking—and so put the individual personality back into psycholinguistics.

These principles of reading also apply to teaching and criticism, although, at first glance, they may seem to swamp us in an overwhelming subjectivity. If each reader responds to even so precise a stimulus as Faulkner's one-sentence tableau or the one word "fathered" according to his own individual personality, then it might seem that no interpretation can claim any authority over others. If there is no way to contrast a good reading with a bad one, there is nothing to teach about literature nor any purpose to literary criticism. There isn't even much point in writing, since the reader, not the writer, creates the literary experience. Or so one might say, if one wished to remain pinioned between two conflicting bodies of evidence: the highly personal way these five readers have read and the fact that people do teach, do write criticism, and do agree with some readings and not with others. The answer to the dilemma is to recognize that the principle we arrive at to understand the dynamics of reading applies to at least four other roles besides that of reader and therefore provides a rationale for understanding our collective relation to literary works.

Teacher, Critic, Author, Audience

To analyze the five readers' readings, I brought to bear four principles, each of which is really only an aspect of one basic principle: *a reader responds to a literary work by assimilating it to his own psychological processes, that is, to his search for successful solutions within his identity theme to the multiple demands, both inner and outer, on his ego.* Now, I can accent different facets of this one basic principle to talk about four different phases of reading. I can consider the identity theme as a kind of mime to think about the way a reader has to make what he reads match his defensive and adaptive capacities, shaping it until it will fit. Alternatively, I can accent the reader's characteristic kinds of pleasure in considering the way, once in, he uses the literary work as a source of pleasure, projecting into it the particular kind of fantasy that unconsciously gratifies him. When he transforms that fantasy to themes that are of particular concern to him, I can use his identity theme to define his characteristic transformations.

Then, in considering his moment-by-moment reading, I can speak of the reader's characteristic expectations, again in terms of his identity theme.

One can also think of these four principles in terms of two broad modalities: taking external reality into and then using it within the ongoing psychological life of the organism. Taking in outside realities, we have seen, involves the ability to give up imaginary satisfactions and really act on one's environment. Hence, it calls for problem-solving thought and a defensive attention to danger. Using what has been taken in, however, is much more primitive, much more a matter of fantasy, immediate gratification, and feelings of omnipotence uncorrected by the external world. One mode is alert and wary, the other relaxed and open to gratification, although both are variations on the basic identity theme through which we take in all external realities.

If we absorb literature like the rest of the outer world, through adaptations that protect gratification in terms of one particular identity theme, then we respond to statements about literature the same way, and you have already seen a number of such reactions in the readers' readings. For example, all the readers more or less automatically equated Miss Emily's South with some sort of ante-bellum image derived from other writings by Faulkner, *Gone with the Wind,* or the movies. In effect, they used statements derived from literature, like any other information they brought to the story, as material for supplementing and consolidating their reactions. A familiar image could be used either to assimilate the South to ideas and stereotypes that had already been absorbed, as Sam and Sebastian did, for example; or in order to reject it as "constrictive benevolence" as Saul did. Either way, the critical idea existed alongside the story in the reader's re-creation of the story.

Sometimes, as when Saul insisted on "precision," a critical standard revealed the reader's defense. In the world of exactions Saul lived in, there had indeed to be precision or he would reject an experience outright. His critical demand, therefore, articulated his defensive pattern, and almost explicitly stated the terms the work would have to meet before he would admit it to his inner self. Finding precision, as he did with Faulkner, he respected it. Not finding precision, as with Fitzgerald, he could reject the work with a kind of moral superiority, as if it had failed to live up to a bargain. Shep did much the same when he demanded "A Rose for Emily" provide a magical system or "The Battler" an initiation ritual. Not finding them, he could dismiss the stories contemptuously. Again, the reader had set down the conditions imposed by his defenses before giving the story much of a chance: Shep needed the magic or ritual to make persons into roles or things within a system.

Most readers are not so readily threatened. Easygoing Sam, for example, liked pretty much everything that came his way—but he did not like "The Battler" because of "critics who tell me that the relationship between Ad and Bugs is essentially homosexual." I felt that throughout our talk about the story, this idea was making him anxious, and toward the end of the interview I gave him an alternative interpretation, that Ad and Bugs are "a pair of rather grotesque and nightmarish parents," Ad supplying the strength and money and Bugs doing the cooking and shopping and nurturing. Sam liked this reading and wondered, "I'm trying to think of why *I* didn't think of that, and I think only of the fact that I do so much of my own cooking." Then, when he realized he also took money from his father, he laughingly said he had "married my father!" But then he went on to say "what I meant, actually, more." "I unfortunately don't have any father-figure that I take money from." "I mean, I wish I had. . . . somebody around here—or perhaps I'd marry the University . . . which is even more fearsome." Yet the very relief implicit in Sam's floundering jokes tells us that the critical interpretation I offered served him as a way of allaying anxiety. Specifically, it said to him that there was a way to nurture and be nurtured without being a homosexual; that he could still keep his boyish masculinity intact; that he could see this in the story and therefore he could be this way himself. The story alone does not yield enough evidence to make me feel I have to choose between the homosexual reading and my familial one. Indeed, I don't think the two readings are really inconsistent. But from Sam's point of view, the familial reading enabled him to deal with a source of anxiety—it enabled him to create a gratifying fantasy from the story through his defensive and adaptive forms, and thus it let the story be a possible source of satisfaction for him.

Criticism can also operate in a more positive way, as in Sandra's discussion of the colors in "A Rose for Emily." I had asked her what she thought or felt about the title, and it was then she reminded me she had written a paper on the "color imagery" in this story. Even so and even having read it several times before, she "never really thought at all about it [the title] until just this afternoon." The idea of writing a paper on the colors in the story and never noticing the rose in the title suggests to me that it meant something special to her. "It's really fascinating, and I enjoyed even looking at it again," as if some wish to look away had to be overcome.

She spelled out her thesis about colors. "Any color that's ever mentioned is . . . either a metallic color, like gold or silver, which is usually tarnished, or a very pale, like an off-white, a faded color, or a yellow," which she pictured as "more of a jaundice color than the lemon yellow or something pretty." "The only time the rose is mentioned is at the very end in the colors of the bridal sort of room that they have set aside [*sic*] and I think that the rose is kind of a large term for all that would have been going on or all her expectations about that room, because that was her . . . bridal chamber. And then rose is mentioned a couple times in the, oh, the draperies, maybe the rug, *faded* rose, of course, at this point, too, and it works very well against all the other colors." Having thus identified the bright rose with Emily's bridal chamber and the faded rose with old Emily, Sandra felt she had coped with the title that earlier she had paid no attention to. "I kind of liked . . . the rose color and the rose whole idea. I didn't think it specifically a flower at all. Although it could be, but I don't think flowers are mentioned at all. [She paused.] So I suppose it's the one [pause] colorful or beautiful—in her own way—kind of thing that she has."

Sandra's comments in general evidenced a concern with what you have that is distinctly your own (often with genital overtones, although here she insists the "rose whole" could not be a flower). She was re-creating the story for herself through that concern and her need to find a source of strength in some inner, private possession, here a strongly colored bridal chamber against a lot of weak colors. I must say, rose is not a strong color in my vocabulary, and I could have pointed out to her that Faulkner himself thought of the rose in the title as a flower. But Sandra's own reading has evidence enough, and it enabled her to consolidate and integrate one part of the story, the title, with her total construction of it. As she said, "This is more a critical—no, it's an emotional thing, too, because it works so well." Indeed, it seems useless to try to separate the two.

Even the sixth, professional reader of "A Rose for Emily" would be hard put to distinguish the two factors. I used a survey of my fellow-professionals' readings to supplement and support my own. I drew on factual information they provided me, for instance, that the narrator refers to himself forty-eight times but always as "we." I drew, too, on total views of the story, for example, to support my idea of denial with other critics' statements that Miss Emily had blurred the distinction between reality and illusion. I enjoyed their discoveries and insights into details, such as the relation of the smell in the story to the couplet—"That which we call a rose . . ."—from *Romeo and Juliet*. I myself brought to bear all kinds of outside knowledge, ranging from general notions about the South to psychoanalytic data that interrelated dirt, smell, forces of control, and those "mute" shoes to mythological lore such as the three colors of the triple goddess as given by Apuleius (a different perception from Sandra's of "faded" colors). And, of course, I omitted a great deal both of my own intellectual stock-in-trade and the accumulation of critical literature around the story.

For both the professional, then, and the amateur, the rule is the same. *Each reader takes in statements about a literary work as he takes in the work itself.* That is, he uses the critics' statements as ways to help achieve and consolidate his own personal synthesis of the story. He absorbs them to the extent he can use them with the story to match his habitual pattern of defenses; he derives fantasy content from them directly or from the story with their help; and he characteristically transforms that fantasy by means of the defenses toward a theme. In short, he uses the critical statements in parallel with the story itself, to achieve a re-creation of his personal style. And it is through statements about literary works that we arrive at a consensus and shared experience of them.

Imagine for a moment a story with a dozen readers, each of whom feels impelled to give a critical account of his response (a situation not unknown in the publish-or-perish atmosphere of the modern American university). These critical statements operate in two ways. In a negative sense, they confront each reader with an accumulation of factual information that he must cope with. He can assimilate some information to the extent it will pass through his characteristic pattern of adaptations. The rest he can simply dismiss—critics do not, after all, write with the same authority as writers of fiction. In a more positive vein, his wish to achieve gratification from the story may support a search through the eleven other readings for particular statements that will aid his individual re-creation of the story. Either way he ends by assimilating some of the others' views in his own way, and he in turn has put forth his own statements about the story, some of which others will assimilate in their own way. And thus a consensus is born, or what looks from outside, as it were, like a consensus: a series of statements about the story all the twelve readers will agree with. But looked at from the inside, each reader still has his own private, personal, and perhaps very idiosyncratic experience that no one else can share or even know.

Thus we come to what could be called, not the "limits" of subjectivity—for subjectivity cannot be limited—but the *terms on which it will take place, through which it will express itself.* That is, each of us experiences a literary work so as to re-create his personal style; this is the first set of terms and they do not change. A second set comes from the objective realities out of which that personal synthesis must be built: certain words applied to Miss Emily in the story, the mention of particular colors, or the psychoanalytic commentary on "strained" facial expression, for example. Paradoxically, these do not impose unchanging conditions on the subjective experience. On the contrary, as our five readers have so abundantly shown, these "objective" realities can be construed, warded off, ignored, or varied in an almost infinite variety—and commonly are. To the extent they are shared by others, however, they represent a sharing of statements about the story that can lead to considerable agreement, like the three closely related interpretations that make up the critical consensus on "A Rose for Emily": just about every critic found the story either a portrait of the South, or a study of denials and controls, or a scapegoat tragedy. Yet a reader might reject any of these readings or any factual information in or out of the story. Only the terms of his identity theme define his subjective response, while "objective " statements must be accommodated to the subjective realities.

Outside criticism achieves its greatest force, I think, when one goes to the theater to see a play or a film. There you meet, not verbal statements, but the physical acts of other members of the audience. People all around laugh or cry, fidget restlessly or sit attentively. They are making words with their bodies. "This is funny." "This is moving." "This is awful." And these statements present themselves, not in critical prose, but as the opinions of people actually, physically present. A number of psychological experiments have shown that judgments so presented have a heavily coercive effect: they will make subjects change their minds about quite unarguable things, such as one line's being obviously shorter than another. If enough people contradict the evidence of the subjects' senses, three out of four subjects will go along with the majority even when they are clearly in error.[6] How much more powerful, then, must be the judgments of value and mood made by an audience in a theater where a person has no way of "proving" he is right and they are wrong.

Each member of the audience achieves the theatrical experience only if he can take in the spectacle before him through his habitual defenses. Suppose he disagrees with the people around him. Suppose, for example, he laughs when they are silent or tries to quiet them because he is moved and they are laughing. To the imagined dangers his defenses must already deal with, he has added their real disapproval. Conversely, if he agrees with the rest of the audience, he subtracts from his task of adaptation whatever threats would be entailed by a contradiction. Further, if the people around him reject the work, they make it that much more difficult for him to trust in the work as an objective something with which to re-create his own defenses. If, however, the audience supports the work, it becomes that much more reliable as a source of personal adaptations. The audience thus has a doubly powerful effect because it presses in two ways on each individual's literary synthesis at precisely the most pivotal point—the matching of defenses—by calling into question that consensus about reality and oneself on which most of us deeply, constantly rely.

Teaching literature presents another situation that affects one's re-creation of a work by statements outside of it and by the reactions of other people. In a large hall, a gifted lecturer can create an almost theatrical situation that supports his statements about literature with the weight of his own personality and the consensus he elicits from his hearers. The usual academic lecturer, however, is no spellbinder, and his lectures simply deliver written criticism in another medium. The best teaching of literature takes place in smaller classes, sized for discussion. There is, finally, the luxurious situation of one teacher to one or two students as in a tutorial program. To all, however, the same fundamental model applies.

Together, teacher and students create a space that contains the literary work and into which some individuals project their own statements about the work and from which all draw resources to synthesize their own experience of it. Such statements range through all the kinds of things we have seen critics say about "A Rose for Emily." They may be factual background, like explanations of Faulkner's language or Mississippi customs. They may be statements about the work itself: its length or form or structure, patterns within it, what it leaves out, and so on. Or they may be total interpretations: the kind of mastery we have seen the critics—and the five readers—seek. From all of them another reader may take what he wishes and is able to construct into his own structure of adaptations.

In this kind of teaching, the teacher is essentially passive: he offers his students insights and they take them or not, as they wish. In a more active mode, he may urge them to contribute insights and dicta of their own from which a consensus can emerge: a series of statements about the story that most of the people in the class agree with although they retain their private experiences of the work. At the same time, as this consensus approximates a total interpretation of the work, some students will perceive it as a coercive force that threatens to overpower them, and they will reject it out of hand.

There is a better way of teaching actively, although it requires some ability to "listen with the third ear" and willingness to go beyond the problem of teaching literature or even of teaching students to the more fundamental problem of teaching *this* student. To set about that kind of teaching systematically, one needs to understand (and therefore to have listened to) the inner dynamics of the particular student. One hears them best, notably the defensive side of his character structure, by listening for his resistances. Having heard Saul's demands for precision in the context of his other remarks or Sandra's and Sam's fears of being overpowered, one can begin to understand the dangers these readers ward off and the defenses they set up against them. It then becomes possible to suggest a slant on a particular work that will enable them to absorb it through their defenses, as I was lucky enough to hit on a way Sam could dissociate nurture and dependency from homosexuality and castration. Once he could do that, he could begin to work with the Hemingway story.

One can also infer these defenses from students' preferences, although indirectly: preferences in literature suggest favored fantasies that are the other side of the defensive structure —what is deeply wished is also deeply feared. Thus, Sandra's tendency to find or create strong figures in the stories she read suggests her more general wish for sources of strength and her defenses against either being overcome or abandoned by them. Sebastian's liking for English aristocratic fiction or for Mrs. Robinson in *The Graduate* (see p. 365) told me about his wish to receive something warm and sexual from those he saw as his elders and superiors. In turn, this wish revealed his ambivalence toward authorities and his defensive way of dealing with forces of control by receiving something from them and giving in return. This kind of insight enables a teacher to direct what he is saying to *this* student, but it is an insight not easily won and rather exhausting to live with. And it is well to remember, too, that some kinds of character structure—Saul's, for example—set up resistance to almost any literary experience. Not everyone can be taught everything.

This kind of teaching based on a psychoanalytic model of the psyche's interaction with external reality allows one final—and still more taxing—mode of teaching. One can make statements about the work available. One can direct one's teaching by means of inferences about students' adaptive patterns. Finally, one can turn students' attention toward their own patterns of rejection or re-creation. Clearly, such a mode requires sophisticated students, ideally those with some insight into themselves arrived at in a clinical setting. I have myself tried this kind of teaching only with advanced graduate students in a program specifically directed to literature and psychology. One must be tactful and discreet. Above all, one must avoid diagnoses or any use of terms that even slightly suggest psychopathology. Needless to say, the old-fashioned kind of symbol-twirling that used to pass for psychoanalytic criticism is completely out of place.

Within a positive and supportive discussion, however, I have seen students—out of their own curiosity about themselves —become strikingly aware of their feelings and associations, and from that awareness followed an understanding of their synthesis of the work. Obviously, this is not therapy, only understanding within and for a limited, literary purpose. If that limit is breached, the whole venture becomes risky, hard to describe, but extraordinarily rewarding.

This last kind of teaching, and all the others, rest on the recognition that one cannot teach or study a work in isolation. I cannot know "A Rose for Emily" apart from my personal construction of it. Nor can you apart from yours. Nor can anyone. Denying this fact only makes it impossible for the teacher or critic to deal with it. Recognizing it, a teacher can at all times know at least how to find out what effect he is having and why.

Unfortunately, recognition or no, the writer can never work even with that minimal security. He knows his reader still less than the teacher knows his student. If literature answered to a stimulus-response model, he could predict how readers in the abstract would respond, but, one cannot predict—as we have seen here and as common sense would say. Shakespeare himself could not imagine what some of his modern critics have made of him. Indeed, if authors could predict readers' responses, they would all be millionaires. No. One cannot tell how people will react merely by looking at the text—one has to see some particular reader at work. This is why, I suppose, so many writers as they write, imagine a reader they write for —often a person who unconsciously images part of their own personality, frequently an avatar of someone from early life who still exists, as it were, in the writer's structure of identifications.[7] Even so, this *public intérieur* who is the writer's twin does not predict the ways of real readers. He assuages the writer's inner needs.

At the end of this book as at its beginning, one can say only that the "what" the writer creates is something that can be used in a variety of defenses by a variety of people who will see it in a variety of ways. The writer creates supplies from which each of his readers will build an individual psychological process. In Faulkner's tableau, the words are precise enough but we still have to give "spraddles" a meaning, Mr. Grierson a position (seated, standing, facing forward or sideways), and "slender figure in white" a height, a shape of hair, a facial expression, or a lateral position in the depth of "background," eyes. And even if Faulkner had spelled out some of these contingencies, others would be left for us to fill in, for this openness to projection inheres in language itself. Nouns, verbs, and modifiers describe classes, but people do not think in classes—at least when they are reading poems or stories. They turn the attributes that define the class into particular instances, as we have seen the five readers do with that one sentence from "A Rose for Emily."

Yet the words can't be just anything. Miss Emily, we have noted, cannot be an Eskimo—at least not without doing violence to the text. The writer creates opportunities for projection but he also sets constraints on what the reader can or cannot project into the words-on-the page and how he can or cannot combine them. The reader can violate these stringencies, of course, but if he does so, he loses the possibility of sharing his reading with others and winning their support for his lonely and idiosyncratic construct. He submits to the same threats of isolation and ridicule as the dissenting member of a theater audience. Yet the choice is his, finally, for this is the psychoanalytic sense of free will: no one can impose a limit on subjectivity from outside, although the whole course of a person's development defines from inside the invariance in that subjectivity, namely, his identity theme.

Freud thought that "the essential *ars poetica* lies in the technique of overcoming the feeling of repulsion in us which is undoubtedly connected with the barriers that rise between each single ego and others." When we are told the fantasies or daydreams of an ordinary person, he said, they

> repel us [him, anyway] or at least leave us cold. But when a creative writer presents his plays to us or tells us what we are inclined to take to be his personal day-dreams, we experience a great pleasure, and one which probably arises from the confluence of many sources. How the writer accomplishes this is his innermost secret.[8]

Now, these five readers have brought us somewhat closer to the solution of that mystery. The writer creates something from his own characteristic processes of transformation that then becomes the treasury from which someone else can draw by means of his processes of defense, project fantasies into, and transform according to *his* characteristic modes. But this, evidently, is the secret of creativity in general, not just artistic creativity.

A Gandhi, a Hitler, a Christ, an Einstein, and, yes, a Freud—all their creations cross the barriers between self and self, ego and ego. Even the literary critic, whose statements work in parallel with the writer's words, creates something "in" his ego that can become a something "in" his reader's ego. Looked at theoretically, from the outside of the transaction, the words of the creative writer, religious leader, politician, teacher, scientist, or literary critic are simultaneously "in" the ego of their author, have an independent existence as "something external," and function "in" the ego of the hearer. But this state of affairs we infer from theory.

We can really know those words only from inside our own mental processes. The literary critic, for example, cannot examine a text apart from his personal and inner re-creation of it. If he could, that would mean he could choose between being in his mind or out of it—surely, not even the most agile of literary critics can achieve the latter, except in a metaphorical sense. The very notion of having an identity, habitual ways of coping with inner and outer reality, means that one interprets reality through that identity.

For some literary critics, this is a troubling idea. Any critic tries to make his own response rational and coherent through his interpretations. He would also like to persuade a community of readers that the meaning he provides is one they should share, for then they would consolidate not only their own responses but, tacitly, his as well. Some critics give themselves that reassurance by saying the literary work is an "objective" fact to which they are responding "correctly" by discovering "things" that are simply "there." As Remy de Gourmont says, every sincere reader will "erect into laws his personal impressions." Accepting the opposite view, that the critic is writing, not the Truth-with-a-capital-T, but his own interpretation that others are free to accept or not as it suits them, this opens the critic to the same risks as the lonely dissenter in a theater. It is for this reason, I think, that some critics cling so tenaciously to a stimulus-response model of the literary transaction that they would reject indignantly in other contexts. Yet, no matter how deeply a critic might need to feel he is telling "objective" truths, it is not given to man to know things outside himself apart from his personal re-construction and synthesis of them. And so it is that our five readers lead us to a model of human experiencing that applies to many situations besides reading.

Experiencing: A Model

Our five readers take us to something very like Freud's earliest models of experience, derived from his studies of slips of the tongue, memory, jokes, and especially dreams. (I am thinking particularly of the so-called "picket fence" model in the last chapter of *The Interpretation of Dreams*.) A man perceives a bit of reality, either inner or outer. His percept sinks down, as it were, through related percepts, now memories, and is thus elaborated unconsciously. It then, so to speak, comes up again to consciousness accompanied by various unconscious elaborations and distortions, making a dream, a motor act, a slip of tongue or memory, or, in our literary context, a thematic interpretation.

What we have seen of readers reading has focused this model of experiencing more sharply. A person takes in a perception, shaping it to match his characteristic pattern of defenses and adaptations, as if they were a kind of tunnel to the underworld that would only admit objects of a certain configuration. Once it has passed into the underworld, a person freely projects onto that perception his characteristic fantasies and associations. He transforms the combination into a conscious interpretation of the percept, which serves as a guide for further thinking, feeling, or action and marks an experience. Alternatively, he wards off the whole experience from the start, again, in his characteristic way.

The key term that five readers reading have added is *characteristic*: characteristic defenses, fantasies, transformations, and interpretations. A man experiences within the medium of a given style, ego identity, *mythe personnel* or, finally, identity theme. The identity theme in turn is the invariant that one can abstract from all of an individual's behavior including (or especially) his verbal behavior. It sets the terms of subjectivity because it defines the organism's criterion for acceptable and unacceptable solutions to its quest for pleasure in response to the multiple demands on the ego. An identity theme in this sense is as ancient as the pleasure principle itself. More properly, beyond the pleasure principle there is an "identity principle": the organism will seek out responses from its environment to establish and maintain its continuous organization.[9]

Human beings engage both principles at conception, because they are, from the very first moment, related to an answering environment. As Erikson so characteristically says, "The human being, at all times, from the first kick *in utero* to the last breath, is organized into groupings of geographic and historical coherence: family, class, community, nation. A human being, thus, is at all times an organism, an ego, and a member of a society and is involved in all three processes of organization."[10] For example, both parents receive the very fact of pregnancy into a matrix of fantasy and expectation. The mother, in particular, provides the fetus with a human environment out of her body, which may be easy or agitated, balanced or disordered. The unborn child, too, brings to that first environment a heredity and a behavior that may mesh easily with it or may be the source of tension, which in turn may accelerate or slow development. The same community continues after birth, but with, of course, greater intensity, more stimulations from the environment, many more chances for the interaction of parent and child, and also many more chances for match and mismatch. Every mother and father knows the difference to a family of a baby who is "easy"—who eats without difficulty and sleeps without crying—and anyone can imagine the mounting spiral of tension that a mismatch between the styles of mother and baby can become.

Usually, of course, mother and child find a loving match out of which the identity emerges: "The mother does not convey a *sense* of identity to the infant but an *identity*: the child is the organ, the instrument for the fulfillment of the mother's unconscious needs." Indeed, "The mother imprints upon the infant not *an* identity, but an *'identity theme.'* "[11] According to this model of Heinz Lichtenstein, humans are born with "infinite potentialities" of adaptation. However, "the specific unconscious need of the mother," her own identity theme, I should think, actualizes "one way of being in the child, namely being the child for this particular mother." This "primary identity," this "zero point which must precede all other mental developments," is "a primary organizational principle without which the process of developmental differentiation could not begin."[12]

There is an innately determined readiness in the human infant to react to the maternal stimulations with a "somatic obedience" experience. This "obedience" represents, however, fulfillment of the child's own needs: in being the in-

strument, the organ for the satisfaction of the maternal
Otherness, the full symbiotic interaction of the two partners
is realized for both of them. It would, however, be a mistake
to see this "organ" or "instrumental" identity as too narrowly defined. The mother imprints upon the infant not *an*
identity, but, an "*identity theme*." This *theme* is irreversible,
but it is capable of variations. . . . What in the adult is
referred to as his social identity . . .—being a worker, a
farmer, a hunter, etc.—is, at its best, a successful variation
of the identity theme imprinted upon the infant. At its worst,
it is an artificially imposed part, the playing of which is experienced as alienation by the individual, because it is in-
compatible with his identity theme.[13]

The achievement of an identity theme thus takes its place
among the other major accomplishments of the first stage of
child development: the differentiation of self from object and
the ability to tolerate feelings of love and hate toward the same
person. The child, by learning to wait for a nurturing other,
learns through delay that he can control the coming of that
other person only to a limited extent, that therefore he is himself a separate being. The child thus acquires an Eriksonian
sense of identity as well as a Lichtensteinian identity theme,
and he or she does so with more or less anger and anxiety
according to the delays and the kind of mothering experienced.
There is still other evidence that the child achieves a fourth
basic ability in the course of self-object differentiation: to
hypothesize and symbolize reality.[14] All the other three take
place within the terms defined by the identity theme. The infant
loves, hates, symbolizes, and acquires a sense of self within his
or her identity theme. It sets the phrase on which these experiences and all later developments improvise.

As in that first transaction the child develops as he, in
Donne's verb, "interinanimates" himself and his human and
nonhuman environment. The infant develops in rhythmic
mutuality. The primary identity or identity theme acts "as an
invariant the transformations of which we could call development." Within its pattern, certain mental developments are
"possible" or "impossible" according to whether or not they

can be transformations of the invariant theme and whether the world makes it possible to translate the "organizing directions" given by that identity into inner and outer actualities.[15]

I have put the process of development through experience in Lichtenstein's terms. One could also look at it through D. W. Winnicott's concept of a "potential space between the individual and the environment, that which initially both joins and separates the baby and the mother when the mother's love, displayed or made manifest as human reliability, does in fact give the baby a sense of trust or of confidence in the environmental fact." "This potential space is a highly variable factor (from individual to individual)," and most important "in that it is here that the individual experiences creative living."[16] Still closer to what we have seen of reading is Winnicott's concept of the "transitional object," that first treasured possession —blanket, teddy bear, or stuffed dog—to be loved and clutched and sucked, which is both found reality and created symbol. "The object represents the infant's transition from a state of being merged with the mother to a state of being in relation to the mother as something separate." Gradually, as the child grows, it puts aside its transitional object, neither repressing that past love nor incorporating the object. "It is not forgotten and it is not mourned. It loses meaning . . . because the transitional phenomena have become diffused, have become spread out over the whole intermediate territory between 'inner psychic reality' and 'the external world as perceived by two persons in common,' that is to say, over the whole cultural field." "This intermediate area of experience . . . is retained in the intense experiencing that belongs to the arts and to religion and to imaginative living, and to creative scientific work."[17]

Sam and the rest, however, suggest that these transitional phenomena apply not only to intense experiences but to the casual reading they were doing for me. They filtered these short stories through a transitional space and adapted them into transitional objects, for the nonce at least. This study of reading implies that each individual adapts *all* the physical realities he meets to fit his personal style. He shapes as he perceives, splitting into parts, adding to and omitting from, until his perception matches his particular defensive and adaptive structures. In effect, someone like Saul or Sebastian who has learned to deal with the world in terms of authority must perceive the world as authority before he can deal with it. Someone like Sam or Sandra who perceives reality as sources of strength does so because sources of strength match the fears and wishes they experience. Only when a person has so perceived a reality that it matches his adaptations and defenses can he admit that reality into his ongoing mental processes and their press toward pleasure and meaningfulness.

> Each new developmental influence, as it is incorporated, is stamped by the existing organization. This viewpoint also makes clear that certain developmental influences "take" in a given style, whereas others, no matter how forceful or compelling they may seem from an objective standpoint, do not "take," that is, are inconsistent with or lack foundation in the existing forms of functioning.[18]

What we have seen is that objective realities "take" only when an individual finds they match his ego style, whether he had to make them do so or not.

In effect, I have refined a favorite analogy of Freud's: the amoeba. At any given moment, this protozoan is immersed in experience—it moves through its world, and the world moves past it. It surrounds pieces of reality it wishes to satisfy itself with, and it absorbs what it can of them through its outer "skin" depending on the balance of chemicals within and without. It excludes (if it can) what would be harmful or painful, and it soaks in what gives satisfaction. It then leaves behind ("ignores," as it were) what it did not want, and it reaches out to the next chunk of edible reality with, now, a modified chemical balance. It filters matter through its defenses into its bodily economy, which is then changed by what has been taken in. Thus, the next edible is filtered a little differently before it, too, changes the inner balance—and so on through the lifespan of the organism.

As the amoeba ingests food, so we take in experiences. For us, too, experiences and the personal style we bring to experience each create the other, and this mutual creation takes place within a determined world of dialectic cause and effect. Hegel and Marx would have recognized their influence in Waelder's original formulation of the multiple functioning of psychic acts:

> Each attempted solution issuing from the ego already carries within itself the tendency to its destruction, for scarcely is it fixed than it no longer constitutes a solution. Through each act the world is changed in all its elements; for instance, the outer world is changed generally, and something in the instincts is changed by what this act contains in the way of gratification or denial, and so on.

"Through the attempted solution itself everything is changed," he concludes, "so that now new problems approach the ego and the attempted solution fundamentally is such no more." Thus, the personality *must* reach actively toward new experiences, and, having absorbed them, it *must* reach again, and again, and again. Each new experience in turn slightly changes the reaching personality. What remains constant are "the methods of solution peculiar to the individual . . . the character and . . . the ego,"[19] in other words, the lifestyle or identity theme.

Thus, we get a picture of man as an endlessly cycling, cybernetic being. His transitory, even momentary, solutions exhaust themselves; he then reaches out for new experiences that cause slight readjustments in his psychic economy. Then these new solutions exhaust themselves in turn. Underneath these rapid cyclings, like the drones below a bagpipe's skirling, plays the steady chord of the individual's constant identity theme, essentially unchanging even after successful treatment. For example, we have seen how Lichtenstein's Anna S. before analysis had to "be another's essence" by fantasying an imaginary mad lover drinking her blood so that she lost her separate identity in him. Then, after treatment, she still felt "part of" her lover, "way down deep inside of him, that his arms are my arms, etc." A growing body of evidence suggests that neither psychotherapy, psychoanalysis, "brainwashing," nor severe physical and emotional traumata, including psychosis have the power to change someone's identity theme. They can, however, radically alter the variations an individual plays upon that identity theme, from unhealthy to healthy, from political right to political left, from a closed, opaque person to one almost raw in his openness, and so on. Nevertheless, the basic polarities around which the individual shapes reality remain the same, and they will form the underlying structures for his experiences, ranging from ostensibly "raw" perception to the most intellectual of interpretations.

Between the unchanging identity theme and the rapid cyclings of everyday life fall the slow cycles of psychosocial development. Though measured in years, not moments, they follow the same cybernetic pattern of active growth toward new experience assimilated into a continuing life style. In terms of multiple functioning, writes Waelder,

> There is change or development on the basis of change or development of the instinctual life, of the outer world, or of the superego. Hence, through the biologically predetermined development of the instinctual life other problems will approach the ego in puberty than in the period before puberty, and accordingly change all happenings in the ego, all attempted solutions. The changing of the outer world places the individual at times before changed problems. We can also speak of a development of the superego . . . becoming constantly more and more independent.

In development, in addition to this constant pressure for change, there is also a continual regressive ingathering of the past as a preparation for the future. This regression takes the form of consolidating and rearranging one's psychic economy in fairly substantial and permanent ways, shaping old strengths to meet new challenges or new experiences. Thus, in a sense, events in the future make changes in the past, and the future, in turn, seems different according to the different constructions of the past we bring to it.

I suspect I am like most post-Renaissance people in carrying as part of my mental baggage a one-direction model of causality. As Noam Chomsky once declared, "The empiricist view is so deep-seated in our way of looking at the human mind that it almost has the character of a superstition."[20] If I say that A causes B, then I also mean that B cannot cause A. If I speak of an "experience" or a "response," I still catch myself meaning that there is an objective *res extensa* that is doing something to a subjective *res cogitans*.

Clearly, however, something more complicated is really going on in the human and social contexts described by Lichtenstein or Winnicott. Consider, for example, Erikson's description of the way a "baby's weakness gives him power."

> A baby's presence exerts a consistent and persistent domination over the outer and inner lives of every member of a household. Because these members must reorient themselves to accommodate his presence, they must also grow as individuals and as a group. It is as true to say that babies control and bring up their families as it is to say the converse. A family can bring up a baby only by being brought up by him.[21]

In effect, a childhood (baby's or parents') creates an adult, as an adult creates a child's childhood. A causes B, but B also causes A. Experience causes development, but what is experienced is determined by what has already developed—indeed, this study of reading shows one can *only* experience what one's developed system of defenses and adaptations permits.

If so, one cannot model experiences by means of a dichotomy between mind and body or subject and object. Such a state of affairs calls at least for a description in terms of cybernetic feedbacks between the two, in the manner (for example) of Gregory Bateson.

> In no system which shows mental characteristics can any part have unilateral control over the whole. In other words, *the mental characteristics of the system are immanent, not in some part, but in the system as a whole.*
>
> In principle, if we desire to explain or understand the mental aspect of any biological event, we must take into account the system—that is, the network of *closed* circuits, within which that biological event is determined.[22]

If this sounds too scientific, one could think instead of T. S. Eliot's description of the relationship between an existing artistic tradition demanding conformity and a new, individual talent:

The necessity that he shall conform . . . is not onesided; what happens when a new work of art is created is something that happens simultaneously to all the works of art which preceded it. The existing monuments form an ideal order among themselves, which is modified by the introduction of the new (the really new) work of art among them. The existing order is complete before the new work arrives; for order to persist after the supervention of novelty, the *whole* existing order must be, if ever so slightly, altered; and so the relations, proportions, values of each work of art toward the whole are readjusted; and this is conformity between the old and the new. Whoever has approved this idea of order . . . will not find it preposterous that the past should be altered by the present as much as the present is directed by the past.[23]

In terms of lifestyle, the new experience conforms to the old style—the old style changes a bit in order to accommodate the new experience. I seem to remember a French critic phrasing this, in a fine Gallic paradox: "Only the really new can be really old. Only the forever old can be forever new." And that is as true for people as for books.

Eliot could have been referring to the two sides of an adaptation as described by Jean Piaget. In "assimilation," the organism takes in experience from its environment, and what is taken in is changed to fit the existing processes that mediate between the organism and its environment. In "accommodation," the movement is opposite: "At the same time that the input is being changed by the mediating processes, the mediating processes are being changed by the input." And these two functions are characteristic of all biological systems.[24]

It seems to me Piaget's theory, by its extreme generality, goes past the essence this model of experience tries to capture. This logical model may apply to all organisms but (I would say) only to the extent they can be said to have a style or identity theme, that is, an invariant that can be abstracted from the continuum of the organism's choices or, alternatively, a theme on which all the organism's choices can be understood as variations. Something as inflexible as an amoeba's chemistry is probably a limiting case. An identity theme for a human being implies rather an idea as infinitely explicable as the ambiguous phrases I have used to describe these five readers. By means of such an identity theme, one can understand a variety of functions: how someone defends or adapts, seeks gratification, knows, or feels emotion. One understands these different functions by applying the identity theme to the different axes of multiple functioning: meeting internal reality or external, warding off anxiety or trying to gain pleasure. Specifically one can arrive at the general model of experiencing this study of reading yields. A human being experiences by adding a variation to his identity theme. In this way he re-creates his identity theme, first, by matching the experience to his characteristic pattern of defenses and adaptations. Then, to the extent such a matching takes place, he admits the experience and transforms it to yield the particular gratifications he prefers. Finally, he interprets the experience intellectually, aesthetically, morally, or socially, according to his characteristic ways of transforming drives into ego-acceptable activities. The identity theme sets the terms (contractual and linguistic) in which realities will be taken in or rejected, and in this sense it limits the ways the organism will experience its world.

Looked at another way, however, the fact we perceive the world in the terms of our own subjectivities has a positive, freeing side. It is only by being different from one another that we can have the experience of sharing. Your having a personal style makes it possible for you to take in something that I have said and make it your own. Thus, paradoxically, only by beginning with different subjectivities can we arrive at that consensus about experience that constitutes all the objectivity subjective beings can have. If we were not different and therefore subjective, we could not sense reality at all—we would simply be compelled by it, having no more personal experience of our interaction with the world than objects do of other objects. It is only by having our objectivity limited that we can have any objectivity whatever. Loving and knowing are inseparable.

8   From Subjectivity to Collectivity

Reading mingles curiously book with person and person with person. Thus, what began as a simple inquiry into the effect of personality on reading has led us far afield. We had to develop and draw on a very general theory of motivation: the human being seeks what looks to him like the best solution to the multiple demands on his ego within the possible variations of his identity theme. This theory of motivation, applied to readers reading, led to an equally general theory of experiencing. In perceiving reality, the individual shapes it to match his ways of dealing with reality. To the extent he succeeds, he can take in an experience from outside, blend into it his characteristic wishes for pleasure, and transform it by means of his characteristic sublimations.

Such a model lets us understand the private re-creation each reader makes as he reads. You can think of the typical nineteenth-century situations of reading: the solitary governess closeted with her novel or the paterfamilias reading aloud to the household, each member of it having his silent, personal experience. But we have also touched on the twentieth-century additions to the picture: reading in the university, discussion in the classroom, studies in the learned journals. And we have seen that our models of motivation and experience account for those situations too.

Criticism and discussion constitute a reality that each reader takes in by the same process that he takes in the literary work itself. Literature and talk about literature work in parallel. Each reader can give of himself to that talk, either by discussion or writing criticism or even by body language, fidgeting or laughing in a theater. He can in turn draw from the collective talk resources with which to construct his own experience of the work. But now, in taking reading from the private experience to a collective one, we approach one of the classic problems of psychoanalytic and other psychologies: extending a model of the individual to groups.

Minicause and Macroperson

In moving from an intrapsychic model to an interpsychic one, psychologists have usually taken one of two strategies. Sometimes, they have made an act of simple faith or imagination and assumed outright that their picture of the individual would serve as a model for the collectivity, much as an engineer, looking at a physical event, "knows" intuitively that a certain type of second-order differential equation will describe it. This was Freud's method, for example, in *Totem and Taboo* and *Moses and Monotheism*. Alternatively, the psychologist tries to sum up the group, as it were, from a series of individual transactions by its members, as Freud did in *Group Psychology and the Analysis of the Ego*. The first method looks for convergence around a style, in the sense we have been giving that word: a series of choices with a discernible pattern. The second looks for something more like the quasi-causality we found in teaching and criticism. The first looks at a large cultural or national group as a macroperson; the second, in terms of minicauses.

It seems to me hard indeed to try to arrive at group traits from their causes. The most successful attempts have applied an Eriksonian paradigm of mutuality to derive large cultural trends from patterns of childrearing, such patterns in turn produce adults who tend to favor those trends in the culture by which they themselves were given a social identity. For example, John Demos and David Hunt have shown how political and historical styles in seventeenth-century America and France followed upon certain family structures.[1] And long ago Margaret Mead spoke of "the mechanisms by which the Manus child's attention is turned toward the outer world, motor behavior insisted upon at the expense of passive dreaming, moral and physical necessity so joined that the Manus are almost unique in the way they handle the mechanical devices of modern civilization." It is only a short step from such a discovery to analyses like Lucian Pye's of more complex "political cultures." He has shown, for example, how patterns of upbringing and adult institutions coact to create in the Burmese civil servant a "peculiar combination of faith in the diffuse and suspicion of the particular" which is "precisely the opposite of what is needed" to effect Burma's conscious wish to profit from the mechanical devices of modern civilization.[2] Even so, such an approach quickly moves from the assessment of childhood causes to the observation of the culture itself as a total personality.

This second approach, positing a leviathan or macroperson, can draw today on a sophisticated psychology of the individual. The concept of multiple function and identity theme derived from and gave rise to various ways of inquiring into an individual. If we can observe a sequence of ego choices and discern patterns in them, then we can infer a style and identity theme. We can recognize from the ego's responses the demands of reality as the ego perceives them. Looking at the ego's choices in other ways, we can infer characteristic defensive strategies or habitual sources of pleasure. These, in turn, enable us to surmise the kinds of pressures to express or inhibit drives that the ego must find multiply functioning solutions for.

The question is, then, is it legitimate to apply these inquiries to a culture or nation as though it were a macroperson, responsive to an identity theme and the principle of multiple function? As it happens, when Robert Waelder originally formulated the principle in 1930, he proposed that it could play a role in social psychology by requiring "the consideration of typically social phenomena in multiple function, that is, an historic movement with regard to its economic side (adjustment to the outer world or overcoming the outer world), with allowance for instinctual gratification, collective ideals, etc."[3] Waelder was suggesting that the mind, perceived as an economy of multiple functions, could serve as a model for larger social phenomena to the extent they, too, could be interpreted in terms of multiple functioning. He was simply projecting the special teleological causality we have seen operating within one mind onto collective mental products. Essentially, Waelder had hypothesized in psychoanalytic terms what has come to be known in sociology

and social anthropology as "functional analysis." I am thinking, for example, of Raymond Bauer's analyses of the total
movement of a business organization toward its goals as the
multiple functioning of sub-systems. That is, one must ask,
"What function does the total behavior serve in terms of the
various sub-systems of the organization, e.g., profit-making,
social gratification, public image, and so on?"[4] One could
analyze the behavior of any group this way—corporation, tribe,
government unit, army, gang, and so on.

This study of reading, however, also shows that one has to
join to the principle of multiple function the idea of a style or
identity theme: characterisitic ways of trying to reach the best
multiple functioning define the essential unity of the organization. Then, applying both principles to a culture brings us to
that combination of a holistic with a functional tradition in anthropology associated with Malinowski, Boas, and in recent
years even more dramatically (and mathematically) with Lévi-
Strauss. Thus, a psychoanalytically oriented anthropologist
like Clyde Kluckhohn can bring out unexpected connections
within a culture by recognizing it plays a theme and variations on "orality." Similarly Ruth Benedict's Kwakiutls or
Erikson's Yurok Indians play out variations of anal themes.[5]
To speak of a culture as working out a structure of fanta: y
and defense, as a "style" in our sense, is to apprehend the
whole culture simultaneously. Weston La Barre sets out what
amounts to a method: "Culture is the observed consistency
in the behavior of a number of individuals in a society; personality is the consistency of pattern in the observed behavior of one individual."[6] In effect, one simply abstracts
from the total behavior of a society to find a style for that
society analogous to an individual's style (or character or myth
or personality).

Extending such a sense of "style" or "culture" beyond
primitive societies to the industrial nations of the Atlantic
community, brings us to the much-criticized concept of "national character." Nevertheless, at least one noted political scientist, Stanley Hoffmann, will accept "the notion of a national
style" provided it is understood as "a postulate and a construct." "A nation perceives the world, and its place in it, in a

fashion which is never quite like that of any other nation, just as no individual ever faces the world like any one else."

A Frenchman of the right and a Frenchman of the left may disagree about every conceivable substantive issue, from the meaning of the French Revolution to the nature of man, and yet they will present their arguments and try to convince their audience in a way that is common to both and not quite like the Englishman's or American's, a manner shaped by education and family customs and based on assumptions about reality, time, or authority that transcend substantive disagreements on issues.[7]

When one thinks in terms of a total style this way, it becomes possible to group together themes of behavior for a nation just as one would for an individual. Thus, we can understand them as part of a consistent national myth or identity analogous to the identity themes of individuals. Not, perhaps, a "modal personality" with mathematical nicety, but a "national style" or, to borrow a term from two Dutch researchers, a "mentality expressed in cultural products," a mental national product (MNP) analogous to the economic GNP or gross national product.[8] One would arrive at a national style (or the style of any definable group) through the analysis of its MNP, that is, its shared documents, behavior, and thought (as one groups the behavior of an individual or the words of a story into themes or traits culminating in a central theme). No detail is too small, as Gertrude Stein realized:

Another thing that interested us enormously was how different the camouflage of the french looked from the camouflage of the germans, and then once we came across some very very neat camouflage and it was american. The idea was the same but as after all it was different nationalities who did it the difference was inevitable. The colour schemes were different, the designs were different, the way of placing them was different, it made plain the whole theory of art and its inevitability.[9]

Collective artistry has its style, just as the individual artist does.

So does collective language. I find it more than a whimsy to hear a distinguished translator say, "The right image for the German sentence . . . is that of a great gut, a bowel, which deposits at the end of it a sediment of verbs." "The Germans roll compound words into sausages of abstraction, and then roll these sausages into bigger ones. This predilection for the sausage shape cannot be fortuitous. It must have some relation to the German love of Wurst and Dachshunds. And why did the Germans invent the Zeppelin? Nor should we forget that the favorite German word of abuse is *Scheiss*." German, like Latin, "affects the thought of those who use it and disposes them to overvalue authoritative statement, will power, and purposive drive." "The drive, the straight purposive drive, of Latin, for instance, is remarkably like the straight purposive drive of the Roman roads. One might hazard a guess that from the use of *ut* with the subjunctive one could deduce the Roman Empire."[10] No more than a guess, I suspect, even though this interpretation does little more than wittily overstate the widely accepted Sapir-Whorf hypothesis: that language determines the constructions of reality its speakers make.

National style, sighs Stanley Hoffmann, is one of those "intellectual tools, which have a way of creeping back into the analysis even after being thrown out for lack of rigor."[11] Yet they need not lack rigor. As in the criticism and teaching of literature, there are at least two criteria we can apply. One is convergence: a quantitative sense of the number of details interrelated and the directness of the connections made. (*Wurst, Dachshund, Scheiss,* and Zeppelin, to be sure, but I do not find the notion of sausage-shaped nouns very direct.) Margaret Mead, in her study of the American national character, describes the method as it applies to a seemingly divergent trait: "This is an excellent example of what the anthropologist means by the regularity of culture: that an apparent contradiction . . . when it is analyzed more closely nevertheless fits in with other ideas in the culture which it appears to contradict."[12] For "regularity of culture" we could read, simply, cultural style or identity theme; and one arrives at it by the same kind of grouping toward convergence as for a literary text. Second, as with teaching and criticism, one looks for truth by sharing ideas, each making his personal synthesis out of the observations and statements made by others until a certain degree of agreement is reached. Working this way, one would, in a free market of ideas, sum different analysts' syntheses of a society, taking what they share as their conclusion.

This is to look at a group as though it were a macroperson, a method that perhaps can work only for very large groups. One can also look at a group, however, particularly a small group, as the sum of the individuals who make it up. Then, if we can understand those individuals (for example, by means of their identity themes), the question becomes, What operation will sum up from the behavior of the several individuals the behavior of the group? Clearly, some kind of meshing takes place. Thomas Mann described what is, in essence, a group of two:

> But lo, the world hath many centres, one for each created being, and about each one it lieth in its own circle. Thou standest but half an ell from me, yet about thee lieth a universe whose centre I am not but thou art. Therefore both are true, according as one speaketh from thy centre or from mine. And I, on the other hand, stand in the centre of mine. For our universes are not far from each other so they do not touch: rather hath God pushed them and interwoven them deep into each other.[13]

By intersecting circles Mann images not only the essentially private quality of experience, anchored to each individual's center, but also the possibility of sharing. Ahab used a similar image to describe the way he won the *Pequod*'s crew to his demonic quest for the white whale: "My one cogged circle fits into all their various wheels, and they revolve."[14] Mann and Melville, one in imagery of cloth, one in terms of machinery, are both describing what we found in criticism and teaching: people come together as each one synthesizes the others through his own style. One person says something. Others take it in through their characteristic defenses and project their characteristic fantasies onto it, thus making it part of their own universe.

This is the way an ideology functions, not just for its content, but in a way that engages the whole personality, especially the unconscious ego. Despite the pioneering work of Kardiner and his associates a quarter of a century ago, people still cling to the illusion that ideas, interpretations, and ideologies spring solely from reason and logic. As Robert E. Lane engagingly puts it,

Asked where ideas come from, most men are as innocent or as misinformed as the child who asks where babies come from. While human reproduction is now the subject of candid, informed, even polite conversation, the production of ideas out of the material of personality and experience is often explained by some equivalent to the story of the flowers and the bees; the process is wrapped in a rationality that does not account for an idea's origins, its private meanings, its power to move and paralyze, its style of expression, the ellipses and lacunae in its uses, and much more.[15]

People use ideological content to express and confirm a total character, either of themselves as individuals or of their group. In other words, people use ideas or ideologies to structure their worlds as our readers have used interpretations to build their experiences of these stories.

The basic principle that describes the way we share the experience of reading through teaching and criticism, then, will model the way people integrate other kinds of experiences through their personalities. As Milton Rokeach has shown, one can find a single language that suits the analysis of personality, ideology, and cognitive behavior. In our terms, each of these is linked to the other through the individual identity theme. We have seen it with five readers. Rokeach showed it for people's attitudes specifically toward religion, politics, and problem solving. He found principles that are similar enough to those we have seen governing the reading transaction to constitute a kind of experimental confirmation of our own conclusions. For example, Rokeach discovered the reason people favor one "belief system" over another:

Such systems are seen to serve two opposing sets of functions. On the one hand, they represent Everyman's theory for understanding the world he lives in. On the other hand, they represent Everyman's defense network through which information is filtered, in order to render harmless that which threatens the ego. The beautiful thing about a belief system is that it seems to be constructed to serve both masters at once: to understand the world insofar as possible, and to defend against it insofar as necessary.

He could almost be describing what we have considered the two aspects of the identity theme: the defensive aspect to which experience must be carefully modeled and the easy projection of characteristic fantasies into experience so as to gain satisfactions from it. Rokeach found, as one of his major generalizations, that

> We generally seem to prefer, to one degree or another, those with belief systems that are more congruent with our own. Our findings suggest that this organizing principle is far more important than other kinds of categorizations, such as race or ethnic grouping, in determining our relations with others. If race or ethnic categorizations are important it is primarily because they are convenient symbols that stand for complexes of beliefs which to one degree or another are seen to be similar to and different from our own.[16]

In effect, our preference for certain stories (and their authors) comes from the same source in unconscious motivation as our preference for certain belief systems (and their adherents). We give belief systems a latent content, and psychoanalysis, Freud thought, would turn metaphysics into metapsychology. Beliefs express for us "unconscious fantasies and object relations (just like dreams, play, the neurotic symptom, or any mental phenomenon)," but at the same time—indeed, precisely because they do—they will be an "absolutely authentic" function of the ego,[17] as much so as responses to stories.

Even looked at without consideration of the unconscious factors involved, as in the psychology of personal constructs developed by George A. Kelly, perception and belief take the same inward-outward form. "It is possible for two people to be involved in the same real events but, because they construe them differently, to experience them differently."

> But does this mean that there can be no sharing of experience? Not at all; for each may construe the likenesses and differences between the events in which he himself is involved, together with those in which he sees that the other person is involved. Thus, while there are individual differences in the contruction of events, persons can find common ground through construing the experiences of their neighbors along with their own.

> People belong to the same cultural group, not merely because they behave alike, nor because they expect the same things of others, but especially because they construe their experience in the same way.

This common construction, then, provides a basis for political and social action: "The person who is to play a constructive role in a social process with another person need not so much construe things as the other person does as he must effectively construe the other person's outlook."[18]

Thus, beliefs, values, culture, or constructs all face in two directions at once. Looked at as within, the individual's experiences of them uniquely express the individual's identity. Looked at as without, however, they are realities that others share. As William Meissner puts it in discussing the assimilation of values,

> Each child assigns different meanings to the cultural heritage and accepts or incorporates these meanings to a unique degree, so that his personal cultural heritage becomes something distinctive and characteristic of himself and no other. The evolving personality, therefore, selects and adapts a personal culture out of the cultural heritage presented him by his parents, family, and society.

> The value-system of each individual personality is something unique and distinctive of that individual. But the unique quality of its integration does not violate its capacity for shared meaning or the familial or communal aspects of its symbolic integration.

While the structure of values can be defined in terms of intrapsychic functions, it nonetheless turns its face to the outer
world and both initiates and modifies itself by continuing
dialogue with a pre-existing climate of values.[19]

This sharing of values and, through them, percepts and beliefs, comes from, but also gives rise to, human society and
community. "Man," writes Lichtenstein, "is a *zöon politikon*
because he is not given, as innate endowment, a naturally
shared perception of what is real." Rather, when we speak of
"objective reality" or "external reality," we need to recognize

that this "reality" is the product of a complex process of
actively "fitting" reality to the given circumstances of one's
existence—namely, to make possible for the individual "the
sense of oneness of man among men." It is, in other words, a
"tendentious" perception of reality, fitting the need of those
who "promote" it at a given time and place. It is "tendentious" even if we acknowledge that only by this "shaping"
of the sense of reality are we enabled to live as humans.

Thus, from Lichtenstein's point of view, psychoanalysis must
surrender the easy use of "reality" in Freud's "reality principle," which assumes a nineteenth-century, Kantian reality of
amiable persistence. In this last third of a troubled century,
psychoanalysis must even give over Hartmann's "average expectable environment," on which the notion of "autonomous
ego functions" was based, for we live in a time when, for many
people, "the only expectable element of their environment is
its unpredictability." Instead, psychoanalysis must accept the
idea that our notions of reality profoundly depend upon family,
community, and society—they are, finally, political. "Psychoanalytic theory needs to apply its very own principles to the
analysis of the unconscious determinants of reality perception
not just of an individual, but of the shared reality of one's
historical existence."[20]

For some of us, as R. D. Laing has eloquently shown, the
politics of shared reality have become so permeated with fraud
or violence as to preclude any sharing at all—and people speak
(not very accurately) of a "psychotic loss of reality." Most of

us are lucky enough to share reality more or less peaceably and honestly with our nurturing environment. Even from the very first moments of life, we are able lovingly to shape ourselves and be shaped by our identifications within—first, the family and later the community—each of us taking in surrounding realities and giving back to them in a continuing dialogue of cultural and individual growth, a "genetic epistemology" in Piaget's sense.

Such outward-inward images of culture expand the social model Freud developed in *Group Psychology and the Analysis of the Ego* (1921). He pointed to the way group leaders take on the role of fathers and therefore assume the functions of a superego (at this stage in Freud's thinking, the father incorporated as a permanent voice of command in the psyche). Today one can generalize this principle to culture at large and the personality as a whole: because of needs and desires, such as those for love, the individual lets the group conduct part of his psychological functioning for him, just as he contributes to the total psychological functioning of the group. Macroperson and minicause cooperate as, in reading, criticism and discussion function to create shared perceptions. This large principle makes it possible to describe not only the inward-outward concept of the individual and his groups but even the way groups themselves collect to form still larger groups.

In effect, I am suggesting a combination of two ways of exploring group behavior: the "multiple function" within an "identity theme" model of individual motivation; the consensus model for the situation in which men combine their interpretations of external realities. Both these models require the abstracting of traits and themes so as to grasp a total style as it converges toward an identity theme. They avoid what seems to me a far more precarious task, tracing fragmentary chains of cause and effect, for example, from ideologies to the behavior of key men to the behavior of the groups they govern. Such methods rest on traditional notions of causality, even though (according to the authoritative survey by Kenneth W. Terhune)[21] experiments trying to deal with national styles by statistics or cause-and-effect have so far proved quite inconclusive.

Rather, this study of reading leads to the conclusion that at all levels, from individual to nation, the same principle applies: each constituent takes from and gives to the group according to his particular style. Looked at from the point of view of the individual, the group's impact on him and his impact on the group both take place in the terms of the individual's identity theme. Within each group, the behavior of each member constitutes a reality which, along with other realities (including other groups), each member synthesizes through his particular identity theme. What the members share becomes the consensus of thought or action that is the group's "ego choices." Then, in turn, looking from the point of view of the group at a record of these choices one can infer an identity theme for the group itself, in terms of which the total group will interact with other groups or individuals. In this sense, the inferring of an identity theme (the way it was done for each of the five readers) constitutes an inquiry by means of which one can relate an individual's identity theme to the identity themes of the groups to which he belongs and vice versa, the identity themes of groups to their constituents, be they individuals or other groups.

That is, if we look at a group from the point of view of the individuals making it up we see a collectivity resulting from a series of minicauses. Each individual has contributed to the collectivity and taken from it through the multiple functioning of his ego in terms of his identity theme. We can trace the effect of each individual as he contributed his opinions and actions to the common store of experiences that could be shared by the other individuals in the group, through their identity themes. Looking at the group as a summing of its members this way corresponds (in a clinical, case-study way, to be sure) to the powerful experiments of Robert Freed Bales.[22] They are powerful precisely because the psychoanalytically trained Bales did not limit himself by the conventional controls and categories of experimental methods but tried to deal with *all* the interactions within a small group and *all* the personalities of the interactors. Such experiments, however, dealing even with small groups, are what keep psychologists nimble, observing here and jotting there as they transcribe the nuances of several personal styles. It is hard to imagine such painstaking methods extended to groups the size of a legislature or nation.

This psychoanalytic view, however, we can supplement with the opposite, inward perspective: looking at the group from outside as though the existence of the group as group opaquely screened off the individuals—the minicauses—that created it. One can then understand the group as a macroperson, having an identity theme and meeting the demands of multiple function apart from the separate, multiply functioning identities that in fact make up the group. In this sense, one grasps the whole style of the group outright, as one would abstract the personality of one of these five readers. As we have seen, such a style can describe a small group, a department, a firm, a village, a linguistic unity, a culture, or even a nation (through its MNP or "national character").

Further, having once formulated such a macropersonal style (multiple functioning through an identity theme), one can regard a group so understood as itself a minicause resulting in the creation of larger groups; these, in turn, can be understood as macropersons with distinctive styles that can give rise to still larger groups, and so on. Conversely, one can look back down the chain of plurality, through each group, to see the behavior of the constituents or "minicauses" that make it up. For each constituent one can infer from that (and other) behavior the identity theme of the constituent. That constituent group can then be treated as a macroperson (with multiple function and identity theme) and looked through in turn for the styles of its constituents and so on down to the single human beings from which any group must be made, leaders, for example, voters, consumers, or opinion makers.

Thus, we can use the concept of style (multiple function plus identity theme) to look at groups in both a macropersonal and a minicausal way and so range back and forth, describing groups as large as nations or as small as a nuclear family. Yet, in so doing, in turning to societies, cultures, and nations, I must seem really to have deserted what is, after all, the supposed subject of this book: reading. I have, however, a particular group in mind that I think lives within these principles like any other group, although it often seems reluctant to admit it does:

the reading public, particularly the public of professional
readers—critics and teachers of literature.

Toward Transactive Criticism

I have been quoting from psychologists, psychoanalysts,
sociologists, political scientists, and anthropologists, all of
whom agree that the political, social, and even physical
realities an individual sees depend heavily on that individual's
personality and the social matrix in which he lives. By and
large, however, teachers and critics of literature have *not*
accepted this position. Indeed, they seem to resist it strongly,[23]
preferring instead to think that literary works cause or define
general responses that particular people experiencing literature
approximate up to the limits of their intellectual and literary
ability.

Consider these conclusions from a learned and influential
theorist—some literary critics might disagree with his particular
philosophical formulations, but few, I think, with his general
attitude. "A poem," writes René Wellek, "is not an individual
experience or a sum of experiences, but only a potential cause
of experiences." One cannot define a poem in terms of states of
mind because of "the simple fact that it might be experienced
correctly or incorrectly." I would query whether that "fact" is
so simple, because I do not know who decides whether a given
experience is correct or incorrect. In other words, I think Professor Wellek is assuming that the poem, in some sense, is its
own arbiter.

> Thus, the real poem must be conceived as a structure of
> norms, realized only partially in the actual experience of its
> many readers. Every single experience (reading, reciting, and
> so forth) is only an attempt—more or less successful and
> complete—to grasp this set of norms or standards.

> We always grasp some "structure of determination" in the
> object which makes the act of cognition not an act of
> arbitrary invention or subjective distinction but the rec-
> ognition of some norms imposed on us by reality. Similar-
> ly, the structure of a work of art has the character of a

"duty which I have to realize." I shall always realize it imperfectly, but in spite of some incompleteness a certain "structure of determination" remains, just as in any other object of knowledge.[24]

Such a theory stems, I suspect, as much from a desire to honor literature and to abase oneself before its beauty or power as from a need for explanation. That is, we surround the aesthetic transaction with an almost religious aura when we call ourselves the imperfect, incomplete experiencers of something that goes beyond what any one human could experience or when we say that we are "always" the inadequate performers of a superhuman duty the literary work imposes. Such a view, moreover, blurs reason and observation with obscurity; it subordinates the lively and human appreciation of human achievement to something transhuman. It puts literature on a pedestal.

This theory, that literary works are structures that impose norms on their readers, will explain the similarity in different readers' readings. It will not, however, account for the equally striking fact of their difference, except as some aberration, some failure on the readers' part. Yet this difference in response can become a particularly pointed issue, for example, to one who comes to these questions from the study of Shakespeare. There, three centuries of opinion have produced an astonishing diversity of experiences and interpretations. At times, particularly with *Hamlet,* it seems as though there are indeed few interpretations that some intelligent person has not discovered and, to some liminal extent, supported by evidence. Difference, individuality, of interpretation seems not a failure but the norm; and while I may disagree with many of these interpretations, I learn by understanding the how of my disagreement.

I offer, for that purpose, the principle developed by this book—that we draw upon the treasury a literary work provides to re-create our own characteristic psychological processes—to account for *both* the difference in experiences *and* their sameness. The difference comes from the differences in character. The sameness comes from the sameness in the resources used to create the experience. Further, the model of experiencing here developed enables us to discover a relation between these samenesses and differences that the simpler assertion of "correct" or "incorrect" obscures, namely, the relation of identity to collectivity. Finally, the model of groups developed in this chapter shows how to share these samenesses and differences to create a critical community, both unified and diverse.

These principles urge us toward a literary criticism that takes as its subject matter, not a text, but the transaction between a reader and a text: a criticism that frankly acknowledges and accepts the critic in his criticism. Indeed, what I have here set forth about the way people read and otherwise interpret their experience suggests that literary criticism can never in fact be the study of the text as a separate, objective thing and need never be the study of the self alone. Rather, interpretation is a function of identity. Therefore, the true focus of criticism has to be the relation between oneself and the text, and the sensible thing for literary people to do is to acknowledge that focus and write and talk accordingly, sharing our samenesses and differences in interpretation so as to create an evergrowing resource of responses that we can share. In the phrase, "transactive criticism," I am advocating a criticism in which we consciously recognize that we re-create literature for ourselves just as the transactional psychologists have shown we create the colors, shapes, and directions of the world we perceive.

In developing these theories of individual and group experience, I have been drawing on the stiff, if precise, language of psychology, but the principles can be stated in the humanistic eloquence of another distinguished teacher and critic of literature:

To seek relief in particular details is inevitable to a finite being. In reading a poem, in contemplating any work of art, we may genuinely feel the active coalescence of the diverse. But when we come to speak about it, we have to proceed consecutively: one thing has to be mentioned before another; in the process of noticing them individually, we find some considerations striking us more than others, if only because in our own phrasing of them we begin to tap essential concerns within ourselves; and we are led by the momentum of our own cooperating eloquence to narrow our interpretation. A great work, of course, not only permits but invites that eager subjective response to different parts of it.

This is the reason, continues W. J. Bate, that for poems as majestic as Keats' great odes, "No single interpretation . . . satisfies anyone except the interpreter."[25]

Rather, then, than confine our estimate of one another's interpretations to a curt "correct" or "incorrect," we do better to engage ourselves in a politics of literary creation and re-creation. We can understand differences in interpretation and absorb them by the psychoanalytic principles developed here, particularly the principles of group psychology evolved in this chapter, which show how individuals can integrate and mutually enrich their several literary experiences precisely by sharing their mutual differences. Such a sharing, be it in a learned forum or the ordinary classroom, leads to a truly critical and humanistic discourse. When critics or teachers pronounce upon the interpretations of others on the premise that the text renders them "correct" or "incorrect," they are proceeding (this study shows) from a highly limiting and limited premise. Such verdicts seek to extend the socially useful fiction of unquestionable judicial authority to literary situations, where authority is neither useful nor justifiable nor, finally, attainable. We do better to give into and take from that communal store of human re-creation that extends from beginning readers (like our five) to the most gifted critics and teachers. We do not attend to that human creativity—we do not share in it at all, really—if we substitute for it the autocratic fantasy of language-as-tyrant, deciding on its own interpretation or imposing a duty beyond the capacities of the mere humans who, after all, create language.

9 Knowing

This book began with a conception of the nature of personality. Using it to understand readers reading enabled us to understand much more: criticism, creating, teaching, or being a member of an audience. Finally, these particular interactions took us to a model of the way human beings apprehend the world and one another, how they retain in very specific terms a private and personal experience, but still reach agreements about a "reality" that we know only as a public consensus among private persons.

This psychological study thus takes its place within a growing philosophical trend. It becomes one more in a series of efforts to bridge that gap that has dominated much systematic thought since the seventeenth century: the belief that the reality and meaning of the external world exist alone, independent of the perceiving self, and that therefore true knowledge requires the splitting of the knower from the known.[1] Alfred North Whitehead traces the development of this position as a shift from a simpler view held since antiquity, namely, that "we conceive ourselves as perceiving attributes of things, and bits of matter are the things whose attributes we perceive." Seventeenth-century thinkers, however, had to come to terms with the more complex "transmission" doctrines of science, notably Newton's connection of light with color. Discovering that sound and light were things proceeding from emitting bodies then established certain attributes (the "secondary qualities" of Locke) as not attributes at all (unlike the primary attributes of mass and size) but as our perceiving a lot of things that are simply "not there." "The result," says Whitehead, "has been disastrous both to science and philosophy,"[2] and a great many people since Kant have tried to bridge the gap.

I have mentioned Whitehead; I could have spoken of John Dewey, with his concept of "having an experience," or F. H. Bradley's thesis that the unity of "immediate experience" is

what "really is" and systems that build on an assumption of
the duality of subject and object or mind and world, with one or
the other primary, will be led into contradiction.[3] The work of
Ernst Cassirer and Susanne Langer on the ways people use
myth, symbols, and language to integrate the external world
with the internal has relevance here as does Husserl's concept
of "intentionality," that is, our power of conferring meaning.
One of Husserl's followers lucidly puts it:

> Once we have realized the connections between subjectivity
> as intentionality and the role of intentionality in bringing my
> world into being . . . we arrive at the point where we have to
> turn the objective hypothesis round 180 degrees and observe
> the subjectivity we are studying, not as a body operated upon
> by forces in a mechanical world, but as a freely emitting
> centre of meanings. We attain a point of vantage from where
> we find out that we are *conferring* meaning upon the world
> instead of letting the world shove its meanings down over us.
> We become *active* in forming . . . decisions about the being
> of things, instead of accepting the usual objective paradigm
> of Lockean *tabula rasa* or some kind of behaviourist-
> Pavlovian conditioned reflex assumption.[4]

It is precisely this epistemological turnabout to which our study
of reading gives empirical support.

Other studies of reading point the same way. I am thinking
particularly of the work of David Bleich that shows ostensibly
literary categories such as period, genre, meaning, one's decision as to the most important word, sentence, or idea in a
work, one's relation to a character, and the like, all express
personal styles and concern.[5] Indeed, more than a dozen years
ago, Caroline Shrodes asserted that

> Reading, like all other human behavior, is a function of the
> total personality. When we read fiction, poetry, or drama, we
> perceive selectively in accordance with our needs, goals, de-
> fenses, and values. Parallel in substance and function to the
> primary phases of psychotherapy, the vicarious experience
> induced by reading includes identification, projection, and
> introjection; transference of emotion from early experience

to current symbols of it; catharisis; and insight. However,
the reader will abstract from the work of art only what he is
able to perceive and organize; what he experiences and feels
will determine the nature of his perceptions and the meaning
he attaches to them.[6]

This book differs from these earlier works in making use of
modern identity theory and the principle of multiple function to
describe readers reading.

In so doing, it develops four principles that inform not only
the act of reading but all other experiencing. These principles
enable us to translate a general ethical or epistemological concern with individuality into an exact way of examining any
given act of experiencing. These four principles also make it
possible to relate personality to perception in considerable detail and within the larger explanatory system of psychoanalysis.
They thus make precise a number of trends in modern
psychoanalytic ego psychology. They also give a precision to
the group psychologies proposed by political scientists, cognitive psychologists, and cultural anthropologists, relating them
all, again, to fundamental psychoanalytic principles.

We arrived at the four principles of experiencing by comparing two kinds of interpretations: one, an analysis of what
someone said about one particular experience; the other, an
analysis of total personality by means of what someone said
about many experiences. Both these analyses, however, used
the same holistic method; that is, both sought out a formulable
unity around which one could interrelate all the details of the
experience or personality. It is this method, fundamentally, on
which all the conclusions of this book rest, a method which, for
me at least, began in literary criticism where it still receives its
most exacting and satisfying application.

Literary Criticism and Holistic Method

When a literary critic explicates a text in the most formal and
rigorous way, he establishes meaningful relations between particular details of the text (specific episodes, for example, or

phrasings) and large, general themes. As a standard handbook
for students of literature puts it,

> The process of academic criticism begins, then, with reading
> a [literary work] through to the end, suspending value-
> judgements while doing so. Once the end is reached, we can
> see the whole design of the work as a unity. It is now a
> simultaneous pattern radiating out from a center, not a narra-
> tive moving in time. The structure is what we call the theme,
> and the identifying of the theme is the next step . . . not
> something in the poem, much less a moral precept suggested
> by it, but the structural principle of the poem.[7]

One listens primarily for repetition and contrast, notably the
repetition of an image or phrase in different contexts. One listens, too, for ambiguities and complexity of meaning in the
words used, for structural and formal patterns, and for what is
not said. Out of all these fervors and recurrences, the critic
creates, by his own act of personal synthesis, "the unity to
which everything else must be relevant," to use another phrase
from Northrop Frye's description of critical method for
graduate students.

Lest you think I am a disciple, not just an admirer, of Professor Frye, let me quote also from Leo Spitzer's statement some
thirty years ago of the methodology that I believe has become
the canonical strategy of the modern literary critic:

> to work from the surface to the "inward life-center" of the
> work of art: first observing details about the superficial ap-
> pearance of the particular work . . . then, grouping these
> details and seeking to integrate them into a creative principle
> which may have been present in the soul of the artist; and,
> finally, making the return trip to all the other groups of ob-
> servations in order to find whether the "inward form" one
> has tentatively constructed gives an account of the whole.
> The scholar will surely be able to state, after three or four of
> these [voyages to and fro] whether he has found the life-
> giving center, the sun of the solar system . . .[8]

One might or might not agree with some of Spitzer's

metaphysics (or his metaphors) but I think most Anglo-American and an increasing number of continental literary critics follow the method either by itself or combined with other critical modes. Such modes include: interpreting a work sequentially rather than as a whole, "decoding" individual details by means of an allegorical schema, tracing a theme through several works, "phenomenological reduction," "structuralist hermeneutics," and so on. All critical modes, I think, serve readers as ways of mastering literary experiences and making them coherent. The search for thematic unity, however, deals particularly with divergencies that many people perceive as vaguely threatening—I am thinking of the dawning discomfort I feel as I slowly realize the reels in a film have gotten out of order or when part of an unfamiliar play feels discordant in tone or causal relation with the rest. Perceiving the work as a thematic unity enables me to experience both convergence and divergence, to have joy in "in active coalescence of the diverse." Evidently many other readers, too—Aristotle being the first on record and W. J. Bate, the critic from whom I have borrowed that Coleridgean phrase—have shared this feeling.

You have already seen me use this thinking and intuiting toward convergency to derive a centering theme for "A Rose for Emily" with which to grasp the many different details of the story in "a consistent, coherent, and intelligible pattern" (a phrase we will see later in a different context). I arrived at a central theme that suited me by grouping subsidiary themes: change, government, retaining, body dirt, voices, the O. Henry-type denouement, and so on. These subsidiary themes, in turn, I derived from the story by listening to its words for patterns of repetition or contrast and by grouping the details of the story in my mind, not only according to plot sequence, but also in terms of repetition or contrast. Thus, by a process of successive abstraction from the particular verbal events of the text, I formulated a central theme with which to unify my experience: "Putting within yourself and so controlling something that is outside where it cannot be controlled but seeks to control you."

Given such a theme, I can proceed the other way, from the

abstract, general pattern of the story to its particular verbal details. Around just two polarities, outside/inside and controller/controlled, I can bring together to my own satisfaction all the different variations of the story: the forces of change acting on the South, the surroundings of Miss Emily's decaying house, her father's domination, her own seizing of Homer, the inside of her house—and body. I can even grasp such tiny verbal details as her thrice repeated, "I have no taxes in Jefferson," in terms of a retention inside herself against outside pressures to give out. The phrasing of the tableau, "the two of them *framed* by the back-flung front door," also involves things being held inside, throwing other things outside. The door and the frame connote boundaries and the violence of the "flung" door suggest both lack of control and the severest, most brutal of controls.

By the same token, I can relate diverging details of the story to one another by tracing their connection through their subsidiary themes to the "central theme" of the story and back through subsidiary variations. For example, I can see relationships between Emily's "strained" facial expression and the repeated references to the legal forces of the town; between Emily's obesity and her keeping of Homer's body; between her father's domination and her choice of a Yankee day-laborer for a lover. The first two are linked through the major theme of control (one inner, the other outer). The second two involve taking things inside one's body. The third could be described as "loving the forbidden one," both defying the forces of control and taking him inside one's body, house, or mind. In effect, I move back and forth from the periphery of the story to the "center" or "unity to which everything else must be relevant" to give superficial details a mutual interrelationship around a single "inward form," which, in turn, gives an account of the whole.

At least one theorist has seen that a similar method operates in psychoanalysis. "Analysis," writes W. W. Meissner, "is not concerned with the repeatability of data from case to case, but rather with the inner consistency and pattern of meaning that obtains within each case."[9] "Meaning is the central fact of human existence with which psychoanalysis has to deal. The

whole direction of the therapist's effort is toward elaboration of
the full context of meaning in which the whole range of data
that he has gathered about the patient falls into a consistent,
coherent, and intelligible pattern"[10]—a phrase we have seen
describe literary as well as psychoanalytic interpretation. Freud
himself sheds light on this "consistent, coherent, and intelligible pattern."

It was as early as 1896 that he analogized the psychoanalyst
trying to make sense of his patient's behavior to an archaeologist confronted with half-buried ruins, fragments of
buildings, and the garbled traditions of the surviving inhabitants. His task, too, is to make sense of these things.

> If his work is crowned with success, the discoveries are
> self-explanatory: the ruined walls are part of the ramparts of
> a palace or a treasure-house; the fragments of columns can
> be filled out into a temple; the numerous inscriptions, which,
> by good luck, may be bilingual, reveal an alphabet and a
> language, and, when they have been deciphered and trans-
> lated, yield undreamed of information about the events of the
> remote past, to commemorate which the monuments were
> built. *Saxa loquuntur!*[11]

In effect, each element in the ruins becomes related to every
other through a knowledge of the themes or traits of the lost
civilization.

In other words, one rates the success of a psychoanalyst's
explanation qualitatively by the coherence, meaning, and convergence with which it interrelates the data. One also rates its
explanatory power quantitatively by the amount of detailed behavior it interrelates and the directness of the connections it
makes. A good psychoanalytic explanation must interrelate not
just large categories of behavior but myriads of small details
from many spheres of activity. In particular, because of the
basic method of psychoanalysis—free association—a "correct"
psychoanalytic explanation must be able to deal with the *words*
the patient uses about what he does, including their form as
well as their content (the reason this book has had to be so full
of quotations).

For example, Freud noted a phrase that his patient, "Wolf-

Man," used: "The world, he said, was hidden from him by a veil; and our psycho-analytic training forbids our assuming that these words can have been without significance or have been chosen at haphazard." Again, speaking of the same patient, "It is," he said, "always a strict law of dream-interpretation that an explanation must be found for every detail."[12] Certainly, his practice with slips of the tongue, jokes, symptoms, lapses of memory, and free associations to dreams showed the absolute necessity of concentrating on the exact words used or the exact details of a particular behavior or symptom.

Then, as we have seen, one puts the particular wording (such as a reader's remark about a short story) into "an integral and meaningful relation to a pattern of meaning," in Meissner's phrase. "This pattern of meaning at its highest level of generalization encompasses the entire life of the patient."[13] That is, it becomes what we have been calling an "identity theme" or myth or *mythe personnel* or lifestyle for that particular person.

The psychiatrist needs this kind of synthesis not only to understand his patient but to make therapeutic responses. He has to have what Ralph Greenson describes as a "working model of the patient," consisting of physical appearance, emotions, life experiences, modes of behavior, attitudes, defenses, values, fantasies, and the life by which the analyst can transform the patient's words into pictures and feelings from actual experiences "in accordance with [the patient's] ways."[14] Freud himself spoke of the reconstruction of "Wolf-Man's" central fantasy as the way to explain a great many details in his analysis,

> how, after a certain phase of the treatment, everything seemed to converge upon it, and how later, in the synthesis, the most various and remarkable results radiated out from it; how not only the large problems but the smallest peculiarities in the history of the case were cleared up by this single assumption.[15]

Probably, however, the first person to systematize this method of reasoning as a *verbal* phenomenon was Franz Alexander in the mid-1930s with his "emotional syllogisms." As a phrase, "receiving or taking something," represents a general dynamic quality that could affect body organs—for example, the stomach functions, swallowing, or breathing in—as well as wishes to receive help, love, money, a gift, or a child and oppositely directed wishes to take away something, to unman, or to steal. Similarly, "to give love, to make an effort, to help to produce something, to give a gift, to give birth to a child," or the wish "to attack someone (especially by throwing something at him)"—any of these impulses could relate to organic functions such as urination, defecation, ejaculation, perspiration, or exhaling, all being different modes of "eliminating." Alexander explored the possibility of understanding large areas of patients' behavior (including organic illnesses) as translations into specific details of such "emotional syllogisms" as "I do not receive and therefore I have to take by force," or "I give so much and therefore I have the right to receive," or "I have never received sufficiently, so I must hold on to my possessions."[16]

You have already seen (in Chapter 3) a number of psychoanalytic writers support the assumption that there is a central theme (which can be expressed in words) that unifies an entire human personality. Heinz Hartmann would include in it moral behavior, and Abram Kardiner ideologies and values. Anna Freud spoke of an "ego style" that would encompass cognitive functions as well as the more traditional concerns of psychoanalysis.* The nonpsychoanalytic psychologist, George A. Kelly, developed a theory of "personal constructs" through which each individual anticipates events, both public and private, that is, within the self and outside it. "The aspirations of the scientist are essentially the aspirations of all men."[17]

Typically, however, the psychoanalytic psychologist wishes to interrelate many kinds of experience. He seeks a concept of the individual personality that will link the anticipation of events to many areas of feeling and behavior. Thus Erik Erikson notes in a subtle analysis of the kind of evidence he used in a particular case, that "that immediate clinical situation . . . the history of the patient's breakdown and a certain period in his adolescence are all found to have a common denominator" in his wish for a certain "countenance" and his fear that his anger

* See above, pp. 57–58.

will destroy it.[18] Similarly, Robert Jay Lifton found that a victim of brainwashing could be wholly understood through three short sentences that represented "convictions which he had been seeking to prove to himself almost from the day of his birth." "To maintain these personal myths required ever-strenuous but ever-exhilarating efforts. He was always on guard against his own inner urges in the opposite direction."[19] After being chained hand and foot, subjected to eight days of continuous interrogation, and imprisoned for three and a half years, he turned his ordinary behavior completely around, becoming frank and open instead of isolated, superior, and self-contained. But he never changed his "identity theme," in the deeper sense of the fundamental polarities and dichotomies through which he perceived and structured his world. As we have seen, it is Heinz Lichtenstein who has defined this "identity theme" in its most general and far-reaching form, as like a musical theme and variations in which not the notes themselves but their correlation to one another remains constant. It is this very general "invariant correlation" that underlies our perception of the myriad behaviors expressing personality or character, "whose transformations . . . provide the developmental sequences with an unchanging inner form or core"[20]— unchanged apparently, even by brainwashing.

Now this establishing of meaningful relations between particular details in order to establish the basic personality structure of a patient seems to me exactly what the literary critic does to establish the unity of the text. I would even state it as an analogy. Unity is to the text as identity is to a person; or you could say, identity is the unity I find in a person if I look at him as if he were a text. At least one psychotherapist has made the same analogy:

A man reads a poem. He reads the poem through, every word of it, and memorizes it. Although the words and phrases are familiar to him and understood in ordinary contexts, he feels his "understanding" of the poem, as a poem, is inadequate; his enjoyment of it is meager. He fails in his attempts at a conception of the poem which will "work" by tying together all the elements. Now a friend, a trained and

sensitive critic of poetry, suggests to him an over-all organization or unifying meaning-scheme which has not occurred to
him. Suddenly, it "clicks."

The words, without some unifying scheme of meanings,
are not a poem. A poem is an experience which is generated
only as there is also brought to bear some unifying scheme
by the one who interprets.

Now I propose that the patient in insight therapy plays a
role analogous to that of the reader of the poem: what the
patient "reads" are the bits and pieces of his life. He brings
these fragments of his life to the therapist who then suggests
a meaning-scheme in terms of which to reorganize and unify
the patient's experience.[21]

While a classical psychoanalyst would not expect a quick interpretation at the level of intellectual meaning to have much
therapeutic effect, nevertheless, he himself must use some such
model in understanding his patient, and he would expect his
patient to acquire such a model of himself as a result of the
analysis.

You have already seen me using such models in relating disparate "bits and pieces" of the five readers' lives. Sam's tolerance for Lyndon Johnson, his concern with manners, or his
wish to be touched by friends all related to his characteristic
quest to be admired as an intact, boyish male—and the same
need led him to assert that masculinity by thrusting into literary
texts interpretations that would really, in his phrase, "stand
up." Saul used fictions as sources of factual data and quoted
from texts as exactly as he could, but he mumbled vague responses to me—seemingly contradictory, the two styles form
part of one larger pattern: making forces from outside small and
precise so they would not take away from him what he wanted
to keep inside. Shep's leftist politics coexisted in his mind with
his being "taken" by Mussolini's nephew's comparison of fascist bombs to blossoms. Although quite inconsistent on the
surface, both express his deeper search for safety by seeing
either himself or others as mere things among things in an
impersonal system. Sebastian's adolescent liking for the
Anglo-Catholic aristocratic tradition had given way to "a ten-

dency now to put my eggs in the hippie basket," and the odd phrasing reminds me of the characteristic pattern that underlies both commitments: his style of giving to and getting from an outside control. Sandra's liking for the narrator in "A Rose for Emily" and other stories served as one variation of her basic wish for an equalizing flow of power from stronger to weaker as did her muting of colors in the story and the Rorschach test.

Since the skills of the clinician and the literary critic coincide in this holistic method of analysis, it seems to me that literary and psychiatric education should meet here as well. While attending clinical conferences, I have often been struck by the skill literary people have of perceiving unifying themes in a mass of disparate detail, which allows them to arrive readily at insights that psychiatrists find useful and significant. Similarly, in a program of internship in a mental clinic that I help guide, I commonly see graduate students in English develop interpretations of "clients" that are at least as good as those of the social workers and medical students who are their fellow trainees. The study of literary texts offers to the physician and the paraprofessional alike a ready source of sharable and safe material on which to develop skills of psychiatric interpretation. I do *not* mean diagnosing literary characters as though they were case histories. I *do* mean that search for "the unity to which everything else must be relevant," which provides the intellectual basis for an empathic interpretation of either a patient or a poem.[22]

And we are not limited to patients or poems. We are dealing with a method of wide applicability in the social sciences and beyond them. Paul Diesing, in his incisive sorting-out of the four basic methods actually used by social scientists, describes the holistic (or case-study or participant-observer) methodology as it applies to social systems ranging from large societies or cultures to a small gang or clique, even a single family or an individual, and sometimes a historical period. Devised by anthropologists, it is commonly used by sociologists, social psychologists, political scientists, organization theorists, clinical psychologists, historians, institutional economists, and—I would add—literary critics. "Its primary subject matter is a single, self-maintaining social system," or, in the literary situation, a text, really, a text *cum* reader, a reading transaction. "In each case the emphasis is on the individuality or uniqueness of the system, its wholeness or boundedness, and the ways it maintains its individuality." The primary objective is to describe the individual in its individuality.[23]

As Diesing describes case-study method, it looks more and more like literary analysis as described by Frye or Spitzer. The lowest level of interpretive statement is, in Diesing's terminology, a "theme." "It asserts simply that a certain uniformity exists in the data . . . some sort of clustering or syndrome." "It is like a pawn, easily gotten and easily discarded." "If only a few [instances] turn up it is inactivated, and if more than one or two negative instances appear it is discarded."[24]

The next level of generality (again, in Diesing's terminology) is a configuration or model, "used to organize a set of themes into a systematic description of a case and in this sense to explain the themes." The model is tested by its explanatory power. "First, how many themes are included . . . and how many are left out; second, how coherent or well-organized the themes are; and third, whether new themes fit into the model as well." From models or configurations, one moves to types that are used to control comparisons, and finally to general theory, which is used to organize types. All are tested by their explanatory power and accepted or rejected depending on the availability of a better alternative configuration, model, typology or theory.[25] In this study, the important levels have been the model of literary experience and the general theory that explained differences in perception by differences in identity theme. I tend to play down the usual psychoanalytic typologies (oral, anal, phallic, compulsive, etc.) in favor of a "smoother" description based in a general principle of motivation.

All these levels, however, use the same kind of explanation. Diesing, following Abraham Kaplan, calls it "the pattern model of explanation." "A theme, and also a relation, is explained by specifying its place in the pattern." As Kaplan says, "For the pattern model, objectivity consists essentially in this, that the pattern can be indefinitely filled in and extended: as we obtain more and more knowledge it continues to fall into place in this pattern, and the pattern itself has a place in a larger whole."[26] So here, I could know more and more about the five readers and their readings, but still understand them in terms of these identity themes and this model of reading. As I encounter new readers of new books, they should provide new instances for the model, which, in turn, can be placed in a larger psychoanalytic model for other kinds of experiencing besides reading.

Whatever its generalizing power, though, I suspect there are many who will object to such a model, precisely because it rests on a holistic or pattern method of explanation, and therefore is "unscientific." For example, there is no way to refute such an interpretation of a person or a poem by contrary data. There is no room in the procedure for repeatable experiments. Its data cannot be quantified and, worst of all, the results rest on explicitly "subjective" interpretations of the data. Indeed, the theory says *my* interpretations must express my personality as much as the five readers' readings do. Necessarily, a method based entirely on some interpreter's sense of convergence must be untrustworthy. Or must it? That is, I think, a question worth lingering over.

The Scientific Issue

The social sciences aspire to the condition of the natural ones, seeking rigor by adopting methods—and attitudes—borrowed from physics, chemistry, or biology. That is, the experimenter appeals (sometimes tacitly, sometimes explicitly) to a consensus of disinterested observers. He tries to make careful distinctions between observation and inference and to keep the results separate from his own personality. He assumes that his subject matter is uniform, passive, and amenable to numbering, that he can make repeatable experiments on it, and that he can strictly control variables. How true this all is of what has come to be known locally as YAHS (Your Average Hippie Subject), I leave to your imagination.

In a more formal sense, as Diesing points out, we see the experimental method in the social sciences, mostly in psychology and social psychology. It takes as its subject matter variables, that is, any natural events that show measurable variations in occurrence. The experimenter tries to locate a lawlike variable by looking in previous experimental results for masking effects that covered over some hidden correlation. Then, he invents an experimental situation in which he can control and thereby remove the effect of the masking and so reveal that correlation. He devotes considerable art to refining variables, modifying his methods, strengthening his correlations, and extending his experiment to new populations in order to formulate a general law.[27]

This all sounds very rigorous indeed, yet some of the assumptions seem to demand an almost superhuman perfection. I have raised the question of bias from the subjects of the experiment. (Do sophomores behave like normal people?) A leading student of psychological methodology, Joseph Masling, has identified other sources of bias; the testing situation, the way the experiment is administered, the investigator himself, and the actual experimenter[28] who is often the investigator's graduate assistant, hoping for a successful dissertation and consequent promotion.

Even in the exalted world of the "hard" sciences, an objectivity untainted by the personality of the experimenter is more an ideal than a reality. As one of the wisest of physicists, Max Planck, put it, "A new scientific truth does not triumph by convincing its opponents and making them see the light, but rather because its opponents eventually die, and a new generation grows up that is familiar with it."[29] He is remarking, in effect, the way personality and previous experience enter into a man's feeling that this or that kind of explanation is satisfying. The psychologist George A. Kelly sees the same variability in hypotheses despite claims of "proof" through prediction:

> The substantiation of hypotheses is really not quite as simple as this. The catch is in the design of the experiment. If the experiment is so designed that other obvious hypotheses would have expressed the same prediction, the question arises as to which hypothesis was verified. As a matter of fact, in scientific research, one never finds the ultimate proof of a given hypothesis. About the time he thinks he has such

proof within his grasp, another scientist comes along with another hypothesis that provides just as plausible an explanation of the experimental results.[30]

The word "plausible" reveals a necessary criterion of truth. As a recent commentator on scientific innovation concludes, "A discovery is premature if its implications cannot be connected by a series of simple logical steps to canonical, or generally accepted. knowledge."[31] Thus, Oswald Avery discovered in 1944 that DNA was the basic carrier of genetic information, but "geneticists did not seem to be able to do much with it or build on it" until 1952. A still more famous example is Gregor Mendel's discovery of the gene in 1865; it lay dormant for thirty-five years because no one could relate it to contemporary anatomy and physiology and because Mendel's statistical methods were quite alien to the habits of nineteenth-century biological thought.

Even the scientist sometimes cannot help behaving like the bishops who refused to look through Galileo's telescope because the discovery of moons around Jupiter or spots on our moon could have no conceivable relevance to their canonical and generally accepted view of the world. If anything, the bishops were more self-aware than people today who claim that the scientist's methods put him in touch with a reality independent of his own personal vision. The true situation is that even in the "hardest" of "hard" sciences, scientists accept "truths" to the extent they can take them into the system of beliefs and values that make up their culture and personality. Even "hard" sciences share the personal interpretation of data characteristic of holistic method.

In comparing holistic and experimental research, then, we are not talking about two methods, one of which is objective and one subjective, one "scientific" and one not. We are talking of two methods, *both* subjective, but having different ways of dealing with the influence of subjectivity on one's acceptance of explanations, framing of hypotheses, or agreement on what constitutes confirmation. What we need is an honest comparison, not the name-calling ("*That*'s not scientific!") into which evaluation of holistic studies sometimes degenerates. In considering my work on reading and psychoanalytic studies in general, if you will put aside the honorifics and polemics and keep in mind the model of the cultural anthropologist (like Freud's archaeologist) rather than a nineteenth-century physicist or the experimental psychologist who imitates that style of physics, then you can usefully contrast methods.

For example, holistic and experimental methods differ in the way they explain things. In the pattern explanation, the thing to be explained and that which does the explaining exist on the same level of generality, and their relation is that of part to whole. "The whole explanation," writes Diesing, "is a description of a particular personality, social, or cultural system," and "No general laws appear anywhere," except as "suggestive guides in the search for directly observed particular connections," within, say, a certain tribal village. By contrast, the experimenter uses the familiar deductive model of explanation by means of a general law, positing a sharp distinction between the thing to be explained and that which does the explaining. The law "is always more abstract and more general than what it explains." "The emphasis in a deductive model" Diesing continues, "is on laws, while in a pattern model it is on facts." "Consequently, to devotees of the deductive model, pattern explanations look like descriptions, since they cannot find the laws they like to use as sources of intelligibility. Sometimes they dogmatically assert that there *must* be laws hidden in the explanation somewhere, since otherwise it would not really be an explanation."[32]

Thus, well-meaning experimentalists sometimes try to legitimate psychoanalytic psychology by stating it in the form of laws. Typically, it is studied in psychology departments this way. Yet, as Michael Sherwood observes, taking Freud's "Rat Man" case as a prototype of psychoanalytic explanation, such laws miss the point.

Whatever cogency and force [psychoanalytic] explanations may possess is acquired only through our close acquaintance with the whole case history of the patient and the whole psychoanalytic narrative Freud weaves about him. Yet once we do know that past history and have some idea as to the conflicts and forces Freud posits as underlying his behavior in general, then the interpretation of, say, the formula *"Glejsamen"* as being an anagram of the name of the patient's cousin may well strike us as being shrewd, immediately understandable, and probably correct. . . . The ultimate basis of a psychoanalytic explanation is a long narrative account applicable to the individual as a whole rather than isolated explanations of particular bits of behavior.

Or, more generally, "Any explanation of a particular piece of behavior must always be studied within its context, as a part of a larger, unified narrative." This is obviously a very familiar idea to a literary critic used to seeking organic unity within extended poems and fictions or to an anthropologist used to studying a culture as a whole. No "laws" apply except an *ad hoc* pattern of parts converging toward centering themes.[33]

While laws or general principles about behavior would

represent a part of the basic commitment of Freud's explanation, it is *not* true that they are the essence or heart of that explanation. The actual explanation is a long and involved narrative tying together a great number of biographical factors into a coherent account. . . . General statements are at best only summaries of the wealth of biographical information which went into the actual narrative. Taken by themselves, however, they appear as rather arbitrary assertions, totally lacking in explanatory power.

A patient's miserliness, for example, is not "explained" because it can be deduced from his "anality." "If we have been convinced, it is because we have followed Freud through a complicated narrative which has attempted to organize a wealth of biographical data into some understandable whole." Given general statements, "Rat Man's" miserliness

might now be predicted with certainty, but the explanation no longer has any general applicability to the rest of the patient's behavior. The explanatory power of Freud's discussion resides in the narrative itself or else is nonexistent. Generalizations abstracted from that matrix will of course

appear arbitrary and unconvincing. But the sense of convic-
tion is restored not by supplying an artificial logical schema,
but by returning those statements to their original explanatory narrative.

Dr. Sherwood had, all unwittingly, pinpointed my difficulty de-
vising experiments and particularly, predictions of literary response in psychoanalytic terms. Such an analysis based on a
general law plus deduction from an if-then hypothesis "could at
best provide nothing more than a rather misleading sketch or
outline summary of the actual psychoanalytic explanation of a
particular piece of behavior."[34]

As you know, it is one of the most common criticisms of
psychoanalytic psychology that it will not predict human behavior. Partly, this criticism simply reflects an attitude, the
demand carried over from the "hard" sciences, where, in
Sherwood's phrase, "control looms large as a goal," intellectually, economically, and politically. Another perspective, that of
the doctor or the patient, tends to equate success of cure with
validity of explanation. The wish to predict is a wish for the
kind of control over future events that a scientist exerts over
matter or an internist over the digestive tract.

The problem is more than attitudinal, however. In a holistic
explanation, notes Diesing, "it is not possible to deduce an
unknown part of a pattern from a known part," because the
relations within the pattern are usually neither those of logical
implication nor cause nor consistency. Functional relations always leave room for alternatives; symptoms can always have
different explanations, and so on. Think of trying to deduce the
missing parts of the *Satyricon*, say, from the fragmentary text
we have; or imagine an archaeologist trying to infer complex
rituals from the catalogue of ceremonial objects and the shape
of the sanctum. "A corollary of this point is that one cannot
deduce specific predictions of future behavior in novel circumstances from a pattern explanation; the symmetry of prediction
and explanation that occurs in a deductive model is not
present."[35]

A pattern explanation thus comes after all the evidence is in,
raising yet another question about its claims to scientific status.

Are there any data that would not fit it? In a frivolous sense, obviously not—it was designed precisely to encompass every detail. The objection really intends, however, the old standard: a scientific hypothesis must be stated in a form that is falsifiable by some observation of fact. That canon seems reasonable enough, and, in one sense, the identity themes I have derived live up to it. If Sandra were suddenly to start worshipping weakness or Shep to begin seeing the world in interpersonal terms, I would have to admit there is something wrong with the identity themes I have given them or with the idea of identity themes in general.

But no new facts about these five readers can now come into being. For the purposes of this "experiment," they exist as so many hundreds of pages of transcript. Although I occasionally hear bits of news about them (and they confirm, sometimes quite pleasingly, the themes I suggest), these items have to remain *hors de combat*. I am rather in the position of the archaeologist or the interpreter of a novel whose data are simply "there," as opposed to the anthropologist or psychoanalyst with live respondents.

To apply the requirement of a hypothesis that can be refuted as well as confirmed by data to the archaeologist's situation or mine, one needs to understand what is meant by refuting or falsifying in this context. Data do not, in and of themselves, falsify any hypothesis in either methodology, holistic or experimental. Rather, new data may suggest that some *other* hypothesis would fit *all* the data, both old and new, better than the old hypothesis designed from the old data alone. Even if no new data are possible, one can still falsify an old hypothesis by showing that a new one accommodates the existing data more neatly—this is the archaeologist's criterion and mine, and also the experimentalist's. The question becomes one, not of true or false, but of better or worse fit, according to one's estimate of the amount and directness of interrelation established.[36]

This pattern of confirmation becomes even more obvious when the interpretations are as generalized as the identity themes for these five readers or the usual full interpretation of a literary work. If one were testing a tightly defined, if-then hypothesis, one or two items of data that didn't fit would require a wholly new hypothesis (although statistical methods sometimes mute this kind of invalidation). A broad convergence hypothesis, however—a "model" or "configuration" in Diesing's terminology—does not fail because of one or two facts but only in response to a substantial deficiency.

In the same way, the generality of this kind of interpretation means that many interpretations will be possible for the same observed data. Some will fit the large amount of data obviously less well than others, but many will not differ very much. Differences in interpretation will ultimately stem from differences in the interpreters' personalities, in the sense that each individual's interpretation will make sense of the data *for him*. Just as in the act of reading, however, this is not to say, "It's all subjective," meaning thereby untrustworthy, unverifiable, and unscientific. On the contrary, it is precisely by accepting and telling about competing hypotheses that one individual can draw on another's interpretation to enrich his own—as we saw in speaking of audiences, criticism, and teaching (in Chapter 8). An open forum of ideas (or, here, interpretations) makes it possible for different investigators individually to arrive at shared truth.

By contrast, the experimentalist tries to elude his personality entirely by wrapping himself in elaborate procedures like questionnaires, product moments, or autocorrelation functions. While such tactics can complement holistic research, we should not ask one method to self-destruct by converting itself into other methods. As Diesing says,

> One should not expect a clinical, holistic theory to be hierarchical-deductive, to contain rigid formal definitions, or to yield predictions and deductive explanations. Its task is to provide revealing classifications of cases and to sensitize one to what is happening in a case.[37]

That is the great strength of holistic method—its ability to deal with the single case, the unique poem, the solitary tribe, the patient like no other.

The experimenting psychologist, however, wants to avoid subjective influence and attain generalization, and he tries to do this by substituting classes for unique experiences. He works, for example, within "objectively" defined categories. He will experiment with twenty creative writers or ten "aggression prone" subjects, as determined by some standardized series of operations that seem to leave little room for argument. He may use categories from test results such as a certain MMPI score for "defensiveness" or "social introversion." He may count publications or arrests. He may adapt clinical classifications such as "schizoid," "depressive," or "obsessional," perhaps by comparing several diagnoses. Yet the very acceptance of these "objective" boundaries involves "subjective" endorsement of the operations that marked them off (MMPI tests, summed diagnoses, or social definitions of creativity or aggression).

Further, if the picture we have arrived at in the preceding chapters is true—if people act out variations on an identity theme—then these categories that are so sharply defined in operational terms may actually overlap and mask over the inner dynamics of the people being studied. Would it have helped us, for example, to analyze Sam's style of reading in terms of his "homosexual" anxieties or Sebastian's through his "authoritarian" fantasies? It may be, for instance, that the important categories are those that involve the defensive or warding-off side of an identity theme as against the aspect of drawing close—although one could scarcely define these in an experimental way.

Literature, taken simply as one human phenomenon among many, offers useful analogies with which to probe psychological methods such as these. Just as each play and author and person in the audience is unique, making generalizations from one to another member in such classes problematic, so in the larger realm of general psychology, each human act may also have to be thought of as unique. The history of criticism is littered with different efforts to sort literary works into one or another class: lyric, dramatic, tragic, comic, and so on. Definitions abound, none universally acceptable, none even universally applicable. As one makes the terms of definition more precise (stories more than ten thousand words long, stories about the South, stories with heroines), sorting becomes easier, but the classes lose significance. Do these classes, for example, tell us anything useful about "A Rose for Emily"?

Thus there is a further question. Even if one could establish such categories, would general principles follow from them? If, for example, we could establish a firm definition of tragedy or aggressivity, could we use it to discover a uniformity in literary response? I doubt it. Nothing in my experience as teacher or experimenter suggests that there is that kind of categorical patterning.

What such a procedure does is substitute commitment to a method of generalizing for an openness to the subject matter. To be sure, the intellectual care introduced by demands for quantification, replicable results, or hypotheses that can be confirmed or refuted is praiseworthy indeed, particularly if these experimental procedures give rigorous insights into the human subject matter to which they are now applied. But if they don't? Many nonpsychologists share, I suspect, the sentiment described by Noam Chomsky:

> To a considerable degree, I feel, the "behavioral sciences" are merely mimicking the surface features of the natural sciences; much of their scientific character has been achieved by a restriction of subject matter and a concentration on rather peripheral issues. Such narrowing of focus can be justified if it leads to achievements of real intellectual significance, but in this case, I think it would be very difficult to show that the narrowing of scope has led to deep and significant results.
>
> The term "behavioral science" suggests a not-so-subtle shift of emphasis toward the evidence itself and away from the deeper underlying principles and abstract mental structures that might be illuminated by the evidence of behavior. It is as if natural science were to be designated "the science of meter readings."[38]

Indeed, when one hears of computers rotating matrices with hundreds of variables, it seems as though the human beings who were once the subject matter of psychology have been quite gobbled up in the methodology. And often the conclusions themselves seem to shrink beside the baroque efflorescence of method.

There is a kind of Faustian grandeur in positing a methodology out of pure scientific zeal without pausing to consider the subject matter to which it will be applied. If the method works, one can only applaud. But if it doesn't, I think a reasonable man would question the assumption of the methodology, no matter how sacrosanct it seems at first. Suppose, for example, people had said at the outset that all questions in the physical sciences had to be investigated by interpersonal methods— what kind of physical science would we have? Suppose it had been laid down that we could talk about history only by means of numbers—what kind of history would have resulted? Now some people insist that we talk about inter- and intrapersonal matters only by the methods of the physical sciences. It seems to me this is an assumption decidedly open to question.

It is particularly questionable when the procedure has a built-in barrier to "achievement of real intellectual significance." Diesing explains why. "In the experimental method, definitions are always at least partly operational." Each improvement or novelty in experimental procedure, therefore, introduces a change in the meaning of the terms and laws being tested. "Consequently, widespread use of the experimental method tends to produce a proliferation of variables and laws, many vaguely overlapping, rather than the single clear network of laws originally anticipated." "This difficulty in producing truly general laws is one of the chief problems in the experimental method in the social sciences."[39]

Where the experimentalist puts method before matter, the holist puts his unique subjects first. Indeed, says Diesing, "This belief in the primacy of subject matter over method is perhaps the most striking characteristic of the holist standpoint." The result is paradoxical: the experimentalist who explicitly seeks classes and categories finds it difficult to generalize beyond any given experiment, while the holist who works with unique cases finds it almost too easy to move from the one to the universal. Indeed, Diesing argues that the holist needs to be restrained.

"Generalization from a single case or a few cases is always a haphazard affair." "The basic solution is to move from the particular to the general and back in small steps rather than in one grand jump. One first compares one's case with a similar case, then to another and another, then to one somewhat more different." "Holist theorizing should always proceed in intimate contact with particular cases."[40] As Freud said, talking about the case of "Wolf-Man," "There is no doubt a great temptation to content oneself with 'scratching' the mental surface of a number of people and of replacing what is left undone by speculation," for example, by working with fixed categories of surface behavior. Rather, "In order to derive fresh generalizations," he said it was "essential to have at one's disposal numerous cases as thoroughly and deeply analyzed as the present one. But they are not easily to be had, and each one of them requires years of labour. So that advances in these spheres of knowledge must necessarily be slow."[41] Slow it has been, but the psychoanalytic study of cases has led to a truly universal theory of human psychology, markedly more general than the fragmentary "laws" of experimentalists. The modern psychoanalyst who tries to substitute experimental rigor for the classical method may find he is playing Esau, selling his psychoanalytic birthright for a mess of empirical pottage.

It may be that the holistic method pays off in an almost irresistible push toward comprehensive theory because it more truly accords with the inner dynamics of the reality being explored. This study of reading suggests, for example, that some of the basic assumptions on which experimentation in the "hard" sciences rests do not hold for the social or (better) "human" sciences. For example, to take one that Masling lists, the "scientific" experimenter assumes that his subject matter is passive and does not form attitudes or expectations that affect the experiment.[42] But this was not at all true when the subject matter was a dozen or so undergraduates reading stories. Psychological generalizations may succeed better if they take the holistic route and become both more specific *and* more general than those one sees in the psychological journals today. It may be that they need to speak of *this* person or *all* persons and not attempt to generalize about "20 Ss."

A similar problem attaches to the assumption of a unidirectional causality on which many experiments rest. Changing a cause (or independent variable) results in an effect (or change in a dependent variable), and the prediction of this effect confirms or refutes a hypothesis. Often these changes seem still more impressive because they are measured in numbers. Yet this study suggests that the classical "A causes B" model will not describe what goes on in reading, nor even a subtler "C causes them both." We could, for example, think of this "experiment" with five readers reading "A Rose for Emily" as holding constant the story and the experimenter and the conditions, varying as independent variable the personality of the reader, and observing as dependent variable the response. Yet we have seen that the response itself affects what the personality puts into the story: only if the reader succeeds in synthesizing his defenses from the materials of the story will he introject it and project his preferred fantasies into it. In other words, A causes B *and* B causes A, or C causes them both *and* is caused by them both. As one philosopher, Abraham Kaplan, has said, the "most fundamental" type of law in the behavioral sciences has to be teleological: statements about the functions served by a phenomenon within a larger, purposeful framework.[43]

Some philosophers and psychologists, however, object to the mingling of teleological or functional terms (like drives, needs, or hopes) with purely formal behaviorist concepts, like reinforcement, or physical terms like afferent, central, and efferent neurological systems. Jerry A. Fodor has shown that there is no contradiction. One set of terms need not rule out the other any more than a term like "bookmark" or "penwiper" rules out—or is ruled out by—a physical description of those useful objects. True, confusion will occur if functional accounts are treated as mechanical ones, if, for example, one assumes there is a "markingness" or "wiperdom" in the physical dimensions of these objects. But the answer to the confusion is not to deny the existence of functions like marking and wiping, but to stop thinking of functions of parts (for example, defense mechanisms) as though they were themselves physical parts.[44]

It may also be that such statements of function must be given in words, as I have done with verbal identity themes in this study. Heinz Lichtenstein has suggested that "the algebra of logic" might be the right language to describe identity themes and their variations, and I have myself suggested elsewhere that they can be expressed as four kinds of displacement and a boundary condition that act on and are acted on by affects, ideas, percepts, and motilities—again, leading to a kind of algebra, which has to accommodate meanings as well as quantities.[45] Numbers alone, however, seem of limited use in describing either identity themes or variations on them, while words offer a supplementary kind of exactness.

Words would seem particularly necessary because of the basic method of psychoanalysis: free association. A "correct" psychoanalytic explanation has to be able to deal with the *words*—their form as well as their content—the patient or subject uses about what he does. The words someone uses represent, quantitatively, a major source of details of behavior (or ego choice), and smoothing those words out by means of the quantitative categories of content analysis tends to eliminate them as a basis for insight. Rather, one deals most exactly with words *by* words, as literary critics since Aristotle have known.

Nevertheless, psychologists demanding rigor often insist on quantification regardless, carrying out the pattern we have seen in several contexts now. What we think of as the experimental method in psychology comes about only partly (if at all) as a result of the subject matter of the discipline, but largely as an a priori borrowing on faith from other disciplines. The assumption is: if the methods of physics are used, they will bring the rigor of physics to *any* subject matter.

People, however, make choices, and matter does not. Subjectivity pervades human activities. No matter what a person does, he or she does it within terms set by an identity theme and the sum of experiences that constitute subsequent variations on that theme. These are unique for each of us. It may be, then, that psychological studies can achieve rigor and generality *only* by working with unique events, arriving at a verbal narrative that relates as many as possible of the details of that event as directly as possible.[46] Generalization then follows by comparing these verbal explanations. As I suggested above, it may be that psychological generalizations will succeed better if they deal either with *this* human being or *all* human beings. If so, then one should consider the very broad theory of motivation developed in this book (multiple function within an identity principle) as not something true or false in itself, but a general organizing principle that tells someone what to look for in a given situation to give it "a consistent, coherent, and intelligible pattern." In other words, it permits one to formulate a procedure that is next used to set up interpretations of particular events. Then, finally, those interpretations are found to fit better or worse, as the case may be, according to (roughly) quantitative criteria about the amount and directness with which a given interpretation enables us to interrelate details.

Again, we are not talking about two methods, one of which is legitimate and the other not, one scientific, the other humanistic, one objective, the other subjective. We are talking of two methods, each of which engages in the objectifying of subjectivity in its own way. Each provides its practitioners with a special way of framing hypotheses, evaluating explanations, and confirming or refuting interpretations. One methodology, the more widely accepted, psychologists have borrowed from the physical sciences and applied to human situations even though some of the assumptions basic to the sciences of matter may no longer hold. The other methodology rests on the sharing of interpretations derived from a principle of convergence; and it is designed to deal with subjects that, first, are unique, and, second, can be seen to have a *style*, that is, some discernible habits of choice or strategy. These two methodologies make different claims on our belief. One comes with the authority of Science-with-a-capital-S. The other seems to me to fit the human subject matter of psychology better—although I hasten to admit I may feel it does so because of my own characteristic demand for generality of explanation.

I should also hasten to add that I have been talking about only two of the four methods that Diesing identifies as characteristic of the social sciences, the holistic (or case study or participant-observer) and the experimental. The other two are survey method and formal method.

In using a survey method, one tries to deal with large and complex subject matters more successfully than experiments based on tightly defined categories can, by substituting statistical controls for experimental ones, notably sampling. Correction and validation come about through the statistical manipulation of data, and the new statistical techniques make it possible to deal with many variables in a variety of relationships, yielding complex correlations. "Thus the austere limits of the classical experimental method are transcended, and the complexity of actual societies can be more adequately handled."[47] It becomes possible, for example, to deal with open-ended responses to questions about stories. A statistical method could discover a correlation between liking men who give things in stories and liking narrators (as Sandra did)—if one knew what to look for from a holistic study. One could, in short, use statistics to investigate styles in large numbers.

Possibly, then, one could transcend one of the severe limitations of holistic method and—for a group—make predictions. That is, as we have seen in Chapter 8, one can (particularly for a large group) arrive at a characteristic pattern of choices from which one can infer the defensive and pleasure-seeking aspects of an identity theme. One might be able to predict that a certain story, film, idea, or political event would "take" in a group with that distinctive style, as, for example, Marvin Opler has shown, in a classic paper, that certain nations favor certain "styles" of schizophrenia.[48] To be sure, there would be no guarantee that any one member of the group would have the style in question or that the prediction would work for him in particular. Nor would one be able to "add up" individuals in some statistical way so as to arrive at a style. But within the two criteria for rigor this study of reading has developed, convergence and consensus, prediction of group behavior might be possible.

Formal methods have long dominated economics, but they also occur more and more often in sociology, international studies, and psychology, particularly the behaviorist variety. "The subject matter of a formal method is a formal system of logical relationships abstracted from all the varied empirical content it might have in the real world." From such a model, interpretation derives rules of correspondence relating formal terms to empirical concepts. Then the researcher looks for *differences* between the model and reality so as to refine the matching of the model to reality. Recently, some literary critics have adopted formal methods, drawing their models from European philosophy. So far, however, their work has been confined to the first stage, asserting a logical model, not the second or third, developing rules of correspondence between the model and literature and empirically refining the model. It seems quite unlikely to me that that type of formal analysis of literary texts, genres, or history will tell us much about reading, unless literary critics go on to investigate the limits of such formal models. It is important to note that discovering *similarities* between the model and reality will not lead to improvements in the model—only *differences* will. By the same token, a formal model is never tested as a whole—since it is a purely logical set of definitions, postulates, and deductions, that would be quite pointless.[49] Thus, for example, behaviorist psychology, being wholly a self-contained logical system, cannot be "disproved."

In short, I see two of the four methods as promising in the study of reading: survey and holistic studies of readers; and two methods as unlikely to lead to a useful result: the formal modeling of texts and the experimental presentation of texts to readers. I see the real difference as between methods that can deal with action within a personal style, that is, methods that look at the reader first and directly, and methods that need to look at the text first and only at the reader indirectly, in relation to the text. In other words, as I see the results of my own work, they lead to what David Bleich has called "the primacy of subjectivity."[50] The contrast in research methods then leads me finally to a contrast in epistemologies.

As we saw at the opening of this long and trying chapter, one epistemology treats the knower as separate from the known and acted upon by it—the "Cartesian gap" between mind and body, *res cogitans* and *res extensa*, traditional since the seventeenth century. The other epistemology treats the knower as actively synthesizing and re-creating his world from the materials reality provides him, and this is a larger law urged by the philosophers I mentioned above, namely, that experiencing can be described adequately only as an intermingling of self and

other. From this point of view, the Cartesian cleaving of *res
extensa* from *res cogitans* is itself a historical and personal
strategy governed by psychological criteria and to be described
by terms like Whitehead's in-mixing of self and other, Dewey's
"having an experience," Cassirer's "myths," or Husserl's "intentionality." Now, however, the psychoanalytic psychologist
can give precision to what the philosophers adumbrated: *identity re-creates itself through experience*, identity that can be
examined in great detail through characteristic defenses, fantasies, ego style, and the principle of multiple function.

As Basil Willey argued some forty years ago,[51] seventeenth-
century science itself came into being as a result of a deep
psychological change in the kind of assurance people sought
from explanations.

> For example, the spots on the moon's surface might be due,
> theologically, to the fact that it was God's will they should be
> there; scientifically, they might be "explained" as the craters
> of extinct volcanoes. The newer explanation may be said, not
> so much to contain "more" truth than the older, as to supply
> the *kind* of truth which was now demanded. An event was
> "explained" . . . when its history had been traced and de-
> scribed.

"Interest was now directed to the *how*, the manner of causa-
tion, not its *why*, its final cause."

In our own time, we, the successors of Freud, Marx, and
Durkheim, find ourselves amidst cultural anthropology, the
new transactional psychology of perception, Gödel's discovery of absolute limits to mathematical axiomatization, the
Sapir–Whorf hypothesis in linguistics, and relativity, random-
ness, and uncertainty even in the "hard" sciences. These and
many other discoverings urge us to recognize and accept the
biases in even our most rigorous knowledge. For our purpose,
the most important of these relativizing discoveries is
psychoanalytic psychology, particularly as I have applied it
here, to explain the relation between experience and identity.
So applied, psychoanalysis enables us to go *through* science, as
it were, to a psychological principle that itself explains science:
any way of interpreting the world, even physics, meets human

needs, for interpretation is a human act. From a medieval, theological *why* to the *how* that underlay the three great centuries of classical science, we proceed to a psychoanalytic *to whom*.

Is this not the final ambiguity—and achievement—in Freud's thought? A nineteenth-century scientist himself, he resolutely sought out the *how* of the human mind. Yet the discovery of the method of free association and each subsequent discovery required him to couple a *to whom* to that *how*. It is in this sense that psychoanalytic psychology asks for a total revaluation—a 180 degree turnabout—in the paradigms of our scientific thought.

That is, the positivist of either the nineteenth or twentieth centuries would see the scientific investigation of cause and effect as a wholly different order of knowledge from the holist's (or humanist's) observation of details converging toward a center. But what we have seen is that no such boundary will stand up under close examination. In fact, it might be possible to say that there is only *one* way of knowing—the convergence, coherence, or "fit" of details toward a centering theme or law—but there are different kinds of "fit." Which "fits" are acceptable depends on "to whom"—the psychology of the researcher. The holist will accept similarity and difference, recurrence, intensity, precondition—patterns of many different kinds, including those the experimentalist insists upon. By contrast, the experimentalist will admit *only* his procedures: correlation between dependent and independent variables, prediction, assertions of cause and effect, and the like. From a larger perspective, however, experimental or "scientific" method is only a special case of man's general way of knowing, not *the* way of knowing to which lesser kinds must aspire.

Another way I can express what I am advocating is in terms of addition and subtraction. Many of the objections raised to this model, with its emphasis on the role of individual identity in experiencing reality, come from thinking in subtractive rather than additive terms. That is, people often speak as though the literary work or, in general, some other existed in all its fullness, while I perceive that fullness imperfectly, subtracting out certain aspects. It is as though my perception of the other equaled the other *minus* something. The other becomes very big and vague (remember René Wellek's description of the poem as "a potential cause of experiences," "a structure of . . . implicit norms which have to be extracted from every individual experience of a work"). The self becomes inadequate (in Wellek's phrasing, "the work of art has the character of a duty which . . . I shall always realize imperfectly"). Thinking this way leads to images like the *prison* of the self or the *limits* of what I can see, or the *risk*, even the *peril*, of interpreting wrongly. All such discomfort within one's mind (which, after all, one can never get out of) proceeds from the debilitating assumption that each of us experiences something imperfectly and someone else knows just how imperfectly. In the case of literature, that superior being is usually a literary theorist, sometimes the critic himself cast in the role of theorist, sometimes a very threatening jury of literary critics (or senior professors) who will cry "Shame!" or "Imbecile!" at your experience.

This is surely both a confusing and a discouraging model. Each of us knows what we know. We cannot suddenly know more by casting ourselves in the role of a critic of critics. None of us can stop being himself or step outside of himself to watch the limitation of his reading or other experiencing. All this confusion and sense of limitation and loss comes from positing a literary work or, in general, an other which is full and complete and from which we subtract.

These supposed risks and shames disappear if instead we think additively. Start rather with the reader and ask how and what he is adding to himself by his act of reading. Ask how he is complicating and enriching himself with the literary text, with what he knows or imagines about its author or its time, with what criticism he has read and what he has been told by others—even others wiser or more experienced than he. If we look at the reading transaction from our own point of view as readers, if we consider experience the same way, from within ourselves as what we are adding to ourselves, we need no longer tangle our minds in epistemological confusions about how and how well we can know an other. And the same principle holds true for scientific investigation.

For example, one answers the question of infinite regress that this "experiment" involves in the same way as the problem of personal interpretation, by adding instead of subtracting. You could see this book as a sequence: Sam looks (through his personality) at "A Rose for Emily." I look (through my personality) at Sam looking (through his personality) at "A Rose for Emily." You look (through your personality) at me looking (through my personality) at Sam looking (through his personality) at one, by now, much overburdened short story. It is a mistake, however, to look at these interactions of personality as though they only filtered and subtracted. Rather, each offers something unique, a new perspective, to the one that follows it. Each provides ideas and perceptions with which to make a further synthesis.

As with teaching and criticism, personal views do not cancel one another out, making all personal views wrong. People can add the personal views of others and so enrich their own syntheses, leading simultaneously to some agreement in statements and an irreducible privacy in experience. But this agreement (for example, that Miss Emily cannot be an Eskimo) is precisely what we usually mean by "objective" truth or reality, on the basis of which we will distinguish the genius from the psychotic. The vision of one we can never share. The vision of the other we share only by stretching our own, but we call him a genius precisely to the extent we feel *both* sharing *and* stretching.

In a curious kind of way, then, the best "knowing" we can have, the final test of objective reality, is itself subjective. But these two words themselves introduce the note of subtraction. What this study asks us to recognize is that in knowing, experiencing, and interpreting the world, we do not fail the world in some way. Rather, we achieve the world in ourselves, just as we add to our own lives when we re-create the poems and stories we read. And this return to reading provides an occasion for a final addition.

In Sum

We began with the so-called transformation model of literary experience developed in *The Dynamics of Literary Response*: a literary work, as a person experiences it, consists of a nucleus of fantasy transformed toward intellectual coherence and significance by psychological processes, which, from one point of view, look like literary forms and, from another, like strategies of defense and adaptation. The question this book set out to answer is: How does the personality of the reader shape this experience?, and the answer came from listening to what five actual readers said about what they read. More than listening was required—it was necessary to relate two kinds of interpretation: an interpretation of the reader's personality on the basis of everything he said, including his responses to personality tests, to an interpretation of what he said about one particular reading experience. I could interpret his particular comments by means of the model from *Dynamics,* but to interpret his character as a whole, I drew on a dual theory of human motivation: a person seeks pleasure within his identity theme.

The first half would be tautological—pleasure, after all, is what people seek—except that it can be unpacked through Waelder's principle of multiple function. Each of us seeks what looks like the right balance among drives for gratification and inner inhibitions of drives, the biological tendency to resist change and the demands of reality that require change. Each of these four poles can be explicated in turn through a wealth of clinical and cultural observations into various stages and types of drive, different sources and styles of superego, and different parts of reality—social, economic, intellectual, and physical—which offer solutions, opportunities, and constraints. Only if we feel we have balanced these functions will we feel pleasure.

The second half involves the concept of an identity theme. Every time the individual tries to achieve such a balance, he works within variations of that original invariant, his identity theme. We can discover such a theme by searching out patterns of repetition, contrast, modulation, structure, omission, and the like, in all the myriad details of the individual's behavior. Given a series of achieved or even attempted ego solutions to multiple demands, one can infer from various small patterns a central nuclear pattern by much the same process of successive abstraction as one uses to infer a centering theme in a literary work. In either setting, the theme expresses in a verbal way what one perceives as the essential, continuing unity in a unique and circumscribed organic entity. The concept can apply, ultimately, to anything that reveals its individuality though a discernible pattern of choice.

Together, these two principles, identity and multiple function, comprise a theory of human motivation with which to interpret the widely varying personalities of Sam, Saul, Shep, Sebastian, and Sandra and the action of their personalities in their reading. Applied to this task of double interpretation, the theory of motivation yielded four specific principles informing the reading transaction.

First, if a reader responds positively to parts of a work, that means he sees them as acting out within the work his expectations toward the work or parts of it as entities separate from himself. In other words, he construes events "out there" so as to act out solutions and satisfactions "in here."

In order for this blending to take place, the reading has to fulfill the second and touchiest of the four principles: defenses must be matched. That is, the reader must have synthesized from the language given him in the literary work at least part of his particular style of defense and adaptation. That includes, explicitly, his tastes and preferences according to his degree of literary sophistication and experience, but these in turn express much deeper fears and wishes. This matching is both delicate and drastic. That is, it must be exact for at least a part of the reader's defensive pattern, and the reader will tone, split, or shape the literary work considerably to make it fit. It is as though he has to fit the work through an admitting procedure before "out there" can take place "in here."

Once passed, however, the third principle comes into play: fantasy projects fantasy. The reader projects into the work the pleasures gained and pains avoided that are characteristic for him: in short, his characteristic fantasy. Typically, but not always, it will be linked to a particular phase of development by body imagery or by the particular type of interpersonal issues involved. The story itself does not "have" such a fantasy—but it serves as a "promptuary" (to restore an old word at a late stage in our endeavor). That is, it acts as a ready reserve of structured verbal information from which the reader builds his fantasy as he did his defenses. With fantasy, unlike defenses, the match is very easy. The reader can freely use everything of the story his defenses have admitted.

Finally, the reader transforms the fantasy he has created by means of his own defensive patterns and specifically the particular elements of the story by which he has synthesized those patterns. He gives to the unconscious values he has created out of the elements of the story a conscious coherence and significance—or, if he cannot, he feels uneasy. Conversely, to the extent he does use an intellectual or aesthetic interpretation to consolidate and affirm his response, he can enrich his experience at the fantasy level as well. In other words, he has built up his characteristic mental processes—his defenses, his fantasies, and his transformations of fantasy—from the materials of the story: "out there" has become "in here" now in still another sense. Where the first principle referred to the *sequence* of the literary transaction, the fourth deals with the *whole* work as a unified, coherent experience.

All four principles can be seen simply as aspects of one: *style re-creates itself*. Each reader builds up an experience from a literary work that is characteristic for him, that is, a variation upon his identity theme. One can look at this act of re-creation as the reader's way of warding off sources of anxiety—that point of view would stress his matching his defenses. One could look at the characteristic kinds of pleasures he seeks —that perspective would single out the fantasy component. One could accent his intellectual and aesthetic construction of the work and so focus on his identity theme as it worked in adaptive and transformational ways. Or one could look simply at the reader's expectations and satisfactions from the work moment by moment, and that view would take his identity theme as a pattern of object relations.

These principles would seem to make reading wholly subjective, but they do not, really. Every reader has available to him what the writer created—the words-on-the-page, that is, the promptuary (a store of structured language) from which he can build an experience. To be sure, the promptuary includes constraints on how one can put its contents together, but these constraints do not coerce anyone. One is always free to go to the extreme of total delusion: perceptions dictated entirely by one's inner impulses, wholly unaffected by the world outside. Such a mode of perception would provide an idiosyncratic, solipsistic, or psychotic experience of a literary work, which, by definition, cannot be shared or communicated since it does not work with the resources other readers have available. But most reading is not solipsistic. To say it is eliminates or minimizes one of the two components in this model of response. Usually, people respond to literary works in two ways together. They work with what is publicly available—the words-on-the-page as a readiness of structured information. They make from that sharable promptuary a completely original and private experience.

Some of these public supplies the writer provides, while others come from other sources. In a theatrical setting, at the very moment he takes in the play or film, each member of the audience also takes in cues from the people around him. Such cues come with all the leverage public opinion can exert, and they can make parts of the theatrical raw material radically more (or less) available to him. In the reading situation, critics and teachers offer observations, data, and syntheses of their own, which each reader may or may not make a part of his personal re-creation of the literary work. Finally, literary discussion (as, for example, in a classroom) can put forward a whole collection of statements that exist, as it were, in parallel with the works themselves as provisions to be used or not in each individual's synthesis of the work according to his identity principle. Those shared resources make up a consensus that is as much as one can say about "objective" interpretation.

There seems no reason, however, why the principles to which reading led us do not apply to other activities besides being a reader, critic, or member of an audience. Thus, although this book began with reading, it ends with a generalized model of human experiencing and hence of human development. We are constantly achieving the world for ourselves by means of our defensive and adaptive structures, projecting into it our wishes and fantasies, and transforming it in fact or fancy to meet our demands for coherence and meaningfulness. Reading provides us with a potential space in which the distinction between "in here" and "out there" blurs as we ingest the external world into our ongoing psychological processes. The world of things and people presents itself to us as transitional objects that are both found reality and created symbol—in varying degrees, to be sure, in different kinds and intensities of experience. But all experience would seem to exist in this dual way. First, it is a private and personal experience within the possible variations of the individual's identity theme—he can have literally no other kind of experience. Second, he builds that experience out of an "external" reality that others can share, that is, that they can bring into their psychological functioning to make their private experience. And psychoanalytic psychology tells us how to relate the two modes of experience: by the terms of subjectivity that inhere in all experience, terms set by each individual's identity theme for himself. Then we create objectivity by giving back to the world words and acts for others to experience and perhaps to build into a consensus.

Development is the cumulation of these dual experiences onto an identity theme established by the child's being the child for the needs and patterns of the particular person who mothers him. Onto this initial theme come the rapid cycles of immediate experience and the long, slow changes of psychosocial development. The ego creates each experience by means of the defensive side of its existing identity and then freely assimilates what it has created into its ongoing mental processes of fantasy, gratification, and understanding. Then the assimilated experience becomes part of the equipment the ego brings to bear on the next new experience. Thus, a complex causality is at work. One's character is, in a sense, continually being changed by new experiences in a small way. At the same time, it is continually changing the new experiences in large ways to keep itself the same. And through this feedback of assimilation and accommodation involving both intellectual and personality structures, development, sometimes rapid, sometimes slow, takes place.

This model reveals an element of subjectivity in all human experiences, including the most disciplined and intellectualized. It thus renders useless the sorting of experience into categories of "objective" and "subjective." The two are inextricably intertwined. Rather than try to subtract one from the other, it is better to accept their addition and ask how it takes place. Thus, you can draw from this model a contrast of two epistemologies.

One, based on the seventeenth-century cleaving of mind from nature, takes as its "God-term" a reality that is only partially perceived by each one of us as we see it in our subjective ways. We subtract from this larger entity, and therefore we arrive at truth by trying to minimize that subtractive role of the self. This epistemology has the disadvantage of asking us to take two points of view at once: perceiving the world normally, through the self, but then standing outside ourselves to try to discount that first perceiving as inadequate.

The other epistemology takes as its God-term the self relating to reality, rather than reality alone or self alone, and finds truth by observing the self adding to itself, replicating its character like the genes in a cell, with the materials inner and outer realities provide. Such an epistemology became possible in our century when psychoanalytic psychology provided a way of talking precisely and rigorously about individuality, repealing the old scholastic adage, *individuum est ineffabile*, so that one could accept subjectivity rather than try to subtract it out.

Epistemology is surely the highest level of abstraction this study of five readers is destined to attain, yet it is surprisingly close to the original problem. These two world-views correspond to the two ways I tried to explain my interviews. At first, I believed that the text contained a psychological process of transformation—the fantasy-defense model of *The Dynamics of Literary Response*. The text embodied the transformation fully, and each reader participated in it partially, filtering it through his personality structure, subtracting from the textual totality what he could accept. "Anal" images in "A Rose for Emily" should appear as such in the response but modified by the reader's contribution from other psychosexual stages. Within the reader's own characteristic defenses, one should be able to discern the denials and incorporations from the story. Alas, responses proved far too idiosyncratic for this subtractive explanation. Then I reluctantly tried the opposite explanation,[52] never separating the reader from the text but asking instead how he added it to himself, how he re-created it in his own experience. I found to my satisfaction that *Dynamics'* fantasy-defense model of the literary experience reappeared, not in the text alone, but in the union of reader and text.

In the same way, I think the contrast between a subtractive and an additive epistemology introduces serious questions about psychological research based on categories, even psychoanalytic categories like "anal" or "denial." They subtract a part from what is undeniably whole—the subject's experience or personality. Similar questions apply to psychological research that does not take into account the personalities of the researcher and his subjects or that tries to subtract them from an experiment by borrowing methods from the "hard" sciences. It seems likely to me that such methods will yield only partial and conflicting results so long as they split up a subject matter into categories that mask the more powerful and unifying holistic description. Those categories, I realize, are an effort to take out personal bias, but it would be wiser, I think, if the psychologist accepted the individuality inherent in both himself and his subject matter and worked positively with it. He can do so by giving up categories that are defined in terms of method rather than subject matter and seeing his work as the interaction of specialized experiences and identity themes, his own as well as his subjects'. He can then seek objective knowledge of these interactions by looking for convergence toward themes (through the methods used here to find centers in people and stories) and by submitting those interpretations to the forum of his fellow interpreters.

If he does, he becomes able to extend this intrapsychic model of experiencing to interpsychic situations. The classical way of doing this is to assume that the intrapsychic model of personality can be applied, *mutatis mutandis,* to a collectivity. In the terms of this study, the assumption would be that a gang, corporation, tribe, culture, bureaucracy, or nation would obey the principle of multiple function within the variations permitted by its identity theme, that is, the pattern revealed by its previous choices. And the methods used to find unifying themes in works of literature will serve to discover patterns in groups that can be said to share certain ego choices. This investigation of readers' interactions with stories suggests still more detail in that model, namely, that the group will construct experiences by means of its structure of defenses and adaptations and then, once they have arrived at an experience, adapt it to their own collective fantasies and transformations.

Thus, the group experience takes on the same two components as the private experience. There is an "external" reality on which several groups draw to make up their several experiences. Within each group, there is also the group's private experience of that reality defined by the identity theme of the group. But that private experience for the group is a public one for the members of the group, a reality they share and from which each member draws to make his own inner individual experience. Thus, the picture of interpsychic relations to which our model leads is a great interweaving or cogwheeling of individuals and groups. Facing outward, their experiences point to a shared reality having a centering theme. Facing inward, their experiences become private assimilations to a series of individual centers.

These two opposed directions combine in a single word, *consensus,* whose original meaning, "feeling or sensing together," bridges these two kinds of experience, the shared and the private. By "consensus," I do not mean agreement so much as a sharing of potentials and the crossing of the barrier between ego and ego. What one of us sees, says, and does becomes material for the other to absorb by his adaptive system and re-create in his own ego style. As when readers read stories. And when you read this book.

Appendix A   The Question of Affect

In this account of responses to literature, there is one area about which a great deal more should be said, but alas, cannot be said: the emotions (or affects) people have when they experience literary works. These four principles, whatever their other powers, simply do not tell very much about affects, for an unfortunately simple reason: there is no satisfactory theory of affect in any circumstances, real life, literary response, dreams, or inner tensions. A great deal has been written (and summarized in a learned and most informative survey by André Green).[1] None of it helps much, however, with our very practical problem of understanding what emotions people feel as they experience a given work of literature. At least part of this difficulty comes from language itself: words do not describe feelings directly with much precision. "One can attempt to describe their physiological signs," said Freud rather wryly in 1930. "Where this is not possible . . . nothing remains but to fall back on the ideational content which is most readily associated with the feeling."[2] That is what I did in this project by relying so heavily on the figurative language these five readers used about the stories they had read.

Two articles on affect deserve special mention. The late David Rapaport worked out in great detail one of Freud's original conceptions of affect—as a drive "discharge resulting in an (internal) alteration of the subject's own body without reference to the external world"—to be contrasted to other body actions that deal with drives by altering the external world to make it yield satisfactions.[3] Rapaport suggested the existence of "inborn affect discharge channels," which change and develop as the individual grows. In particular, they take form as his ego differentiates itself from his id, and their existence enables him to experience small quantities of affect as signals of inner and outer danger.[4] For Rapaport, then, we experience affect as such, as body action within the body instead of outside, because it meets an adaptive need.

Edith Jacobson has gone beyond him to show (quite convincingly, I think) that we experience affect not only because of discharge, but because of nondischarge—tension.[5] She distinguishes several different possibilities:

Affects stemming from *intra*systemic tensions:
   a. from drives in the id (e.g., anger, sexual excitation).
   b. from the ego (e.g., fear of reality, physical pain, love, hate, etc.).
Affects stemming from *inter*systemic tensions:
   a. from tensions between ego and id (e.g., disgust, shame, or fear at drives).
   b. from tensions between ego and superego (e.g., feelings of guilt or depression).

From this point of view, we experience affect from both discharges and tensions leading to discharge. All discharges are pleasurable, but only some tensions are, like the tensions aroused in such appetizers as sexual foreplay. Most entail discomfort or pain.

If we simplify Jacobson's model somewhat, we can adapt it to arrive at a table of the affects people experience from literature. I developed such a table in *The Dynamics of Literary Response*. Now, I offer a version of my conclusions with the shift in emphasis demanded by my experience with real readers reading: fantasies, defenses, transformations, affects, meanings, and all other psychological moves take place as readers assimilate texts, not in texts alone. Once we understand that, we can distinguish a series of dualities.

First, in a broad way, readers can be said to respond to literary works either positively or negatively. A positive response tells us the reader has been able to compose from things he found in the text some or all of his own lifestyle, especially some or all of his characteristic structure of defenses. If he responds negatively, he has been unable to make such a synthesis. And he can respond to a work partly negatively and partly positively.

Second, we can distinguish two components in any imagined gratification of fantasy. There is straightforward, direct gratification (analysts speak of discharge or falling excitement), and there is imagined gratification that begins to arouse tension (rising excitement). Some tensions imply pleasurable anticipation; others, anxiety, guilt, disgust, boredom, shame, fear of consequences, or a struggle between inconsistent drives—in general, conflict among or within various psychic agencies.

We can simplify Jacobson's picture, then, by speaking simply of pleasure, combining in one word gratification and pleasurable tension. We can further simplify by calling the fantasy component that moves counter to pleasure just "conflict" without trying to distinguish among the different permutations and combinations of conflict possible.

Third, we recognize that sometimes when readers experience a literary work they defend very strongly and sometimes they defend minimally. The extent to which they defend depends on how much conflict their fantasies arouse and also on how much of the work they can use for defense and how much of their own thinking and defending, quite apart from the work, they have to introduce. To analyze affect, we can consider "defense" as a way of taking the pain out of conflict, specifically, reducing the reality fears of the ego, the frustrations as drives oppose one another, the guilt aroused by superego threats, or countering the loss-of-identity feelings associated with shame. Generally, coping this way will involve giving up some pleasure to avoid pain.

At the risk of losing those humanistic readers who have stayed with me this far, I wish to offer a diagram devised with the ingenious help of Michael Brill, my colleague in systems analysis. I think it may help you to follow the various interactions of these polarities and possibilities, particularly the way affects serve to feed back to the reader information about the success or failure of his efforts to adapt the work to his own identity and lifestyle. Necessarily, the diagram shows fixed points and choices, but you should understand that the whole situation shifts and flows. Each position represents a complex exchange and feedback between the gratification of drives and the warding off of unpleasant affects; each equilibrium position rests on many precarious balances that are not self-correcting. Therefore, as he reads, a reader will move from one mode or

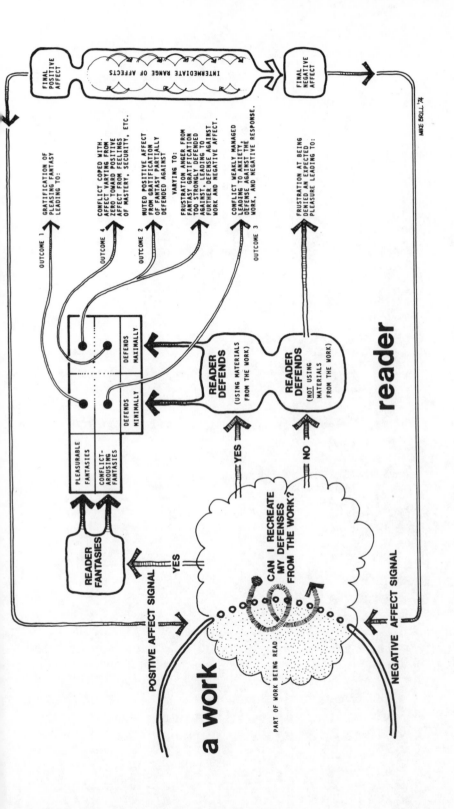

FINAL POSITIVE AFFECT

INTERMEDIATE RANGE OF AFFECTS

FINAL NEGATIVE AFFECT

MIKE BASILL '74

OUTCOME 1 — GRATIFICATION OF PLEASING FANTASY LEADING TO:

OUTCOME 4 — CONFLICT COPED WITH. AFFECT VARYING FROM ZERO TOWARD POSITIVE AFFECT FROM FEELINGS OF MASTERY, SECURITY, ETC.

OUTCOME 2 — MUTED POSITIVE AFFECT FROM GRATIFICATION OF FANTASY PARTIALLY DEFENDED AGAINST

VARYING TO:

FRUSTRATION ANGER FROM FANTASY GRATIFICATION TOO STRONGLY DEFENDED AGAINST—LEADING TO FURTHER DEFENSE AGAINST WORK AND NEGATIVE AFFECT.

OUTCOME 3 — CONFLICT WEAKLY MANAGED LEADING TO ANXIETY, DEFENSE AGAINST THE WORK, AND NEGATIVE RESPONSE.

FRUSTRATION AT BEING DENIED AN EXPECTED PLEASURE LEADING TO:

DEFENDS MAXIMALLY

DEFENDS MINIMALLY

PLEASURABLE FANTASIES

CONFLICT-AROUSING FANTASIES

READER DEFENDS (USING MATERIALS FROM THE WORK)

READER DEFENDS (NOT USING MATERIALS FROM THE WORK)

reader

READER FANTASIES

CAN I RECREATE MY DEFENSES FROM THE WORK?

YES

YES

NO

POSITIVE AFFECT SIGNAL

a work

PART OF WORK BEING READ

NEGATIVE AFFECT SIGNAL

transaction to another, and the final affective outcomes represent a continually changing range of affect.

To maintain a positive relationship with the work, the reader must be gratifying his drives. Ordinarily, since people seek pleasure rather than the lack of it, a reader will be actively expecting and trying to get pleasure from a literary work. He will gratify his drives if he can, but sometimes he can't, usually because he cannot synthesize his own pattern of defense and adaptation from the materials in the work. Thus there is a first, pivotal question (at the left of the diagram): the reader tests whether he can or cannot re-create his own defenses from the work. If he can't, he cannot gratify his drives, he will feel he has been denied a pleasure he anticipated, and he may even feel angry because he has been frustrated. He will take his negative feelings as a signal that he cannot match his defenses, and he will defend against the work by means outside it, thus reinforcing a feedback that negates the possibility of an experience. Among our readers, Saul and Sebastian often took this route, and we noticed with them a kind of irreversibility in the negative direction: once the flow of satisfaction or pleasurable affect is broken, it is difficult to re-establish contact.

More typically, however, a reader achieves satisfaction. Positive affects signal him that he can construct—is constructing—his defenses by means of the work. Therefore, he is projecting into the work a fantasy that matters to him and that he builds up from various features of the text. (By "fantasy," I mean a representation in the ego of a cluster of wishes derived, finally, from basic drives.) A fantasy may evoke in him a sense of straightforward gratification or of conflict—usually both— for, as the old psychoanalytic maxim has it, what we deeply wish, we also deeply fear. One must think, not of two fixed positions, but of degrees and ranges in which pleasing combines with the arousal of conflict. At one extreme, the reader fantasies simple gratification, often sexual. At the other, the reader fantasies gratification mixed with a good deal of fear; hence his fantasies are in conflict.

Take the first extreme. If the reader's fantasy involves simple gratification, he has no need to defend strongly. He can simply accept the pleasure without further ado (outcome 1). Sam, for example, could imagine everyone in the ante–bellum South being "kept in their place" and "being a born baby to one of these people" and how he "would have whipped" his "share of slaves" with this simple, direct satisfaction and a minimum of defense.

Forces within the work or outside it, however, may lead a reader to defend more strongly. For example, he might find the work so complicated (like the puzzles of Emily's wedding night) or he might become so involved with its purely formal features (Faulkner's clauses, for example) as to lose the fantasy he was enjoying. Conceivably, such pressures to defend could come from outside the work, for example, if it were assigned by a domineering teacher whom the reader needed to ward off. (To some extent, Saul perceived me in this role and defended accordingly.)

If the reader has reduced the pleasure from the fantasy (as in outcome 2a), we can infer that he has defended strongly, either because of his reaction to the work or the circumstances around it. He may perceive a "dull patch" in a novel or "a singsong quality" in a poem, the way Sebastian objected to the controls he perceived in "A Rose for Emily." It was, he said, "programmatic, . . . outlined." "It seemed more stark than it had seemed in my memory." "It should be mitigated somehow, the explicitness of it." "It tries to save it for the end and be suggestive, but it seemed too strong." A reader in this position may go so far, his bond of pleasure being broken, as to defend against the work and shift over to a generally negative response (2b). As I said before, once the flow of pleasure is broken, it is hard to re-establish. Hence the irreversible arrow associated with that final negative affect.

To the extent, however, a reader's fantasy ties gratification to a lot of conflict, the role of the defenses becomes reversed. Now the reader needs more, not less, defense. If he has enough, his defenses will take care of the conflict, and he will arrive at a new pleasure (outcome 4, which is a more complex version of outcome 1, straightforward gratification). He experiences the positive feelings appropriate either to having picked out the satisfying parts of a mixed fantasy from the threatening parts or perhaps to feeling he has mastered a conflict-arousing idea. This, for example, is the way Saul responded to the Faulkner story, balancing the "masterful authority" he attributed to Faulkner with the way "he gets away with lots of things," notably, "a wild, wild paragraph in which he just lets out all the stops." Similarly, Shep could like the story despite its Southern system of values, so contrary to those he consciously held, because he attributed powers to Emily and the South that were mythic and magical in the style he liked. Finally, however, those magical powers could not succeed in reality and actually threaten him with those values. He thus achieved the right balance of defense with gratification.

If, however, a reader cannot build the right amount of defense from the work (for example, if he finds it "cheap" or "obvious"), he will experience the conflict and the negative affects he derives from it unmediated (this is outcome 3). The work will cease to gratify him, he will experience a negative affect signal, and he will—or may—reject it, shifting into a totally negative affectual response to the first pivotal question. Then he begins to defend against the work from outside instead of meshing with it to re-create his own adaptive modes. Thus, Sam denied the wedding night: "You're kind of loath to think about it, because it's kind of disgusting." Or—a case in which the reader's need for defense drove her to seek defenses from outside—Sandra's reality-testing of Fitzgerald's "Winter Dreams." She could not, she said, tolerate a woman with as much power as that heroine. "I don't believe in her . . . It's a very simple way to criticize the story but . . . I don't *believe* in this mysterious power she's supposed to have." "I don't believe I would ever meet anybody like that, see? That's the thing."

Thus, the diagram's outcomes (1–4) reveal a certain symmetry in what we ask from a literary work. We need to feel that, through it, we have balanced our defenses and our needs for defense. Thus, outcomes 1 and 4, the modalities of positive response, represent a balance of the defenses we are able to achieve through the work and the need we feel to defend. Outcome 1: there is not much need for defense and not much defense, the modality of simple success. Outcome 4: much is needed and much is found, the modality of complex greatness.

Outcomes 2 and 3 show the situation when we feel a work has failed: we sense a mismatch between our need for defense and the defense we manage to synthesize. In outcome 2, we get more defense from the work than we need, while in outcome 3 we cannot create enough. Either mismatch can lead us to a temporary negative affect signal or, if it continues to break the flow of gratifications long enough, to a permanent rejection.

Notice what this model of affect imples: *we will enjoy and value those literary works from which we can achieve an exciting balance of fantasy and management of fantasy. In a model of literary experience based on readers reading this balance equals literary value.*

To me, this model of literary affect looks promising (if complicated), but I must quickly confess that I know of no way to see affect directly or to infer it reliably. Rather, I have arrived at this model by understanding the dynamics of response first and then inferring what affects would be likely to accompany the various types of inner re-creations revealed in what these five readers said about what they had read. This is, then, a formal model in Diesing's sense,[6] that is, a structure of relations and a claim that that structure exists in the real world.

Indeed, the feedback system sketched out in this diagram seems to me to model adequately the whole theory of response this book has developed. A human being begins with the hypothesis that he can re-create his identity (understood as defenses, fantasies, and ego style) from what he is experiencing. To the extent he receives a positive payoff from his hypothesis, he does indeed have an experience. To the extent he does not, he rejects the intruder. Stated this generally, the diagram could model experiences ranging from the simplest perception and the earliest suckling to the most sophisticated scientific thinking.

Here, however, I offer it as a formal model of affects, hinging on the field of relationships possible between fantasy and defense. To pursue this formal exploration of affects further (according to Diesing), two steps would be required. First, one would have to specify with greater formal clarity the relations within the structure, notably the contrast between "pleasure" and "conflict," and the effect of "defense" upon them.

Second, one would have to investigate discrepancies between this formal description and the real feelings people experience in reading (or in relating to any entity outside themselves), in order to refine the formal description. One might, for example, try out in this model the twenty-five different affectual situations described in *Dynamics*.[7]

Any such attempt to analyze affect formally, however, confronts the notorious difficulty of using words (instead of mathematics) in formal systems and also of using words to describe feelings. At that crux, a psychology of literary response might turn, not to psychology, but to poetry.

Appendix B Further Evidence: Sam, Saul, Shep, Sebastian, and Sandra Read Fitzgerald's "Winter Dreams" and Hemingway's "The Battler"

The Stories

Stories never turn out to be as simple as they seem at first, but one that looked unusually clear and straightforward, and therefore suited to an early probe of five readers reading, was F. Scott Fitzgerald's "Winter Dreams."[1] It tells of Dexter Green, who by brains and determination satisfies the "winter dreams" he had when his summer caddying at the country club ended. He rises from his obscure lower-middle-class origins to become fabulously rich and successful, thereby winning the praise and admiration of powerful older men. The dream he does not satisfy, however, is to win Judy Jones, the pink and gold American dream girl he meets along the way. "Inexpressibly lovely," "arrestingly beautiful," she keeps all the eligible young men of the city circling about her, although ultimately, "She was entertained only by the . . . direct exercise of her own charm." Dexter tries to give her up and becomes engaged to Irene, "sturdily popular . . . intensely 'great.' " Judy, however, beckons him back, and he returns for a month's romance. Once that is over, he flees East to a Wall Street success. Years later, by chance, he hears of Judy as a faded, young matron married to one Lud Simms, who drinks and "runs around." Of the girl who was once a great beauty, Dexter's informant says, " 'She has nice eyes,' " or, more damningly still, " 'Most of the women like her.' " Dexter realizes his dream is dead and weeps, depleted.

Consciously, the winning, losing, and fading of Judy Jones evokes for me—perhaps for many readers—some kind of American Dream of total success and absolute well-being. Less

300

consciously, that well-being takes me back to my earliest, uto-
pian satisfaction of hungers. As the story says, her kisses
"aroused in him not hunger demanding renewal but surfeit that
would demand more surfeit . . . kisses that were like charity,
creating want by holding back nothing at all." Judy draws on
my feelings toward, if not a withholding mother, an unpredictable, fickle one. "She had come . . . to nourish herself wholly
from within." As for Dexter, "He loved her, and he would love
her until the day he was too old for loving—but he could not
have her. So he tasted the deep pain that is reserved only for
the strong, just as he had tasted for a little while the deep
happiness."

The metaphor of taste reminds me of the earliest love of
woman, based on feeding and nurture, but Judy also gives me
feelings of a later kind of love in which a man proves his manhood to himself by winning a woman away from more powerful
rivals. Dexter "had wanted Judy Jones ever since he was a
proud, desirous little boy." But, of course, such a love Dexter
"simply could not have." Thus, I find the end of the story acts
out feelings I can find in myself about such rivalries and
jealousies. If the woman can be won, if *he,* this so obviously
inferior Simms, can win her, she must therefore not have been
the ideal I thought she was. Or, to put the story in terms of
defense, once Judy really, really belongs to another, she can no
longer be desired.

That plot ending is one way the story allows me to fantasy
within it. Another is Fitzgerald's language, which seems to me
breathless, sentimental, self-indulgent: a diction that mythol-
ogizes the story while realizing it, and that, even as it makes
Judy and Dexter most desirable, destroys their credibility. In
the same way, the inclusion in the story both of Dexter's real
mother, an unglamorous immigrant, and the over-glamorous
but frustrating Judy Jones, makes me feel given to and taken
away from at the same time. So also does the plot: once Judy
becomes a mother, she ceases to be desirable.

Very briefly, then—too briefly—"Winter Dreams" comes
together for me around a feeling of submitting to and being
frustrated by an infinitely desirable woman who both gives and
takes away. She seems to promise pleasure, but in fact she

gives pain, as both another kind of pleasure and a way of buying off the anxiety I feel as Dexter arrogantly rises above other
men.

Quite a different set of psychological issues comes to my
mind as I read another story the five readers read, Hemingway's
"The Battler." This story is considerably less open than
"Winter Dreams," and it therefore raised questions about the
psychology of obscurity and interpretation. "The Battler" is
one of the seven stories in the 1925 version of *In Our Time,*
which tell of the youthful adventures of Nick Adams and what
he learns from them about men and manners. In this brief and
enigmatic story, Nick is riding a freight when the brakeman
calls him over ("Come here, kid," "I got something for you.")
and knocks him off the train. Feeling like a stupid child, Nick
keeps on walking the track until he sees a campfire off to one
side. When he goes to it, he finds a mutilated man sitting there
who turns out to be Ad Francis, once a champion boxer. They
talk, and Ad has Nick feel his pulse to count the slow heartbeat
that, he says, enabled him to win his bouts. At that moment,
they are joined by Bugs, a soft-spoken Negro who travels with
Ad, tending and cooking for him. When the crazed, punch-
drunk Ad begins to pick a fight with Nick, Bugs knocks him out
with a blackjack he keeps specially for this purpose. Then, over
the unconscious Ad, he tells how the fighter fell upon bad days:
he married his manager, a woman who had been posing as his
sister, " 'and that made a lot of unpleasantness.' " The marriage didn't work, and she left him, but she still sends him
money. Bugs met Ad in jail (where both men had been sent for
violent assaults), liked him, and joined up with him. Now, as
Ad stirs, Bugs sends Nick off to walk the track again, pressing
a ham sandwich on the dazed guest.

The story leaves a number of puzzles unsolved, notably the
relationship with the sister-manager. This enigmatic, mysterious quality dominated the students' readings, and professional
critics seemed equally baffled. All the readers—professionals
and amateurs—however, agreed that the story dealt with an
initiation of Nick "into the painful and disruptive circumstances of life in our time." "This is a story of a boy coming in

contact with violence and evil," writes Philip Young, and the story stresses the effect of the encounter on Nick (William B. Bache points out) "by underlining the appeal of the action to the senses: references are made to feeling, hearing, tasting; in its various forms *look* is used twenty-five times, and *see*, fifteen times."[2] Professor Young added another piece of factual information, which was useful—perhaps—but intruded into some of my readers' readings: "Hemingway surely had in mind Ad Wolgast, the 'Michigan Wildcat,' who became lightweight champion of the world in 1910 but lost most of his mind in the process."[3]

Such observations carry an air of authority, more so than interpretations, even by professionals. Some analyzed the story in terms of Hemingway's concern with playing the game and keeping the rules. Being "on the track," suggests John Hardy, perfectly symbolizes what is called for, a single-minded determination to keep going—where does not matter. Similarly, the swamp stands for something it would be unsporting and undisciplined to be distracted by. In a mythological reading, Joseph DeFalco suggests the track represents "the Way," and the swamp "the labyrinthian passages of the unconscious and irrational." "Whenever the hero is lured from the tried and proved pathway the dangers symbolized by the swamp threaten to swallow him and to terminate his journey into self-discovery."[4]

From John Hardy's point of view, however, what Nick learns from his encounters is "that a man's gallantry, true self-esteem, is measured precisely and only by his capacity for living according to his code—whatever the code may be." "Bugs in the end is Hemingway's spokesman. We are meant finally to see old Ad Francis, after the Negro has explained him to Nick, as not merely human but the best of humanity—as a hero, indeed. And, therefore, we are meant to accept Bugs' office of attendance upon him as a truly noble one, the true life of the 'gentleman.' " Randall Stewart and Dorothy Bethurum find it significant that "the action takes place in a lighted area surrounded by darkness," and they imply "the vast enveloping darkness . . . stands for the disorder and chaos of a hostile world or universe, and the spot of light for the small amount of order and discipline and civilization and security that the individual has been able to wrest out of the surrounding chaos and old night."[5]

Such a reading, however, neglects the violence and danger Nick experiences by the campfire, and there is much to be said for a more negative view, such as Clinton Burhans's. Burhans suggests that what Nick learns is that the world is a confused and treacherous place; that the friendly brakeman isn't; that Ad is praised for hitting in the ring, but punished for hitting outside it; that the fans like his "sister," but not his wife to be his manager; that the Negro who knifed a man has sympathy and understanding for Ad.[6] As William Bache puts it, Nick has to learn that the world does not run in a simple dichotomy between "kid things—naïveté, friendliness, candor—and adult things—cruelty, deception, hypocrisy."

The second direction the professional readers take is psychological (or pseudopsychological), beginning with Professor Young's suggestion, first put forward in 1952, that the story deals in what is for Hemingway "a kind of ultimate in evil"—homosexuality. "It is not only Ad who is queer." "The tender, motherly, male-nursing Bugs is too comfortable in the relationship." He "blackjacks his companion in sweet good humor . . . with a love that was present even in the blow."

I think, however, one can really understand the story psychologically by taking a larger psychological view of its author. Consider, for a moment, a general characterological type described by Wilhelm Reich that bears at least a recognizable resemblance to the late Ernest Hemingway and to many characters in his fiction.[7] "Self-confident, often arrogant, elastic, vigorous, and often impressive." "It is not by accident that this type is most frequently found among athletes, aviators, soldiers and engineers. One of their most important traits is aggressive courage." "Their narcissism expresses itself not in an infantile manner but in the exaggerated display of self-confidence, dignity and superiority," "pride." Reich gives Napoleon and Mussolini as familiar historical examples of the type. I would suggest Stanley Kubrick's film, *Dr. Strangelove* (1963), for a virtual anthology of such fantasies and character types. Two of our five readers, Sam and Sandra, also showed traits of this kind of personality, although in a complicated mixture, such as one finds in real life.

If we were to imagine this type of personality in its purest form, we would have to observe a child in that early stage of development in which he most prides himself on his muscular achievements: he can stand erect, run, and perform tasks that call for motor skills, and he can control his own body functions. The man who most resembles this child measures achievements in power, range, distance, or size, and he hopes his own body will be admired and loved in those terms. Thus, he will want to ignore, deny, or reverse facts that might blemish that image of self or, ultimately, body, which he wants others to admire. He will try to deal with the world by imposing himself on it, by modes of force, thrust, height, and speed. A man of this type needs to be active and autonomous, and he deeply fears passivity, helplessness, or feminity. Even in loving, he will use others as mere instruments whom he dominates to prove his own potency. A woman of this kind will often use her physical attractiveness—her body—to dominate powerful men in a subtler, more Circean way. In general, a person of this type—a "phallic character" in psychoanalytic shorthand—will want to relate to reality by thrusting into it and imposing himself on it, yet at the same time, he will have an exaggerated fear of getting *in* some situation (like an emotional triangle) and being trapped there, losing his autonomy and his active, aggressive independence. This is the pattern, I think, that underlies "The Battler."

Thus, Hemingway himself wrote to Edmund Wilson about arranging vignettes between the stories of *In Our Time:* "That is the way they were meant to go—to give the picture of the whole between examining it in detail. Like looking with your eyes at something, say a passing coastline, and then looking at it with 15X binoculars. Or rather, maybe, looking at it and then going in and living in it—and then coming out and looking at it again."[8] This, of course, is exactly what Nick does in "The Battler": look from a distance, look close up, then enter, live in the "whole," experience the danger, escape, and look back from a safe distance. This same keeping to the surface, the outside, applies to Hemingway's style in general. As he himself described it: "If a writer of prose knows enough about what he is writing about, he may omit things that he knows and the reader, if the writer is writing truly enough, will have a feeling of those things as strongly as though the writer had stated them. The dignity of movement of an ice-berg is due to only one-eighth of it being above water."[9] This would be that "display" of "dignity" that Reich mentioned. In Hemingway's writing, it takes the form of "a careful attention to the details of the business in hand," so that "One comes," say Professors Stewart and Bethurum, "to have great confidence in the author's accounts of things; one comes to feel that here is a reliable author and no fake."

The hero of this type, as well as his author, must keep himself safely outside and aloof, and this seems to be the moral of "The Battler." The danger of getting *into* things first occurs in the brakeman episode. Here I find a distinctly childish, bribing quality in the brakeman's phrasing: " 'I got something for you,' " says Professor DeFalco, "echoes some sort of offer of candy . . . that a child might expect to be given by an adult." "They would never suck him in that way again," Nick thought; but, of course, this is just the first of two occasions in the story in which he fails to keep out. In effect, says DeFalco, he has "been lured by the authority figure into playing the role of the child."

The second occasion also involves a kind of bait: Nick is hungry and he sees a fire. Just like a trapped animal, he is caught in the dangerous ménage of Ad and Bugs. On the one hand, Ad is always described as "the little man." "His mutilated face looked childish in repose." He is, in Professor Bache's phrase, "a figurative kid." As for Bugs, Bache asks, "His relationship with Ad is at once servile, responsible, and personal. Isn't he reminiscent of the conventional mammy?" Young found him "motherly," and DeFalco says, "The Negro here is the cook and soother, the hermaphroditic figure who resembles the mother."

If Bugs is a mother, then Ad is a child but also a father. He, in DeFalco's reading, "is also the ogre figure with whom Nick must do battle on the threshold of maturity. In this sense he is symbolic of the father-authority who is both helpful guide and

the dangerous presence guarding the entrance into the unknown. The fighter here stands as the father who has held out
the promise to the hero as a child but who withdrew the promise,'' like the brakeman, and, on both occasions, the promise
was a bait. In other words, to the extent Ad is powerful and
threatening, he is a father. To the extent he is childish, dependent, and maimed, he is the victim, not of the father, however,
but of the dark, sinister mother. The title, "The Battler," could
thus apply to any one of the three principal characters.

In short, as I put the story together, "The Battler" cautions
against getting into situations. It is a story about the wisdom of
staying "on the track" or, conversely, about situations off the
track where the promising (the brakeman, the firelight, the
meal) turns into the painful because of some unforeseen
danger. Even so, the victim comes away from the dangerous
situation with a trophy—a sandwich, money, black eye, or
headache, and so (ultimately) wisdom. In a way, as in the last,
long story of *In Our Time,* a baited fishhook images the human
condition; the wise man refuses the gambit or, perhaps takes
the risk of trying both to eat the bait and get away.

As I create its core of fantasy, "The Battler" plays off a set
of wishes transformed out of one phase of development against
two others, one from an earlier, one from a later phase.
Dominating "The Battler" is the wish to be a powerful,
forward-moving, autonomous man, nobly and stoically suffering the hard blows thrown at him by the world, which is his
opponent. I think the story worships the kind of strength Ad
apparently had, and that Nick would like to have. But there are
two dangerous temptations—combinations of wish and fear—
that beset Nick on either side. One is to hunger and become
dependent on someone like Bugs (or the sister-woman,
perhaps) out of one's earliest and most basic human need: to be
succored. The other is to blunder or be lured into taking part in
a world of sexual triangles and complexities—that world that
awaited the child once he had dealt with his own body and
one-to-one relations with his parents, once he had learned to
dominate with his body and still to keep the rules and the code.
In figurative terms, "The Battler" is a story about the wishing
and fearing to be suckered/succored into a dangerous triangle

and the defense against that temptation: keeping single-mindedly on the track, playing by the rules, and settling for the stoic security of solitary manliness. Or so *I* see the story.

Both "The Battler" and "Winter Dreams" could use, indeed they deserve, more critical attention, but our concern here is with the five readers. Did Sam, Saul, Shep, Sebastian, and Sandra find the same combination of longing and denial I did in "Winter Dreams"? Did they, too, find threats to masculinity in "The Battler"? The Hemingway story in particular raises cultural issues. These interviews took place in 1969 when most young Americans were vigorously rejecting the high value placed on individual power and virility by middle-class and middle-aged America. Hemingway being the most eloquent spokesman in our literature for those values, it is—in one sense—hardly surprising that his story found little favor with these four readers. Yet I leave it to you to say whether they rejected the "American" values of Hemingway (and Fitzgerald) from general, sociological causes (youth culture against the hardhats, to put it bluntly) or as individual psychological transactions.

Sam

As we have seen, Sam saw the world primarily in terms of his own (and its) need for love, admiration, direction, security, and the like. He kept his own narcissistic supplies intact by two complementary adaptations, both in a way spatial. To defend against a danger, perceived as a threatening withdrawal of attention, he would, physically or psychologically, distance himself from the potential frustration. Conversely, he would draw close, physically or psychologically, to whatever would give him reassurance, control, or admiration, fusing or identifying, if need be, with such a source of nourishing love as to take it right into himself. Often, for dapper Sam, such nourishment involved wishes and fantasies that he was being loved and admired for his intact and decorous boyishness.

Understood in terms of this pattern, Sam reacted to "Winter Dreams" according to our four general principles. He liked the story, he said. In our terms, that means he found he could share to some extent his own habitual adaptations with it. Then, defended, he could project into the story his own preferred type of fantasy. Evidently, this process worked out quite neatly for Sam because he said of "Winter Dreams":

> I liked it a whole lot . . . first of all for the kind of lesson it teaches. I think it's an important part of—although I admit that in Fitzgerald it gets a bit draggy. We're taught this lesson through every damn novel, you know. . . . The lesson of the past, the knowledge, the realization in every hero throughout the damn thing that it cannot be retraced, that you try ceaselessly to recapture the past and that it forever eludes you.

It may seem odd that Sam should take pleasure in a sense of loss, but it is less odd when we recognize that his alternative adaptations of fusion and flight might correspond almost exactly to the longing and denial he could find in the story.

Sam presented the picture of a young man who showed a fair amount of anxiety toward sexually attractive women who demanded that he progress beyond his own boyish concern with self-esteem. In his tests and in his general remarks about life and letters, he responded to this anxiety from a higher level by retreating from man-woman relations to a simpler, younger aim: admiration of his own unshared maleness. Therefore, he found Dexter's loss of the sexual woman in "Winter Dreams" reassuring, and he took pleasure in Dexter's triumphing as a strong male all by himself.

Thus, in talking about "Winter Dreams," he concentrated more attention than the other readers did on Dexter, and, in particular, on Dexter as a powerful, solitary man. "I have a strange faith in Dexter," he said. "I didn't worry about anything that happened to him." "We don't even have any description at all of the way that he works and the way that he builds things . . . but yet you have an overriding sense of the kind of determination and hard work it all must have taken." "Underneath you have a sense that it's taken all a lot of hard work and that he's a pretty strong fellow." "He's sturdy stuff." "Never seemed to me that he needed [emotional support from a wife]. It seemed to me that he was totally capable."

"He was able to stand on his own two feet forever." "He's clear-headed and hard-nosed."

The faint traces of symbolism in Sam's last two phrasings suggest what might cause him "to worry" about his hero. Thus, commenting on the scene where Dexter takes up with Judy again after his engagement, "It doesn't seem that he really does anything wrong in the story,' said Sam, "not even going into the house. . . . Nothing really got injured. Nothing of practical importance got injured." "Unfortunately for their relationship," Dexter's and Judy's, that is, "Dexter did go inside." Even so, Sam felt that Dexter in New York did not lack women. "I don't think that this last month of— with Judy has crippled him in any way. He did break it off with Irene. . . . I don't think that he would therefore break it off with all other girls. I think he'd go to dances and things like that."

In other words, the Dexter Sam admired was a man who survived sexual relationships that threatened to injure or break his masculinity. "First of all, he was able to stand on his own two feet, and first of all he was making his money, and first of all he was functioning in the world without Judy Jones." "I knew that whether it came out for better or worse he would be able to go on . . . I mean, this kind of self-made confidence." That echo of the marriage ceremony and the phrasing "it came out" illustrate to me, at any rate, Sam's tendency to regard marriage as a risky enclosure. He preferred the single, autonomous male, who, in a way, creates himself.

Thus, Sam compared Dexter to a more famous Fitzgerald hero, Jay Gatsby. "James Gatz dreams of becoming Jay Gatsby who is, in his imagination, such an unutterable figure that it is forever impossible for him to become it." "Dexter," Sam said, "feels superior to his peers, say, his own generation around him, because he recognizes that he's stronger than they are, just as their parents were stronger than they are. In other words, chronologically he's their peer, and yet actually he's older than they are, because he's a peer with their father. And it's that sense of oldness, I think, that you get, that sense of strongness." In effect, Sam saw Dexter as self-made: quite literally, he had become his own father.

When I asked Sam to talk about Dexter's parents, he expressed this trend even more strongly. He emphasized the details that downgrade Dexter's parents, and he worded them more harshly than the story did. They were a "peasant family," "of peasant stock and of the working class." "There's that bit about his mother being a Rumanian peasant who spoke broken English to her dying day." (Actually, the story said "Bohemian," but Sam supplied a word with no glamorous overtones.) They were "rough hewn," and at one point he called them "bad parents," but immediately retracted. "Uh, now, 'bad parents.' I don't think of them as that at all. I think of them as honest, thick-blooded, hearty workers. The mother probably wore aprons and was stout." Finally, Sam simply erased Dexter's parents. "The parents very seldom come into the picture, and it seems to me they function only in a minor way as . . . keeping the hero of the story alive long enough so that the story can be told about him." "The mother is just over from Rumania or wherever, and I imagine they must be providing a good home, yet . . . one that Dexter Green's imagination would not let him participate in at all." In effect, what Dexter can make himself—his money—substituted for his family, "because if you have enough money . . . one's background is forgotten about, but when you don't have the money, the background becomes everything." Finally, toward the middle of the interview, "He had— He was of no family to speak— You know, he had no family. All he did have was the money."

Evidently, Sam wanted to reduce Dexter's parents because he thought they threatened a son's wholeness and power. For that reason, he wanted Dexter to remain independent of both his parents and Judy. He was to be the strong, virile male alone. For example, when we talked about a line in the story, "For the second time, her casual whim gave a new direction to his life," Sam confessed, "That was a strange line. I had trouble with that." "Lucky," he went on, "lucky that he didn't undergo too many ecstasies, lucky for his business, for his work. . . . I didn't like that sentence because I always thought that his work would go on anyway."

In the same way, Sam could readily accept the notion of a strong, independent Judy, even one resembling an overpowering mother—anything but a wife. "She apparently conquered

him totally in the first couple of months of their relation." "All
the women— All the Fitzgerald women are just the same
woman to me." "The Fitzgerald woman is always an utterly
beaut— . . . such an idealistic woman— That's because, well,
first of all, they're rich, very beautiful. They're terribly conscious of the powers that they have, especially over men."
Yet, he went on, "Actually what they're after is the kind of
middle-class family life that the middle class is so happy with."
He was saying Judy Jones wanted to be a mother rather than an
enchantress!

I asked him, "What do you think it takes to win a Judy
Jones?", and again he faintly hinted that this quasi-mother desired a mutual giving with a tabooed son rather than sex with a
lawful husband. Sam even came up with the image of a mother
hen. "Well, I hate to say— The first thing that pops into my
head is, she always wants what she can't have or she always
wants something that's new. She always wants the difficult
thing. Whenever a new man comes into town everyone else is
immediately dropped until she had him under her wing." He
went on, then, to say how "trite" the story would be if Dexter
had played hard to get and Judy had had to "pant after him all
the time." Abruptly, he decided Judy's husband "didn't have
as much on the ball as Dexter."

Sam's sympathies in the triangle are clear enough. It is sex
and marriage that cause the trouble, ruining men and women,
causing physical changes and bodily loss. "I didn't conceive of
Judy Jones as being, once married, the same way that she was
before she was married." "When you look at her as a person
. . . then you begin to balk at the fact that she does fade like
that. Why does she fade?" But the only reason Sam could find
that satisfied him was "that something is lost." "I see her," he
said, referring to the married Judy, "as even plump. As the
man said, . . . she just faded overnight." "The picture you
have of her . . . is rather pathetic considering that you know
her early life. You know, at home with the children and a bit
haggard and a bit moist from housework and stuff like that."
Sam even volunteered that the married Judy made him think of
"my poor mother," "as being even kind of dumpy and . . . a
bit haggard." "That's kind of like the fallen— that sense of the

fallen that I get in Judy Jones, a kind of mentally run down."

I asked Sam if he could compare Judy to anyone we both knew, and he mentioned a rather glamorous older woman, a divorcée. "Feminine," he said, "perfect in so many social ways"—that was Judy Jones before marriage, and he felt the divorcée had been that way, too. But now, he visualized her "as she makes the stew over the stove at nighttime," dreaming of a Judy Jones life. "I don't think she'd wish [the kids] dead, but I can see her wishing them away, disappearing in a bunch of clouds." Again, it seemed to be the mistake of marriage that marked off the glamorous woman from the overburdened housewife.

Before marriage, Judy represented the ideal, the dream, and, in the story, "It is the sanctity of those winter dreams that dies. In the end." "Dexter went on, in a way that I don't think most men would, to romanticize, to build up, to encase her in her case of glass, making her an ideal of sorts, a timeless thing that was untouchable in all ways." As for this sexual woman, Sam said, "The ideal is false." "He lost the falsehood and gained a truth, no matter how saddening it was. That has to be looked at as good, I suppose." As he went on, however, some of the body fears that were giving rise to this view of marriage showed through: "It was more in the end Judy Jones— I mean, it was more in the end Dexter that lost something.,"

Thus, when Sam imagined marriage, he wanted it to be very impersonal, as he had described the divorcée, perfect in social ways. Marriage for Dexter and Judy was to leave them essentially separate. "I like that kind of [self-made] man, and I like [that] kind of woman. They're fascinating, and I love the air of their irresponsibility. How nice it must be to actually live that way." Sam's real image of the marriage was social, an occasion for mutual admiration and self-esteem. "While she would have been charming and gleaming and glittering socially, and she would have bestowed all her smiles and cares on a million other men, I think that Dexter would have been intelligent enough to know that that was her being a woman, and she would not have carried it further than just the smiles at the parties, say. I think they would have been a lovely couple."

When he talked about her "actual" marriage with Lud

Simms, he inhibited it—or him. "He apparently didn't have as much on the ball as Dexter Green did, and Judy Jones should have known that and so why, therefore, marry him?" He saw Judy as staying home nights rather than going to parties, because "she's forever embarrassed by the fact that her husband is drunk or flirting with any unmarried that might be there." Why did he say "unmarried"? For one thing, his phrasing left homosexual possibilities. For another, couldn't Lud have affairs with married women? Evidently not in Sam's anti-oedipal fantasies. As for Judy's loving Lud, "Was she ever in love with the man she married?" I asked. "Well, yes," he replied. "At one time, if they got married real quick. Maybe when they got married, but certainly not for any prolonged period of time."

She "stays home with the kids," he said, picturing the marriage, "and I'm sure she's miserable." His ultimate image for the marriage was a trap. "That would be . . . a terribly ironic twist of it all, if she did fall terribly head over heels in love with him, just as Dexter was in love with her, and then to have him be the one not caring and have her trapped in it for the rest of her life." "We don't know . . . whether she forgives him because she's truly in love with him or whether she forgives him because there's-no-backing-out-of-it-now type thing."

In Sam's metaphors, Judy's marriage was just a gamble, a wheel of fortune. He visualized Judy saying, " 'Well, I'd better get married now' or 'Let me be swept away by this man, because I'm getting too old to play this game any more.' In other words, finally, kind of like when you spin one of these wheels with the thing, it just happens that it came to a stop on . . . the one that she married, and that happened to be him, and she plopped down into his arms." In the same way, Sam referred to Judy's premarital seductiveness as just play or game. "She plays off of these men, watching for one whose interest is lagging . . . and, you know, just kind of playing off the— Socially, it's done very nicely, I mean her social awareness in order to keep as many irons in the fire as possible." That final cliché—that to be entranced by Judy is to be an iron in a fire—suggests the sexual anxieties that made Sam want Dexter to keep clear of her.

Another way he dealt with those anxieties was to blur or merge the sexes, in a way, denying there was any male or female. There were, for example, Freudian slips, as in the sentence central to his response: "It was more in the end Judy Jones— I mean, it was more in the end Dexter that lost something." "I never thought of Judy as being the kind of woman who would help a man's career in any sense except the fact that she had him for the wife, you know." In the same way, about a minute before he called Dexter "clear-headed and hard-nosed," he had commented on the symbol Judy "rather blatantly, and hard-nosedly, comes to be at the end." He saw that ending—and you should remember the possible body meanings of "end" or "ending"—as "terribly ironic, that she would fall in love with somebody and be done dirt by him . . . after she did so much dirt." "I mean, it seems that the roles are reversed more than anything else." Thus, Sam's second way of dealing with the sexual anxieties was to deny the difference between male and female, making them equally powerful. He would exchange or fuse them, so that they were doing each other dirt with their endings. As he referred to another marriage, "Once he was hers, once she was his."

In short, Sam perceived marriage in this story, not as a desirable outcome, but as physical corruption or loss. He tried to deal with marriage by variously denying the sex in it: it was all a matter of dominance or social show or an exchange of roles and a merging, so there was no real difference between maleness and femaleness, hence no sex. In an alternative defense to this desexualized sexuality, Sam turned to dependence on great, vague benevolences.

Thus, he described Judy as "just a kind of a bunch of diamonds and clouds that you have in your mind, something that you have glimpses of flashing and flowing forms, whisking out of doors and things. You really don't have a portrait." The same image came up in imagining Judy as a mother: "Wishing [the children] away . . . in a bunch of clouds." Sam attributed this tendency to magnify to Gatsby and, by inference, Dexter: "His mind builds Daisy up into a kind of Platonic ideal of a woman."

If you think of it as the kind of dream he had as young caddy, being a kind of a boundless, totally spiritual, imaginative dream . . . And along comes this girl . . . who immediately renders the Platonic uncatchable and unreachable and unutterable, who immediately renders it earthbound. . . . When Dexter meets Judy, the dream becomes in human form. The dream becomes reachable, and hence it's sought after, and though it is never reached in this particular story, the dream does remain, the dream of something being there, though now it is not . . . that high-in-the-sky dream. It is the dream now embodied in Judy Jones and when he sees that Judy Jones has wilted and died, the Judy Jones that he knew, all is lost, because this had been lost to be taken up into her, and now she is gone, and there is nothing.

Sam came back twice more to what, I take it, is a response to the first, nurturing, ineffable source and the sense of total loss that losing her would bring.

In this rather confused passage, Sam showed how Judy embodied his earliest longings for the huge, true, ideal dream-mother, who, in a later phase of his development, would take a frightening form—the woman who is the opposite of an ideal because she lacks what men have—

The ideal is false and the thought that you can come back to it and things like that is false . . . he lost the falsehood. . . . Dexter . . . lost something that he caused himself to lose, I mean, simply because it would never have been there. If it wasn't there, he couldn't have lost it, and it was his own mind that put it there. . . . Judy Jones didn't cause it to be lost. She was just the vehicle. I mean, the thing became again greater than her, while it was tied down through her, and she became the vehicle. The thing, the dream, the illusion became bigger than her.

In such phrasings and vague memories of *Gatsby*, Sam recreated a child's situation of building up massive expectations toward the person he depends on and the child's fear of total depletion should those expectations fail. (However, Sam described the rise and fall of expectations in terms of years rather than hours.)

> Your separateness from the past goes on for a few years while your idealism builds it up and idealizes it and makes a bit of something that never was, and then you learn about how it's unreachable, untouchable, can never go back— It all crashes down and you're kind of left empty. I like that.

Yes, he did, and this sense of loss, as we have seen, provided the very reason Sam liked the story. "I like it a whole lot . . . for the kind of lesson it teaches . . . that you try ceaselessly to recapture the past and that it forever eludes you." Thank heaven! he might have added, for to capture woman—in this case, mother, since Sam *now* was an adult—would involve him in those dangerous sexual touchings and traps. In losing Judy, Dexter lost the kind of thing "that you would be better equipped to face the Wall Street life without."

Thus, at the deepest level of his response, Sam took a double pleasure in "Winter Dreams": first, a pleasure in fusing, or imagining a fusion, with a vast, timeless, glass-encased, Platonic ideal of Woman; then, in welcoming the loss of such a woman, as a way of remaining autonomous and masculine.

Notice the distinction Sam drew between "A Rose for Emily" and "Winter Dreams," although someone else might have found the two stories very similar. Both create and then take away romance (do and undo denials). Both have strong, achieving heroes and dangerous heroines. In both, sex destroys. What was different for Sam, however, was the fate of the hero. Fitzgerald's Dexter goes on to his safe but solitary Wall Street career, a prospect that by no means displeased Sam. Faulkner's Homer ends up a skeleton, and the one point that seemed to arouse the most anxiety for Sam in the Faulkner story was Emily's lying beside Homer's corpse.

It is in this context that we should hear Sam's statement that he preferred the "story of a young man and his girl that I find myself closer to than I would be to something [*sic*]." "A story about an old lady" was less satisfying "from my identification point of view." At one level, I take it, he simply meant he could enjoy Fitzgerald's sexy Judy Jones but not Faulkner's grisly Emily. Plausible as this sounds, Sam's preference for "Winter Dreams" was by no means universal: Saul, Sandra, and Shep all preferred the Faulkner story to the Fitzgerald. Sam's response was special in its effort to get sexual satisfaction from the story—to penetrate it. Also, as we have seen, Sam could be happy getting in only if he could get out again. That Dexter could flee but Homer couldn't made a lot of difference to a young man who liked to be able to get away.

In short, Sam showed an almost cyclical psychological pattern: seeking a masculine splendor, he would try out sexual, man-woman roles; then he would fall back to his original solitary autonomy or, perhaps, regress still further toward a mother-infant relation; finally, however, he would give up that feeding and nurture to find again, with pleasure, his boyishly masculine self. In the interview this regression showed in the ease with which Sam would take the various characters of the story—notably Dexter, but others too—into himself and playact their several roles. Sam showed his boyishness in the interview by his unusual energy and productivity: his talk about this story took almost twice as many pages as any of the other four readers. Finally, Sam's total psychological pattern showed most strikingly in his enthusiasm for precisely the theme of loss in the story.

About "The Battler," however, he was anything but enthusiastic—a graphic demonstration of the importance of matching defenses. That is, the story (at least as I see it) should easily admit fantasies of the strong but isolated maleness Sam admired in others and wanted to have admired in himself. Of Sam's defenses, however, I can make only one in the story—and that intermittently. If the theme of "The Battler" is "staying on the track," it advocates a flight from or avoidance of dangerous entanglements, but this, of course, Nick fails to do in the story. He draws close to a strong, masculine figure, but that proves very risky indeed, although the story finally permits him to escape. Thus, I do not see how Sam could find his pattern of defensive maneuvers in the story. In a general sort of way, therefore, although I did not realize it at the time, I should have expected that Sam would not like the story.

As matters turned out, I and some other critics gave him ways of dealing with the story. At first, though, he admitted frankly: "I think it's not one of his best." Later, he began to say the kind of things English majors say when they are unwilling to admit their true dislike: "I did like the story, and I think it's a valuable look at Nick Adams." "On the whole, I did like the story, yet strangely enough, [though] I'm able to in most— I didn't identify as strongly with Nick here as I could in other stories." "As far as the plot goes, the story is strange. I mean, all this stuff about the sisters [*sic*] and— I don't know what it's doing if it's not doing symbolic things." By the end of the interview, Sam succeeded in making symbolic interpretations that allowed him to defend and to project pleasure-giving fantasies into the story. Thus, he had not one, but a sequence of attitudes.

Sam talked much more than the other readers. Thus, it may help if I outline rather directly the structure of his response, as I see it, even if I risk creating the impression of a far more schematic and less rambling interview than he in fact gave. In general, in what he said about this story, Sam sought to avoid dangers to his autonomy and to ally himself with manly strength, provided doing so posed no risks. This phrasing is so general—yet so much the essential Sam—that it does little more than restate the themes of his Rorschach and TAT.

More particularly, we can separate out three themes, presumably unconscious, in Sam's response. First, he perceived Nick as a young man facing physical threats to his manhood, and Sam wanted to distance his hero and himself from them. Second, he saw the possible perversions in the story as examples of unmanning—he almost spoke of castration literally —and he perceived the characters according to that overpowering danger. He feared a homosexual assault from Ad, whom he thought of as having "lost things" (although he thought the "sister" all right for not having caused losses). Most of all, he feared Bugs. Third, at a defensive and more conscious level, Sam tended, first, to merge the strong and weak characters, and, second, to deny and otherwise distance himself from the story, except as he could impose himself on it and master it by interpretation.

The pattern of merger showed most directly in a series of "Freudian slips." For example, five times Sam substituted the name Nick for Ad. "Nick has— uh, Ad has seen the brakeman jumping along . . . feeling proud of himself." The first of Ad's challenges comes out: "Nick says— uh, Ad says, 'You're tough, aren't ya?' " "Ever since that time [the woman ran off], Nick had— uh, Ad had been kind of popping off into himself." "Nick looked— the men looked at Nick . . ." and Sam went on with a description of the mutilated fighter. Describing Bugs' befriending Ad, out of pity, Sam slipped again: "He did take a liking to Nick— I mean, to Ad."

In a later slip, Sam mixed up Nick with Jake Barnes, the impotent hero of *The Sun Also Rises*. He also confessed, "I would never read *The Sun Also Rises* without seeing Hemingway and just blatantly associating everything that's done in the book, not to Jake Barnes, but to Ernest Hemingway. . . . I'll even make slips of the tongue, and say, 'Oh, well, Hemingway did this at this point,' you know, and Barnes did this at this point." Still other slips mixed up Ad and his pseudosister; he would say, "sisters" instead of "brother and sister." "He [Bugs] just got done saying, 'They're not sisters' " or "If they were sisters, well, they did a— I don't know what the hell they did."

A like pattern pervaded Sam's sporadic identifications with other characters. He "did" Bugs, complete with Chinese accent, as a Fu Manchu. Similarly, Sam playacted Ad on the attack: "Ad begins to approach [Nick], says 'Put up your dukes. Fight like a man,' that type of thing." In the same way, he identified with Nick's discomfort at having to touch Ad. "I think it says he was uneasy, doesn't it? And I says, 'Damn right he's uneasy!' " "I was as wary as he was." Again, projecting rather than playacting, Sam invented thoughts for Nick: "He'll get a bite to eat . . . after he's washed up, of course, and the ritualistic Hemingway washes all the dirt under his nails . . . feels his eye, realizes he's going to have a black eye and figures himself lucky for not having anything more happen to him. He could have broken a leg or something."

The sample is tiny, but it shows a theme and variations. In general, Sam's projections into the characters served to let him resolve a fear he felt because of some show of strength or aggression by the character. At the level of least control, by Freudian slips and unintended blurrings of the characters, Sam matched their weaknesses with their strengths. Somewhat up the levels of control, in impulsive actings out of the characters—sudden projections into and identifications with them—Sam compensated for his own fears of weakness by fusing with their strengths. Finally, at a still higher level of control, conscious interpretation, Sam tended to balance the characters, as equally penetrating, questing, manly types, physically thrusting into things. Thus, Nick "is searching for a sense of the good place, that type of thing, which you find Jake Barnes concerned with. Of course Jake fails, whereas Nick only goes a certain way." Nick, he concluded, is "a whole Hemingway character, whom we can even extend into being Jake Barnes." (This, although Barnes was impotent!) Sam decided that Hemingway was cheating a little in creating Nick's supposed ability to identify Bugs as a Negro by his walk: "attributing a power over consequential things— inconsequential things, I mean, to the character of the story." Hemingway "attributes more powers to his characters, uh, in this way of awareness and observatory powers, than are usually found or usually at any rate observed in other people."

In these interpretations, Sam was equating the impotent man to the potent, the weak to the powerful, the passive to the active, the observer to the actor, and so on. Ad, he imagined, "started out [looking] perhaps very much as Nick looked starting out." Thus, he concluded, "the real battler of the story" was not Ad, but Nick. "Nick is the one who . . . has to do the battling, who has to stick to the railroad track, you know, through the symbolism of it all and to watch out for the pitfalls to reach whatever goal it is."

Fusing Nick and Ad was one defense Sam brought to bear on the anxieties about helplessness the story aroused in him. Denial—erasing or refusing the reality of painful aspects of the story—was a second. It was, of course, Sam's characteristic mode of flight away from threats. "I found the story kind of remote," he said. "Everybody seems rather phantasmic, kind of ghostlike." "Strangely, I . . . really feel like I'm reading a story when I read this. I really feel like I'm reading a piece of fiction, and I don't know why." "I feel curiously detached from any of [the characters]."

At times, as when Sam denied the likelihood of a homosexual relation between two prison companions, one with money, one without, the motive for Sam's denials (or flight) would become clear. "I originally liked the thought," but "I kind of reacted against it." "I now think that it doesn't do the story any good to have it so." Sam was revealing in this quite different context the same attraction and repulsion toward other men his Rorschach and TAT responses showed: he wished to fuse with a strong man and so gain strength, but he also feared the help-lessness and femininity a homosexual relationship would imply.

Inevitably, a fair amount of puzzlement went along with these denials. For example, Sam said he was bewildered by the strange story about the sister. "I can't figure it out—that's my feeling towards the sister." "What *is* going on?" Of Nick, he said, "Just what the hell he's doing with his life, you know, we just don't know at all." We have already seen his uncertainties about Bugs: "a kind of strange figure." "He's a kind of evil presence . . . [that] Hemingway wants you to think of him as, and I don't know what reason, why." Sam even wondered about the speed and length of the freight train and went beyond the story to ask, "What does 'impotence' mean exactly?" and how was it related to sterility and the lack of sexual desire.

Such denials betray a good deal of anxiety. "The whole story has an atmosphere about it of a bad dream of sorts. The fact that it's nighttime throughout the entire story, that Nick ap-pears in the story with a bang, falling off the train, and kind of fades out of the story walking down— and moonlight and this kind of fireside happening with no more light than the flickering shadows of the firelight, and the strangeness of the things, the oddity of the people." "Bugs came across as kind of the nightmare element . . . kind of the devil of the nightmare."

To be sure, to achieve his denials Sam made use of those the story makes possible: Hemingway's elliptical style and the

theme of avoidance. But Sam could not find enough denials in
the story to control his anxieties, perhaps because dangers
from being close to other men would be so quintessentially
dangerous to him, perhaps because he could not accept (either
emotionally or intellectually) the unknowns in the story.

At any rate, Sam was presenting a classic case of that
malaise readers feel when confronted by the inexplicable in
their reading, and Sam responded as most readers do, by looking for explanations that would control the story. Sam's third
line of defense, then, became interpretations. They ranged from
the jaunty question with which he opened the interview,
"Okay, what would you like to know about 'The Battler'?" to
the nagging uncertainty with which he puzzled away at Ad's
relation with his sister. He supplied explanations (typical for
Sam) in terms of body position and movement, explanations he
felt he needed, even at some cost in enjoyment. "I should have
read it in a more relaxed manner, I suppose." At any rate, he
decided it was a story that showed Nick "moving away from
home and moving out into the big, wide world." "It shows the
relative state Nick has reached by this time." All kinds of
explanations were possible, from an old-fashioned realism ("I
seem to remember having read someplace that it was based on
someone named . . . Kid Francis") to the odd notion that Ad's
idealism led to his final defeat.

Sam's favorite form of explanation, however, was what he,
using the term in a very broad way, called "symbolic." "You
have to look at the symbolism. You have to look at the images,
because the story as it stands is of such trifling importance. . . .
we really learn nothing," and the word "stands" tells us what
"symbolism" meant for Sam. The very *act* of interpretation,
apart from its content, served Sam's needs and fantasies of
mastery, as, for example, when he spoke of Nick, "whom we
can even *extend into* being Jake Barnes," an odd phrase in this
context. "I just don't know how far out I'm gonna draw this
stuff. It is drawoutable, I suppose." "If you take the story just
as sitting there, what is Nick doing? . . . He's young, apparently. That we know even if the story just stands by itself."
The uncertain story is a sitting story; the certain story stands
by itself, or "What I've done . . . to bolster it up is to infuse in

it all the symbolism, the context of this whole group of short stories, and it gives it more character. It's able to stand up more." He tried applying the symbolism of "Big Two-Hearted River" to this story, but "you wonder if the symbols are going to hold up like that." "Maybe you could have . . . a younger Nick Adams making his little foray into the swamp and scurrying on back to the well-paved, easy-treading road . . . and that's about all he can stand."

As we have seen, Sam was afraid of the homosexual themes in the story. As he put it, early in the interview, "My mind has been poisoned by reading critics who tell me that the relationship between Ad and Bugs is essentially homosexual." By the end of the interview, he was showing a good deal of anxiety, and I thought I ought to offer him reassurance in the form of a symbolic reading that matched his interpretation without requiring Ad and Bugs to be homosexuals. I suggested that, Ad being the one that supplied the money and fought off enemies and Bugs being the one who bought the groceries, cooked, and tended, they symbolized a distorted, dreamlike father and mother, the family Nick had to escape from.

Perhaps I was successful with this alternative interpretation simply because it was a good reading; or perhaps it was because I offered myself as a fatherly, professorial expert with a masculine reading of the story he could accept and identify with (as against critics who "poisoned" him). In any case, this reading suited Sam just fine: "That's really, it really holds up." And he was able to see himself as taking money from his father and cooking (illicitly) in his dormitory room and hence, "Oh, my God! I married my father!" He had identified, finally, with—Bugs! In short, once Sam could get a reading that "really holds up," that had the upright, phallic strength he needed, he could get close to the story, even to the point of realizing his unconscious wish to identify with that character in it who (as we shall see) he consciously felt was *the* most violent, threatening, and dangerous.

In general terms, Sam dramatically instances the notion of "meaning-as-defense," the theory that readers need a sense of intellectual theme and meaning to manage the anxieties they experience from literary works. Such a theory comes directly from Freud's theory of play. Freud discovered that children enjoy games, such as peek-a-boo, because they provide experiences of mastery. When the mother apparently disappears, the child is afraid, but he uses the controlled and ritualized pattern of the game to control and end his fear. Precisely because he knows it is a game, he can be sure she will reappear.

We play the game of literature the same way. We use a story to deal with the anxieties we have let it arouse in us. We do so in two major ways. One is form, for example, the flat, Hemingway style of this story, which, as Sam realized, one uses to avoid "getting into" dangers. The other is meaning, making a social, ethical, or intellectual sense out of the story. That, too, serves to manage anxiety. Thus, when I was able to offer Sam an interpretation that satisfied him, he was better able to accept the story, and he spontaneously identified with the positive side of Bugs, the character he formerly could think of only in a fearful way.

It was very near the end of our interview, however, when I suggested this interpretation to Sam. For most of our discussion, he dealt with the anxieties the story aroused by his three other defenses, evidently less effective for him than my interpretation. In his "Freudian slips," playacting and other projections, and the way he merged himself with the characters, them with one another, with the hero of *The Sun Also Rises,* or with Hemingway himself, Sam showed his major defense: the balancing of weak and strong, potent and impotent characters, by fusing them. He also distanced or denied the story, making it remote and unreal. Third, he tried to master the story's puzzles by thrusting his interpretation on it. No one of these three defenses worked out very well, and only the sense of remoteness and unreality matched a defense already in the story. As a result, Sam engaged with the story, but he was not securely defended and he could feel mostly the negative, fearful side of its fantasy. He could not (as he had done with Dexter in "Winter Dreams") take much pleasure in Nick's male strength, power, and achievement.

Even so, Sam's first impulse was to identify with Nick as a single, isolated principle of male power moving through space. The story, he said, "would be the kind of romance that I'd be

interested in. . . . It's always uncertain just exactly where he's
going. Says he must get to somewhere he really has no idea.
He's just traveling, you know." In such phrasings, Sam
tried being Nick Adams, enjoying Nick's life of adventure
and romance (as Sam saw it), but he also worked out a well-
known fantasy: the identifying of one's total ego, his whole
body or mind or both, with a disembodied maleness, not unlike
the winged *phalloi* on Greek vases. Acts of mind or body take
on the emotional value of thrusts, quests, or risks of that one
member thought of as one's total being, as when we speak of
someone's having a "penetrating mind" or "entering a new
field" or "being out on a limb" or "sticking his neck out."

In this context, Sam saw as a basic theme of the story the
risk that Nick "might have really gone in over his head" in the
situation with Ad and Bugs. Sam identified them with a swamp
in contrast to "the straight and narrow," "the more protected,
the easier runway" of the railroad track. At this point in his
life, Sam said, Nick should stick to "the railroad track, clear
and well-paved [*sic*] . . . to reach . . . the good place or something like that." Nick, he said, has to achieve freedom "at this
particular point, moving away from home and moving out into
the big, wide world."

Sam also saw Nick as having big, vague dangers in front of
him, in his "personal facing-up to life's demands." "Nick is
the one who has his whole life in front of him." "Nick is the,
one who has his whole life against him, who has . . . to watch
for the pitfalls to reach whatever goal it is that you have to
get."

One way Sam dealt with these phallic dangers was to make
Nick primarily an observer: "He's just moving around, seeing
the country, seeing people, and— he *saw* it!" It must, then,
have been as much a reflection on Sam's defenses as
Hemingway's style for him to say: "We don't get much into
Nick's mind." Not getting into big situations, being a mere
watcher, served as defenses against dangers to Nick of being
phallicly entrapped: instead, one has "little glimpses," an
"awareness of small traits."

The nature of the danger was clear enough. "It's okay," said
Sam, "to plop yourself down in a dangerous situation and try

and react with it and . . . worry it, work it out, and see, and come out of it okay. But . . . touching of strangers and of dirty old hoboes makes me a little nervous." As for Bugs, "There's something behind the politeness that you can't deal with until it comes to the front, till you see it." In the same way, Sam told of Nick's seeing the firelight, "and, inexplicably—I think it's inexplicably—he says he must take a look and see what that is." The "inexplicably" that Sam contributed suggests the puzzlingly double value seeing had for him in the story. First, it defended against unknown traps and pits, but second, looking and being looked at gave pleasure in one's own or others' wholeness—if one *is* whole.

That was, of course, the real issue for Sam, in this story as well as elsewhere: the loss of masculinity. "It is weird that . . . you have the two perversions in such a short story," said Sam. "It may be clear-cut, yet it is kind of weird." "There is this suggestion of a weird relationship between Ad and Bugs, and then this comes up strangely enough: a weird relationship between Ad and some woman who may or may not have been his sister." It is worth noting, I think, that, in addition to the two relationships Sam responded to as perverted, each of the other characters individually involves some kind of bodily or mental "difference" some people associate with a loss of male power or intactness: the defaced, punch-drunk fighter, the Negro, the woman. Each of these characters played a different part in Sam's reaction.

Sam partly wanted to glorify Ad. Although the story describes him as a "little man," even boyish, Sam described him as "a heavyweight." Similarly, the story calls him simply "a former champion fighter," but Sam saw "this kind of romance . . . starting out low as a prize fighter, aspiring to being world champion, and actually reaching it." Part of Sam's romancing involved the quite contradictory fantasy of Ad as a stubborn loser in the struggle of life: "Having been beaten the first time, [he] went back into the ring again, and having been beaten a million times still kept going back into the ring." That, I take it, is not the kind of record world champions make.

I think Sam was recreating Ad as "a fallen hero—of sorts," a man who had suffered losses. He was using Hollywood

stereotypes of the champion to develop his fantasies. "Once
. . . he has reached it [the championship] . . . there's a loss
of all the other things because he sees the dirt and sees the
inside of— what goes on behind all of the prize fights. Undoubtedly he's been bribed and gone through all the sordid
little things . . . or big things." The sense of getting into a dirty
place, behind and inside, of little and big, suggests ever so
faintly the mutilation this dangerous penetration implied for
Sam. Thus, he concluded, "Though he is champion, he has
been beaten because the idealism with which he started off has,
of course, been crushed." Why "of course?" And where did
he get the idea Ad was ever an idealist? But the use of
"crushed" reveals the unconscious body meaning for Sam of
idealism: a youthful male power that one could physically lose.

Sam built on the symbols the story gave him: that defeat was
mutilation of mind and body. "His mind had been rendered
rather simple by the beatings he'd been given." Sam quoted
Bugs, "He wouldn't be bad-looking without his face all
busted," and then he added his own interpretation. "You
know, he started out perhaps very much as Nick looked starting out. . . . perhaps in an idealistic frame of mind and the
occurrences of his life . . . have just beaten him to a bloody
pulp who is now more insane than anything else." "Perhaps his
increasing simplicity and child— you know, just being more
and more punch-drunk— she couldn't stand it or perhaps because he became so ugly as his ears got flattened more and his
face got pounded in. And she went off and never came back."
Mutilated, insane, left by his woman—Sam was developing a
theme of Ad's unmanning. "The embarrassment of having . . .
such a . . . pretty girl and saying they were like twins, and then
having such a, such a brute-looking man there." Of Ad's relation to Bugs, Sam said, "It's just one more perversion that Ad
Francis has fallen— as fallen hero, falls into. I mean, look how
he's even fallen lower. He's hanging around with faggots now,
you know, and stuff like that." "It seems that words like 'mis-
shapen' and 'mutilated' and 'dead-looking' and the whole sense
of perversion of normality . . . Ad becomes, in my mind, a kind
of fallen hero."

Ad's "fallen" state mobilized anxiety for Sam about being—or touching—a man. "I was fearful for what might happen to Nick," he said, "and especially the touching business, because, you know, touching is a whole different thing." "I could share in his terror of touching this man at all who's painted for us in such a grotesque, mutilated shape. . . . I think both Nick and the reader at this point are still feeling out just what the hell this guy's all about." Touching—feeling—then was double-valued: it suggested dangerous homosexual touching, but if done gingerly enough, it could be a way of knowing and hence reassuring (as in Sam's remarks above—p. 71— about affectionate Italian touchings).

Mostly, however, Sam found Ad someone to be afraid of. "It's in the middle of the night. It's miles and miles from anywhere. And one fears for Nick," he said excitedly. "This business of touching the wrist. You— I think I felt that Nick ought to be sitting exactly on the other side of the fire and watching out for this guy." "There's a sense that he may leap on Nick any moment, with a knife and stab him in the heart. It's still in my mind, anyway."

In short, Sam put Ad through much the same pattern he created on his own TAT and Rorschach responses. At first, he tended to glorify and idealize Ad in an exaggerated way. Then he talked about Ad's various mutilations of mind and body. These mutilations in turn took him into anxieties about being a man, in particular, violent, dangerous images of homosexual rape. In effect, Sam seemed to be working out the opposite, fearful side of the original idealizing. If he is an ideal, he is a strong, phallic man, and I am safe. But if he is mutilated, I can be, too.

The character who really mobilized anxiety for Sam, however, was Bugs.

I got the feeling that whatever happened Nick could deal with Ad, yet whereas I think he might have really gone in over his head if he would have had to deal with whatever it was Bugs wanted or Bugs was going to do. I think if Ad weren't there, Nick would have had a rougher time at that

little campfire, just by walking in and sitting down and eating
dinner with Bugs alone. I don't know what would have happened. I don't know whether he would have killed him or
taken his money or what. I just don't know, but he's a kind
of evil presence.

"I had more fear of him than I had of Ad, really."
"Even though Ad is the one that threatens violence?" I
asked.
"Right," he said.
"And Bugs is the one who prevents the violence from happening?"
"Yeah, even though that happened." "Bugs came across as
kind of the nightmare element. I mean, I'm a bit afraid of his
'low, polite, smooth, nigger voice.' " He was, Sam said, "a
kind of evil Fu Manchu. Fu Manchu *was* evil, wasn't he? Well,
a kind of Fu Manchu type of person. A kind of polite mingling
with merciless from whom you never know what to expect, and
I had more fear of him than I had of Ad."

> He's kind of the devil of the nightmare, and the excruciating
> type of oriental torture where [and Sam put on his best
> Chinese accent], "Oh, you very nice. I'm now going to rip
> your ears apart and put—" you know, this kind of exquisite,
> terribly polite type of torture which is to me more frightening
> than brutality, where he walks out: "I'm going to punch the
> crap out of you, buddy!" That I can handle. But this kind,
> where you're kind of helpless before the politeness of the
> enemy . . . and you've got to react only to his front which is
> politeness.

As we have seen, Sam admitted his mind had been "poisoned"
by critics who suggested Bugs was homosexual. Sam was
doubtful: "I think you can milk it out of the story, but—"
I think Sam's fears of Ad began as a boy's feelings for a
father who is both loved and dreaded as a big, physical maleness. He becomes (in fearful fantasy) a male lover who muti-
lates or (in the boy's wishes) who is mutilated. However, Sam
saw Bugs as "a kind of shy man who does take care of— but
I'm not saying whether he has any milk of human kindness in

him, in every vein, you know, or anything like this." Sam's image of Bugs as oriental torturer or this echo of Lady Macbeth suggests a more unfocused, deeper anxiety than fears of a homosexual relation with a father, fears rather of a total overwhelming or engulfing. With Bugs, Nick "might really have gone in over his head." I believe one would find Sam's fears of Bugs rooted in deeper, more global anxieties about a mother, associated with milk or the poison of homosexuality.

Thus, here, Sam fought the homosexual theme, denying the realistic bases for it (the two men meeting in prison, one moneyed and one not, one black, one white), but he worried about what you can "see" in "the front," what is "behind" Bugs's politeness. He thus hinted at very primitive fears about females as beings whose defining physical feature is within rather than in front, anxieties about, finally, the mother on whom one is totally dependent and who therefore can be (must be?) the ultimate torturer.

What, then, of the shadowy woman in this story, the sister-and-no-sister, who managed Ad, whom Ad married, and who left him? "She," Sam decided, "seems to be kind of pretty much on the up and up." Specifically, this upright, erect phrasing apparently meant for Sam, not causing Ad any loss. "She hasn't been unfair to him. She hasn't stolen his money or anything of the sort." "She was not responsible for running off with his fortune on top of his heart. Other managers and fight promoters and stuff like that could have sucked money out of him," but she did not. A few minutes before saying this, he had quoted the story's comment on the brakeman episode with which it began: "They would never suck him in that way again." Sam himself commented contemptuously on Nick's naïvely falling for the brakeman's offer to give him something: "Now, what could the brakeman be wanting to give him? What? A couple of dollars to buy lunch with when the train pulled in?" For Sam, as for Hemingway, food baited a trap, and women might also be part of that trap—unless they were desexualized. "She went off and never came back with not even mention of another man, not even infidelity of any sort."

"The story is strange, anyway," he said. Indeed it is, and it is also strange that Sam did not like it, although his attitudes toward food, women, and virility were so like Hemingway's and although he liked youthful exploration and the other Nick Adams stories. I know of no way to account for Sam's gingerliness about "The Battler" save by considering his response in the light of the fourfold structure of a literary response.

In brief, Sam reacted to the characters in the following ways. What he said about Nick showed that he unconsciously perceived Nick as a male body, or member, facing risks—swamps, pitfalls, traps, "his life"—all "in front of" him. He (it) could be safe by being a passive observer rather than one who gets "into" situations, for seeing not only enables one to avoid dangers, it guarantees that one is separate and distanced.

As for Ad, Sam at first glorified him, then saw him as a man who had lost his ideals, finally as a man suffering bodily and sexual losses. Sam felt toward him as one might toward a father: if he is ideal, I am safe; if he is mutilated, I can be, too. Touching such a man is dangerous if homosexual (Ad he saw as posing a threat of homosexual assault), but all right if informative only. Sam feared Bugs as one might some ultimate, terrible mother: he was the really evil character, an oriental torturer, the final terror. "Poisoned" by critics, Sam perceived a homosexual relation between Ad and Bugs, but denied it, too. The "sister" he saw as neither damaged nor damaging, hence "on the up and up." She didn't take anything away.

Neither did Sam, with respect to the story. As we have seen, for a reader to respond fully, he must—first and foremost —either find in the story defenses that match his own or impose his own defenses to manage anxieties mobilized by the literary work. Here, Sam found threats to maleness and dangers from an overpowering, engulfing female. To these anxieties he brought three related lines of defense. He used denials to make the story puzzling, remote, and unreal, and the story provided a basis for such an approach, as exemplified by some of the critics cited at the outset. But this flight through denial, so characteristic of Sam, could hardly bring him "into" the story. He tried getting closer to the story, in his preferred mode of defense, by "Freudian slips," playactings, projections, and identifications that tended to merge Ad and Nick, Nick and the hero of *The Sun Also Rises* and Hemingway, Ad and his sister.

In general, he tended to fuse weak and strong, potent and impotent characters so as to balance and equalize them. While this eased some of Sam's anxiety, it was not a defense he could derive from the story directly and therefore it did not tend to bind him closer to it. Finally, Sam provided explanations and interpretations as a way of getting a virile mastery of the story's puzzles.

In one sense, critical remarks and interpretations stem from "higher" ego functions: one's sensitivity to the unity or intensity of the literary work, one's problem-solving skill, one's ability to empathize, one's experience of literature, and so on. But like all human activities, criticism and interpretation have their roots in our deepest unconscious selves as well. These roots were particularly clear with Sam who was so much and so obviously concerned with themes of bodily loss and mutilation in this story. Appropriately enough, then, he put forth as his first interpretation the theme that Nick Adams ought to stick to the "more protected . . . runway," and that he made a mistake in getting off the direct road to his goal and going to Ad's campfire. In further interpretations, Sam regressed from this virile, venturesome singlemindedness to a fear of Bugs, although—or precisely because—it was Bugs who provided food and protected against Ad's violence. Bugs he represented as an oriental, thereby, I take it, adding distance as well as interpretation to mask Bugs's prosaic American self and perhaps too, to mask his being not only no stranger, no exotic, but the one person in everyone's life who could not possibly be a stranger.

Other critical remarks by Sam suggested flight, notably his shifting to *The Sun Also Rises* or insisting that one could not understand this story without first considering all of the stories of *In Our Time,* even though he admitted most of them had nothing to do with Nick Adams. Finally, Sam accepted my reading of Ad and Bugs as a distorted father and mother. Perhaps he did so because he wanted to feel closer to me, perhaps because he found this an acceptable way of merging those two enigmas. I think he would have enjoyed the story more if he had had that interpretation at the beginning of the interview, but I do not know.

What is clear is the role of conscious interpretation in Sam's response. By keeping the story a puzzle, he could distance himself from it, escaping as need be, but he could also confront the mystery, puzzle, or trap head on and impose his powers on it—mental powers, poetic, Hemingwayan, or, at their deepest level, phallic. If he succeeded, he made the story strong, able to stand on its own feet, something he could merge with enthusiastically. In effect, he would make the story, like the sister-manager, a mystery, but nevertheless something on the "up and up" that would not cause him to lose anything. For Sam, as for all readers, the act of interpretation is not a dry affair of the intellect, but an act of synthesis and creation, the construction of a new human experience out of the very roots and depths of personality.

Saul

Every reader seeks from a literary work a pleasurable acting out of his own inner structure of expectancies. Most importantly, he tries to create from the work a match for his own pattern of defenses so that he can safely introject from it fantasies at the levels of drive that matter to him. Scholarly Saul, we have seen, defended against fears that a superior power would tear something out of him by insisting on a world of exact boundaries and bargains that he himself controlled. He could hardly be expected to like Fitzgerald's mythologizing mode, and he didn't.

He sharply criticized the story for what he called its "indulgent" quality. "I don't like it. It's that sort of self-indulgence with the . . . charming and dying sort of things. I find it repellent but . . . repellent while it bothers." He himself diagnosed his reaction: "Maybe this is my own anal things happening here. . . . It seems very, very soft-edged and shadowy, this fantasy about this girl . . . and then I worried a little about the contours of that fantasy in that relationship. You know, soft-edged like— Well, indulgence is another . . . reaction." I think he was finding in the story the fantasies that could make him anxious—fantasies of losing something, letting something slip away—but I also think he was asking for a visual defense as much as rejec.ing a fearful fantasy: if boundaries were "soft-edged and shadowy," he felt threatened and angry. "This damn romant— you know, this beautiful, exquisite sensibility, you know, turns me off." Saul feared being hurt by what he did not comprehend, even the vagueness in his own fantasies about the girl, and he responded by angrily asserting a hard-edged self, even giving up the fantasies, if he had to, in order to get down to a hard, secure core. Precision was what Saul wanted, not indulgence.

In other interviews, Saul told me he liked authors with "authority," but it became clear he meant by that a kind word of definiteness and precision, not Fitzgerald's mythologizing in this and other stories. He objected to "the method there, the point of view, with the author kind of there. 'I tell you this: the rich are—such and such and such' . . . the way he doesn't fold it out. He doesn't let the story happen; he tells you *how* it happened . . . part of the time he lets it fold out, then jumps back to this and this." Saul was never easy to understand, but I think he was telling me here he felt manipulated by Fitzgerald, just the way he objected to letting down his guard in response to the "self-indulgence" in the story or its "soft-edged" quality. It was not giving him the precisely defined authority he needed to sense to be sure things would not be yanked out of him. The romanticism that charmed other readers repelled Saul. "You know, 'This is transient beauty,' and all this decadent crap."

Saul's phrase, "repellent while it bothers," tells us that the story was reaching him in some sense, that he was engaged with the story to some extent, projecting some fantasy into it. It was not at all the same fantasy, however, that Sam attributed to the story, of Dexter as a strong, solitary, and admirable male. Only one thing in the story held any real interest for Saul: the exchange between Judy and Dexter and the question of who lost what. As for things like Dexter's business successes, his chain of specialty laundries, "They bore me. I was thinking about a guy sitting there writing off for English recipes for cleaning socks. Yeah, that's a nice funny thought," and he laughed.

It was very characteristic of Saul to make sure these things needn't concern him by reducing them to trivial particulars. When I asked Saul, "How do you visualize Dexter's parents?" he remembered one detail from the story: "They run the second-best grocery-store in Black Bear Lake." But he went on, "He could easily . . . be an orphan the way Jay Gatsby is. He could easily make himself in this way, spring from the Platonic form of himself or whatever, to get himself into this position vis-á-vis Judy Jones." Similarly, Dexter's business "is peripheral to the story. It's one of the social preconditions to get him in the position where he can meet Judy Jones." In both instances, he seemed to be saying that the rest of Dexter's life, all that isn't involved in his relation with Judy, serves only to set him in a fixed position toward her, to define a kind of distance and boundary.

Alternatively, "One of my reactions is that it's a nice dream," he said of Dexter's financial success. "It's probably . . . not nearly as much fun to do as it is to tell about someone who's done it, who's become this sort of material success. Here, we are in the province of the American dream again." Shifting from the achievement itself to writing about it, turning a "material success" into a "dream" or a story, placing Dexter's male world on the periphery—all these served to put a guard rail, as it were, around Dexter's power and drive.

He managed Judy's powers much the same way, but even so, he gave very direct, explicit statements of some unconscious themes: love for the earliest nurturing mother and for her later, sexual incarnation, followed by the loss of desire if she is actually won. Thus, he described Judy Jones in a series of oral images. First, she was "this sweet young thing," then, "this sweet young bitch," until finally he was saying, "She's lost her pouty young glow." In his words, she began the story as "absolute beautiful," both an "attraction" and a "check." She was, as the story was, "attractive and repellent." "There's something terribly . . . death-wishy about it," that is, about this love for "the charming and dying."

Drawing on a "higher" stratum of development, concerned with adult sexuality, he began the interview with a joke about virginity. He later spent a good five minutes ruminating on Judy's virginity, or lack of it, complete with statistics on virginity at Midwestern colleges. In a symbolism we shall see in other male subjects (Sebastian, for example), he abruptly took the conversation from "the girl he can't have," the girl of the dream, into what I took to be a quite free association, to *Portnoy's Complaint* and "fantasizing about retiring to a cheap furnished room in Newark with a whore who will do all sorts of wild, wild . . . things."

Many men share this combination of fantasies about women, the dream of virginal innocence and of powerful and degrading passion. It derives from a set of impossibilities: a boy's wish for a virginal mother and his inconsistent, but equally strong wish (and fear) that she become his as passionately and genitally as she has become his father's. Saul's seeing Judy first as virgin, then as the cheapened means of his gratification, neatly parallels his degrading of the "sweet young thing" at the level of nurturing. Both shifts reveal hostility.

"It's not a calm and cool thing . . . like, I under*stand* this longing for this, for this sweet young bitch." Perhaps recalling a line from the end of the story, " 'He [Lud Simms] treats her like the devil,' " he repeated the thought several times. "She needs to be . . . treated like the devil." "I'm insisting on this, I guess, that she has to be treated like the devil." Whoever marries her, "it would need to be somebody who would treat her like the devil." Possibly it was just his repetitions, but looking at the typed transcript of the interview, I realized there was an ambiguity in Fitzgerald's phrase: it could mean Lud treats her as a devil would or that he treats her like the devil she is. Unconsciously, I think Saul did see her as a devil, but consciously, he was speaking of her "need of someone being the devil to her." He was talking as though the male, the father, and a Judy Jones could marry only in a sadistic attack. That was the only way to balance Judy's power to hurt.

In the actual words of the story, however—and, not just Saul, but all the male readers had to be reminded of this—Dexter's informant from Detroit says, " 'I can't understand how a man like Lud Simms could fall madly in love with her, but he did.' " Saul, however, saw the Simmses' courtship quite differently. Dexter couldn't win her, because he's too much in love with Judy, he said. "The guy that does win her

. . . is mean to her." "I think that she needs to be kept in line, needs to be commanded. . . . She plays around with a dozen guys who are just nice and adoring . . . and apparently this character from Detroit came along and whipped her into line."

At the beginning of the interview, Saul confessed to a special feeling toward this story. "Some of it gripped me a good deal more because . . . My reaction is, is polluted," because of "a girl that shot me down," who, it turned out, resembled Judy Jones in some particulars. This experience may account for some of the force with which he voiced his sadistic attitudes or the number of times he would repeat a phrase like "treat her like the devil." Nevertheless, Saul's phrasings, his saying "gripped me," or "polluted" "my reaction," or "shot me down," suggested the fantasies about women that might make a defeat all the more threatening to him and might make him seek gratification from his own fantasies of vengeance rather than the fantasy of mutual loss that Sam found.

Mostly, then, Saul responded to Judy and the entire story by reducing Fitzgerald's romantic legend to coarse realities. Even so, Saul proved able to use Fitzgerald's mythologizing, too, as a defense, at least slightly. First, he used it to distance and reduce threats (as he had made Dexter's financial success a "nice dream"). He came back to the word "fade" over and over again, using it to achieve his own defensive pattern with remarkable accuracy. Thus, he said the real story "is him dreaming about this . . . fadedness, this inevitably fading chick . . . fading and receding." " 'Fading' is the word that keeps coming back to me." And then he was pleased to find, on one of his scans of the story, "He *does* use the word 'fade.' I thought I'd, uh, done that myself."

Second, Judy's fading, as Saul saw it, kept her from being the overpowering woman he feared. She became a possible mate, because she would not take something away from the man—rather, she would lose something herself. Thus, he could say quite bluntly, "She's just unwinnable until the point where she starts to fade." "She's not winnable until she fades." Saul went even farther, to say that part of Judy's attractiveness lay in the very inevitability of her fading. "An element of Dexter's thing about this type of girl is that . . . she *will* fade at twenty-five."

Third, I think Saul was saying fairly explicitly that, in some sense, Judy was psychologically taboo for Dexter. "I think this longing for something that you can't have, for various reasons, is kind of the same impulse like standing outside the gym, outside the prom . . . when he couldn't afford proms. The music passed— The girl who's bound— The girl who he can't have and who (I think) he knows but doesn't know will fade. And it does come as a certain shock to him that it does fade, but I think that's implicit in this kind of check or this kind of attraction."

In the unlikely event that Dexter had won her, he said, "She wouldn't have been staying home taking care of the kids, and so forth, because—I'm insisting on this, I guess—that she has to be treated like the devil, to stay faithful or stay at home with the kids or whatever. . . . That's the mechanism of her ruin, her decline, from absolute beautiful to being just a pretty girl with nice eyes." Saul seemed to be saying right out, that when Judy Jones becomes a wife and mother—a parent, a trainer of children—she must "fade" as a sexual object. She has to be treated aggressively lest she prove destructively sexual. Saul, however, stated this oedipal theme in terms from his own preferred level of fantasy. He spoke of losing something unique and precious from the body (as contrasted to the narcissistic disfiguring Sam posited). Sam's Judy became ugly. Saul's remained pretty, but merely pretty. She had lost her precious quality.

Thus, Saul stated in still a fourth way his defensive maneuvers toward Judy. "Her image keep[s] receding. You keep following her, giving up things . . . and various things fall by the wayside . . . and then finally giving up his dream." "He gives it up or has it yanked out, or whatever." "How would you feel if Dexter had married Irene?", I asked. "The dream would have still remained to be smashed by this Detroit businessman or some other plot mechanism," he replied. Saul's image suggests to me, at any rate, the violence he feared from women or husband-fathers who control. He described the ending as saying, "Another thing is gone. The thing is gone." "The thing that hits Dexter in the last part, you know, the dream-was-gone thing. Something had been taken from him." Precious things falling by the wayside or being yanked out—Saul seemed to find in the story an enactment by a foolish Dexter of his own basic anxiety-arousing fantasy. Dreaming is bad. Precision alone is safe.

In short, only in the most limited way could Saul create his own defenses from elements of the story. Fitzgerald's mythologizing ran squarely contrary to his own need to avoid threats by exactness. Saul therefore provided a series of defenses on his own: focusing the story exactly on the dangerous relation between Dexter and Judy; distancing the events he could safely dismiss, and converting the more dangerous ones to crude realities; degrading Judy, attacking her; finally, reaffirming in his own terms the sexual taboo against Judy. Within the story thus narrowed and guarded, he introduced a fantasy about mutuality, but a fearful fantasy about mutual hurt; he dealt with the fears by angrily attacking Judy and her story. Thus, in this very special way, he could feel his "expectancy enacted," but unpleasurably. For Saul, as for all of us, whether we experience something with pleasure or displeasure, we nevertheless experience it in our own individual style, if we permit ourselves to experience it at all.

Saul refused any relation at all, for example, with "The Battler," at least as far as our interview was concerned. He had recently seen a television production of this story, and he resolutely diverted all my efforts to get him to talk about the story into narrations of and comparisons with the screened version. Thus, he established his control over the interview. He set the terms on which we were to bargain in such a way that I could get nothing out of him that *I* wanted.

Shep

Shep liked "Winter Dreams"—or said he did. While he didn't sound very enthusiastic as he passed overall judgment, he did become excited and pleased at moments when he talked about particulars of the story. Those moments mean that Shep was using the story to enact his preferred defenses and adaptations: flight-and-fight or merger into a system of things.

Shep seemed not to involve himself in the story by way of flight, however, although he did identify Judy as an ideal, "the Grail," never to be won. Dexter's pursuit of her, he said, was mythic, "the old voyage from the earthly to the divine plane." What flight Shep did find had the up-and-down, aerial quality he favored, but there was not much.

Rather, Shep meshed with the story by creating a theme closer to his own psyche. The story, he said, treated people as property or as things, and he went on to develop some fairly far-removed associations.

> You could even plug it into the fear of the whites that all the black man wants is a Cadillac and a white woman. Well, if you didn't make your white women into the highest-priced objects in the showroom, maybe they wouldn't be so desirable to the blacks. Some of the blacks are beginning to realize that, you know, price tags ain't everything, and they don't want them any more. They think that the whites, all they want is a black woman, they've got almost as much, maybe even more, statistical backing for that sort of a statement.

What he here called the white man's opinion of the black man, he had earlier said was being imposed on himself. "I see it coming at me all the time out of the advertisements. I mean, get a hard on over the new car, not the girl who's standing beside it. She's just something you can get if you've got next year's model. She's next year's model, too. You get 'em both at the same time. And I think that's obscene."

Equally striking were the images Shep used for Dexter's final sense of depletion and loss. "Ultimately he loses even his fantasies, and he's left absolutely flat out, and he's lost . . . Utter desolation . . . He's almost destined to utter desolation in this story." He saw all of Dexter's relationship as a "void . . . almost as hard to cope with as the one you live with, on top of." "His sole basis in the world is this nothingness. This is the real thing that's happening behind all the forms. He won't pay any attention to it. He just ducks away from it, and eventually it comes sneaking in through the back door—Whang!—catches

him right about the head and shoulders." He contrasted Dexter
with his immigrant mother, who had learned "how to live
within her environment, rather than be constantly striving to
get outside of it. She learned to live where she was. He never
did find out, kept going further and further East till he dropped
in this ocean of nothingness—right where he started from, you
know, trying to avoid it." "Hell, he may commit suicide in the
next two or three pages. He may just fall back and say, 'Ah,
hey, wait, I'm on the thirtieth floor!' Write some sort of impas-
sioned letter to Judy Simms, leave it sealed and addressed on
his desk and leap out. So then he lives [*sic*] on Wall Street
permanently. He's soaked into the concrete. He becomes almost a fixture in Wall Street." And that sadistic fusion, that
ultimate becoming an object, dominated Shep's view of the
story.

In effect, Shep used Fitzgerald's mythologizing to satisfy his
own need to depersonalize. Given this matching of defenses,
Shep could create a variety of fantasies from the story. For
example, his idea of Dexter as completely emptied and living
on top of nothingness derives from some sense of overwhelming loss. As his associations to Dexter's mother suggest, or
words like "flat," "soaked," "right where he started from,"
Shep was finding feelings derived from the total, overpowering
hungers of earliest infancy and a sense of despair at his
mother's self-sufficiency. Notice, too, that Shep treats Dexter's
becoming a thing as a fall, just the opposite of a flight (Shep's
other mode of defense).

There are other levels of fantasy, however. I think Shep's
imagining Judy as a high-priced car derives from a child's fantasies about his body products. Are they a part of him and alive
or are they separate and dead? Are they precious and high-
priced or are they disgusting wastes? Shep's fantasy of black
man and white woman (or Cadillac) derives from a still later
phase of childhood, this Southern boy's imaginings about his
parents' sexual life and his own wishes and fears toward it.
Who is the dark, tabooed lover? Father? Or son?

Not all fantasies, however, were equally available to Shep.
His psychological tests showed that his defenses armed him

against a withholding mother, and he avoided fantasies of that kind. He did not perceive Judy as a mouth (as, for example, Saul or I did). For Shep, that original "taking in " and all subsequent dependencies had become fierce traps. Thus, talk about Dexter's mother led him to say that Dexter was "caught up in the whole bag, you know, that everybody's in nowadays: I gotta own something. I gotta knife and fork? I gotta cut something. Just mad possessiveness." He went on about the " 'thing' fetishism of America" and described the story as about "economics junkies—people who need money injections regularly in order to be able to function or they have severe withdrawal symptoms, perhaps even including suicide." Part of Shep's fears about nurturing mothers led him to want to see Judy as separate from children. Thus, he singled out "that phony scene where she breaks down, crying ' "Take me home. I don't want to go back to that idiotic dance—with those children," ' you know, in a way, even though she's probably putting him on, there's certain things that she says in the course of this put-on that seem more honest than others." Still more pointedly, when Shep was discussing the scene where eleven-year-old Judy charms Dexter and beats her nurse on the bosom, calling her an old thing, he said, "She reminded me of a little girl I saw on the . . . [bus], who couldn't have been more than nine or ten, but was dressed just like her mother and talking with her mother and answering with the same facial expressions, mannerisms, gestures, virtually a carbon copy of a thirty-five year old upper-middle-class or upper-class woman. And she was a child! [laughing] I mean it was really scary!" (and he laughed again). As for Dexter, he went on, "I don't understand why he is so taken in by her, you know. I would think he'd find it terrifying, the way she was acting."

In general, he tended to see Judy as the strong, active one in the relationship and Dexter as relatively passive.

When he was starting to leave her for Irene Scheerer, she came back and socked it to him right away. Fitzgerald's handling of what actually was going on there, that orgasmic kiss that he got out there on the porch, really blew my mind.

I mean, he stated what was happening, I think, but he insisted on substituting the word "kiss."

NNH: I was going to ask you that. Do you think she was —well, the idiom of my generation would be, "sleeping around"?

Shep: Yeah, I reckon as how she was. I mean, who— Ah, where the hell is that? [leafing through the text] "They [her kisses] aroused in him not hunger demanding renewal but surfeit demanding more surfeit, creating want by holding back nothing at all." That doesn't sound like kissing to me!

Similarly, he saw Judy as the active one, pulling Dexter back when he looks as though he might get away. On hearing of his engagement to Irene, said Shep, she "lures him back to her place and makes it with him." After a month, "She finally decides she's done her bit—leaves."

In effect, Dexter becomes a mere thing in the hands of this powerful, sexual woman, as, in another context, she becomes a mere automobile to the "black man." In an almost classic symbolism, Shep said of Judy, "Very high rate of turnover, to use a nice economic phrase. Low overhead, high turnover, et cetera. It's a profit-making business. I mean she's making a great deal inasmuch as she gets paid for her whoring, not in money, but in admiration and attention."

Yet this is the woman Shep had earlier called "divine," "the Grail." By such images of virgin and slut, Shep was setting out mixed wishes and fears that this powerful, dominant woman be—and not be—sexual. These images combined in a rather odd statement of Shep's: "She's losing hers [her virginity] all over the place!" "Well," I demurred, "you really can only do that once." "O-o-o-ah, well," he replied, "she can do it so many times because she can make people think she can do it so many times."

Shep's view of Judy was still more drastic because of his deeper, underlying fantasies about the cosmically powerful mother associated with food and nurture. Thus, it takes, among other things, bravery to win a Judy Jones. For Shep, this explained Lud Simms's drinking and wenching:

Anybody who went through even what was left of the Judy
Jones initiation test would be entitled to do a little drinkin'
and runnin' around afterwards. . . . He's outmaneuvered
Dexter and everyone else, you know, top of the heap, so
he—Wow! 'Gotta relax. Boy, do I need a drink and several
hundred women!'

To me, he seemed to be talking about a father seen as a powerful, sexual man who had survived the dangers represented by
an equally powerful, woman-mother. Shep had trouble, however, visualizing Dexter with Judy Jones:

Anybody can have fantasies on that level. I saw a guy having
a fantasy about making it with a White Russian princess. . . .
[But] I can't visualize him [Dexter] as really doing it, primarily because I can't visualize myself really doing it. I mean, if
I try and put my own—try to put him into that place, either
I'm still living in fantasy, or it's me that's there, and I'm
leaving!

Lud Simms or the "black man" might be strong enough to be
"really doing it," but Dexter or Shep himself, the "sons" in
this fantasy, were less sure of themselves, needed toughening.
"What he [Dexter] needs is a very tough seventeen-year-old
Mexican chick to lead him a time." Then he could get to the
"top of the heap" and stay there.

Thinking of lovers as a "heap"—this was the major theme
Shep attributed to the story: treating people as things. He
found in the story "the whole business of more money, and the
peculiar definition it gives the people." "I found it almost an
obscene story . . . the pornographic fascination with things that
money can buy . . . the same way *Bonnie and Clyde* is an
obscene movie because there's an obsessive, dirty fascination
with seeing them get shot to pieces in slow motion." "It's
obscene in . . . getting people all hot and bothered about seeing
two human beings shot to death by half a dozen sheriffs." He
himself, however, called the story a pattern of "accumulation
and loss, almost profit and loss," with Dexter's profit being his
business success, "and then on the loss side, you've got this

failure to move in on Judy Jones, and the fact that she loses even her beauty; he loses his dreams, maybe even loses his virginity to her." Shep saw Judy as "some sort of plastic replica of a dollar bill" and Dexter's quest of her as his going after "the right thing," "one of the best *things* available to him." At the end, when Dexter loses his dream of Judy, "he's unable to imagine her any more even as being his property."

It is typical of Shep's way of dealing with the world that one cannot tell from what he says whether he thinks it is he who converts the characters into objects, or the story, or America, or Fitzgerald, or the characters. (Nor, from the point of view of our model, is it necessary to decide.) Judy, he said, "was doing the whole existential thing of turning him [Dexter] into an object, because only as an object could she retain her subjectivity [*sic*] and therefore be able to put up with him. If she were confronted with a real human being, apparently she would have just abandoned him." Similarly Lud Simms is "the only thing she's got left . . . he's one of her more valuable possessions, a husband." To Shep, Dexter's love for Judy was the quest for "an attractive thing to get, probably *the* most attractive thing to get," and, of course, he could point to a great deal of this in American life generally. "Where you've got the principle of acquisitiveness virtually determining everything . . . the only alternative is whether the man turns the woman into an object or whether the woman turns the man into an object." "I think it's tied in with . . . capitalism as a way of structuring your life. So long as you still have the basic pattern given by profit and loss, hell, you know, the acquisition and the departure of gold, then you're going to tend to either be placed as an object by your beloved or obtain her as an object."

The symbolism is classic and firmly proven in clinical experience. One could say with absolute assurance that Shep's seeing this story as about "the acquisition and the departure of gold" represents an "anal fantasy" on his part. But to say this would be to stunt the whole complex and creative role of Shep's ego in his response.

In order for Shep to respond positively to the story, it was necessary (but not sufficient) for him to find a match for his own defensive patterns in the story. Shep evidently found no correspondence to his flight-and-fight defense except raising Judy to a divine plane and dropping Dexter down to earth. But what he could create was a close mesh between Fitzgerald's breathless sentimentalizing and mythologizing and his own need to make himself and others into "things" in a "system." Thus, the theme he found of "making people into things" is not "in" the story nor simply "in" Shep—it is in his synthesis of the story, his creating it anew for himself.

Once meshed, Shep was protected by defenses, and he could introduce several pleasure-giving and anxiety-arousing fantasies into the story. Thus, Shep used particular words and details of the story to sustain fantasies that acted out his own wishes and fears. He took the story's portrayal of sexual relations to be an economic competition between beings who could only relate to each other as profitable objects—types, really: black man, high-priced white woman, inexperienced youth, Russian princess, Mexican chick. In a still more reductive way, Shep thought the story treated all people as precious and desirable things to be possessed by way of accumulation and loss. And at a still deeper level, he interpreted Judy as the totally self-sufficient woman—active rather than passive, dominating but not giving—whom he wanted separate from children. He felt Dexter lost a battle to her over "taking in" that would lead to his utter desolation, suicide, and thingness (being soaked into concrete).

These are the unconscious themes I find in Shep's response. To me they seem relentless and inflexible restatements of a single idea: people as things. What he could enjoy seemed sharply limited in range to this one theme, so narrowing in its effect.

I felt, too, that although Shep liked the story, he accepted it grudgingly. He thought it obscene, he said, and I think he wanted from Fitzgerald a moral condemnation of the story's treating people as money or things—even though this was a theme he himself needed to find. In a way, he was seeking a rejection of a part of himself, presumably the very self that needed to relate to others as things. Thus, someone as involved as Shep was in rejecting his past, including the past he himself embodied, was necessarily also involved in breaking that per-

ceptual circle in which one finds one's own fantasies and defenses enacted in the external world. To reject oneself is also to
reject that interaction of self and other that alone sustains a
self.

In this context, Shep's reaction to "The Battler" was simple
and straightforward—he detested it. "It's *coitus interruptus*.
You know, it doesn't make it" he said, giggling. He ranked it
"around six or seven" "on a one to ten scale, working down."
In response to my question, how would he rewrite it to make it
more satisfying, he would, he said, rather than rewrite it, "give
up on it and toss it out." This is, of course, a perfectly obvious
result: radical Shep, thoroughly immersed in the American
counter-culture, would not like a Hemingway story. Anyone
should know that.

Yet Shep's reaction had something more subtle in it, something more personal to Shep. He disliked the story for a specific
reason; it denied him something he wanted. "I was expecting
something maybe along the general lines of Faulkner's 'The
Bear,' . . . you know, the wilderness confrontation with
perhaps the wilderness guru involved in some way. Rite of
passage, you know, particularly inasmuch as Nick was so
young. He's ripe for rites of passage."

At the outset, he said, giggling, his real interest in the story
"was starting to lie with the area [Nick] was walking through."
"After that got taken away from me, I guess it lay with Nick,
because I wanted to see if he was going to experience anything
meaningful."

> I hoped for something there. I thought, Hey! here's the pat-
> tern. They're going to dump him down in the land, and he's
> going to have to get in tune with it . . . and even when he
> came into the firelight I thought perhaps this fellow might
> represent some sort of earth spirit equivalent. . . . kind of
> guardian of the geography of the area, and that Nick would
> have to go through almost a ritual performance with him and
> pass some sort of test or another, but it didn't turn out to be
> that at all.

"Maybe the test was going to be that he had to fight this guy.
. . . perhaps an antihero form of the wilderness spirit or

something." Nick, he said, "was the crucial figure. He was obviously the ritual candidate, is another way to say what I'm getting at. These people could be priests, they could be onlookers, they could even be part of the landscape, but . . . he was the one who was set out from the beginning to make the journey that it turned out he never made. All he really got to was . . . four miles down the road." "There's [no] test for him to pass. He just comes in there, has a fairly innocuous meeting, finds out a few things about the world, and splits."

Shep came to dislike the story almost violently for its failure to provide him with this ritual pattern, so close to his own needs to test himself against father, mother, and others (he had spoken, for example, of the "Judy Jones initiation test"). Sometimes his images conveyed the anger of frustration: "Wham! the interruption. It's taking a boiling kettle off the stove," he said of Bugs's intervention. Other phrasings suggested a breakdown of a regular pattern of something like feeding: "There was no rite. It was . . . postponed until the next story which is why I think it's a disappointing story." "The ritual pattern of it was violated . . . and trickled off into something unobtrusive."

In the terms we have been using, the story was not enacting Shep's expectancies. He could not find in it a ritual test that he could pass, and so transcend the testers, or fail and so become part of the landscape. The story, in other words, was not yielding a match for either of Shep's major defenses: becoming a "thing" in a "system" or achieving flight-and-fight. As we have seen, Hemingway thought he was providing certain stylistic limits: staying on the surface of things (his iceberg image). This, however, would be exactly the wrong position for Shep, who needed either to be submerged in things or quite distant.

Hence, Shep could not create his own characteristic defenses from the story. Therefore, he could not mingle with it directly—he had to defend against it. Of his two defenses, he brought to bear the one we have been calling flight-and-fight. That is, he would flee from the experience to question and challenge it from a safe distance.

For example, part of his response took the form of what might best be called a "flight to reality," whence he would compare the story's characters with real people, often in a combative way. Thus, he said he felt "respect or awe or something" toward Ad "even given this as a fictional character, rather than somebody actual like [William] Burroughs." Given enough psychological knowledge, he felt, he could "plug in and figure out what is going on in there [in the sister-manager relation], whether it takes place inside an Ernest Hemingway story or actually out in the real world." In other phrasings, he seemed to imagine the story was a reality he could be in: "He [Nick] meets a couple of men there, and they have, of course, past histories, but I don't think you'd run into too many men who didn't." (I felt like answering his challenge by telling him I hadn't said one would.)

Similarly, he would pull out general principles from the story. It made sense, he said, for Nick to agree that Ad's pulse was slow whether he believed it or not, because "in a very fragmented social group, you do your best to pull it together." Well, do you? Ad had to keep up his sense of independence; so did the sister—"Women have to be individuals unto themselves first, too." He doubted whether this was a satisfactory short story because, "I've always understood short stories to be almost along a Joycean line of, you know, crystallized epiphanies." He saw Bugs's relation to Ad as "benevolent exploitation," but "I don't reckon the Marxists would let me get away with that!" Similarly "a straight Freudian line" might have helped him explain the sister.

In addition to this "flight to generalization," he ran on about (or off to) other authors. Hemingway's tendency to irrelevancies was like Kerouac's. Ad was like Burroughs. This wilderness story could have been like Faulkner's "The Bear." Nick could have had a journey into "kind of a B. Traven sort of Mexico," like (he said) Wallace Stevens. "The Battler" compared unfavorably to Ken Kesey's *Sometimes a Great Notion*.

Some of these homilies and comparisons seemed sensible enough, some seemed silly, but all served the same purpose in the interview setting. They worked as a kind of flight for Shep, away from the story into something he had himself created and introduced. They also enabled him to assert things that could provoke me.

Some of these generalizations Shep did use to interpret the story. On the assumption Bugs had begged rather than bought food, he was puzzled about how he brought it back: "They usually invite you inside to eat it." Do they? In the brakeman episode, Hemingway, he decided, was not only trying to show how young and inexperienced Nick was, but also how "he's trying to retain the possibility of agency which, you know, is open to almost all children." Well, do I know that? Did he want me to argue the matter? At first, Shep thought the story took place in "it seemed like, Louisiana, and then there was that name in there, Kalkaska, or something like that, which is an Algonquin name, which just threw it up above Tennessee immediately," and he giggled as he came to this (I now know) fragmentary notion.

I asked him about the possibility that had so troubled Sam, of a homosexual relationship between Ad and Bugs, but he didn't see any point in talking about an overt homosexual relationship because Ad "climaxes by getting uptight and trying to kill somebody and would have not too much interest in any sort of overt homosexual relationship." Besides—"Christ, there are so many . . . the railroad crew . . . the whole fight game." Again, I suppose we could have argued whether trainmen and boxers were necessarily homosexuals.

I got a clue as to what these invitations to disagree meant to Shep when he mentioned a very "square" cousin of his, with whom he contrasted himself and competed. Whereas, he, Shep, resembled Nick, his cousin "was one of the paying passengers on the train, probably." "We haven't spoken really to each other for the past three–four years." "I don't feel he's going to— In a way, he's a safe person to talk with. He's not going to throw me in any sort of consternation, make me realize that I've been wrong all this time." In effect, Shep was telling me he saw contradiction—speaking contrary—as a threat to autonomy, not only his own but his cousin's, mine, and especially Hemingway's (who came in for an impressive unmanning at Shep's hands, or, more accurately, in his speaking).

Thus, in *The Sun Also Rises*, Hemingway was just "running off into this mawkish sentimentality about whether a guy with no balls is ever going to be able to lay a chick." As for this story, he snickered, "It doesn't make it." When Hemingway was living in Cuba, said Shep, "from what I've read about it, he didn't have too much contact with the *campesinos*, that it was usually the Havana expatriate nightclub set." The people in the story, by reminding Shep of a couple he had met once while hitchhiking, gave him a chance to set himself up against the author. "Take that, Hemingway!" he laughed. "I've seen better cats than you write about!"

Both the conscious and unconscious hostility to Hemingway came through clearly enough in the last part of the interview: "a physical culture fascist," with "*such* bad politics." Hemingway's politics were "right of the democratic thing," said Shep, coming up with a startling theory of voting:

> Somebody told me, apparently had checked it, that the way voting got started, the whole democratic thing in Greece, was that they used to have fights at the meetings, and then it got to the stage of too many people being maimed by this, so they proposed a question and people would raise their fists, and the most fists carried the question. They just assumed that the people with more fists could beat up the people with fewer, and, in a way he's [Hemingway] right back there in that first turn toward the phony structure of democracy . . . because really what it rests upon is the right of the majority to beat the shit out of the minority, and Hemingway is very much into that. That's the way his majority operates. His majority is always unzipping his fly [*sic*] and checking to make sure the testicles are still there.

The castrator castrated.

It was no surprise, then, when I asked Shep if Ad reminded him of anyone in his family, that he readily answered, "a little bit my father." He described his father's anger at his own traveling "further and further down the road to debauchery or whatever it is, but I think he also knows there's nothing he can do about it, so he gets about four times as frustrated." He called his father a business failure: "He knew he'd been outgrown by a lot of things," so he developed "an obsessive belief in scientific fact and rationality and . . . almost the sort of claim that [Lyndon] Johnson has, to that statement in the early days,

'Come, let us reason together,' as though *that* were going to solve something. 'Come, let us make it together' might.'' With a father or Lyndon Johnson?

Both in his view of voting and his remarks about his father, Shep seemed to be describing an all-or-nothing world. We have already observed (in his psychological tests and his response to "Winter Dreams") his twinned defenses of total submersion or total flight. Here, he seems to be saying one can either have total flight or "the phony structure of democracy," "making it" with a father-figure or seeing him as futile and irrelevant.

The flight side of the coin, we have seen as Shep's direct reaction. The submersion side showed when I asked him how he would rewrite the story. "Have Nick make some sort of presumably violent confrontation with Ad in which one of two things— Either he rejects him [Ad], pushes him away almost as if he's repulsed by what's happening, or he triumphs over him." I thought Shep was assuming Nick could outfight a boxing champion, and I was puzzled.

"You visualize him as beating up Ad?"

"In some sense, let's say. He needn't necessarily grab his shirt, throw him down, and start stomping him." Rather, Shep defined a kind of oral battle against the father-figure Ad through words, ideology, vomiting, frustration:

Maybe just in some way coming out of it without having Ad do to him what Ad had intended to do with him, you know, beat him up and throw him out. Either to stop him himself from doing it or to go into the contest and come out victorious or even to say something particularly clever that struck through the fog and brought him [Ad] back down to his depressive state again. It could even operate on a verbal level, though that would be the most tenuous of them. . . . The opposite possibility would be . . . when Ad came at him, to push him down and run out of the camp retching, to put it in its most extreme form . . . to flip out, to freak out, to really have a bad trip out of it, to get unsettled by the environment and run screaming into the night.

Part of this rewriting into ritual took its form from Ken Kesey's novel, *Sometimes a Great Notion,* to which Shep had compared the story—quite unfavorably. Kesey's hero, a lost, flaccid, pot-smoking student (not unlike Shep), has to face his massive, powerful, seemingly infallible brother-father. The hero betrays his lumberjack brother in economic battle and in bed, cuckolding him. Finally, in being beaten physically, he triumphs over his brother and allies himself to this (perhaps) guardian of the wilderness. At any rate, the novel is rich in just the kind of ritual elements Shep liked. He wanted Nick to face Ad in that ritual way and "to wrench his sense of self away from him. You know, he [the Kesey hero] realizes that's what he's doing." Again, one could see the roots of Shep's comparison in the deep conflicts we first found in his tests and his response to "Winter Dreams": a need to reduce himself or others to objects, particularly in situations of dependency or "taking in." Now we can see how myth or ritual served that need.

In *The Dynamics of Literary Response*, I suggested that such mythic substructures as that of the Kesey novel, or the one Shep resented not finding in "The Battler," allow readers to find a nurturing matrix, a kind of timeless maternal security encouraging regression and fusion, ultimately a loss of sense of self. Shep's anger at not finding a ritual, informally at least, confirmed this view, as did his figures of speech, like "trickled off into something unobtrusive," "I found it flat and fairly empty," which ever so faintly recalled the frustrations of suckling. His more mature aggressions sought that same fusion aggressively: losing the fight means having one's sense of self taken away. In effect, Shep was demanding that the story give him a ritual matrix, and his anger at the story reflected the way it frustrated him.

Frankly, Shep's myth-and-ritual reading seemed to me a rather promising construction of the story (and I later learned that at least one professional critic, Joseph DeFalco, took the same view). Shep, however, felt it was not clear-cut enough for him. He wanted the story, first, to impose a psychological transaction on him (the struggle between Ad and Nick for a sense of self), and second, he wanted this transaction to match his own struggle with, let us assume, his parents. That is, he wanted either to see Nick gain a self by wrenching it away from

Ad or to have Nick relax into thingness by passively accepting the mythic matrix: "They're going to dump him down in the land, and he's going to have to get in tune with it."

The same alternatives underlay his conscious interpretation of the theme of the story. He saw Nick as following Ad in "sort of a journey toward whatever you want to call it, 'awareness' for a nice, general term." More specifically, Shep found a "difference between Bugs and Ad Francis, that Ad is down to compulsively repeating a reaction pattern and that Bugs is able to move through the world independently. . . . Those are really the two choices open to Nick, and I think the emphasis on youth is a way of stating that the question is still open for him." Nick is "not going to commit himself to one or another of the two possible states before he finds out what they mean."

Nick himself is trying to keep the "agency" that children have. By "agency," Shep meant "the power of action rather than the power of reaction. The power of initiating possibilities in the world." Because Ad is dependent on Bugs and on the woman who sends him money, "he is losing his own power of agency." "I think that's the crucial test that's facing Nick, whether or not he will manage to retain the ability to initiate possibilities in the world or whether he'll lose it and become somebody as down and out as Ad Francis. There's no way of telling."

Just at this point, the difference between Shep's reading and Sam's becomes quite clear. That is, both saw the story as in some way involved with the gaining or losing of masculinity. Sam revealed a good deal of specific anxiety about attacks on his body, fears of homosexual rape, for example. These made him see Ad as overtly dangerous and Bugs as more subtly powerful and, therefore, even more sinister and threatening. Sam allayed his fears by finding a symbolism that would "hold up," that is, by bringing to bear on the story a reassuring substitute, his own mental version of manly power.

Although Shep also took the issue to be gaining or losing power, he saw that power as genderless and in a very global, undifferentiated way: "the ability to initiate possibilities in the world," which children have but lose as they grow up. Shep's ritual interpretation sought a matrix with which he could fuse: a timeless "rite of passage" that would magically transform Nick, freeing him from any dependency that implied the loss of "agency." Otherwise he would become like Ad, and "Just . . . in one moment, I think, you transition between the two stages."

Just as Shep saw the conscious theme of the story in terms of his own unconscious need radically to submit or radically to fight free of dependency, so he interpreted the characters. For him, Ad had to be weak and helpless, because he was dependent. Thus, when I asked Shep to tell the story in his own words, Nick's encounter with Ad came out curiously pale and eviscerated. "He finds this older man sitting there, who invites him to have a cup of coffee, settle down. Talks with him. Has a fairly messed up face." Shep described the moment the fight is about to start as, "Ad starts getting very uptight about all sorts of imagined offenses, generally imagined offenses, and comes out as if he wants to fight him." (Whereas, Ad's actual words at this moment are: " 'You yellow-livered Chicago bastard. You're going to get your can knocked off. Do you get that?' ")

Shep seemed to want to tone Ad down, and that was why I asked him what he thought about his having been a boxer. "It seemed like rather a tawdry way to give a causal explanation to the state he was in, to say that he was punch-drunk." " 'Boxer' seemed like a fairly obvious choice as a matter of fact." Shep offered a suggestion that fitted Ad more into a system, it seemed to me. "He could have been a steel worker, got hit on the head with an I-beam or something." "The way he starts coming on has really very little connection with his having been a boxer. I mean, he could have been an alcoholic businessman and still get into a reaction pattern of that sort. . . . It becomes almost an addiction for him to react that way." Similarly, Shep saw Ad as losing sexual potency. "I think most of Ad's energies have gone into this manic-depressive cycle, which doesn't seem to have anything particularly sexual about it."

In effect, Shep was reversing positions: Ad, the strong boxer, was weak because he was dependent, and the butler, Bugs, was strong, because Shep saw him as independent. "Ad is down to compulsively repeating a reaction pattern, and . . .

Bugs is able to move through the world independently." "In a way, Ad is the 'nigger' in the story . . . because he's the one in the subject position or, more accurately, in the object position because he's controlled by the forces round him. He's lost his subjecthood." Bugs, however, has "a sense of self which is going to preserve him." Notice that Shep had again, as he had in Miss Emily's "tableau," reversed black and white.

In this story, Hemingway speaks at one point of Bugs's "low, smooth, polite nigger voice," and, throughout, he associates him with words like "gently," "soft," "softly," "soft-voiced," "soothed," "smoothed," and so on. Shep decided, however, "Hemingway goes to apparently great pains in the dialogue to show us that this is not just an ordinary nigger, that this is an educated nigger." "It's a very crude way to put across the fact that he's independent." Shep needed to polarize Ad and Bugs into dependency and independence, even though Bugs lives on Ad's money.

Shep's polarization raised still another question: his own and Hemingway's use of racial terms. Ad was the "thing" in a "system," while Bugs would not be. Thus, Shep decided Hemingway was using racial stereotypes oddly. The phrase, "all this in a low, smooth, polite nigger voice," "That whole phrase," said Shep, "is a set of tensions . . . between the fact that 'niggers' don't speak low, smooth, and polite. . . . They just don't do that. Now, your 'nigger' speaks like, oh, wow, any number of conventional stereotypes of it. Shufflin', says 'Yassuh, boss,' that sort of thing. That's how a 'nigger' speaks. . . . And [Hemingway] he's setting up this tension here saying this person is not really a 'nigger.' "

I asked Shep about another odd feature of the story, Hemingway's statement, "Nick knew from the way he [Bugs] walked that he was a negro." "He had rhythm," laughed Shep. "All of 'em got rhythm. Probably got a straight razor, was picking watermelon seeds out of his teeth with it, and everything." "I was a little bit leery of that . . . It did sound an awful lot to me like plugging the stereotype [that] 'they got rhythm.' "

As in his comments on "Winter Dreams," Shep himself made dependent characters into stereotypes or mere things, but he blamed authors if they did so. "Hemingway would be very puzzled by somebody like Stokely Carmichael or Dick Gregory, saying that it's possible to attain selfhood within the black skin. You don't really have to bleach it out . . . go through the white educational process." As with Fitzgerald, I think Shep was projecting onto Hemingway his own need to make people into things.

I think Shep was again finding in being a thing safety for an identity in a position of dependency, this time for Bugs's identity. Shep went right on from the "they've got rhythm" stereotype to say. "In a way, that's true, you know. What they have is not so much rhythm as a peculiar sort of a freedom of the oppressed: that when you're down there at the bottom you can get away with things you couldn't get away with up there on top, just as there are some things you can't get away with [at the bottom] that you could if you were further up."

Clinical experience says that an adult's reversing between two such extremes, being a thing in a matrix or fighting free of it, derives from a childhood alternation between fusion with a feeding mother and independence from her—a transition that was apparently forced into extremes with a great deal of anger in Shep's infancy. Be that as it may, Shep tended to see this story in terms of feeding, even introducing extraneous elements to do so. Thus, the main event begins when Ad "invites him [Nick] to have a cup of coffee" (there is nothing to this effect in the story). Ad could have been "an alcoholic businessman"; probably his sister also suffered "alcoholic decay."

Being fed seemed to imply to Shep the opposite of being autonomous, as when he compared Bugs to Ad's supposed sister: "They've both taking care of him. They're in a sort of power relationship to him." Shep had considerable trouble seeing how Bugs obtained ham and eggs. At first, he assumed theft. Bugs "could even have stolen the eggs if he wanted, but sliced ham? [And he laughed.] Not only did he kill the pig, but he sliced it up, cured it, cooked it, brought it back, and— 'Hey, look! Been gone fifteen minutes.' Amazing!" I had automatically assumed Bugs had simply bought the groceries, but Shep didn't. Food seemed to him inconsistent with independent action, even action to get food. In the same way, he diagnosed Ad: "He seems to lose touch with reality when he gets up about that thing about smoking my cigars and drinking my liquor." Similarly, Shep saw the whole story as "flat and fairly empty" (to me, an image of depletion), because Nick "just . . . splits, stuffing his ham sandwich in his pocket." "The opposite possibility would be, say, for him to . . . run out of the camp retching, to put it in its most extreme form."

Thus, too, Shep had a highly idiosyncratic misreading of the brakeman's trick at the start of the story: "Nick has apparently hopped the train and apparently had some sort of arrangement with the brakeman. Apparently the brakeman told him to come on or something. At any rate, he [Nick] trusts him enough to go over to him." Now, there is nothing in the text to suggest any reason for Nick's trusting the brakeman—Nick's own comment is, "What a lousy kid thing to have done. They would never suck him in that way again." There is nothing in the text, really, but a good deal in Shep, to explain why he might re-create through a "break man" his own fears about trusting and sucking in a matrix that would try ("a-parent-ly") to destroy him.

As one might expect from Shep's oral conflicts, he associated the one woman in the story to deprivation and loss. When I asked him if Ad's sister reminded him of anyone in his family, he countered by telling me how he, his brothers, sisters, parents, and other relations had become separated from one another. Ad's sister, he saw primarily as a puzzle: "Not knowing what was intended there leaves me very vague about the woman." "What it means to have his so-called sister as the manager—that's a real groovy psychological-type question." He took it as a cue to try to build Hemingway's "thing" for him, although, he said, "I feel unsure about it."

> He is trying to cast a parallel light upon her and the repetition implies that she may now still be enough like him to be his own twin and perhaps universalize the process of [decay]. That she has also gone through a period of probably alcoholic decay. Losing contact with the world around her. That when

she left him, she went downhill, too, and she perhaps is a part-time hustler in a big-city hotel room or something. . . . that her position in the world right now is a twin of his.

Shep could accept a parallel between the "sister" and Ad, and even Nick, but not Bugs.

NNH: The Negro sort of takes care of Ad and this sister-woman sort of takes care of Ad. Do you see a kind of parallelism between the Negro and the sister?
Shep: [Definitely] No! [and he giggled].

This, mind you, although he had called the sister a "hustler," and, a minute before that, had said of Bugs, "That boy's a hustler." But he saw no parallel: "I don't. I mean, except insofar as they're both taking care of him. They're in a sort of power relationship to him." And thus Shep never mentioned the woman's closeness to Ad or the money, care, and love she gave him. Shep took no pleasure in such thoughts—at least consciously.

Two patterns, it seems to me, stood out in Shep's lifestyle, two ways in which he was able to find an identity for himself: one, fighting free from a system, the other, finding a kind of freedom to hate by being its victim. These strategies both satisfied Shep's drives (notably his aggressive drives) and served as defenses and adaptations, helping him cope with the demands of inner and outer reality. Both helped him maintain an identity while relating to an other he feared as all-powerful, for the premise underlying both these strategies is that one confronts in this world a hostile system or matrix or oppressor.

In the more active pattern, Shep would speak defiantly, seeking occasions for argument and aggression. From the deepest level of his being, where his identity was focused on his mouth (like an infant's), he seemed to fear dependency and even food as threats to his autonomy, and therefore he put words out instead of food in. Speaking contrarily enabled him to assert himself and, at a higher level, where his identity more concerned being a son—a male—than an infant, he gained a manhood by wrenching one away from Ad or Hemingway—or me.

In the passive version, Shep would accept his position in the matrix, being "at the bottom," a stereotype or a thing with the "freedom of the oppressed." In the later stage associated with his sense of his own maleness, he could see himself "making it" with his father or Lyndon Johnson, at the bottom in a different sense.

These two patterns totally pervaded Shep's three major comments on the story. He sought in the story—and did not find—a ritual matrix, which would provide a transition for Nick into a state of selfhood. That is, Shep sought, on the one hand, a fully spelled out ritual into which Nick could fit, as a stereotype into a pattern, but he also wanted this fitting to guarantee freedom and a sense of self. The story, he said, did not impose the ritual pattern strongly enough, nor did it give Nick a true passage to freedom, and the anger he felt at the story for not doing these two things suggests the extent to which he wanted them.

Combining an ethical view with this wish for a ritual, he saw the story as posing Nick with a choice. Would he become like Ad, who was losing his "power to initiate possibilities in the world," being "victimized by his reactions?" Or would he become like Bugs, "able to move through the world independently?" But Nick makes no choice. "He just . . . splits" (and both senses of that word apply).

Finally, Shep did fit the characters into this pattern, even violating the sense of the story to do so. For example, he saw the sister-manager solely in terms of power and deprivation, although she was providing the money that supported Ad and Bugs. Ad, he felt, had sunk into a passive, victimized state, and the attack on Nick did not give him back any sense of self. In other words, he took Ad to embody both of his own defensive patterns (total fusion and total aggressive break-out), but with unsuccessful outcomes. Bugs, whom he admired, embodied the same two patterns, but successfully. That is, although Hemingway (or Shep) imposed a stereotype on him, he had "the freedom of the oppressed." By controlling and being in a "power relationship" to Ad, he showed, "He's got a sense of self which is going to preserve him."

Shep's reaction highlights two features of our general understanding of the literary experience. First, he disliked the story, but what he said about it shows that readers use the same psychological patterns to dislike stories as to like them. In one sense, this is obvious enough—Shep is Shep whether he is liking or disliking. Perhaps it is less obvious, though, if we recognize that his adaptations are working in two different ways despite the similarity in pattern. If he had responded positively, Shep would have been making parts of the story act some part of his defenses for him. His adaptations would have found a basis in the story for allaying his anxiety. In responding negatively, however, Shep's defenses acted *against* the story, putting up a wall separating him from it.

Second, even in responding negatively, Shep tended by his deliberate rewritings and his unintended forgettings and misinterpretations to turn the story into one with a style that matched his own. As we know (from the "principle of multiple function"), Shep's need to polarize the world into either things in a system or freed rebels worked defensively, to reduce anxiety, but it also gave him pleasure by satisfying drives (both aggressive drives and Shep's deeply buried need to be nurtured by an all-powerful other). Thus, Shep's very *defenses against the story*, looked at from the point of view of his total psychic economy, represent an effort to get pleasure from it even, if need be, by reworking it considerably.

Sebastian

Sebastian, we have seen, had two adaptive strategies. In one he sought out an authority or controlling figure into which he could merge himself in a loving, tender way. Such authorities could range from his adolescent infatuation with the Roman Catholic Church to what might be called his "Anne Bancroft complex" at the time of the interviews. Second, he created his own mental products as substitutes or exchanges for the controls he sought from these authorities. These two strategies could combine into one: a mutual giving in which he drew close to a desired, controlling person, who gave him something sexy, fleshy, or "dirty" to which he answered by giving his own intellectual creations. (And it is only now, years later, as I write that sentence that I realize he may have—indeed, must have—perceived his interviews with me that way. No wonder we enjoyed our conversations.)

At any rate, one would think that Sebastian could take pleasure in Dexter's final independence (as Sam had). In Dexter's escaping Judy and succeeding on his own, Sebastian probably perceived his own pattern of substituting his creations for the controls imposed on him by others. But these matchings of defense, for all their subtlety, demand precision. Dexter's business success did not count for Sebastian as an intellectual or verbal product. As he phrased it, he didn't like the story because "Dexter Green isn't interesting enough, because it doesn't seem that he's ever going to develop enough breadth of vision to . . . be truly self-critical. At the end, it appears that he's just going to settle in a half-unconscious way for the abandonment of ideals . . . and just sink into a sort of miasma, that kind of brown fog that [T. S.] Eliot talks about."

Much more important in Sebastian's response was his other defense—finding an external controlling force to which he could join himself in a loving way. He found such a force even though he had to go outside the story for it. "It's an American story, although it has the overtones of the aristocracy and everything. It could be European . . . if she were a countess and he were a tutor or something." In this image, Sebastian made Judy into the kind of maternal authority he favored and he turned Dexter into a loving and seducible servant, although the story shows him only as a driving, powerful business success.

Sebastian's vision of Judy had its roots in his wish for control and sustenance from a mother; and they showed when he called Dexter's love "the old hunger," "the unquenchable desire," "the old aspirations." She "just keeps tantalizing him with the real goal." "She's the point of reference, she's the goal behind all the money business, which almost in a way is presented secondarily, I mean, it's so vague." "I sense a potential in Judy Green [*sic*] . . . it's probably just total romanticism on my part, but it would seem that she would be capable of developing." Perhaps in the sense that one's mother becomes the prototype for all significant later women.

If a mother, however, Judy was a withholding mother, and she could not meet Sebastian's defensive strategy of finding a maternal control to receive from and blur himself into. But Judy wasn't giving. "She seems to be some way tied up with narcissism, to a point where an external object would seem to be unimportant." He called her, twice, a *femme fatale*, and identified her with the Grail, so that once Dexter's dream was gone, "it's a very grim kind of executive existence that he leads, a bachelor, who's been almost a knight in the service of this love and now that the object, the Grail, has been devalued, apparently a celibate without hope of emotional involvement."

What Sebastian wanted, both by way of drive and defense, was for Judy first to be holy and Grail-like and then become less exalted, more giving, and more available as a physical, sexual, even dirty, object. Because his lifestyle demanded that he physicalize Judy, Sebastian had nothing but contempt for Fitzgerald's efforts to romanticize her. For instance, he quoted Fitzgerald on her kisses: "They aroused in him not hunger demanding renewal but surfeit demanding more surfeit, creating want by holding back nothing at all." "That," he said, "seems to be the most utterly absurd statement . . . It's really a salesmanship job. If he could really believe that, that's the ultimate in romanticism, it would seem to me."

Similarly, he thought Dexter silly to idealize her. In an unsympathetic moment, he could speak of Dexter's "dumb medieval lovesickness." To win such a woman, "The thing to be avoided at all costs, is any appearance of doglike devotion. You can't worship on that altar. That's out of the question." Thus, in Sebastian's world, Judy sees Dexter's idealizing as naïve and unloving. "A good part of her contempt for him is the fact that she knows that in a way he devalues her by making her the ideal. In a sense, it's impossible for her to love him, because what she is to him and what she is are . . . two different things."

Sebastian's Dexter is helpless, caught in an unrealistic, idealizing attitude. "If he's somehow dimly aware of the strength of the ideal, as opposed to the real, maybe [he's reluctant] to see the ideal crumble. Even though it makes it more attainable. Somehow it may devalue it by moving it down a couple of notches to bring it within reach." "Dexter Green is . . . in love with Judy Green [*sic*] the ideal, not necessarily Judy

Green the real, because to Dexter, she's never real. She translates his idealism into kisses, and he . . . sort of agonizes over the fact that when he wants to be in love, she just wants to kiss and hug. She translates everything, everyone's ideals, to physical terms."

Ultimately, Sebastian found Dexter simply silly. He recalled Mike Nichols's film *The Graduate*. "Somehow Dexter reminds me of Hoffman, his responses are always so . . . idiotic." When Sebastian thought of Dustin Hoffman and Mrs. Robinson, some of his attitudes toward Judy Jones became clearer. "That's so much of a fantasy of mine that I was really upset with his stupidity. . . . I'd so much like to make it with Anne Bancroft myself . . . I suppose everybody, you know, dreams about the glamorous older woman, but it was like a TV thing. It was that stereotype American male, who has to be so vigorously seduced that he practically has to be tied down." Sebastian felt only contempt for the daughter in the movie: "It was a perfect touch, I thought, where she has to think that the mother was raped, that she couldn't admit to the mother's sexuality." Again it is silly to idealize a mother. Mothers should be sexual.

In other words, Sebastian made the possibility of Judy as mother far more explicit than the other readers did, and he even went a step further, making her explicitly seductive (like Mrs. Robinson in *The Graduate*). Something of the intensity with which he needed to do this came across in his recurring "Freudian slip." He referred to Judy Jones as Judy Green a half a dozen times in the interview. These slips tended to come when he was saying things like, "Judy Green is a materialist desire," or when he was talking about her fading. Once he even corrected himself, "The only thing that's real is Judy Green in terms of— or, uh, Judy Jones, as far as material concrete goals are concerned." When I asked him about his "slip," he confirmed this pattern. "Ah," he said, "an identification of the ideal with the— I mean, it's a tension that you want to resolve. I mean you'd like to see him get her." Also, he said, "It sounds so ordinary . . . for this fabulous heroine to be named Judy Jones" (although, to me, Judy Green seems not much of an improvement in that respect).

So far as I was concerned, the crucial phrase was, "You'd

like to see him [Dexter] get her," and Sebastian's phrasing revealed both the intensity and the somewhat sadistic quality of his desire. She was *not* to be idealized, or, if idealized at first, she was to be brought down to earth, sexualized, and so dirtied—gotten. "In a way, I was glad to read that Lud Simms drinks and runs around, because that kind of reversal . . . fleshes a heroine like Judy Jones. It makes her seem more concrete, more real, more embraceable." He surmised that "the notion that maybe an unworthy knight—not Dexter —discovered the Grail maybe perversely pleased me."

Such words as "fleshes," "concrete," "unworthy," suggest the level of drive—in Erikson's terms, the concern with "holding on and letting go"—that gave rise to Sebastian's concern with a control that could turn into a physically cruel coercion. For example, I asked him what it would take to win such a woman, and he answered, "There has to be enough physical advantage on your side, on the male side, to engage her interest." "The only thing that's real is . . . Judy Jones, as far as material concrete goals are concerned." For Dexter, "Apparently there's an idealism of glamour behind his materialist dreams or—I don't know whether it's behind it or in front of it—but somehow making it with physical objects is supposed to open to him the kind of world of Judy Jones." Words like "money," "concrete," and "behind" suggest fantasies about the body's creating physical objects, dirt. So does this odd image: "Every time she appears, it just crumbles those minor and compromise sand castles for the real thing, for the real sand castle that just never gets washed over because it's too far up the beach, or something."

For Sebastian, with his concern about exchanging his creations for external controls, such body creations, sometimes seen as precious, sometimes as dirty, represented important features of his sense of identity. To lose them or give them up—have them crumble—meant, in a way, loss of one's very self. For example, as Sebastian saw it, Judy had a very ordinary life from twenty-seven on, because of "the loss of her distinguishing feature." "There's always that . . . continuum or spectrum in any male-female Western relationship where the mystery has to be on one side or the other as long as the relationship is going to continue." Then, once Judy is married, "apparently it's passed [the mystery] from Judy's hands to Lud's so now she's the slave to the relationship." "Mystery really is a chess piece finally," and evidently Judy had lost hers.

Another type of sadistic impulse showed when he said, "Any kind of difficulty that a woman like Judy Jones experiences, any reversal, is glamorous, too, just because it's a fall from such a high place." "I would have preferred," said Sebastian, "that he [Dexter] married her and let it [her 'withering'] be a more biological process than it is. I mean, as it stands now, it's too much like the idealism that makes him unhappy, the fact that her aging is presented . . . not even dramatically —narratively. He *hears* about it. It's so bloodless that I would have preferred it if he had married her."

In short, Sebastian reworked the story, quite strikingly, to achieve his pattern of fantasy and defense. His strongest need was to establish a closeness through mutual giving and getting with an all-powerful or overpowering authority, in this story, a woman. Thus, unlike Sam, Sebastian paid practically no attention to Dexter's economic or social rise, and he seemed to care relatively little about male power. What bothered him was Judy, and it is worth noting here that in three out of four TATs he produced a total, mind-and-body identification with the females. Here, he saw Judy as all-powerful because she was totally self-contained. He became almost angry at Dexter's failure to see her the way he, Sebastian did: as a Mrs. Robinson offering herself. Instead, Dexter was fool enough to idealize her and even to resent her turning ideals to kisses that revealed the "material concrete reality." Rather, once she revealed this lower sexual or dirty self, the man could become sadistic and take a more active role—*he* would be the authority coercing the giving. "You'd like to see him get her," make her "devalued," "withered," "fleshed." Then there could be a fall from a high place, events no longer bloodless, and the loss of her distinguishing feature. But, having neither a Judy degraded nor a Judy idealized, Dexter now sinks into a brown miasma. And the brown and concrete and sand express the level of drive that gives rise to Sebastian's strategies of control and that he needed to satisfy through the story, adaptively re-creating it to match his own lifestyle.

However, when Sebastian tried to create an experience for himself from "The Battler" within these adaptive strategies, he simply could not. He ranked the story very low, lowest of the few stories he had read for me at that time. "Fear," he said, was his gut reaction. "Just one of anxiety and fear. And it's not Nick's fear, especially, so much as it seems to be . . . just there—the atmosphere." "At first, all I thought was fear." "The reaction was all fear. It started as soon as Nick walked into the campfire scene, and . . . it was this sort of anxiety as long as he was with those people, and it wasn't over until he was walking down the track with the fire disappearing."

Sebastian's fear, I felt, came from his sense that there were not enough controls and specifically his feeling that a taboo was broken at the moment when Ad asks Nick to count his pulse. "My only reaction first seeing it was the taboo business, the danger . . ."

> That's a big, tense moment, because of his reluctance to take [Ad's] wrist in the first place. Any man who asks another man to, like, feel my heart or feel me, put your hand on me, in a strange situation like this, in a traveling situation like this, that's—even in my own experience—a taboo that only a crazy man could break. You don't ask a strange man to touch you except under very special circumstances, so that was sort of a frightening moment because it breaks a strong taboo of the road.

One might have expected Nick's touching Ad to suit Sebastian, to be the kind of drawing near to an authority that he used in his own adaptations. The trouble was, he did not see Ad as an authority or a force for control, because he found Ad unpredictable. "The chance element is too scary," he said. "The man's craziness . . . gives that quality of unpredictability." "When you find out that the man is crazy, it localizes the feeling of tension for me, because now there's a matter of real unpredictability," he said, "that kind of manic thing he has going for him."

The same thing held true for the story as a whole. "When [the author] doesn't draw any conclusions himself and when his characters draw no conclusions, when they seem to be bewildered by the action, I'm, in my turn, bewildered."

Inevitably, then, he appreciated—even if I did not—his being rescued from his fears. He had been using the ordinary intellectualizations of the student of literature: "As I was sitting there, I was underlining the number of times 'fire' appeared in the story . . . and [another student] came up to me and said, 'Oh, Hemingway, huh? Isn't it weird? That's the story about the homosexual.' Yeah! And it is! . . . That's an explanation for all that tension, for one thing." His friend had resolved the uncertainty he had been trying to end by himself.

Thus, when Sebastian tried out the homosexual interpretation himself, he did so by introducing phallic symbols and behavior in a rather intellectual way. He playacted: " 'Let me take your knife, Nick.' 'No, you just hold onto your knife.' " Again, imitating, " 'She was a mighty fine woman, though. Mighty good-looking woman.' " He mentioned "the sexual symbols of trains and train tracks and all that business going forth, which is a reflection of that illegitimate homosexual thing." "It's a way of accounting for the tension."

Even so, Sebastian was not satisfied because he was not sure how the theme of homosexuality managed the fearful content of the story in an intellectually satisfying way. "I want to know why. I want to know what's the purpose of it. Why tell me?" "Somehow you want Nick to draw a moral from his experience." In terms of his adaptative strategies, Sebastian was asking two things: that Nick make an intellectual creation, a "moral," from his experience; and that the story control its material with meaning.

Still feeling then, despite the homosexual reading, a lack of control, Sebastian himself offered ritual (as Shep had done) to manage this chanciness and random aggression. Nick, he said, "just can't get along with other men except in certain ritual circumstances." Thus, Sebastian tried to place the story in various fixed patterns: "a big American tradition of riding the freights and making the breaks, whether good or bad, and then the other kind of traditional thing of going into the camp scene, like the encounter on the road." But nothing would fit this story—"it's not seemingly ritualistic."

Here again, Sebastian found he could not creatively synthesize the story into his own character. The obvious ritual in "The Battler" is initiation into manliness, conceived in a rather aggressive way. This did not suit Sebastian:

> I somehow feel it's awfully adolescent . . . that real preoccupation with initiation all the time, with being good enough, somehow making it all the time, making it again and again and again. And the rituals that go along with it finally irritates me [*sic*] because it's scary to have to make it all the time. It's a kind of tension that I really don't want. I'd like to think that I made it or that I don't have to make it. I just don't like making it, I guess. I'm just not at all that competitive.

"It's because I'm not really that much of a man's man." Just as he could not take Dexter Green's independence through business success seriously in "Winter Dreams," here he could not take athletic manliness as a solution. Sebastian's substitutes or exchanges for control had to be his own achievements of a mental or verbal kind. Hemingway, he found "too simple-minded and . . . too much of a jock." "The characters are not seemingly socially aware or aware of their effect on each other, but seem to be interested, as Nick is, in following his own line of development or his own journey, and Ad is interested seemingly only in Ad's life." Rather, as he had said, "You want Nick to draw a moral." "You want to know why. Why this detail? Why is this being told?"

Thus, he found Hemingway's use of detail (usually regarded as one of his great stylistic achievements) simply tiresome. "I was . . . irritated," in the description of the cooking, "by the extreme detail of the fat and of the— 'Well, it's better after dinner than before'—it's such a typical Hemingway touch. 'I won't have this cigarette until five minutes after dinner because that's the best time to have it and the only time when you're out in the woods alone.' Sometimes all that detail is a bringdown when you're not really attuned to it, and somehow I wasn't." Not only did Hemingway's details fail to give him the sense of trust he needed, Sebastian even felt drawn into a con-

test of wits. "Because the story draws so much from
Hemingway's personal experience . . . somehow you feel that
you have to call your experience in to corroborate his, so that
any details that he presents, you have to, like, riff back through
the cards of your memory to see if this doesn't jibe with what
you know, and if it doesn't, it's like a really horrendous clang."
In general, he said of things like the cooking, "There's not
enough feeling of ritual there." Detail would only work for him,
he seemed to be saying, if merged into a larger controlling
pattern, "a conclusion implicit . . . something that you could
grab onto."

Sebastian, then, found control not in plot or style or theme,
but in one of the characters. Bugs, for him, balanced "chance"
and "necessity": "He's the only known quantity." "I respond
to him [Bugs] with a certain amount of, well, let's say relief,
because he seems to be the only spot of sanity or of predictable
social behavior in the lot." "The Negro seems to be the most
sane individual of the bunch, counting the brakeman who was
totally violent." "He seems to be the only superego in the lot."
"Without his ministrations . . . the scene would be over because Nick would be eliminated."

Because Bugs had become a source of control, any possibility of the unpredictable in Bugs aroused anxiety in Sebastian.
As he had said, "The chance element is too scary . . . the fact
that it could have turned out so differently so easily; that
maybe the Negro's violence— Maybe he could have been
satisfied just to see what— Suppose he had been a little bit
curious to see how Nick would handle himself." "It was lucky
that the Negro was there. It was lucky that he wasn't farther
off . . . that he hadn't left the fire for some other housekeeping
reason."

In general, he associated Bugs strongly with food: "He's the
fire-maker. He's always connected with tending the fire, making the food, preserving order." "The ham and eggs were part
of . . . the Negro's ethos and his situation." Sebastian could
even speak of Bugs's words as food: "The Negro pays him [a]
compliment, which is a sop."

This reassuring role took on special images: "I respond to
the Negro's centrality. I mean, it's like a parable almost of the

country . . . founded on slave labor." "The Negro, although
being the basis, the fodder, for this story, is in the same position as the slaves, really, in a kind of . . . love-hate thing . . .
There he is, and he's necessary." "He's the anchor of the
scene," "the anchor of the whole situation." "I do see Bugs as
the center, the only thing that keeps Nick from being physically
obliterated."

To the third ear, a character who is both food provider and
"fodder" in a "love-hate thing," the "center" in a conflict
between two men, the anchor that keeps the "son" from an-
nihilation, represents someone quite specific. And Sebastian
himself bluntly made the interpretation. "The Negro is obviously a mother to [Ad]; and you sense that immediately. As
soon as the Negro makes his appearance, in the way he comes
down off the bank, he's taken a kind of magisterial, house-
wifely attitude." Indeed, as if to prove that this was not an
intellectual gimmick but that Bugs really had this meaning for
Sebastian, he made a "Freudian slip": "It was such a logical
thing for the Negro's mother to be making food and to be giving
them food."

Perhaps the slip testifies to an ambivalence, fears Sebastian
felt toward Bugs as mother, maybe toward mothers in general,
as his slip "Judy Green" revealed sadistic impulses toward the
mother-figure of "Winter Dreams." Thus, he said, "Bugs does
not seem to represent a threat to me until—there's a sort of
flash—when he . . . volunteers the information, 'I was in
[prison] for cutting a man.' Then we see that there's also violence in Bugs, but somehow the maternal element is overriding.
You feel that Bugs is benign." He worried about Bugs's black-
jacking Ad: "He commits an act of violence, as Nick wonders
at this himself. Obviously Nick is responding to this characteristic, too [that is, Bugs's controlling the others' aggression].
' "You hurt him yourself." "Yeah, but I know how to do it." '
And he does know how to do it. He does know what he's
doing." "The Negro seems to be the one who holds the other
two in check as far as violence is concerned." Nevertheless,
something in Sebastian must have wanted to find violence in
Bugs, for he misremembered: "He sympathizes with Nick's

plight, and he advises him how to get him [the brakeman] with a rock the next time through."

For all Bugs's functioning as a check, however, he did not serve as a satisfactory resolution for Sebastian because he did not offer enough in the way of verbal or intellectual creation. "Maybe . . . if Bugs made some sort of social observations." "The Negro . . . should be aware of himself and aware of his effect on everyone else." "If he were more self-reflective or more openly self-reflective or confessional— I suppose if I were writing it . . . I'd make him more aware of himself and more ready to expand on his situation, say, 'I know that I'm not what I seem,' or something like that."

> If the Negro had seemed to be more aware of his own situation, of the fact that he speaks so politely . . . that he's very careful in his diction and very unctuous in his treatment of both parties [and Sebastian did some imitations here], if he broke down and admitted that there's something incongruous about this or something to produce a wonderment that we're aware of in Nick . . . it wouldn't be a conclusion, but in a sense it would bring [the story] down to a much more didactic kind of thing.

In effect, we are seeing Sebastian try to create a Bugs that matches his own characteristic strategies. Bugs is to be a tender, motherly controller, and he is to provide verbal and intellectual creations. The story gave Sebastian materials with which to match his first demand on Bugs but not the second.

Nick did no better. To approach him, Sebastian recreated in his own terms Hemingway's concept of manliness: a man is a controlling, authoritative other. "Nick's preoccupation with learning and developing and not being a boy and being a man and getting the credentials that he doesn't have to show finally— I suppose that's the Hemingway criteria for manhood: any other man will recognize you as a man, if not immediately, at least pretty soon after you appear, without any kind of initiation."

In this new form, then, Sebastian was bringing back his need for predictability and certainty. "You feel that any episode is liable to get out of his control, because his sensibility is so beshrouded with himself as 'the kid,' as the comer, as the learner." "Nick, obviously, is anxious not to be a child—like Coriolanus" (whom Sebastian then explicated—a little verbal creation of his own). "Nick's hostility, outsiderness, battlerness"—this was Sebastian's explanation of the story's title—"He's too tough. He's too unsure of himself to let anyone be sure of him." A good observation, I thought, true to human nature. One can count on a man who can count on himself. One cannot count on a man who still needs to prove himself to others. And it was precisely Sebastian's own wish for certainty and control that enabled him to experience Nick's unsureness in this re-creative way. "Somehow he just seems to precipitate violence [in the Nick series as a whole], and I suspect that it's that kind of phony masculinity at work." "It seems that it's always productive of this tension whenever he's around other men." "He just can't get along with other men except in certain ritual circumstances . . . when they're doing something together that's bigger than both of them, like building a fire or doing something ritually."

The reference to fire and ritual suggests that Sebastian was seeing men in relation to maternal controls, as, in effect, fathers or sons. "So Nick's the kid," he decided at one point, "and Ad is the child. I mean you . . . couldn't call Ad the kid, because it implies a kind of potency that he just doesn't have anymore." At another point, however, Sebastian said of Ad (whom the story always calls "the little man"): "Ad's emanation is very bull-like. It's like the childlike powerful athlete. Sort of a Lawrentian figure, almost, except for the violence." "I mean it's saved from D. H. Lawrence's kind of massive-buttocked, Midlands, slow-blooded violence by . . . his sort of twitching nerve kind of unpredictability." "So it's in character. . . . The fact that his pulse goes only forty beats a minute, too, along with the fact that he has one ear and is a mass of scar tissue. But a sort of childlike potency, somehow." "In the fact that his pulse is so slow [there's] a kind of potential energy."

Potent or impotent? Sebastian could also say, "Ad is a perpetual child and without . . . possibility of developing into a man." I think we are seeing an ambivalence, that Sebastian creates some fatherly elements in Ad—who is, after all, the "man" to Nick's "kid"—but he also needs to bring Ad down to manageable size. Thus, when Nick recognizes Ad's name as that of a famous fighter, "it's possible that there's an element of awe, that he doesn't want to topple a god even if it's a very tarnished god at this point."

In effect, Sebastian used the theme of incest to turn an especially big man (a father) into an especially small one (a child). "The fact that there was this incest thing in his past, which wasn't real, but which looked real, it makes him more believable as a fallen celebrity. It gives that sort of spice to the past. It makes him seem to have fallen from a higher plane to a lower one, and it gives that touch of perversity and also of fear."

He was using phrases much like those he applied to Judy Jones whom he also wanted to bring down from a high level to a more reachable and slightly degraded plane. What Sebastian wanted was a controlling authority whom he could get close to in a physical, sexual way. Judy played hard to get, so she had to be brought low. Ad was sexually taboo. He was also unpredictable, therefore no source of control. So he, too, had to be brought low. And yet Sebastian's finding in "the little man" that Lawrentian, bull-like power tells us how deeply he really longed for that nurturing yet controlling other whom he tried—and failed— to find in Hemingway's story.

Sebastian's response to "The Battler" reminds us of something we have seen before, to be sure, but which it is important to remember. Our four principles do *not* describe either a passive process or a pathological one. According to "the principle of multiple function," any given psychic transaction both gratifies drives and avoids anxiety—it partakes of both defensive and instinctual functions. Hence, when one says that Sebastian had two adaptive or defensive patterns, these are not only ways he avoids threats but also the avenues along which he actively seeks satisfaction.

Sebastian sought from "The Battler" an authority he could be tenderly close to and he tried to create a character who would create his own inner products, but the story yielded materials for neither. Bugs came closest to offering maternal control, but he could satisfy Sebastian only partially, because he was not "self-reflective" or "confessional" enough; that is, he did not give out in verbal or intellectual ways. Sebastian saw Nick as seeking the same kind of controls he himself wanted and therefore only to be relied on in "ritual circumstances." Ad he made partly into a father and partly into a child, according to whether the need for Ad's power or the fear of it was uppermost. The story offered him neither any character who really controlled the threatened violence nor any ritual or thematic pattern that gave a satisfactory meaning to the whole. Instead, Sebastian found Hemingway's cult of manliness (which did not suit his own adaptation of mental creation) and details that would not come together into a total pattern.

Sebastian's response thus shows the importance of theme or meaning to the reader's re-creation of the story. *The Dynamics of Literary Response* spoke of "meaning as a defense." That is, from a literary work a reader develops moral and philosophical themes, giving the text a "point" around which its details converge, as a way of assuaging the reader's anxieties. "We need meaning, but we can accept a wide variety of possible meanings to achieve literary pleasure." "Almost any kind of coherent thought about the work will open up the paths of gratification, so long as it 'makes sense' of the text."[10]

In reading this story, Sebastian encountered no less than three possible interpretations. His fellow student supplied him Philip Young's reading[11] of the story as about a pair of homosexuals. On his own, Sebastian arrived at the interpretation I favored, Ad and Bugs as grotesque and dangerous parodies of a mother and father. Also on his own, he tried out the theme Shep had proposed, an initiation ritual. Although the homosexual reading enabled him to assuage his fears of the story temporarily, none of these three interpretations gave him a permanent way of achieving a satisfactory experience.

Apparently, then, we can accept a theme as a way of opening the paths of gratification only if those paths have already been opened. If we can accept a theme at all, we can indeed accept a variety of them as the final transformations of our deeper responses. But I can accept themes only if they consolidate and perfect *a pre-existing transformation* that re-creates my particular identity theme.

Sebastian found in "The Battler" practically no match be-tween the story (even as his friend helped him interpret it) and his own characteristic adaptations and fantasies—his identity theme. Therefore, he could have practically no positive experi-ence of the story, no matter how coherent the interpretation offered him. In a sense, we leave Sebastian just where we found him, underlining words in the story, looking for a con-trolling theme but not finding it, because at a deeper level his style was not finding itself. The story would not yield him words on which he could base a perception of the control and exchange he so deeply needed. His identity could not re-create itself.

Sandra

"It didn't have that much in it for me," said Sandra. It "didn't involve me." It gave her "no real tug." She was, in effect, telling me that she was unable to use "Winter Dreams" to express her own characteristic adaptation: namely, to find a source of strength or nurture and draw from it. More precisely, Sandra approached experiences as if she were seeing something that could tug at her. If it seemed threatening, she would take steps not to see it. If it seemed promising, she would try to see it more closely, even touch it, hoping for a flow of power or nurture that would neutralize differences between male and female, older and younger, stronger and weaker, and so on. The key lay in what she *saw*.

Thus, she had an astonishingly detailed memory of the story, which she tended to put in visual terms. She described Judy, for example, as "the *vision* and this, you know, extraordinary person in his life," "his constant vision." He can never exactly be disillusioned, she concluded, "because he's always got this same vision," nor would Judy fade for Dexter "because some-how the first impression . . . was so strong." "He might not have cared about her fading because you always kind of have your first impressions."

In effect, in her reading of the story, Dexter had looked at Judy and been hooked but she, Sandra, refused to. Instead, she brought her characteristic defense of not seeing into play against "this kind of fatal woman " with her "mystery" or "unnamed quality." Asked a question posited on her meeting someone like Judy, she dodged. "I don't believe I could ever meet anybody like that, see? That's the thing." "How do you feel toward her?" I asked.

> I don't believe in her . . . It's a very simple way to criticize it [the story], but . . . from all the different experiences I've had of girls who were, quote, "popular," girls who were enchanting and mysterious in some ways, at their *best*, all of them combined would never command this, *this* string of men. I don't *believe* in this mysterious power that she's supposed to have. If it were just over the one man in the story, you could, say, well, that's just the way he *feels* about her, but I think in the story you're meant to accept this fact, you know, that she could keep half a dozen men, you know, just up and down and waiting, and he [Fitzgerald] said [she is sarcastic now] there would be dozens of men who would carry that impression of her smile like to their *grave* or something.

Actually, Fitzgerald's phrase is, "the memory of which at least a dozen men were to carry into middle age." Sandra's exaggerating to "dozens" and to the "grave" suggests the degree of power she feared in Judy.

So does her disbelief, her unwillingness to see Judy. For example, she said she didn't believe there really were women with these powers: "I've read, you know, about these kind of women in stories . . . and here she's probably one of the most extraordinary— It would certainly be interesting if there were, but I just—" and finally, she just laughed. But when I asked her about these other stories, she shifted. "I suppose I tried to think right away of real life experience, somebody in real life experience where they *never* fail." Then she turned once more from life to fiction, and finally to a *lapsus memoriae*: "I'm almost sure I've read something else like that [ending], and I wish I could think of what it was. But— . . . I'll have to see if I can think of it."

That last figure of speech expressed her fantasy of vision as dominance and control. "She [Judy Jones] had a mystery or whatever that very special quality is that would have set her so apart from other people that even just—well, . . . as you're told here, that maybe even one look could do it." At this point, I had asked her, "What kind of woman do you see for Dexter?" After many hesitations and false starts, she decided, "Well, you know, she can be all the things that Irene is . . . with maybe just a little bit *more* mystery without having it be that almost destructive kind. At one point he [Fitzgerald] says that anything Judy does—though you kind of see her just mowing over all these men—is not malicious, which is kind of hard to accept."

In short, she saw Judy as having a dangerous mystery, and like a Medusa, one look at it enabled her to "mow over" numbers of men, rendering them helplessly passive. She felt there was no way a man could actively win Judy: "It's almost like there would be nothing you could *do*; you would just have to *be* a certain way." As for Judy, however, men are an "easy conquest." "It's as if the poor man never had any choice. She was sort of presented as the aggressor, and if she came up and said, 'You're it,' that was *it*, and you went along with it until you weren't it, and then you were kind of dropped." In this version she saw the men as passive; what she admired in Dexter was "that he does have something more in him than average," and I cannot help feeling that that "something" and that "it" have the unconscious meaning of active, manly power.

Perhaps not, but in any case Sandra's answer to Judy's power was an equalizing. "Somebody that loved her less than she loved him was what appealed to her," a man who "could intrigue her more than she intrigued him, maybe."

I suppose there's a certain kind of [pause] mystery. I grant that there certainly is in some women, and even though I don't believe that this woman could have such unqualified success, she could have—it's so hard to say what I'm trying to think of—that power to attract somebody in that very special way, but not to the point where it was such an . . . unlimited *power* over the other person. So like maybe the *right* person for him [Dexter] is somebody that has an extra-ordinary quality about her, yes, but not to the point where it takes him over so completely that he's not like in control of himself anymore. If you know what I mean.

Earlier, when she talked about Dexter's impulsively quit-ting as a caddy, she had said, "Both of these things work: his pride that he doesn't want this little girl to have the power maybe to boss him around, and . . . not wanting to be on inferior terms with her right away." That word "inferior" came up, inevitably, to describe Irene, who clearly offers little more than "an addition to his own sort of successful life. She's in such an inferior position because she's so pale beside his *constant* vision, really, of Judy." In Judy's own case, once she was caught in this inferior position, it was a disaster. "That's why the end seemed obvious to me: that it was inevitable you'd have to hear at some later time that finally she's met someone who really crushed all the life—it does remind me of something else, and when that ending came—I'm almost sure I've read something else like that." In her phrasings, in her concern with the "end" and the "ending" and being "crushed," we hear, I think, one of the unconscious fears reflected in the theme of deficiency in her TAT stories: that a man or woman might crush the other in the "end."*

Thus, in spelling out further the person who could be right for Dexter, she developed again the theme of equalization in images that seemed to derive from a little girl's idea of a 'bigger-is-better' power associated with man's anatomy as against woman's.

I suppose I think this about almost anybody, say, in this case, a man, who has superior qualities or something. . . . I think it works both ways. I guess we're talking about mar-riage partners or the kind of person you're going to establish this long relationship with. To find somebody with equally superior *something*, whatever it is— Well, I like the idea of— I can accept the idea of this mysterious force that she has.

* These words were important in the same way for Sam: "end" and "ending" in "Winter Dreams" and "crush" in "The Battler" (see above, pp. 313 and 328).

It's partly her physical appearance. It's partly the way she handles people. And it's partly just an unnamed quality that some people have, and I do believe some of them, some people do. And so I guess I'd like to see him and anybody else like him, that's got a little bit something more than average, find a person who has mystery, maybe, a unique attractiveness, even if it's only for that one other person. *But* [and she paused] but only to the point where it doesn't overpower the other person . . . where each partner, each individual can meet the other person . . . where each partner, each individual can meet the other one on his own ground . . . where one isn't overtaken by the other, which I suppose wouldn't be the case if each had his own unique qualities to begin with.

After this generalization, as I began to wind up the interview, she laughed a little at herself. "I should have really thought about that before I began developing a whole theory of marriage, or something. Frightening!"

Those last words bring together all of Sandra's modes of adaptation. That is, she has found a way of making the "frightening" not frightening at all, by equalizing man and woman, different kinds of strength, and the younger generation with the older (as they become husbands and wives). "To find somebody with equally superior something." But she does all this outside of and away from a story in which one person is overtaken or overpowered by the other's "mysterious force."

In terms of our four principles, then, she was not able to enact through the story her own general expectancies from experience. More specifically, finding nothing in the story with which to re-create her own adaptive patterns (her need to draw near a source of strength without being overpowered), she defended against the fiction by turning to reality—"some people"—instead. Her avoiding the story shows she felt some anxiety from it. She must have felt, therefore, the kind of danger that mattered to her, the feeling that men and women can be overwhelmed unless they have a "mystery," "an unnamed quality," or "superior qualities or something" "equally superior *something* whatever it is" that "works both ways."

For her, Judy's superior powers were *too* superior—a source of
anxiety rather than pleasure. Yet she could find nothing in the
story from which she could re-create her defensive and adaptive strategies. Dexter was, by the very fact of Judy's strength,
not strong enough to be a source of protection. The story, then,
remained something that "didn't have that much in it for me,"
and she turned away from it to reality.

One reason I always found Sandra's comments interesting
was that she had such exact likes and dislikes, often markedly
different from the other readers'. For example, in answer to my
standard question as to how she reacted to "The Battler" generally, she told me she had read it twice and reacted differently
each time. The first time she just said, "Ech!" "I was reading
it for what was happening and reading the dialogue and skip-
ping to the parts where something was really happening, where
the action was; and I missed so much of what, when I read it
the second time, really appealed to me." "You know how your
eye catches on dialogue," she said, and it was precisely the
dialogue that she found implausible and bad. "The second
time, what I got was . . . the sections of, well, description, I
guess, in which I found myself really stopping to say, 'This is
really good. . . .' Which I missed entirely the first time."

In a general way, she did not like Ad. She shared with Nick,
she said, "this *uneasy* feeling of his first glimpse of him." She
did like Bugs, however: "He's probably the easiest character
to like in the story." "Big and— Big and gentle and helpful."
"He's just— he's all gentleness. Even when he's hitting his
friend over the back of the head, he's being [as] gentle as he
could possibly be." (A far cry from Sam's image of him as an
oriental torturer!) And, of course, Sandra liked Nick with
whom she strongly identified: "I almost can't think of how I
feel toward him [Ad] without thinking how Nick feels." Evidently, then, in at least part of the story, Sandra was building
fantasy in her own adaptive style.

Sandra approached the story by sight (as in Hemingway's
image of the "15X binoculars"). She would use sight to try to
remove uncertainty about things like Bugs's "Negro walk." "I

didn't know exactly what he was getting at," she said. "Whatever that was, it was lost on me." Nevertheless, she took a stab at the problem in specifically visual terms. "I remember kind of puzzling over what was a 'Negro walk.' The only thing I can think of is some kind of stereotyped . . . Amos and Andy thing, somebody kind of shuffling along. I don't see how anybody can shuffle along as they're jumping over an embankment so [she laughed] I didn't really see what he was talking about there." She often used "see" for "understand," this way. "You sort of see how [Ad] could have gotten that way . . . punchy, anyway. And crazy." For example, she said (quite unconsciously), "I can see a Negro voice" (meaning, obviously, she could understand Hemingway's use of that stereotype). There is, to be sure, a tradition for this use of "vision" reaching back to proto-Indo-European, but the other readers did not use it to anything like the extent Sandra did. Among these readers, she alone answered my question, Can you picture that woman?, by using the story's visual datum: the woman looked like a twin of Ad's. "He's blond and almost a childlike face, so . . . I picture her as blonde, a sweet-faced blonde, no particular characteristics."

She would go so far as to provide visual effects to explain dialogue she did not understand: "I look at the line, and I think, 'This sounds kind of strange.' Well, without [its] saying, Nick could be smiling, saying, 'Well, you gotta be tough.' " She was able to make sense of Ad's crazy spell that way:

It could be like in movies or something . . . I imagine I've seen movies where this kind of situation occurs, where somebody comes along, and things are good, and then it's a sort of a comic thing—it works very comically here, too —where the person like, say, Ad turns on Nick and says, 'You were here, drinking my liquor, smoking my cigars, and now you come and get all snotty.' Of course, he's serious in his own way, too. . . . To make it even more comic in a way, Nick never even said a word. And it was his friend [Bugs] who said 'Put down the knife,' 'Just don't give it to him,' or something like that. That kind of thing I think I've seen done,

although I couldn't think of any place [in written literature]. I
almost pictured it more as being done in a play or a movie or
TV show or something rather than a— I don't think I've *read*
this kind of situation is what I mean, I guess.

Indeed Sandra's powers of visualization so far exceeded mine,
anyway, that it wasn't until I cast Laurel and Hardy or Chaplin
and Turpin into the roles that I could conjure up what she was
getting at.

So intense a use of one sensory mode shows how seeing
served Sandra not only as an early warning system, but as a
source of pleasure in itself. In her attitudes toward "The Battler," she used seeing both ways.

When what Sandra saw seemed dangerous, she took steps
not to see it (to avoid it physically, to block the perception, or,
once seen, to erase it or feel no pain). Inevitably, these avoid-
ances came into play against Ad, whom the other readers found
to be either a frightening father or a victimized child or some
combination of them. Both of these would be threatening for
Sandra, who needed evenly balanced strengths, and she defended against him. When she first mentioned him in the interview, it was in connection with "the description of [Nick's]
looking at—what was the guy's name?" "Ad," I answered. "His face," she finished, but her forgetting was a classic *lapsus memoriae*.

Another way Sandra dealt with threatening parts of the story
was to dodge back and forth from fiction to reality (as she had
with "Winter Dreams"), when one or the other became too
risky. She appealed to experience to get at Nick's first feelings
toward Ad. "At first, you're feeling discomfort, like your first
reaction to somebody that has a badly mutilated face." But
when I asked her if she felt anything but sympathy for Ad, she
wavered. "I suppose anybody would be— I would be somewhat frightened about it. Say you were meeting it, not in the
story, but . . . talking about the person himself. You— I'd be
frightened by somebody like that." I asked her, "Does he [the
Negro] remind you of anybody? Anybody in your experience?"
She said, "I was trying to think of the stories first of all," and
she came up with "somebody like Jim in *Huck Finn*. Then she

shifted to life. "I suppose I know a lot of generous people." Similarly, when she thought of the story as a whole, she generalized: it recalled "any time" "you've" ever been picked on. When I asked her if Ad reminded her of anyone she knew, she laughed, "Anybody I know!" as though that were quite impossible. Then she turned to movies and television, as we have seen, to explain his explosion.

She had other ways of dealing with Ad's threatening aspects: "Even at the same time when he's sort of turning on Nick and, you know, ready to, you know, ready to beat up on him for the incident of the knife, you kind of understand what's going on." Elsewhere she used "understanding" to substitute for emotion. For example, she contradicted herself to say she didn't feel angry when Nick was knocked off the train: "Nothing quite that strong. No. [But] I can understand an anger." She was pitying him for being so stupid as to fall for the brakeman's trick, "but at the same time understanding how he was furious about it." "Understanding" in this sense almost classically illustrated Freud's notion of isolation as a defense: not letting one idea "touch" another, particularly the emotion appropriate to it.

Those were Sandra's unseeings, triggered by threatening sights. If what she saw was promising, however, she wanted to draw closer to it and take strength or nurture from it. Thus, she liked the story's progression from mystery or trap to succor.

Sandra said that, on her second reading of the story, "The first thing that got me was the feeling of Nick when he was walking the railroad tracks after being kicked off, and how he would hurt all over and the loneliness of it and fear somewhat, not knowing *where* he was going, exactly *what* was ahead. The darkness . . ." The second thing, she said, was looking at Ad's mutilated face. Then, regression to safety: "After that, it was where he was being fed."

After the feeling of loneliness and kind of searching for something was conveyed so well, that coming up to a light is sort of a feeling of, well, promise, perhaps, relief. But it's a strange feeling, too, because there's always the element of whatever is unknown, is— You know, what kind of person is it? Is it somebody who's going to be happy to offer you some warmth with maybe some food? Or is it somebody that— You know, it could have been somebody who would have turned on him right away.

Food, in effect, replaces aggression.

Sandra took a simple, sensuous, oral and visual pleasure in the food in "The Battler." "It was really, *really* well described, like *watching*, how he [Nick] was *watching* him cook something was so good, and just the way everything was described as he put together the sandwich and just how good everything tasted. It came across very well." Indeed, Sandra and I even got into a discussion of the right way to fry eggs, "basting" them.

Sandra's straightforward enjoyment of food contrasted quite neatly with Shep's conflicts. Asked how he felt about the food, he had said, "Seems like tolerable food. You know, I'm not in the habit of dragging my bread through the ham fat, but I can see how I would be if I lived out there. Then I wouldn't have a can in the kitchen I could pour the grease into to use it to cook with later on. So I'd eat it probably." Before this, our "oral" reader had brought in nonexistent coffee, alcohol, and addiction, and after this statement he puzzled out how Bugs might have stolen the eggs or slaughtered the pig.

Sandra's uncomplicated pleasure in the food and in being nurtured enriched her response to Bugs. "So warm, hospitable . . . he adds so much to what I was saying about the feeling of how good the food is going to be. It's always so much better if somebody's there, making it for you [she laughed], helping you enjoy it, not begrudging it to you. He was, you know, so happy to be cooking this for them. Just a line or two seemed to bring that out." (Not, I must admit, a line or two that I could find.) "He asks Nick if he wants some food to take with him, and he says 'No,' sends him off; and then, after he's on his way, he finds out he's got a ham sandwich. [Bugs is] one of those kind of generous people that, I suppose, it's hard not to like." Again, this time misreading the story slightly to do so, she singled out the element of feeding and maternal protection (or overprotection) without using the idea of "mother" as such. Instead, she spoke of Bugs's "gentleness" and "generosity."

Hospitality's really a better word in its very best sense. A lot of people can bring you over and throw a lot of food at you. . . . [Hospitality's] very different from just entertaining people, and it carries over, I think, to all kinds of different relationships. It involves a lot of things, and I would say that it's probably the one quality that I would single out as the most attractive thing about him.

Again it comes up . . . [when] Nick is about ready to leave, and he says, 'I wish you'd leave.' . . . I suppose he's thinking first of his friend Ad. At the same time, he's as nice as he possibly can be to Nick; and each one is handled— You have the feeling that he could handle a whole roomful of people and give each enough attention, make each feel pretty special.

We begin to see another reason she enjoyed Bugs so much. Not only does he give food—he also acts out the very equalizing Sandra herself wanted to give and receive. He could "make each feel pretty special." With him, everybody has the same power. "You *almost* get the feeling that— . . . I shouldn't generalize that—that *I* get almost the feeling there's a servant-master relationship between this Bugs and Ad. It could, I suppose, carry over to his relationships—to Nick." "In effect, if anybody's really in command, it's Bugs, the one that can hit him on the back of the head and wake him up. He's really in control."

Bugs's control would have served to prevent the fearful fantasy Sandra associated to the story as a whole. Her wording is central:

Something like this in its very most isolated sense probably calls on any time that you've ever been kind of maybe bullied or picked on when . . . for some reason . . . the other person ran away or was out of range—this could even be a verbal situation—or for some other such reason, that, say, the person was an authority . . . Any time when *you* were put down and didn't have a chance to stand up and fight back on your own terms, either verbally or physically [and she laughed]. Verbally mostly, I suppose, in my case . . . Nothing that physically violent ever happened to me.

The issue of whether one would "stand up" or be "put down" evokes (as with Sam) questions of power and strength, understood particularly as erectness.

By contrast, Sandra liked Bugs because he was so gentle, controlling, and giving. According to our principles, if she liked Bugs for these qualities, these were things she hoped for from experiences generally, and, if she liked the story, she would like it for having these qualities. Sandra established what amounted to a personal relationship to the story. She would talk to it (or the characters in it). After the brakeman's trick, "Actually, I . . . said, 'That's too bad that you fell for something like that.' " Of her first reading of the story, she said, "I even found myself saying, 'Oh, this is bad' in a couple of lines." The second time, "I found myself really stopping to say, 'This is really good. This is really getting across the feeling that he's trying to portray.' "

Sometimes she treated the story as a person in other ways, for example, regretting she had read it too fast. "I figure, well, that's not being fair to the story." She could recall in the story "the first thing that got me," and evidently she thought of fiction in general this way. "Even if I read something fast, if there's really something that I'm going to like in it, it gets me the first time." The story could be a trap, or it could be a source "getting across" to her, just as earlier, she had rhapsodized about Bugs's food—"It came across very well." Or as she had imagined Nick wondering whether the distant fire represented somebody who would give him warmth and food or somebody who would turn on him.

Closely linked to her feelings about a source that could also be a trap was Sandra's concern with strength and power. Thus, the description of Nick looking at Ad: "It came out almost as strongly," she said, as the description of Nick's lonely walk, not knowing where he was going, what was ahead in the darkness "That was, I thought, very strongly presented." Sandra's mind puts opposite the trap something thrusting out strongly, and throughout her comments on this story, she seemed concerned with a sense of the one, the loner on his heavy quest. Thus, trying to justify what she took to be the wretched language given Nick in the story, "He could [be] . . . very impressed with his own sense of being alone and against the world." In praising the descriptions, she singled out "a tiny detail like Nick walking over the railroad tracks when he goes over the bridge. Hemingway describes the way he sees the water through the railroad ties down below, black in between the railroad ties. Then kicking one spike into the water—it gives a sense of how high up he is and how it would kind of echo in the dark and all alone." This is a common fantasy: a body (or a spike) moving in isolation through space, either climbing or riding or falling, avoiding damage or entrapment. We see it in such common phrasings as "a rise to power."

In "The Battler," the character who expressed this theme most was, of course, Ad. She was impressed by his power:

> You have a sense of his strength, because, even though he is beaten up, he still has this certain amount of strength back. And he has a great desire to prove it, too, which is the main thing to worry about, and that, coupled with the fact that he is behaving, like, irresponsibly, then that adds an extra degree of it.

She referred repeatedly to Ad's being mutilated, too. "I think I kind of figured that [that he was a boxer] when he shows his ear and his messed up face. I think I was surprised . . . when he said something like he was a former *champion* boxer. You know, you almost didn't expect him to have ever made it that big." The three male readers all expressed anxiety about the moment when Ad has Nick touch his wrist. Not Sandra. "I don't remember feeling any emotion, but feeling in the sense of almost being able to touch it." "You could almost feel it. I remember describing the thickness of his wrist and his muscles and the real slow, slo-o-o-ow pulse beat."

All these phrasings about something coming out strongly, a lone spike or man, something with thickness, and a pulse, which you didn't expect to be *that* big—all these relate to

Sandra's other level of drive satisfaction, her concern with manly power conceived in phallic images. As in her remarks on "Winter Dreams," she wanted to match herself with a strong man, neither overpowering nor overpowered. In part, she found him in the solitary venturer, Nick Adams, with whom she so strongly identified. In fact, she had difficulty separating her own feelings from Nick's. The first three things in the story that she said "got" her were all feelings Nick had: his feelings of loneliness and hurt after being kicked off the train; "the kind of uncomfortable feeling he had with [Ad]"; finally (in her words), "After *you*'d had the earlier feeling of loneliness . . . *he* began to build up a sense of hunger." In general, she felt the story was "seen through his eyes," and she entered into "the description of his looking at" Ad, his "watching [Bugs] cook something," "this uneasy feeling of his first glimpse of [Ad]," and so on.

She also took part with Nick in various moves toward equalizing power. For example, on seeing Ad, "At first you're feeling discomfort, like your first reaction to somebody that has a badly mutilated face, and then his [Nick's] discomfort when the guy comes right out and says, 'What's the matter? Don't you like my face?' or something like that." Similarly, after the brakeman's ruse, "You feel this kind of rage he has, especially when it isn't a fair fight." "You feel his physical hurt and you feel his sense of outrage . . . to be taken in by a trick, really, and then to be hit when he didn't have a chance to hit back or to even put up his guard or anything." And she sort of laughed. "You'd think, . . . tough kid that he is, he'd know better." "I was a little bit surprised that he was taken in." "That was a little bit hard to even accept, that he would do that." In Sandra's structure of adaptations, the lonely, virile thruster was not supposed to be "taken in by a trick."

Curiously, Sandra's interest in the loner thrusting through space against the traps of the world underlay her complicated reaction to Hemingway's language. In her first reading, she said, her eye caught on the dialogue, and it was not until she read the story a second time that she discovered the descriptions, which she liked very much. I asked her to describe her feelings about the style, and she responded instead in images like "short," "straightforward," "blunt":

> Like the obvious things that you always think of, the short, the kind of short sentences, the kind of straightforward description of things, fairly blunt, and just about the opposite of anything— [complex? feminine?] I suppose it comes out of a newspaper style, but with an amazing feeling for description, *hitting* at the things that'll make something stand out. Like if he uses an adjective maybe, just using the right one that'll— but not always relying on [several] adjectives to carry the weight of it.

We have already heard her praise language that makes things come out strongly, like Ad's wrist that she could almost feel, or the "one spike." "It's the little things like that that work for the descriptive part of the style."

She went right on to say, "The dialogue—you don't have a whole lot of it here. I know some of the stories rely almost completely on it, it seems. *That* is very, very blunt," to be contrasted, presumably, with that which is "fairly blunt." (By the way, she found "an arrow that's blunted" in Rorschach Card VI, the "phallic" card.)

In general, she responded to the dialogue with incredulity: "I look at the line, and I think, 'This sounds kind of strange.' " "All that stuff. Come *on!*" she said, laughing about all the "tough" talk. "I think you're supposed to believe they said these kind of things." When she spoke more specifically about the dialogue, she seemed to find it just the opposite of the descriptive style. The dialogue—"It's usually just line, line, you know, alternating." She kept saying the description worked "strongly," but in the dialogue, "I think he usually avoids, where he can, saying, 'He said bravely,' or 'He said boldly.' " In effect, she was saying, if the description is solitary, thrusting, hitting—in short, virile—the dialogue is just the opposite, alternating, not brave or bold, unconvincing—you can't believe it's true. At the root of her complex distinction between the two parts of Hemingway's style (as she saw it) lay her own adaptive style: the need to draw near a source of virile strength. Hemingway's descriptions became for her such a source, but his dialogue didn't.

In general, then, Sandra could give life to this story with just those characters or mannerisms that she decided she could safely draw near to and touch and take manly strength or gentle nurture from. Sandra used touching precisely for the emotions she could enjoy and not have to "understand." She could feel Ad's pulsing wrist: "I don't remember feeling any emotion, but feeling in the sense of almost being able to touch it." She could "feel [Nick's] physical hurt and feel his sense of outrage." "You have the feeling" that Bugs could "handle" a roomful of people. You "get the softness of" his voice. She could find exactly her defense of not seeing dangers by getting away from them or keeping out of them in the plot and language. Equally she could gratify her wish to see sources of strength and support in order to draw power and sustenance from them (but not to be overpowered).

Given such a style of response, obviously, it would be Ad who posed her the most complicated problem. Basically, she said, she felt "Sorry for him, I guess."

"Sorry for him," I repeated, having thought she would express fear.

"Yeah," she said, pausing, "Yeah, I think so. If I were to say one thing above another."

"Suppose you were to say two things," I suggested hopefully, and she did come through with the anxiety I had expected.

"Well, I think I'd be somewhat—" and she stopped sharply and paused. "I suppose anybody would be— I would be somewhat frightened about it." She went on, then, to place him in a worrisome but acceptable range. "He still has this certain amount of strength." "You almost didn't expect him to have ever made it that big," that is, to have been a champion. In short, Sandra came into the interview defended against Ad. Once she could feel sorry for him, she was able to get him into a range of power acceptable to her. Then she could, with some hesitation, reexperience the fear that Ad's overpowering strength would put her down, which had frightened her into the denial in the first place.

More generally, Sandra's defenses were what determined her response to Ad. To be sure, her comments, like those of the other readers, formed a seamless web, from which it is not easy to tease out separate threads of response. Nevertheless, she drew some sharp lines that made her patterns clearer than most. In particular, she responded to Ad primarily in terms of defense, and, although she was finally able to manage him, she took no pleasure from the character.

By contrast, she positively enjoyed Bugs and Nick. Bugs, she saw as a gratifier of people's needs for food and nurture; he was the gentle and happy cook, and (important for Sandra) one who balanced the roles of controller and controlled, equalizing among the people he cared for with true hospitality. In short, for Sandra, he was "the easiest character to like."

Nick, she responded to in a more complex way. She was content to receive from Bugs, but Nick she almost merged with, seeing through his eyes, feeling as he felt, touching what he touched. I think she did so because she found in Nick a pattern of drives that was both more complex than Bugs's and more like her own. At the beginning of the story, Nick was the virile, manly loner, thrusting and questing his way through space, entering unknown dangers. He meets Ad, and at first they seem to have a friendly relationship; they are different but equal. Then Ad turns out to be very dangerous, and Nick regresses: he becomes passive, saved by the nurturing, protective, or maternal, Bugs. As Sandra said at the end of the interview, she associated being bullied or picked on to this story, and evidently the Bugs-Nick solution appealed to her.

Just as she sharply distinguished Nick and Bugs from Ad, Sandra set off the story's descriptions from its dialogue. She talked about the descriptions in language that suggested they gratified the same quest for virility that Nick did. The terms she used for the dialogue came out just the opposite, suggesting that the reason she disliked and disbelieved the dialogue was that it frustrated some of her deepest drives.

Finally, then, because she had such exact likes and dislikes and because they were so distinctly hers, Sandra illustrates with unusual precision the four principles of response.

Notes

The following notes are for reference only. All notes that make substantive comments on the text appear as footnotes in the text itself.

I have used only one abbreviation: *The Standard Edition of the Complete Psychological Works of Sigmund Freud* (trans. James Strachey, Anna Freud, Alix Strachey, and Alan Tyson), ed. James Strachey, 24 vols. (London: The Hogarth Press and the Institute of Psychoanalysis, 1953–), is hereafter referred to simply as *Std. Edn.*

Preface

1 Norman N. Holland, *The Dynamics of Literary Response* (New York: Oxford University Press, 1968).
2 Ibid.
3 Norman N. Holland, *Poems in Persons: An Introduction to the Psychoanalysis of Literature* (New York: W. W. Norton and Co., 1973).
4 Paul Diesing, *Patterns of Discovery in the Social Sciences* (Chicago: Aldine-Atherton, 1971).

Chapter 1

1 Walter J. Slatoff, *With Respect to Readers: Dimensions of Literary Response* (Ithaca and London: Cornell University Press, 1970), p. 188.
2 Ibid., p. 35.
3 Otto Rank, *The Myth of the Birth of the Hero* (1914) (New York: Vintage Books, 1959), Chapter 3, p. 89n.
4 Marie Bonaparte, Anna Freud, Ernst Kris, eds., *The Origins of Psychoanalysis*, trans. Eric Mosbacher and James Strachey (New York: Basic Books, 1954), letter of October 15, 1897.
5 Jacob Levine, "Response to Humor," *Scientific American* 194 (1956): 31–35.
6 I. A. Richards, *Practical Criticism: A Study of Literary Judgment* (New York: Harcourt, Brace, 1951).
7 James R. Squire, *The Responses of Adolescents While Reading Four Short Stories*, NCTE Research Report No. 2, 1964. James R. Wilson, *Responses of College Freshmen to Three Novels*, NCTE Research Report No. 7, 1966. Alan C. Purves with Victoria Rippere, *Elements of Writing about a Literary Work: A Study of Response to Literature*, NCTE Research Report No. 9, 1968. All published by National Council of Teachers of English, 508 South Sixth Street, Champaign, Illinois 61820.

8 Leo A. Handel, *Hollywood Looks at its Audience: A Report of Film Audience Research* (Urbana: University of Illinois Press, 1950), particularly Chapters 11 and 12, provides an accurate sample of what is being published currently, although the work is twenty years old.

9 Slatoff, *With Respect to Readers*, pp. 13–14.

10 Richards, *Practical Criticism*, pp. 347–349.

11 David Bleich, "The Determination of Literary Value," *Literature and Psychology* 17 (1967): 19–30.

12 Erik H. Erikson, "The Dream Specimen of Psychoanalysis," in Robert P. Knight and Cyrus R. Friedman, eds., *Psychoanalytic Psychiatry and Psychology*, Clinical and Theoretical Papers of the Austen Riggs Center, Vol. 1 (New York: Hallmark-Hubner Press, 1954), p. 140.

13 Norman N. Holland, *The Dynamics of Literary Response* (New York: Oxford University Press, 1968). Robert Waelder, *Psychoanalytic Avenues to Art* (New York: International Universities Press, 1965). Ernst Kris, *Psychoanalytic Explorations in Art* (New York: International Universities Press, 1952). Simon O. Lesser, *Fiction and the Unconscious* (Boston: Beacon Press, 1957). Philip Weissman, *Creativity in the Theater: A Psychoanalytic Study* (New York: Dell Publishing Co., 1965). In addition to Freud's essays on *Jokes* (1905) and "The 'Uncanny' " (1919), see my attempt at a synthesis: "Freud on the Response," in Holland, *Psychoanalysis and Shakespeare* (New York: McGraw-Hill Book Co., 1966).

14 I am exceedingly grateful to Ms. Betty Jane Saik, Ms. Mary Z. Bartlett, and Mr. Stephen Gormey for assembling and helping me punch-card as complete an index of studies of response to the arts as *Psychological Abstracts* affords. It was after our own work, in 1972, that an excellent survey appeared by Alan C. Purves and Richard Beach, *Literature and the Reader: Research in Response to Literature, Reading Interests, and the Teaching of Literature* (University of Illinois at Urbana-Champaign: National Council of Teachers of English, 1972). It supports our general conclusion that results are many but unsystematic.

15 When I am not using these studies substantively, I shall simply list them by author and *Psychological Abstracts* (*PA*) reference. Edward Opton, Jr., *PA* (1967): 5663. Jack Block, *PA* (1963): 7682. Richard C. Pillard et al., *PA* (1967): 6610. Luigi Gedda et al., *PA* (1956): 443.

16 Lutz von Rosenstiel, *PA* (1967): 4630. Marvin Spiegelman, "Effect of Personality on the Perception of a Motion Picture," *Journal of Projective Techniques* 19 (1955): 461–464.

17 E. M. Scott, *PA* (1958): 4129. G. Foulds, *PA* (1943): 994.

18 Eleanor E. Maccoby et al., *PA* (1960): 4080. Paul I. Lyness, *PA* (1952): 7218. Robert S. Albert, *PA* (1959): 4603.

19 Stanley E. Fish, *Self-Consuming Artifacts: The Experience of Seventeenth Century Literature* (Berkeley: University of California Press, 1972), p. 406. Slatoff, *With Respect to Readers*, pp. 55–56.

20 Morse Peckham, *Man's Rage for Chaos: Biology, Behavior, and the Arts*

(New York: Chilton Books, 1965). See also my review article, "Psychoanalytic Criticism and Perceptual Psychology," *Literature and Psychology* 16 (1966): 81–92.

21 Lilli E. Peller, "Libidinal Phases, Ego Development, and Play," *The Psychoanalytic Study of the Child* 9 (1954): 178–198; "Reading and Daydreams in Latency; Boy-Girl Differences," *Journal of the American Psychoanalytic Association* 6 (1958): 57–70; "Daydreams and Children's Favorite Books: Psychoanalytic Comments," *The Psychoanalytic Study of the Child* 14 (1959): 414–433. Kate Friedlaender, "Children's Books and their Function in Latency and Prepuberty," *American Imago* 3 (1942): 129–150.

22 Gordon Globus and Roy Shulman, "Considerations on Affective Response to Motion Pictures" (unpublished paper, Department of Psychiatry, Boston University School of Medicine); also cited in Holland, *Dynamics* (note 13), pp. 94–95. David V. Forrest, "The Patient's Sense of the Poem: Affinities and Ambiguities," in Jack J. Leedy, ed., *Poetry Therapy: The Use of Poetry in the Treatment of Emotional Disorders* (Philadelphia: J. B. Lippincott Co., 1969), Chapter 20, pp. 231–259.

23 Avery D. Weisman, "Reality Sense and Reality Testing," *Behavioral Science* 3 (1958): 228–261. Edith Buxbaum, "The Role of Detective Stories in a Child Analysis," *Psychoanalytic Quarterly* 10 (1941): 373–381. Gilbert J. Rose, "Creative Imagination in Terms of Ego 'Core' and Boundaries," *International Journal of Psycho-Analysis* 45 (1964): 75–85.

24 Caroline Shrodes, "Bibliotherapy: An Application of Psychoanalytic Theory," *American Imago* 17 (1960): 311–319; "The Dynamics of Reading: Implications for Bibliotherapy," *ETC.: A Review of General Semantics* 18 (1961): 21–33. Both articles are based on her "Bibliotherapy: A Theoretical and Clinical Experimental Study" (Ph. D. dissertation, University of California, Berkeley, 1949).

25 David Bleich, "The Determination of Literary Value," *Literature and Psychology* 17 (1967): 19–30; "Emotional Origins of Literary Meaning," *College English* 31 (1969): 30–40; "Psychological Bases of Learning from Literature," *College English* 33 (1971): 32–45.

Chapter 2

An earlier version of this chapter has appeared. Readers interested in the change in critical practice implied by the change from the conceptual framework of *The Dynamics of Literary Response* (1968) to that demonstrated here may wish to compare "Fantasy and Defense in Faulkner's 'A Rose for Emily,'" *Hartford Studies in Literature* 4 (1972): 1–35, with the present analysis of the story. The changes may meet the objections leveled by Wayne A. Tefs in "Norman N. Holland and 'A Rose for Emily'—Some

Questions Concerning Psychoanalytic Criticism," *Sphinx*, 1 (No. 2, December 1974): 50–57.

1 Northrop Frye, "Literary Criticism," in James Thorpe, ed., *The Aims and Methods of Scholarship in Modern Languages and Literatures* (New York: Modern Language Association of America, 1963), pp. 57–69, 65.
2 Freud, *The Interpretation of Dreams* (1900), *Std. Edn.*, 4: 179. See also Norman N. Holland, "Why Organic Unity?", *College English* 30 (1968): 19–30.
3 Holland, *The Dynamics of Literary Response* (New York: Oxford University Press, 1968), Chapter 6, "Meaning as Defense."
4 *Interpretation of Dreams*, *Std. Edn.*, 4: 219.
5 Georges Poulet, "Phenomenology of Reading," *New Literary History* 1 (1969): 53–68. Robert Gorham Davis, "Literature's Gratifying Dead End," *Hudson Review* 21 (1968): 774–775. Ortega y Gasset, *Notes on the Novel*, quoted in Roy Harvey Pearce, ed., *Experience in the Novel* (New York: Columbia University Press, 1968), pp. vi–vii. In general, see Holland, *Dynamics*, Chapter 3.
6 Marcel Proust, *Remembrance of Things Past*, trans. C. K. Scott Moncrieff and Frederick A. Blossom, 2 vols. (New York: Random House, 1927–1932), 2: 1024.
7 Elmo Howell, "Faulkner's 'A Rose for Emily,' " *Explicator* 19 (1961): Item 26. Arthur L. Clements, "Faulkner's 'A Rose for Emily,' " *Explicator* 20 (1961–1962): Item 78. Sister Mary Bride, ibid.
8 William O. Hendricks, "Linguistics and the Structural Analysis of Literary Texts" (unpublished paper, Department of English, University of Nebraska, Lincoln, Nebraska), pp. 139–140.
9 Floyd C. Watkins, "The Structure of 'A Rose for Emily,' " *Modern Language Notes* 69 (1954): 508–510.
10 Irving Howe, *William Faulkner: A Critical Study*, 2nd ed. (New York: Vintage Books, 1962), p. 265.
11 William Van O'Connor, *The Tangled Fire of William Faulkner* (Minneapolis: University of Minnesota Press, 1954), p. 162.
12 Austin Wright, *The American Short Story in the Twenties* (Chicago: University of Chicago Press, 1961), pp. 42–43.
13 Frederick L. Gwynn and Joseph L. Blotner, eds., *Faulkner in the University: Class Conferences at the University of Virginia, 1957–1958* (New York: Vintage Books, 1965), p. 185.
14 Ray B. West, Jr., "Faulkner's 'A Rose for Emily,' " *Explicator* 7 (1948): Item 8; (with Robert Wooster Stallman) *The Art of Modern Fiction* (New York: Rinehart and Co., 1949), pp. 270–275; *The Short Story in America* (Chicago: Henry Regnery Co., 1952), pp. 92–94; *Reading the Short Story* (New York: Thomas Y. Crowell, 1968), Chapter 5, "The Use of Atmosphere in *A Rose for Emily*," pp. 79–85.
15 Cleanth Brooks and Robert Penn Warren, *Understanding Fiction*, 2nd ed.

(New York: Appleton-Century-Crofts, 1959), p. 351.

16 O'Connor (see note 11), p. 68n. C. W. M. Johnson, "Faulkner's 'A Rose for Emily,' " *Explicator* 6 (1948): Item 45.

17 *Faulkner* (note 13), pp. 58–59.

18 Kenneth P. Kempton, *The Short Story* (Cambridge, Mass.: Harvard University Press, 1966), pp. 104–106.

19 Brooks and Warren (note 15), p. 352. D. Streatfeild, *Persephone: A Study of Two Worlds* (New York: Julian Press, 1959).

20 John V. Hagopian and Martin Dolch, "Faulkner's 'A Rose for Emily,' " *Explicator* 22 (1964): Item 68.

21 West, 1968 (note 14), p. 83. Hendricks (note 8), p. 87.

22 George Snell, *The Shapers of American Fiction* (New York: E. P. Dutton and Co., 1947), p. 98.

23 William T. Going, "Faulkner's 'A Rose for Emily,' " *Explicator* 16 (1958): Item 27.

24 Johnson (note 16). West, 1952 (note 14), p. 93. Brooks and Warren (note 15), p. 352.

25 Robert A. Jelliffe, ed., *Faulkner at Nagano* (Tokyo: Kenyusha, Ltd., 1956), p. 70. West, 1968 (note 14), p. 83.

26 Freud, "Obsessive Actions and Religious Practices" (1907) and "Character and Anal Erotism" (1908), *Std. Edn.*, 9: 117–127, 169–175.

27 West, 1949 (note 14), p. 272. Irving Malin, *William Faulkner: An Interpretation* (Stanford, Calif.: Stanford University Press, 1957), p. 37.

28 Freud, "On the Universal Tendency to Debasement in the Sphere of Love" (1912), *Std. Edn.*, 11: 186–187, 182–183, 181.

29 Karl Abraham, "Contributions to the Theory of the Anal Character" (1921), in *On Character and Libido Development: Six Essays by Karl Abraham*, ed. Bertram D. Lewin (New York: W. W. Norton and Co., 1966), p. 186.

30 Erik H. Erikson, *Identity, Youth and Crisis* (New York: W. W. Norton and Co., 1968), pp. 107–114. West, 1968 (note 14), p. 84.

31 Erik H. Erikson, *Childhood and Society*, 2nd ed. (New York: W. W. Norton, 1963), pp. 252–253.

32 Erikson, *Identity*, pp. 108–109.

33 Benjamin Spock, *Baby and Child Care*, 2nd ed. (New York: Pocket Books, 1957), Sections 380, 383.

34 Otto Fenichel, *The Psychoanalytic Theory of Neurosis* (New York: W. W. Norton and Co., 1945), pp. 312–313.

35 West, 1948, 1949 (note 14). Brooks and Warren (note 15), p. 351.

36 Compare the suggestion that the town makes Emily into a non-person (an idol, institution, etc.) as she does Homer. The town understands her but lacks sympathy, while we sympathize but without understanding her. Terry Heller, "The Telltale Hair: A Critical Study of Faulkner's 'A Rose for Emily,' " *Arizona Quarterly* 28 (1972): 301–318.

37 Ruth Sullivan, "The Narrator in 'A Rose for Emily,' " *Journal of Narrative Technique* 1 (1971): 159–178.

38 Ibid.
39 In this connection, I should mention three readings of the story that I found interesting but that I came to too late to incorporate in the text. T. J. Stafford, "Tobe's Significance in 'A Rose for Emily,' " *Modern Fiction Studies* 14 (1968): 451–453. Helen E. Nebeker, "Emily's Rose of Love: Thematic Implications of Point of View in Faulkner's 'A Rose for Emily,' " *Bulletin of the Rocky Mountain Modern Language Association* 24 (1970): 3–13. And the Heller article cited in note 36. Had it been available to me at the time of writing, a most useful collection of exegesis would have been: M. Thomas Inge, ed., *William Faulkner: A Rose for Emily*, Merrill Casebooks (Columbus, Ohio: Charles E. Merrill, 1970).

Chapter 3

1 Marvin Magalaner and Edmond L. Volpe, eds., *Twelve Short Stories* (New York: The Macmillan Co., 1961).
2 William Van O'Connor, *The Tangled Fire of William Faulkner* (Minneapolis: University of Minnesota Press, 1954), p. 70. Ray B. West, Jr., *The Short Story in America* (Chicago: Henry Regnery Co., 1952), p. 93. C. W. M. Johnson, "Faulkner's 'A Rose for Emily,' " *Explicator* 6 (1948): Item 45. Cleanth Brooks and Robert Penn Warren, *Understanding Fiction*, 2nd ed. (New York: Appleton-Century-Crofts, 1959), p. 352.
3 Irving Howe, *William Faulkner: A Critical Study*, 2nd ed. (New York: Vintage Books, 1962), p. 265. Floyd C. Watkins, "The Structure of 'A Rose for Emily,' " *Modern Language Notes* 69 (1954): 508–510. Harry M. Campbell and Ruel E. Foster, *William Faulkner: A Critical Appraisal* (Norman, Okla.: University of Oklahoma Press, 1951), p. 99. Sister Mary Bride, *Explicator* 20 (1961–1962): Item 78.
4 Norman N. Holland, *The Dynamics of Literary Response* (New York: Oxford University Press, 1968), p. 317.
5 Freud, "The Psychogenesis of a Case of Homosexuality in a Woman" (1920), Section 4, *Std. Edn.*, 18: 167–168.
6 W. B. Yeats, "At Stratford-on-Avon," *Ideas of Good and Evil* (London: A. H. Bullen, 1903), p. 162.
7 William Congreve, "Concerning Humour in Comedy" (1695), in J. E. Spingarn, ed., *Critical Essays of the Seventeenth Century*, 3 vols. (Oxford: Clarendon Press, 1907), 3: 248–249.
8 William C. Schutz, *COPE: A FIRO Scale* (Palo Alto, Calif.: Consulting Psychologists Press, 1962).
9 Charles Mauron, *Introduction to the Psychoanalysis of Mallarmé* (Berkeley: University of California Press, 1963), p. 110. See also, by the same author, *Introduction à la Psychanalyse de Mallarmé* (1950), 2nd ed. (Neuchâtel, Switzerland: Editions de la Baconnière, 1968); *Des Métaphores Obsédantes au Mythe Personnel* (Paris: José Corti, 1963); *Psychocritique du Genre Comique* (Paris: José Corti, 1964); *Phèdre* (Paris: Libraire José Corti, 1968).

10 Otto Fenichel, *The Psychoanalytic Theory of Neurosis* (New York: W. W. Norton and Co., 1945), pp. 467 and 523. Fenichel is referring to the classic paper by Robert Waelder, "The Principle of Multiple Function: Observations on Over-Determination" (1930), *Psychoanalytic Quarterly* 5 (1936): 45–62.

11 Freud, " 'Civilized' Sexual Morality and Modern Nervous Illness" (1908), *Std. Edn.*, 9: 198.

12 Heinz Lichtenstein, "Identity and Sexuality: A Study of Their Interrelationship in Man," *Journal of the American Psychoanalytic Association* 9 (1961): 179–260.

13 Charles Mauron, *Psychocritique du Genre Comique* (Paris: José Corti, 1964), pp. 141–142. Heinz Lichtenstein, "Towards a Metapsychological Definition of the Concept of Self," *International Journal of Psycho-Analysis* 46 (1965): 117–128.

14 Heinz Hartmann, "Technical Implications of Ego Psychology," *Psychoanalytic Quarterly* 20 (1951): 31–43, 35, 38.

15 Anna Freud, "Obsessional Neurosis: A Summary of Psycho-Analytic Views as Presented at the Congress," *International Journal of Psycho-Analysis* 47 (1966): 116–122.

16 *Psychoanalysis and Moral Values*, The Freud Anniversary Lecture Series, The New York Psychoanalytic Institute (New York: International Universities Press, 1960), p. 53.

17 See, for example, the series of papers on language by Maria Lorenz and Stanley Cobb in *AMA Archives of Neurology and Psychiatry*, Vol. 69–70, 1952–1953. The assumption in the text corresponds to the *Stilforschung* of Leo Spitzer—see, for example, Spitzer's famous discussion of an odd use of the phrase *à cause de* in "Pseudoobjective Motivierung bei Charles-Louis Philippe" in *Stilstudien* (1928), 2 vols. (Munich: Max Hueber Verlag, 1961), 2: 166–207. Spitzer, however, did not have a psychology adequate to the problem of relating linguistic choices to personality. For an application of psychoanalytic psychology to generative grammar for this purpose, see Norman N. Holland, "Prose and Minds: A Psychoanalytic Approach to Non-Fiction," in George Levine and William Madden, eds., *The Art of Victorian Prose* (New York: Oxford University Press, 1968), pp. 314–337.

18 Abram Kardiner and Associates, *The Psychological Frontiers of Society* (New York: Columbia University Press, 1945), p. 372.

19 Alexander Thomas, Stella Chess, and Herbert G. Birch, "The Origin of Personality," *Scientific American* 203 (August 1970): 102–109. David Shapiro, *Neurotic Styles*, Austen Riggs Center Monographs, No. 5 (New York: Basic Books, 1965), p. 179.

20 James Barrie, *Peter Pan*, The Uniform Edition of the Plays of J. M. Barrie (New York: Charles Schribner's Sons, 1928), p. xii.

21 Heinz Lichtenstein, "The Role of Narcissism in the Emergence and Maintenance of a Primary Identity," *International Journal of Psycho-*

Analysis 45 (1964): 49–56.

22 Erik H. Erikson, "The Life Cycle: Epigenesis of Identity" (1950), in *Identity: Youth and Crisis* (New York: W. W. Norton, 1968), pp. 95–96.

23 Elizabeth R. Zetzel, "A Developmental Model and the Theory of Therapy" (1963), in her collection, *The Capacity for Emotional Growth* (New York: International Universities Press, 1970), p. 268.

24 Roy Schafer, "The Mechanisms of Defence," *International Journal of Psycho-Analysis* 49 (1968): 49–62.

Chapter 4

1 William C. Schutz, *COPE: A FIRO Scale* (Palo Alto, Calif.: Consulting Psychologists Press, 1962).

2 Heinz Lichtenstein, "Towards a Metapsychological Definition of the Concept of Self," *International Journal of Psycho-Analysis* 46 (1965): 117–128.

3 Vittorio Mussolini, *Voli Sulle Ambe* (Florence: G. C. Sansoni, 1937), pp. 47–48.

4 You may wish to compare Saul's and Sandra's responses to this TAT picture; see Norman N. Holland, *Poems in Persons: An Introduction to the Psychoanalysis of Literature* (New York: W. W. Norton and Co., 1973), pp. 63, 88.

5 See Holland, *Poems in Persons*, Chapter 1, "A Maker's Mind."

6 See Norman N. Holland, "A Touching of Literary and Psychiatric Education," *Seminars in Psychiatry* 5(1973): 287–299, 288–290, 298; and "An Identity for Rat Man," *International Review of Psycho-Analysis*, forthcoming.

Chapter 5

1 *Ulysses*, The Modern Library Edition (New York: Random House, 1934), p. 210.

2 Roy Schafer, *Aspects of Internalization* (New York: International Universities Press, 1968), pp. 100–101, 109.

3 *Std. Edn.*, 5: 601.

4 Arnold Modell, *Object Love and Reality* (New York: International Universities Press, 1968), pp. 159, 103, 164, 31.

5 Selma Fraiberg, "Learning to Read and Write" (paper distributed in 1968), cited in *Shady Hill News*, Fall 1970, 178 Coolidge Hill, Cambridge, Mass. 02138.

6 D. W. Winnicott, "The Location of Cultural Experience," *International Journal of Psycho-Analysis* 48 (1966): 372.

7 Louis Sullivan, *The Autobiography of an Idea* (1922) (New York: Peter Smith, 1949), p. 115. I am grateful to Professor Albert Stone of Emory University for calling my attention to the anecdote.

Chapter 6

1 Ernest Jones, "Anal-Erotic Character Traits," *Journal of Abnormal Psychology* 13 (1918): 261; *Papers on Psycho-Analysis*, 2nd ed. (London, 1918), Chapter 40. Karl Abraham, "Contributions to the Theory of the Anal Character" (1921), in *On Character and Libido Development, Six Essays by Karl Abraham*, ed. Bertram D. Lewin (New York: W. W. Norton and Co., 1966), pp. 165–187, 185.
2 Kenneth P. Kempton, *The Short Story* (Cambridge, Mass.: Harvard University Press, 1966), pp. 104–106. Ruth Sullivan, "The Narrator in 'A Rose for Emily,' " *Journal of Narrative Technique* 1 (1971): 159–178.

Chapter 7

1 Heinz Lichtenstein, "Towards a Metapsychological Definition of the Concept of Self," *International Journal of Psycho-Analysis* 46 (1965): 117–128, 119 (italics omitted).
2 For earlier explorations of this problem, see Norman N. Holland, *Psychoanalysis and Shakespeare* (New York: McGraw-Hill Book Co., 1966), pp. 296–308, 318–347; *The Dynamics of Literary Response* (New York: Oxford University Press, 1968), Chapter 10, "Character and Identification."
3 Chapter 6, sect. E (added in 1909, 1914, and 1925), *Std. Edn.*, 5: 350–353, 359–360.
4 Ferdinand de Saussure, *Course in General Linguistics* (1916), ed. Charles Bally and Albert Sechehaye with Albert Riedlinger, trans. Wade Baskin (New York: Philosophical Library, 1959), pp. 7–17, 65–70.
5 Noam Chomsky, *Aspects of the Theory of Syntax* (Cambridge, Mass.: M.I.T. Press, 1965), especially pp. 59 and 141–147. Jerrold J. Katz and Jerry A. Fodor, "The Structure of a Semantic Theory," in *The Structure of Language, Readings in the Philosophy of Language* (Englewood Cliffs, N.J.: Prentice-Hall, 1964), pp. 479–518.
6 A continuing line of research into this phenomenon is described by Solomon E. Asch, "Opinions and Social Pressure," in Stanley Coopersmith, ed., *Frontiers of Psychological Research* (San Francisco: W. H. Freeman and Co., 1966), pp. 107–111.
7 Michel de M'Uzan, "Aperçues sur le processus de la création littéraire," *Revue Française de Psychanalyse* 29, No. 1 (January–February 1965): 43–77.
8 Freud, "Creative Writers and Day-Dreaming" (1908), *Std. Edn.*, 9: 153.
9 Heinz Lichtenstein, "Identity and Sexuality: A Study of Their Interrelationship in Man," *Journal of the American Psychoanalytic Association* 9 (1961): 179–260, 246, 253.
10 Erik H. Erikson, *Childhood and Society*, 2nd ed. (New York: W. W. Norton and Co., 1963), p. 36.
11 Lichtenstein, "Identity and Sexuality," p. 208.

12 Lichtenstein, "The Role of Narcissism in the Emergence and Maintenance of a Primary Identity," *International Journal of Psycho-Analysis* 45 (1964): 49–56, 53–54.

13 Lichtenstein, "Identity and Sexuality," p. 208. "Role of Narcissism," pp. 55–56.

14 David Bleich, "New Considerations of the Infantile Acquisition of Language and Symbolic Thought," paper presented to the Group for Applied Psychoanalysis (Buffalo), March 18, 1971. For a nonpsychoanalytic account, see Jerome Kagan, "Do Infants Think?", *Scientific American* 226, No. 3 (March 1972): 74–82.

15 Lichtenstein, "Towards a Metapsychological Definition" (note 1), p. 126.

16 D. W. Winnicott, "The Location of Cultural Experience" (1966), in *Playing and Reality* (London: Tavistock Publications, 1971), Chapter 7, p. 103.

17 Winnicott, "Transitional Objects and Transitional Phenomena" (1953), in *Playing and Reality*, Chapter 1, pp. 14, 5.

18 David Shapiro, *Neurotic Styles*, Austen Riggs Center Monographs, No. 5 (New York: Basic Books, 1965), pp. 179–180.

19 Robert Waelder, "The Principle of Multiple Function: Observations on Over-Determination" (1930), *Psychoanalytic Quarterly* 5 (1936): 45–62, 60, 59.

20 Quoted by Daniel Yergin, "The Chomskyan Revolution," *The New York Times Magazine*, December 3, 1972, p. 43.

21 Erikson, "The Life Cycle: Epigenesis of Identity" (1950), in *Identity: Youth and Crisis* (New York: W. W. Norton and Co., 1968), pp. 95–96.

22 Gregory Bateson, "The Cybernetics of 'Self': A Theory of Alchoholism" (1971), in *Steps to an Ecology of Mind* (New York: Ballantine Books, 1972), pp. 316–317.

23 T. S. Eliot, "Tradition and the Individual Talent" (1919), *Selected Essays*, new ed. (New York: Harcourt, Brace and Co., 1950), p. 5.

24 See John L. Phillips, Jr., *The Origins of Intellect: Piaget's Theory* (San Francisco: W. H. Freeman and Co., 1969), particularly Chapter 1.

Chapter 8

1 John Demos, *A Little Commonwealth: Family Life in Plymouth Colony* (New York: Oxford University Press, 1970). David Hunt, *Parents and Children in History: The Psychology of Family Life in Early Modern France* (New York: Basic Books, 1970).

2 Margaret Mead, *Growing Up in New Guinea* (1930) (New York: Mentor Books, 1953), p. vi. Lucian Pye, *Politics, Personality, and Nation Building: Burma's Search for Identity* (New Haven and London: Yale University Press, 1962), p. 186 and passim.

3 Robert Waelder, "The Principle of Multiple Function" (1930), *Psychoanalytic Quarterly* 5 (1936): 45–62, 58.

4 Raymond A. Bauer, "Problem Solving Behavior in Organizations: A

Functional Point of View," in Merwin M. Hargrove, Ike H. Harrison, and Eugene Swearingen, eds., *Business Policy Cases with Behavioral Science Implications* (Homewood, Ill.: Richard D. Irwin, 1963).

5 Clyde Kluckhohn, "Myths and Rituals: A General Theory," *Harvard Theological Review* 35 (1942): 45–79. Ruth Benedict, *Patterns of Culture* (1934) (New York: Mentor Books, 1948), Chapter 6. Erik Erikson, *Childhood and Society*, 2nd ed. (New York: W. W. Norton and Co., 1963), Chapter 4.

6 Weston La Barre, *The Ghost Dance: Origins of Religion* (Garden City, N.Y.: Doubleday and Co., 1970), p. 46.

7 Stanley Hoffmann, *Gulliver's Troubles: Or the Setting of American Foreign Policy*, The Atlantic Policy Series (New York: McGraw-Hill Book Co., 1968), pp. 87, 89.

8 H. C. J. Duijker and N. Y. Frijda, *National Character and National Stereotypes* (Amsterdam: North-Holland Publishing Co., 1960).

9 Gertrude Stein, *The Autobiography of Alice B. Toklas* (1933) (London: Arrow Books, 1960), p. 190.

10 Willa Muir, "Translating from the German," in Reuben Brower, ed., *On Translation* (Cambridge, Mass.: Harvard University Press, 1959), pp. 95–96.

11 Hoffmann, *Gulliver's Troubles*, p. 87.

12 Margaret Mead, *And Keep Your Powder Dry: An Anthropologist Looks at America* (New York: William Morrow and Co., 1943), p. 196.

13 Thomas Mann, *Joseph in Egypt*, trans. H. T. Lowe-Porter, 2 vols. (New York: Alfred A. Knopf, 1938), 1: 4.

14 Herman Melville, *Moby-Dick or The White Whale* (1851), Chapter 37, "Sunset."

15 See Abram Kardiner and Associates, *The Psychological Frontiers of Society* (New York: Columbia University Press, 1945), 9th printing (1967), generally. Robert E. Lane, *Political Thinking and Consciousness: The Private Life of the Political Mind* (Chicago: Markham Publishing Co., 1969), p. 334.

16 Milton Rokeach, *The Open and Closed Mind: Investigations into the Nature of Belief Systems and Personality Systems* (New York: Basic Books, 1960), pp. 6–7, 400–401, 391.

17 Freud, *The Psychopathology of Everyday Life* (1901), *Std. Edn.*, 6: 259. Willy Baranger, "The Ego and the Function of Ideology," *International Journal of Psycho-Analysis* 39 (1958): 191–195.

18 George A. Kelly, *A Theory of Personality: The Psychology of Personal Constructs* (1955) (New York: W. W. Norton and Co., 1963), pp. 90, 55, 94, 95.

19 W. W. Meissner, "Notes Toward a Theory of Values: Values as Cultural," *Journal of Religion and Health* 10 (1971): 77–97, 88–89, 77.

20 Heinz Lichtenstein, "The Challenge to Psychoanalytic Psychotherapy in a World in Crisis," *International Journal of Psychoanalytic Psychotherapy* 2, No. 2 (1973): 149–174, 154, 165, 155, 168.

21 Kenneth W. Terhune, "From National Character to National Behavior: A Reformulation," *Journal of Conflict Resolution* 14 (1970): 203–263.

22 Robert Freed Bales, *Interaction Process Analysis, A Method for the Study of Small Groups* (Reading, Mass.: Addison-Wesley Publishing Co., 1950). *Personality and Interpersonal Behavior* (New York: Holt, Rinehart and Winston, 1970). It is Paul Diesing who points out that Bales's studies, although thoroughly experimental, are also holistic or semiholistic. Diesing, *Patterns of Discovery in the Social Sciences* (Chicago: Aldine-Atherton, 1971), pp. 78–79 and 214–215. I will discuss questions of experimental rigor and holistic methodology in the next chapter.

23 Alan C. Purves, Review of Norman N. Holland, *Poems in Persons*, in *Research in the Teaching of English* 8 (1974): 9–12.

24 René Wellek, "The Mode of Existence of a Literary Work of Art," in René Wellek and Austin Warren, *Theory of Literature* (1942), 3rd ed. (New York: Harcourt, Brace and World, 1956), Chapter 12, pp. 150, 152.

25 Walter Jackson Bate, John Keats (New York: Oxford University Press, 1966), p. 486.

Chapter 9

1 I am indebted to Professor Murray Schwartz for this phrasing and for many ideas throughout this chapter. See his essays, "Where is Literature?", presented before the Buffalo Group for Applied Psychoanalysis, December 1972, and "The Space of Psychological Criticism," *Hartford Studies in Literature* 5 (1973), x–xxi. I am deeply grateful for his help before, during, and after the writing of this chapter, so unaccustomedly philosophical for me.

2 Alfred North Whitehead, *The Concept of Nature* (Cambridge: Cambridge University Press, 1920), pp. 26–27.

3 See T. S. Eliot, *Knowledge and Experience in the Philosophy of F. H. Bradley* (London: Faber and Faber, 1964).

4 Roger Poole, *Towards Deep Subjectivity* (New York: Harper and Row, 1972), pp. 92–93, explicating Edmund Husserl, *The Crisis of European Sciences and Transcendental Phenomenology* (1934–1938), trans. David Carr (Evanston, Ill.: Northwestern University Press, 1970).

5 David Bleich, *Readings and Feelings: An Introduction to Subjective Criticism* (forthcoming, National Council of Teachers of English). *The Subjective Reader* (in preparation).

6 Caroline Shrodes, "Bibliotherapy: An Application of Psychoanalytic Theory," *American Imago* 17 (1960): 311–319; "The Dynamics of Reading: Implications for Bibliotherapy," *ETC.: A Review of General Semantics* 18 (1961): 21–33. Both articles are based on "Bibliotherapy: A Theoretical and Clinical Experimental Study" (Ph. D. dissertation, University of California, Berkeley, 1949). The quotation in the text is from p. 22 of the *ETC.* article.

7 Northrop Frye, "Literary Criticism," in *The Aims and Methods of Schol-*

arship in Modern Languages and Literatures, ed. James Thorpe (New York: Modern Language Association of America, 1963), p. 65.

8 Leo Spitzer, *Linguistics and Literary History: Essays in Stylistics* (Princeton, N.J.: Princeton University Press, 1948), p. 19.

9 W. W. Meissner, "Freud's Methodology," *Journal of the American Psychoanalytic Association* 19 (1971): 265–309, 303.

10 W. W. Meissner, "The Operational Principle and Meaning in Psychoanalysis," *Psychoanalytic Quarterly* 35 (1966): 233–255, 249.

11 Freud, "The Aetiology of Hysteria" (1896), *Std. Edn.*, 3: 192.

12 Freud, "From the History of an Infantile Neurosis" (1918 [1914]), *Std. Edn.*, 17: 99, 42n.

13 Meissner, "Operational Principle," p. 251.

14 Ralph R. Greenson, "Empathy and its Vicissitudes," *International Journal of Psycho-Analysis* 41 (1960): 418–424, 421.

15 "History of an Infantile Neurosis" (note 12), 17: 52.

16 Franz Alexander, "The Logic of Emotions and its Dynamic Background," *International Journal of Psycho-Analysis* 16 (1935): 399–413.

17 George A. Kelly, *A Theory of Personality: The Psychology of Personal Constructs* (1955) (New York: W. W. Norton and Co., 1963), p. 43 and Chapter 2 generally.

18 Erik H. Erikson, "The Nature of Clinical Evidence," *Insight and Responsibility: Lectures on the Ethical Implications of Psychoanalytic Insight* (New York: W. W. Norton and Co., 1964), p. 67.

19 Robert Jay Lifton, *Thought Reform and the Psychology of Totalism: A Study of "Brainwashing" in China* (London: Victor Gollancz, 1961), p. 115.

20 Heinz Lichtenstein, "Towards a Metapsychological Definition of the Concept of Self," *International Journal of Psycho-Analysis* 46 (1965): 117–128, 125–126.

21 Herbert Fingarette, *The Self in Transformation: Psychoanalysis, Philosophy, & The Life of the Spirit* (New York: Basic Books, 1963), pp. 20–21.

22 Norman N. Holland, "A Touching of Literary and Psychiatric Education," *Seminars in Psychiatry* 5 (1973): 287–299.

23 Paul Diesing, *Patterns of Discovery in the Social Sciences* (Chicago: Aldine-Atherton, 1971), pp. 5–7.

24 Diesing, p. 229.

25 Diesing, pp. 229–232.

26 Diesing, pp. 158–160, referring to Abraham Kaplan, *The Conduct of Inquiry* (San Francisco: Chandler Publishing Co., 1964), p. 335.

27 Diesing, pp. 2–4.

28 Joseph Masling, "Role-Related Behavior of the Subject and Psychologist and Its Effects upon Psychological Data," *Nebraska Symposium on Motivation, 1966*, ed. D. Levine (Lincoln: University of Nebraska Press, 1966).

29 Max Planck, *Scientific Autobiography and Other Papers*, trans. Frank

Gaynor (New York: Philosophical Library, 1949), pp. 33–34.

30 Kelly, *A Theory of Personality* (note 17), pp. 31–32.

31 Gunther S. Stent, "Prematurity and Uniqueness in Scientific Discovery," *Scientific American* 227, No. 6 (December 1972): 84–93.

32 Diesing, pp. 160 and 163.

33 Michael Sherwood, *The Logic of Explanation in Psychoanalysis* (New York and London: Academic Press, 1969), pp. 218–219, 202.

34 Sherwood, pp. 239–241.

35 Diesing, pp. 163–164.

36 Diesing, p. 230.

37 Diesing, p. 258.

38 Noam Chomsky, *Language and Mind* (New York: Harcourt, Brace, and World, 1968), p. v.

39 Diesing, p. 4.

40 Diesing, pp. 182–183.

41 "History of an Infantile Neurosis" (note 12), 17: 105.

42 Masling (note 28), pp. 68–69.

43 Abraham Kaplan, "Noncausal Explanation," in *Cause and Effect*, ed. Daniel Lerner, The Hayden Colloquium on Scientific Method and Concept (New York: The Free Press, 1965), pp. 145–155.

44 Jerry A. Fodor, *Psychological Explanation: An Introduction to the Philosophy of Psychology* (New York: Random House, 1968), p. 114.

45 Lichtenstein, "Towards a Metapsychological Definition" (note 20), p. 119. Norman N. Holland, "Defence, Displacement and the Ego's Algebra," *International Journal of Psycho-Analysis* 54 (1973): 247–257.

46 I have explored these criteria with both psycholiterary and psychobiographical examples in *Psychoanalysis and Shakespeare* (New York: McGraw-Hill Book Co., 1966; Octagon Books, 1975), pp. 126–129, 282–285.

47 Diesing (note 23), p. 5.

48 Marvin K. Opler, "Cultural Differences in Mental Disorders: An Italian and Irish Contrast in the Schizophrenias—U.S.A." in *Culture and Mental Health* (New York: The Macmillan Co., 1959), pp. 425–442.

49 Diesing (note 23), pp. 8–10, 94.

50 David Bleich, *The Subjective Reader* (in preparation).

51 Basil Willey, *The Seventeenth Century Background: Studies in the Thought of the Age in Relation to Poetry and Religion*, 2nd ed. (Garden City, N.Y.: Doubleday Anchor Books, 1953), pp. 12–14.

52 I am deeply indebted to David Bleich for his extensive comments on an earlier version of this book, which persuaded me to recast the prototypes of the four principles presented here in a more subjective frame of reference. Personal communication, June 14 ("Flag Day"), 1971. I have chronicled this indebtedness and the relation between my *Dynamics of Literary Response* (New York: Oxford University Press, 1968) and this book in "A Letter to Leonard," *Hartford Studies in Literature* 5 (1973): 9–30.

Appendix A

1 André Green, "L'Affect," *Revue Française de Psychanalyse* 34, No. 5-6 (September 1970): 885–1169.
2 Freud, *Civilization and its Discontents* (1930), Chapter 1, *Std. Edn.*, 21: 65.
3 "The Unconscious" (1915), section III, *Std. Edn.*, 14: 179n.
4 David Rapaport, "On the Psychoanalytic Theory of Affects," *Psychoanalytic Psychiatry and Psychology, Clinical and Theoretical Papers*, Austen Riggs Center, Vol. 1, ed. Robert P. Knight and Cyrus R. Friedman (New York: International Universities Press, 1954), pp. 274–310, especially p. 307.
5 Edith Jacobson, "The Affects and Their Pleasure-Unpleasure Qualities in Relation to the Psychic Discharge Processes," in Rudolph M. Loewenstein, ed., *Drives, Affects, Behavior* (New York: International Universities Press, 1953), pp. 38–66.
6 Paul Diesing, *Patterns of Discovery in the Social Sciences* (Chicago: Aldine-Atherton, 1971), p. 42 and Chapters 2–9 generally.
7 See Norman N. Holland, *The Dynamics of Literary Response* (New York: Oxford University Press, 1968), pp. 289–301. In these instances, the affects of items 9 and 10 (p. 290) and consequently of *e* (p. 292) became reversed. I am indebted to Professor Arthur Efron for pointing out this inadvertent misapplication of the Berkowitz studies of aggressive films cited on p. 289.

Appendix B

1 As this 1922 story appeared in Marvin Magalaner and Edmond L. Volpe, eds., *Twelve Short Stories* (New York: The Macmillan Co., 1961), pp. 50–70.
2 Robert M. Slabey, "The Structure of Hemingway's *In Our Time*," *Moderna Språk* 60 (1966): 273–285, 277. Philip Young, *Ernest Hemingway: A Reconsideration* (New York: Harcourt, Brace and World, 1966), p. 39. William B. Bache, "Hemingway's THE BATTLER," *Explicator* 13 (1954): Item 4.
3 Young, p. 37n.
4 John E. Hardy, *The Modern Talent: An Anthology of Short Stories* (New York: Holt, Rinehart and Winston, 1964), pp. 32–36. Joseph DeFalco, *The Hero in Hemingway's Short Stories* (Pittsburgh: University of Pittsburgh Press, 1963), p. 73.
5 Randall Stewart and Dorothy Bethurum, eds., *Modern American Narration*, Vol. 3 of *Living Masterpieces of American Literature* (Chicago: Scott-Foresman, 1954), pp. 68–70.
6 Clinton S. Burhans, "The Complex Unity of *In Our Time*," *Modern Fiction Studies* 14 (1968): 313–328, 321–322.
7 Wilhelm Reich, *Character-Analysis*, 3rd ed. (New York: Noonday Press,

1949), pp. 200–207, "The Phallic-Narcissistic Character."

8 October 18, 1924. I am quoting from Professor Burhans's essay.

9 From *Death in the Afternoon* (New York: Halcyon House, 1932), p. 192. The quotation appeared in the anthology we were using: Marvin Magalaner and Edmond L. Volpe, eds., *Twelve Short Stories* (New York: The Macmillan Co., 1961), p. 88.

10 Norman N. Holland, *The Dynamics of Literary Response* (New York: Oxford University Press, 1968), Chapter 6 and pp. 314, 185.

11 See note 2.

Index